Accounting, Finance, Sustainability, Governance & Fraud: Theory and Application

Series editor

Kiymet Tunca Caliyurt, Iktisadi ve Idari Bilimler Fakültesi, Trakya University
Balkan Yerleşkesi, Edirne, Turkey

This series acts as a forum for book publications on current research arising from debates about key topics that have emerged from global economic crises during the past several years. The importance of governance and the will to deal with corruption, fraud, and bad practice, are themes featured in volumes published in the series. These topics are not only of concern to businesses and their investors, but also to governments and supranational organizations, such as the United Nations and the European Union. *Accounting, Finance, Sustainability, Governance & Fraud: Theory and Application* takes on a distinctive perspective to explore crucial issues that currently have little or no coverage. Thus the series integrates both theoretical developments and practical experiences to feature themes that are topical, or are deemed to become topical within a short time. The series welcomes interdisciplinary research covering the topics of accounting, auditing, governance, and fraud.

More information about this series at http://www.springer.com/series/13615

Iffet Kesimli

External Auditing and Quality

Springer

Iffet Kesimli
Lüleburgaz Vocational School
Kırklareli University
Lüleburgaz/Kırklareli
Turkey

ISSN 2509-7873 ISSN 2509-7881 (electronic)
Accounting, Finance, Sustainability, Governance & Fraud: Theory and Application
ISBN 978-981-13-0525-2 ISBN 978-981-13-0526-9 (eBook)
https://doi.org/10.1007/978-981-13-0526-9

Library of Congress Control Number: 2018942522

Printed on acid-free paper

This Springer imprint is published by the registered company Springer Nature Singapore Pte Ltd.
The registered company address is: 152 Beach Road, #21-01/04 Gateway East, Singapore 189721, Singapore

I dedicate my book to my lovely mom, who passed away during my endeavor.

Foreword

The aim of the book is analyzing in detail the topic "quality of external audit," which has been put on the backburner for years, but suddenly rose to prominence with Enron case. The book not only examines the issue from international perspective, but also connects the reader with a comprehensive research about Turkey. This research is done by my meticulous doctoral student and elaborated and approved with the demanding jurors' vigorous efforts. Another aspect of this research book is the research being conducted, completed, and presented at a time period when external auditing had been mostly discussed, and the new Turkish Code of Commerce (TCC) had been introduced and applied. The auditing seen in Ninova 3000 BC, in China 1100 BC, and in 1800s in England started being applied by banks in Turkey in 1987. At the time external auditing started for public companies upon regulations of the Capital Market Board of Turkey implemented in 1988, the accounting circles started discussing the necessity and merits of external audit.

In 2003, Turkish Auditing Standards Board was established in order to prepare the auditing standards in line with international auditing standards. This body is dissolved upon formation of Public Oversight–Accounting and Auditing Standards Authority, which is an American PCAOB kind of organization. Nonetheless, there are fundamental dissimilarities between the managements, missions, and implementations of these two institutions. Furthermore, in 2012 a very important shift was lived and TCC, completion of which lasted 10 years, has gone in effect. The act that is to be accepted as the breeze of Sarbanes–Oxley Act (SOX) in addition to public companies demanded the SMEs to be audited and international accounting standards to be applied.

In 1995, when I started working at Horwath Istanbul, the external audit sector was unknown. On the contrary to important developments in Turkey that pave the way of it, external audit still did not reach the rightful place as it deserves. In-depth information is presented in this book by the author.

As the series editor, with my wishes that this research keeps going on with different country samples, I gratulate Dr. Iffet Kesimli for her success and book work.

Prof.Dr. Kıymet Çaliyurt
Book Series Editor

Preface

Business entities have been tying a lot of money in audit engagements historically; disappointments in forms of accounting scandals are apparent. Investors have been putting their savings into business entities trough the history; disasters come one after the other. Public authorities have been showing efforts in bringing legislation and regulations; inevitable misconduct always prevails.

Business entities are profit maximizing units in economy. Maximizing profits also encompasses looking after their interest by carefully watching cost/benefit ratio of audit engagements. The audit firms are entities as well. Though producing not material goods, they render services. Services are abstract and not easy to be classified from quality perspective. Quality is a concept not easy to describe. It totally depends on the person assessing the aspects of quality. The assessment depends on the culture, environment, age, education, background, ethics perception, and interests of the person who makes the assessment. It is not that easy to conclude that this/that audit is high/low quality, as it is to tell how delicious an apple is, or how high quality a fabric is woven. The expectations of the person assessing the audit quality are quite determining the result.

What about investors, who we think most benefit from high quality audits? Do they have experienced finance literacy? Are they good in research to find out whether a business entity will be prosperous in the future or not? Mostly investors, except for the institutions who professionally handle investment issue, are ordinary people with poor understanding of even accounting let finance. Corporate investors have the means to make research for investing opportunities, whereas the ordinary investor who has tiny saving does not. So, who will be the gatekeeper for those disadvantageous in investment decisions?

Public Company Accounting Oversight Board and SEC in USA, and Public Oversight–Accounting and Auditing Standards Authority (POA) and Capital Markets Board in Turkey are some examples to these authorities who will act as the regulators in the audit market. For the moment, the audit market has an oligopolistic character. This had been the reality of this industry since long. Once there were Big Eight, then they became Big Six, now they are called Big Four. From revenue to staffing, from numbers of audit clients to number of countries they are active;

today's Big Four make up more than two-thirds of the audit market from several aspects. Each of the Big Four audit firms has yearly revenue around $30 billion, each one operates in around 150 countries all over the world, and each one employs around 200,000 people in these offices. Mid-tier audit firms almost do not have any chance in getting big-sized companies' audit engagements. Contrary to size, here comes the question: Does being big means that all the audits done are perfect?

With this book, based on the research done in Turkish audit market and an immense literature survey, I wanted to present my findings and suggestions in order to contribute to audit quality. Why do we need high-quality audits? How can we achieve this? What are do's and don'ts? My book will tell you about these. Moreover, I proudly present my Audit Firms Quality Index (AFQI) and discuss a Payment Pool.

Hope this book will be beneficial for the reader.

Lüleburgaz, 2018 Iffet Kesimli

Acknowledgements

First, my sincere gratitude goes to Kıymet Çalıyurt. She is not only the editor of this book and the book series, but also my doctoral thesis advisor, who inspired me to make audit quality research, and consequently encouraged me to write this book. My research took three years to complete. There were times of frustration, times of misery and times of joy. During all those seesaw, Prof. Çalıyurt stood behind to help overcome obstacles. Many thanks to her!

The knight during this journey is my dear spouse Oğuz, who showed patience during my doctoral studies, and kept supporting afterward when I was up to my knees in writing this book. Here, I do not want to miss the opportunity to thank to my only child, Cengiz, who also showed patience during my researches.

Besides, I would like to acknowledge the help of all the Springer Nature Singapore Pte Ltd. lovely people, involved in this book project to express my opinions and suggestions about audit quality and more specifically Divya and Ritu, who built the bridge for me to accomplish my goal. Without their collaboration, this book would not have become a reality.

The research part of this book is supported by Trakya University Scientific Research Projects Unit (TÜBAP) with the Project Number 2013/70. I owe TÜBAP commission members and the staff of a debt of gratitude for financially supporting my research.

Iffet Kesimli

Contents

Table of Audit-Related Institutions

Abbreviation	Organization
AAA	American Accounting Association
AAC	Audit and Assurance Council
AAERs	Accounting and Auditing Enforcement Releases—SEC
AAOIFI	The Accounting and Auditing Organisation for Islamic Financial Institutions
ACAP	United States Treasury Department's Advisory Committee on the Auditing Profession
ACFE	Association of Certified Fraud Examiners
AICPA	American Institute of CPAs (abbr.)/American Institute of Certified Public Accountants
AMEX	The American Stock Exchange
AMU	Audit Monitoring Unit (Scotland)
ARSC	Accounting and Review Services Committee
ASB	Auditing Standards Board
ASG	Accounting Study Group (EC)
AUASB	Auditing and Assurance Standards Board (Australia)
CalPERS	California Public Employees' Retirement System
CAQ	Center for Audit Quality
CEPA	Code of Ethics for Professional Accountants
CEPC	Code of Ethics for Professional Conduct
CFE	Certified Fraud Examiners
CICA	Canadian Institute of Chartered Accountants
CIMA	Chartered Institute of Management Accountants
CMB	Capital Markets Board of Turkey
CNCC	La Compagnie Nationale des Commissaires aux Comptes
COBIT	Control Objectives for Information and Related Technologies
COSO	Committee of Sponsoring Organizations of the Treadway Commission
CPA	Certified Public Accountants

(continued)

(continued)

Abbreviation	Organization
CPAB	Canadian Public Accountability Board
CCRC	Conseil Canadien Sur la Reddition de Comptes
CPC	Code of Professional Conduct
DFSA	Dubai Financial Services Authority
DIPAC	La Délégation Internationale Pour l'audit et la Comptabilité
	International Auditing and Accounting Delegation
DTI	UK Department of Trade and Industry
	Department of Treasury
EFFAS	European Federation of Financial Analysts Societies
EFRAG	European Financial Reporting Advisory Group
EGAOB	European Group of Auditors Oversight Boards
EGIAN	European Group of International Accounting Networks and Associations
EQC	Engagement Quality Control
FAF	Financial Accounting Foundation
FASAC	Financial Accounting Standards Advisory Council
FASB	Financial Accounting Standards Board
FCM	Fédération des Experts Comptables Méditerranéens
	Federation of Mediterranean Certified Accountants
FED	Federal Reserve System
FEE	European Federation of Accountants
	Fédération des Experts comptables Européens
FRC	Financial Reporting Council
FSA	Japanese Financial Services Agency
FSA	UK Financial Services Authority
GAAP	Generally Accepted Accounting Principles
GAAS	Generally Accepted Auditing Standards
GAO	Government Accountability Office
GASAC	Governmental Accounting Standards Advisory Council
GASB	Governmental Accounting Standards Board
IAASB	International Auditing and Assurance Standards Board
IAG	Investor Advisory Group (PCAOB)
IAS	International Accounting Standards
IASB	International Accounting Standards Board
ICAEW	The Institute of Chartered Accountants in England and Wales
ICAS	The Institute of Chartered Accountants of Scotland
IDW	Institut der Wirtschaftsprüfer
	Institute of Public Auditors in Germany
IESBA	International Ethics Standards Board for Accountants
IFAC	International Federation of Accountants
IFIAR	International Forum of Independent Audit Regulators
IIA	Institute of Internal Auditors

(continued)

(continued)

Abbreviation	Organization
IMA	Institute of Management Accountants
INTOSAI	International Organization of Supreme Audit Institutions
IOSCO	International Organization of Securities Commissions
OICV	Organisation Internationale des Commissions de Valeurs
IRS	Internal Revenue Service
ISAs	International Standards on Auditing
ISO	International Organisation for Standardisation
ISQC	International Standard on Quality Control
ISSAI	International Standards of Supreme Audit Institution
JICPA	Japanese Institute of CPAs
MPG	Market Participants Group
NAO	National Audit Office
NASBA	National Association of State Boards of Accountancy
NASD	The National Association of Securities Dealers
NCFFR	National Commission on Fraudulent Financial Reporting
NYSE	The New York Stock Exchange
PCAOB	Public Company Accounting Oversight Board
PCPS	Private Companies Practice Section
PEEC	Professional Ethics Executive Committee
PIE	Public Interest Entity
	KAYİK—Kamu Yararını İlgilendiren Kuruluş
PIOB	Public Interest Oversight Board
POA	Kamu Gözetimi Kurumu (short)
	Public Oversight Authority
	Kamu Gözetimi—Muhasebe ve Denetim Standartları Kurumu
	Public Oversight—Accounting and Auditing Standards Authority
POB	Professional Oversight Board (UK)
SAG	Standard Advisory Group (PCAOB)
SASs	Statements on Auditing Standards
SASsfARS	Statements on Standards for Accounting and Review Services
SCAS	Special Committee on Assurance Services
SEC	Securities and Exchange Commission
SFO	Serious Fraud Office
SOX	Sarbanes–Oxley Act
SQCS	Statement on Quality Control Standards
TAC	Transnational Auditors Committee
TCC	Turkish Code of Commerce
TELFA	Trans European Law Firms Alliance
TESMER	TÜRMOB Temel Eğitim ve Staj Merkezi
	Training and Education Center of TURMOB

(continued)

(continued)

Abbreviation	Organization
TIDE	Türkiye İç Denetim Enstitüsü
	Institute of Internal Auditing—Turkey
TMUD EAAT	Türkiye Muhasebe Uzmanları Derneği
	Expert Accountants' Association of Turkey
TÜRMOB	Türkiye Serbest Muhasebeci Mali Müşavirler ve Yeminli Mali Müşavirler Odaları Birliği
	Union of Chambers of Certified Public Accountants of Turkey
WFE	World Federation of Exchanges
WPK	Wirtschaftsprüferkammer
	Chamber of Auditors

Abbreviations

Ar. or Art.	Article
B.A.	Bachelor of Arts
Board	Public Company Accounting Oversight Board
BRSA	Banking Regulation and Supervision Agency
CMB	Capital Markets Board of Turkey
CoEPA	Code of Ethics for Professional Accountants
CPA	Certified Public Accountant
e.g.	exempli gratia (for example)
EMRA	Energy Market Regulatory Authority
et al.	et alibi (and others)
EU	European Union (EU)
i.e.	id est (that is)
IAbL	Independent Audit By-Law
ibid.	ibidem (in the same place)
IFRS	International Financial Reporting Standards
ISQC 1	International Standard on Quality Control 1
IT	Information Technologies
Law 3568	The Law dated 1/6/1989 and Numbered 3568 on Certified Public Accountancy and Sworn-in Certified Public Accountancy
NA	Not available
NAS	Non-audit services
No.	Numéro (number/numbered)
PCOAB	Public Company Accounting Oversight Board
PDP	Public Disclosure Platform
PIEs	Public Interest Entities
POA	Public Oversight—Accounting and Auditing Standards Authority
R&D	Research and Development
SEC	Securities and Exchange Commission
SiCPA	Sworn-in Certified Public Accountant
SPV	Special Purpose Vehicles

SQC 1	Standard on Quality Control 1
TAS	Turkish Accounting Standards
TCC	Turkish Code of Commerce
TLA	Turkish Language Association
TSAs	Turkish Standards on Auditing
UK	United Kingdom
US/USA	United States of America
vs.	versus

Symbols Used

&	and
≈	approximately
$	dollar
€	euro
>	greater than
<	less than
%	percent
TL	Turkish Lira

List of Figures

List of Tables

List of Graphics

Abstract

Corruption, defective audits, frailties, and bankruptcies caused by them distrusted the confidence of investors; countries' economies and financial structures being damaged raised the significance of auditing and stimulated reengineering in organizations. The anticipated efficacy of external audit would be derivable on condition of audit service being efficient. The future of auditing profession is related to the quality and effectiveness of external auditing as well as to the perceived value of it. The source of inspiration of this book is the International Standard on Quality Control 1 (ISQC 1), which is established by International Federation of Accountants (IFAC) and deals with the auditing firms' responsibilities for their systems of quality control for audits and reviews of financial statements, and other assurance and related services engagements. The deterministic features of audit quality have been presented through research along with the literature survey.

First section of the book emphasizes the importance of high-quality financial reporting and continues with a brief history and description of auditing. Section II reviews auditing in USA and European Union along with Turkey and profiles Turkish auditing firms. Section III focuses on audit quality. Section IV presents the results of surveys separately conducted on auditors, on managers of auditing firms, and managers of audit customers. Conclusions and recommendations complete the book. According to findings of the survey, answers from auditors and auditing firms' managers show that auditing firms have succeeded neither in establishing, nor disseminating the quality control policies and procedures in written forms, yet. Managers of audit client companies, the third stakeholder group also needs to alter its stance and follow regulations regularly. The debut of rating auditing firms by an index to be created is the recommendation of the thesis. In order to fortify the auditor independence, a Payment Pool, to be applied in conjunction with a random match of auditing firm to the customer is opened for discussions.

Keywords External auditing · Public companies · International quality control standard · Quality index · Payment Pool · Turkey

Introduction

Not only in United States and European Union, but also in Turkey, the way audit industry operates has been considerably transforming. In Turkey, the establishment of *Public Oversight—Accounting and Auditing Standards Authority* (POA) in late 2012 caused turmoil in Turkish auditing market. Against this backdrop, the parties involved in auditing have been facing a steam of radical changes. This ended up with the revision of the auditing function. Based on observations since 2012, we may put forward that POA initially adopted the European Union legislation, whereas Turkey stood close to American regulations as well. American regulations reshaped by Sarbanes–Oxley Act (SOX) and European Union legislation gradually become closer (Çalıyurt and Kesimli 2015). The source of inspiration of this book is the International Standard on Quality Control 1 (ISQC 1), which is established by International Federation of Accountants (IFAC) and deals with the auditing firms' responsibilities for their systems of quality control for audits and reviews of financial statements, and other assurance and related services engagements (Kesimli 2015). An exact translation of ISQC 1 has been adopted by the POA. The literature survey and reviews on American, European Union, and Turkish legislation helped to draw the frame of audit quality and derive a list of audit quality indicators. Some of these indicators pointed public authority; however, we assumed that public authority is out of our scope, because of its poor accessibility in the short run. Therefore, three surveys conducted with auditors, managers of auditing firms, and audit clients followed, to depict the stance of parties involved in auditing on audit quality.

All kinds of events in business world stem from utilization of inputs, background processes within the system established by businesspersons, and production of outcomes given the environment of the business. The environment comprises all kinds of stakeholders, including regulating authorities and average investors. Most of the time, non-institutionalized investors lack the necessary financial background and accounting knowledge. If not so, there is even the possibility of a competent investor to err, unless the proxies are determined to be honest. However, corruption and slyness have been ever present on the stage. The public that is agitated by accounting scandals perceives audit as a saving blanket/life buoy. Yet, it is apparent that the existence of auditing alone does not fix financial markets turmoil. This forces us to question the quality of auditing. The list of determinants impacting audit quality, derived from the literature survey and review of legislation, is as follows:

1. *Independency of the auditors and auditing firms* (American Institute of CPAs; International Ethics Standards Board for Accountants; Arens et al. (2012); Turkish Auditing Standards),
2. *Transparency of auditing firms and audits* (IOSCO Consultation Report 2009; Abma 2009; Financial Reporting Council—FRC 2012),
3. *The design of network firms* (IOSCO Consultation Report 2009),
4. *Local office or partner* (Skinner and Srinivasan 2011; Banker et al. 2003; Block 2011; Fraser 2010),
5. *Quality control system* (IOSCO Consultation Report 2009; Turkish Auditing on Standards)
6. *Human resources plans and procedures* (IOSCO Consultation Report 2009; Turkish Standards on Auditing)
7. *Ethical policies and practices* (IOSCO Consultation Report 2009; ISQC 1 2009; Quality Control Standard 1 (QCS 1)—Turkish Public Oversight Authority, 2013)
8. *Effective public oversight* (Fédération des Experts comptables Européens—FEE 2010; United States Treasury Department's Advisory Committee on the Auditing Profession—ACAP 2008),
9. *Rotation of the auditor, and/or of the auditing firm* (Capital Markets Board of Turkey (CMB); Turkish Code of Commerce (TCC) 6102; POA; European Union; Soo et al. 2014; Cameran et al. 2013).

Factors impacting audit quality are called as *audit quality indicators*. These are not country specific, and having focused on Turkish audit industry, here we grouped them into four: (1) factors related to the auditing firm, (2) factors determined by auditor merits, (3) audit client-related factors, and (4) factors stemming from public authority.

Chapter 1
External Audit from Quality Perspective

Abstract This Chapter gives the definition of external audit, types of it, and displays the importance of external audit under quality control perspective title. Then follows developments in auditing, importance of high-quality audits, the interactions between financial reporting and the audit quality, the relationships between external audit and fraud, and frauds in the twentieth century. This way the increasing demand for high-quality external audits are presented under the title emphasizing the necessity of external auditing. The extent the external auditors are involved and responsibilities of them in those frauds are discussed. The Chapter also discusses the Sarbanes–Oxley Act, which is perceived as a reaction to frequent frauds in the last quarter of twentieth century.

Keywords External Audit · Audit History · Accounting Scandals
Fraud · Sarbanes-Oxley Act SOX

Definition of external audit, types of it, and the importance of external audit are handled under quality control perspective title. Developments in auditing, importance of high-quality audits, the interactions between financial reporting and the audit quality, the relationships between external audit and fraud, frauds in twentieth century; thus, the increasing demand for high-quality external audits are presented under the title which emphasizes the necessity of external auditing. The involvement and responsibilities of external auditors in the above-mentioned frauds are discussed, and the title also comprises Sarbanes–Oxley Act, which is perceived as a reaction to frequent frauds in the last quarter of twentieth century.

1.1 Audit Types and Importance of It

There are lots of classifications of audit/auditing in literature. According to the reason why there is an audit, according to the objectives of an audit, auditing according to Securities and Exchange Commission (SEC) in the pre-era of Public Oversight—*Accounting and Auditing Standards Authority* (POA), auditing within the scope of Turkish Code of Commerce (TCC), auditing according who makes the

I. Kesimli, *External Auditing and Quality*, Accounting, Finance, Sustainability, Governance & Fraud: Theory and Application,
https://doi.org/10.1007/978-981-13-0526-9_1

audit, auditing compulsory due to regulations, and auditing based on the statute are several types of auditing.

This book is about external audit, and wherever the term "audit" solely is used, it substitutes "external audit," and dichotomously classifies auditing as "auditing according to purpose" and "auditing subject to regulations" or "audit from statutory point of view."

1.1.1 Definition of Auditing and Properties/Characteristics of It

According to Oxford Dictionary published by Oxford University Press in 1977, audit is defined as an official examination of accounts to see that they are in order. Contemporary version of the same dictionary develops the definition as an official examination of business and financial records to see that they are true and correct (www.oxfordlearnersdictionaries.com, 23.02.2012, Oxford Advanced Learners' Dictionary). Thesaurus dictionary defines auditing as "an inspection, correction, and verification of business accounts, conducted by an independent qualified accountant" (www.thefreedictionary.com, Free Online Dictionary, 23.02.2012). According to Turkish Language Association (TLA) lexicon, auditing is examination and inspections of accounts of commercial firms in order to find out whether they are in accordance with laws, codes, and regulations and that the accounts are in order (www.tdk.gov.tr, 23.02.2012, Türk Dil Kurumu). We can add numerous lexical definitions to the above-given ones, by enriching them with attributions like independence, objectivity, and the like.

The reports of the studies of the committee, which had been established in USA to inquire the role and function of audit, bring suggestions for research projects, to investigate issues related to evidence, and to depict the stance of auditors to audit; conducted between 1969 and 1971 had been published in Accounting Review journal as an extra issue in 1972. According to this report, auditing is a systematic process of objectively obtaining and evaluating evidence regarding assertions about economic actions and events to ascertain the degree of correspondence between these assertions and established criteria and communicating the results to interested users (Committee on Basic Auditing Concepts, 1969–1971, 1972: 18).

Within the framework of Sarbanes–Oxley Act (2002), the passage of which had been urged in the aftermath of Enron Scandal, audit is defined as an examination of the financial statements of any issuer by an independent public accounting firm in accordance with the rules of the Public Company Accounting Oversight Board (PCAOB/sometimes will be used as Board) or the Securities and Exchange Commission (SEC), for the purpose of expressing an opinion on such statements (http://uscode.house.gov/, 12.12.2011, United States House of Representatives). External audit is done by an auditor. The auditor can be an individual Certified Public Accountant (CPA) or a CPA firm registered with PCAOB (http://pcaobus.org/, AU 1, 16.01.2015). Knechel et al. define audit as a professional service rendered by specialists in response to economic demand, and in accordance with audit regulations (Knechel et al. 2013: 386).

In Turkey Independent Audit By-Law (IAbL) mentions the term *Statutory Audit* and defines it as the auditing of financial statements and other financial details on books, records, and documents by applying required statutory audit techniques specified in the auditing standards with the aim of obtaining sufficient and appropriate statutory audit evidences, which would ensure a reasonable assurance with regard to their compliance with financial reporting standards and accuracy, then evaluating and reporting them (www.kgk.gov.tr, http://www.kgk.gov.tr/content_detail-219-1020-bagimsiz-denetim-yonetmeligi.html, 01.01.2015).

Article 4 explains *Statutory Auditor* as the natural persons authorized by the Public Oversight Authority (POA) to perform statutory audit among members of the profession, who acquired certified public accountant or sworn-in certified public accountant license in accordance with the Law dated 1/6/1989 and Numbered 3568 on Certified Public Accountancy and Sworn-in Certified Public Accountancy (Law 3568) (*ibid.*).

1.1.2 Types of Audit

Audit activities may be classified according to several criteria. When evaluated in accordance with the **cause of audit**, it can be classified as *Statutory Audit* and *On Demand Audit*. Classification according to the **frequency of audit** can also be considered, where *Continuous Audit*, also called *End of Year Audit*; *Custom Audit*; and *Partial Audit*, namely *Interim Audit* definitions follow. Classification **regarding the auditor** brings types of audits as *External Audit*, *Internal Audit*, and *Public Audit*. Trichotomy comes out when classified according to **purposes of audit**, *Financial Table Audit*, *Compliance Audit*, and *Operational Audit*. **Audit from statutory point of view** or auditing subject to regulations is another classification, which also splits into three: external audit, internal audit, and public audit.

Literature research displays that the last two classifications overlap. Thus, the definition of *Internal Audit* matches *Operational Audit*; *Public Audit* pairs with *Compliance Audit*; and *External Audit* overlaps with *Financial Table Audit*.

1.1.2.1 Audit from the Point of Purpose

Audit from the point of purpose encompasses subgenres as financial table audit, compliance audit, and operational audit. Operational audit and especially compliance audit are types of audits specific to public sector. Below these subgenres are handled in detail.

Financial Table Audit

Statutory audit is the auditing of financial statements and other financial details on books, records, and documents by applying required statutory audit techniques specified in the auditing standards with the aim of obtaining sufficient and appropriate statutory audit evidences, which would ensure a reasonable assurance with regard to their compliance with financial reporting standards and accuracy, then evaluating and reporting them (IAbL: Part 1, Art. 4). The aim of financial table audit is to build an opinion about whether financial tables reflect the financial position and the results of operations of the business in a fair and decent way in accordance with generally accepted accounting principles (GAAP), and legislative regulations (Bozkurt 2006: 27). *External audit* is inspection of financial tables and underlying records by CPAs with the main aim of expressing an opinion (Weston 1966: 157).

In place of financial table audit, financial table audit, external audit, and accounting audit terms are also being used. Financial table audit ought not to be confused with the term financial audit. TLA lexicon explains the term financial as an adjective meaning something related to money and finance (www.tdk.gov.tr, 05.01.2015). This term pursuant to Turkish lexicon causes confusion. Hasan Kaval enlightens this issue as follows (Kaval 2008: 10):

> However, most of the time what is meant with financial audit is tax audit. Financial audit differs from accounting audit. Subject of inspection of financial audit is the basis of tax. Specifically issues affecting the basis of tax are made the subject of inspection, not financial tables as a whole. …assessment criteria are different than accounting audit and are tax laws.

It is observed that in many sources financial audit term is being used instead of financial table audit. *Financial audit* or *certification audit* assessed from public scrutiny perspective is an auditing technique as an improved and efficient form of traditional duties and functions of regularity audit (Gülen 1998: 3). Financial audits are conducted to communicate an opinion known as the "regularity" opinion; as to whether the accounts and financial tables are free from material misstatement and show a true and fair view, and transactions in the accounts comply with appropriate parliamentary authority. The audit report also comments on the progress made by audited bodies in embedding risk management systems and other best practice within corporate governance (www.nao.org.uk, 05.01.2015).

Among others, external audit is the core of this book, and independent audit is the term used interchangeably. Throughout the text, the terms "audit" and/or "auditing" are shortly used in place of independent audit and external audit. Having a healthy definition of independence is prerequisite in understanding independent audit conceptually, which is handled in the book from several aspects. **Independence** as defined in Ethical Codes of Conduct for Independent Auditors is (a) the state letting to announce the results without being affected by factors that may cause concessions to professional reasoning; thus enabling the person to act in integrity and managing his/her objectivity, and professional skepticism, (b) preventing the settings and conditions which may cause a third party, who is logical and has knowledge, by assessing all existing special conditions and circumstances at the moment to conclude that the auditing firm or a member of an audit team has concession to his/her integrity, objectivity, or professional skepticism.

Operational Audit

Operational audit, also called performance audit, value for money, or managerial audit, is an audit to determine the efficiency and effectiveness of the organization.

Operational audit may be conducted by internal auditors, government auditors, and CPAs. As long as the aim of the test is determining the effectiveness of any part of an organization, the term operational audit is preferred. If the purpose is to help an organization operate its business more effectively or efficiently, testing the effectiveness of internal controls by an internal auditor, and determining whether a company has adequately trained assembly line personnel, may also be considered part of operational auditing (Arens et al. 2012: 666).

This type of audit, which is called operational audit when classified from the point of purpose, is named as *internal audit* when classified according to the auditing person. Internal audit is the review and evaluation of financial and other activities by members of the same organization (Weston 1966: 157). The concept, description of which had been done in a very simple way and in general terms in the 1960s, had been expended by different bodies in different ways and in much more detail.

Internal audit service provides management with an objective assessment of whether systems and controls are working properly. Since internal control system measures and evaluates the adequacy and effectiveness of other controls; the management board can know the extent to which they can rely on the whole system; and individual managers can know how reliable are the systems and controls for which they are responsible (National Audit Office of England, www.nao.org.uk, 26.02.2012; NAO England 2009: 134).

Pursuant to the definition done by Institute of Internal Auditors (IIA) internal audit is an independent, objective assurance and consulting activity designed to add value and improve an organization's operations. It helps an organization accomplish its objectives by bringing a systematic, disciplined approach to evaluate and improve the effectiveness of risk management, control, and governance processes (https://na.theiia.org, 15.01.2015). Internal audit activity has to assess the effectiveness and congruousness of the control over organization's governance, operations, and information systems. According to this description, internal audit has to include (Fraser and Lindsay 2004: 7);

- Reliability and integrity of financial and operational information;
- Effectiveness and efficiency of operations;
- Safeguarding of assets;
- Compliance with laws, regulations, and contracts.

Findings and comments based on the research (2010) conducted by Turkish Industry and Business Association Internal Auditing Sub-Working Group follows as such (Uzun et al. Internal Auditing Implementations in Real Sector: Findings and Comments. Seminar Presentation: Uzay, cited slide no. 41–42, 44–45): (1) the role of internal auditing is on the rise during economical crises, (2) Independence of internal auditors is important in the sense of fulfilling the expectations from internal auditing, (3) Internal audit, along with audit committee assists external audit, (4) Internal audit function at small and medium sized enterprises can be provided by outsourcing, (5) Adaptation level to international internal audit standards should be increased, (6) In Turkey, there is no such regulation toward internal control and/or internal audit for the real sector, which has very close relations with financial sector. Therefore, internal audit has to be legally compelled for big size companies and public companies.

Independence as the most important factor of auditing and competency keep their importance at operational audit as well. Timing, design of methodology, reporting by emphasizing details, collection of evidence, and communication through meetings are other factors to be considered during internal audit implementation (Uzay, *An Overview of Operational…*, 2008: 279).

Compliance Audit

Compliance audit is measuring the level of conformity of the executives to the predefined rules accepted as criteria set by the organization's management or government agencies. Compliance audit is a type of audit undertaken to confirm whether a firm is following the terms of an agreement, or the rules and regulations applicable to an activity or practice prescribed by an external agency or authority (www.businessdictionary.com, 26.03.2013, compliance-audit.html).

This type of audit, which is called compliance audit when classified from the point of purpose, is named as *public audit* when classified according to the auditing person. In literature, *supreme audit* frequently substitutes public audit expression.

The International Organization of Supreme Audit Institutions (INTOSAI), which is an autonomous, independent and non-political organization, operates as an umbrella organization for the external government audit community. Supreme Audit Institutions (SAIs) of several countries are under this organization. In order to understand *supreme audit*, reference is made to Mexico Declaration on Independence, which emphasizes the importance of SAIs' independence. Eight core principles recognized by SAIs generally as essential requirements of proper public sector auditing are compiled below (www.intosai.org, Mexico Declaration, 28.01.2017).

Principle 1: The existence of an appropriate and effective constitutional/statutory/legal framework and of de facto application provisions of this framework.
Principle 2: The independence of SAI heads and members (of collegial institutions), including security of tenure and legal immunity in the normal discharge of their duties.
Principle 3: A sufficiently broad mandate and full discretion, in the discharge of SAI functions.
Principle 4: Unrestricted access to information.
Principle 5: The right and obligation to report on their work.
Principle 6: The freedom to decide the content and timing of audit reports and to publish and disseminate them.
Principle 7: The existence of effective follow-up mechanisms on SAI recommendations.
Principle 8: Financial and managerial/administrative autonomy and the availability of appropriate human, material, and monetary resources.

The orderly and efficient use of public funds and resources constitutes one of the essential prerequisites for the proper handling of public finances and the effectiveness of the decisions of the responsible authorities. SAIs can accomplish their tasks only if they are independent of the audited entity and are protected against outside influence. To achieve this objective, it is indispensable for a healthy democracy that each country have a SAI whose independence is guaranteed by law. SAIs cannot be absolutely independent; however, SAIs should have the functional and organizational independence required to carry out their mandate. Through the application of principles of independence, SAIs can achieve independence through different means using different safeguards.

Except when specifically required to do so by legislation, SAIs do not audit government or public entities' policy but restrict themselves to the audit of policy implementation. While respecting the laws enacted by the Legislature that apply to them, SAIs are free from direction or interference from the Legislature or the Executive in the (1) selection of audit issues; (2) planning, programming, conduct, reporting, and follow-up of their audits; (3) organization and management of their office; and (4) enforcement of their decisions where the application of sanctions is part of their mandate. SAIs should not be involved or be seen to be involved, in any manner, whatsoever, in the management of the organizations that they audit. SAIs should ensure that their personnel do not develop too close a relationship with the entities they audit, so they remain objective and appear objective. SAI should have full discretion in the discharge of their responsibilities, they should cooperate with governments or public entities that strive to improve the use and management of public funds. SAI should use appropriate work and audit standards, and a code of ethics, based on official documents of INTOSAI, International Federation of Accountants (IFAC), or other recognized standard-setting bodies.

SAIs should submit an annual activity report to the Legislature and to other state bodies—as required by the constitution, statutes, or legislation—that they should make available to the public (www.intosai.org, Mexico Declaration, 28.01.2017).

When Mexico Declaration on Independence is read between the lines, it is apparently seen that independence is the most important thing in supreme audit, as it has to be in external audit. Independence will be handled throughout the text and will receive the emphasis it deserves.

Naturally, there are differentiations in terms of audit terminology between private sector organizations' auditing and public sector institutions' auditing. As expected, the definition of compliance audit for public sector institutions involves different components.

As observed from the Fig. 1.1, compliance audit involves *regularity audit* as well as *performance audit*, and the stages of regularity audit are shown in Fig. 1.2, and stages of performance audit are displayed in Fig. 1.3.

According to INTOSAI, performance auditing carried out by SAIs is an independent, objective, and reliable examination of whether government undertakings, systems, operations, programs, activities, or organizations are operating in accordance with the principles of economy, efficiency, and effectiveness and whether there is room for improvement. Economy means minimizing the costs of resources, efficiency means getting the most from the available resources, and effectiveness concerns meeting the objectives set and achieving the intended results (ISSAI 3100, 7–8).

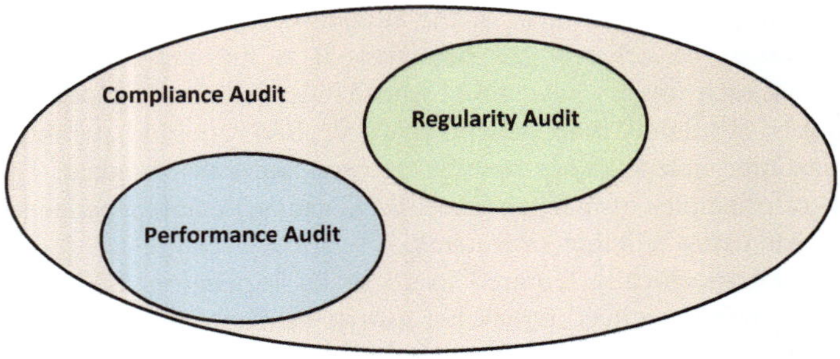

Fig. 1.1 Scope of compliance audit in Turkish public sector. *Source* Gülen, F. (1998). Finansal Denetim. 1st Edition. Ankara, Turkish Supreme Audit Institution. T.C. Sayıştay Başkanlığı. Figured from pp. 1, 3. http://www.sayistay.gov.tr/yayin/yayin2.asp?id=39. Accessed 26 Feb 2012

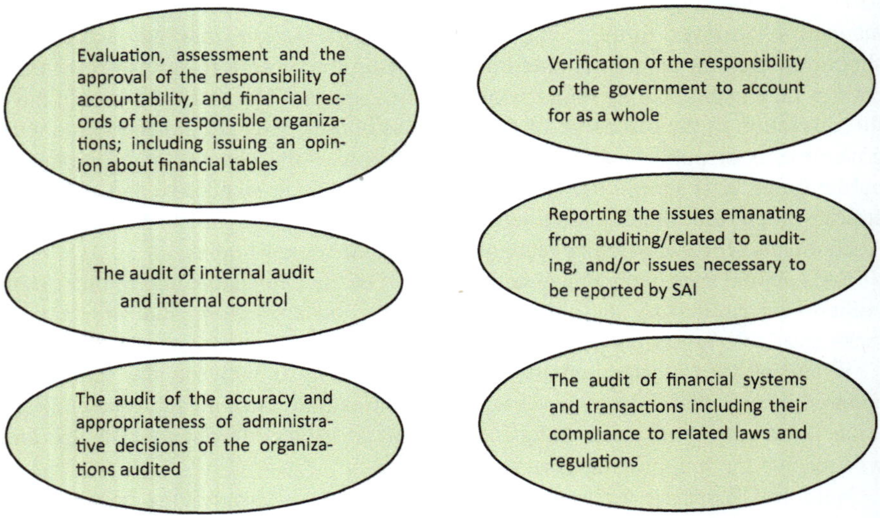

Fig. 1.2 Stages of regularity audit in Turkish public sector. *Source* Gülen, F. (1998). Finansal Denetim. 1st Edition. Ankara, Turkish Supreme Audit Institution. T.C. Sayıştay Başkanlığı. Figured from pp. 1, 3. http://www.sayistay.gov.tr/yayin/yayin2.asp?id=39. Accessed 26 Feb 2012

National Audit Office of Finland states that performance audit emphasizes sound financial management, while financial audit is more concerned with legality and compliance with the budget. Performance audit is focused and audit questions are formulated from the perspective of economy, efficiency, and effectiveness and attention is also paid to any problems that may be observed regarding the legality of financial management and compliance with budget (National Audit Office of Finland, www.vtv.fi, 26.02.2012, NAO Finland, 2007: 9).

Another term employed in describing oversight of government is *economic audit*, which is a review of recent government expenditure to determine the effectiveness of budget outlays. The objective of this review is to ensure value for money for taxpayers —that is, government is involved in the right activities, they are being delivered for the

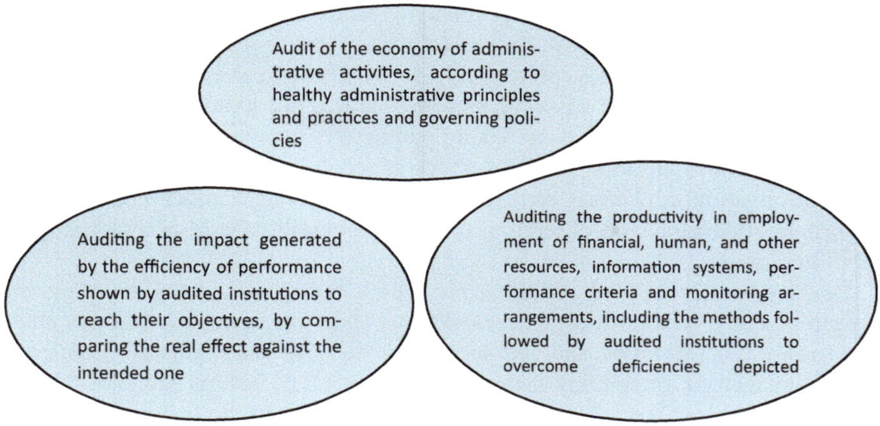

Fig. 1.3 Stages of performance audit in Turkish public sector. *Source* Gülen, F. (1998). Finansal Denetim. 1st Edition. Ankara, Turkish Supreme Audit Institution. T.C. Sayıştay Başkanlığı. Figured from pp. 1, 3. http://www.sayistay.gov.tr/yayin/yayin2.asp?id=39. Accessed 26 Feb 2012

least cost, and they contribute to the achievement of improved outcomes for citizens. It includes a transparent and comprehensive assessment of the financial performance of state departments, authorities and commercial entities, with a focus on identifying potential savings from bureaucratic waste and mismanagement. Furthermore, it is an examination of the current structure of government agencies to determine whether changes are warranted to better support the efficient and effective delivery of government services, and an evaluation of the effectiveness of existing performance metrics and options for greater transparency and accountability through improved public reporting (www.treasury.wa.gov.au, 29.01.2017, Department of Treasury, Government of Western Australia).

1.1.2.2 Audit from Statutory Point of View

External audit, internal audit, and public audit are subclasses of audit from statutory point of view. This classification is in harmony with the classification regarding the auditor. European Union (EU) legislation employs the term **statutory audit**. Internal audit matches with performance audit; public audit composes a pair with compliance audit, and external audit overlaps with financial table audit. Since these are handled under the title Audit from the Point of Purpose in detail, these topics will not be repeated here.

1.2 Developments in External Auditing

Economic life emerged as a natural consequence of people's need to live together as a society. Economic life requires making decisions which bear consequences at differing significance levels; decision making necessitates making a choice among alternatives. Making a healthy choice totally depends on the accuracy, validity, and reliability of the data especially collected for assessment. At an opposite position, there will be the possibility of not only the decision makers, but also a large segment of the society and stakeholders being harmed due to interaction; thus, their faith in the system being shaken. Today's intensive, complicated, and multisided economic relations are in need of assurance of reliability, relevancy, and accuracy of the information, which may have the possibility affecting transactions. Following the historical development of audit, it can be admitted that audit as a fact arose to fulfill this need.

Development process of auditing, interactions between financial reporting and the audit quality, relationships between external audit and fraud, frauds in twentieth and twenty-first centuries and the increasing demand for high-quality external audits, engagement of auditing firms in these frauds, and last but not least the link between Sarbanes–Oxley Act (SOX) as a turning point in the history of auditing and quality are discussed under this title.

1.2.1 The Evolution of Auditing and the Importance of Quality Audits

In the paper published in 1962, where he gave coverage to changing targets and techniques, R. Gene Brown also handled the history of auditing. According to the paper, prior to sixteenth century, accounting concerned itself with governmental and family units. Two scribes were keeping independent records of the same transactions, in order to prevent defalcations within the treasuries of the ancient rulers. The secondary objective was the assurance of accuracy in reporting. Inventories were periodically taken to prove the accuracy of the accounting records (Brown 1962: 696).

Auditing during Roman Empire was primarily concerned with preventing fraudulent acts by the quaestors. In the aftermath of the Roman Empire, auditing developed in cooperation with the Italian City States. Brown states as (*ibid.* 697).

> The merchants of Florence, Genoa and Venice used auditors to assist in the verification of the accountability of the sailing-ship captains returning from the Old World with riches bound for the European Continent. Auditing was primarily fraud-preventive during this era.

As embedded in the history and under circumstances depicted above, an early era definition of audit objectives done by L. Fitzpatrick[1] is as follows (as cited in Brown 1962: 697): "Auditing as it existed to the sixteenth century was designed to verify the honesty of persons with fiscal responsibilities." Basically until Industrial Revolution, there had not been distinct modifications of audit objectives, though attitudes noticeably changed. The recognition that an orderly and standardized

[1] L. Fitzpatrick (1939). The story of bookkeeping, accounting, and auditing. Accountants Digest, IV, 217.

system of accounting was desirable for both accurate reporting and fraud prevention was the first attitude that changed. The second was a general acceptance of the need for an independent review of the accounts for enterprises disregarding the size.

Great Britain lived the greatest economic growth between the years 1850–1905, and one of the outcomes of Industrial Revolution had been incorporation of enterprises. The passage of management from the owners to professional managers greased the skids for auditing to emerge as a profession. Brown states that the last decade of nineteenth century was the decade witnessing the implementation of testing as an auditing procedure, and evidence of sampling laid in London & General Bank case dated 1895 (1962: 698). Lawrence R. Dicksee, the author of the highly valued book of auditing in its period, says that the object of an audit may be said threefold (1907: 7): (1) the detection of fraud, (2) the detection of technical errors, (3) the detection of errors of principle. In the following epoch, American auditing profession progressed independently of its British origins. The main objects of an audit listed below, replaced the former objectives of formative days of auditing (Montgomery 1919: 11): (1) to ascertain the actual financial condition and earnings of an enterprise for (i) its proprietors, (ii) its executives, (iii) bankers or investors considering the purchase of securities, and (iv) bankers considering discounting/purchasing of its promissory notes; (2) the detection of fraud or errors as the secondary objective.

As Brown points at; Montgomery states these objectives in the first, second, and third editions of his valuable book. This epoch is also the one, when internal control started gaining importance. The period encompassed by 1933 and 1940, during which the reflections and consequences of McKesson & Robbins[2] case were felt, was a period when there was confusion about audit objectives, and incongruous ideas had been put forward; however, there was near consensus on audit techniques. In the next epoch, 20 years ahead of 1960, there were minor changes regarding audit techniques and audit objectives, but many audit techniques were specifically designed to assist in the detection of fraud.

The attitude expressed by American Institute of Certified Public Accountants (AICPA) and most accounting writers was, that the primary objective of an audit by a CPA is to enable him to express an opinion as to the fairness of the financial statements, and that the ordinary examination incident to the issuance of an opinion respecting financial statements is not designed and cannot be relied upon to disclose defalcations and other similar irregularities (Brown 1962: 701). Porter et al. (2005) define the 1960s through the 1990s, as an era when the world economy continued to grow; important developments in technological developments and the size and complexity of companies had been witnessed; and auditors in the 1970s played an important role in enhancing the credibility of financial information and furthering the operations of an effective capital market (as cited in Lee and Azham 2008: 4).

[2]McKesson & Robbins case will be handled in detail in the following pages.

This book mainly focuses on contemporary auditing; therefore, history of auditing is shortly captured in a table. Table 1.1, starting with ancient times, divides audit history in meaningful eras; where unique approaches, common objectives, and methods of audit are observed. The first column shows the time period, the second one shortly tells about the stated objectives of the specific era, the third column gives the extent of verifications—tells about the methods used, and the last one gives hints about the existence of internal control and how much it is considered important. This table is a result of integrated data derived from several sources. The period up until 1960 is almost the replica of Brown's (1962). The following periods are used as they had been determined by the original source.

1.2.2 The Interaction Between Financial Reporting and Audit Quality

Accounting as a system, an *economic information system*, refers to the transformation of an organization's economic data into economic information useful for purposes of financial decision making with regard to that organization. Accounting information is used by a wide variety of groups concerned about the economic activities of business organizations. The parties benefitting from accounting information can be separated into internal and external users. Management is responsible for the content of the financial accounting statements. It is essential for the investors, creditors, and public in general to take decisions by being well informed. Thus, there exists a need for an independent party to examine or audit financial statements. CPA examines the financial statements and supporting evidence prepared by management's internal accounting staff (Johnson and Gentry 1980: 13–17).

At his speech given to American University Kogod School of Business students PCAOB member Steven B. Harris by laying emphasis on the fact that American households invest their savings in the capital markets either directly or indirectly, pointed to the importance of accounting and auditing. According to the most recent U.S. Census Bureau survey, 42% of households have 401(k)[3] or thrift savings

[3]401(k) plan: A qualified plan established by employers to which eligible employees may make salary deferral (salary reduction) contributions on a post-tax and/or pretax basis. Employers offering a 401(k) plan may make matching or non-elective contributions to the plan on behalf of eligible employees and may also add a profit-sharing feature to the plan. Earnings accrue on a tax-deferred basis.

Caps placed by the plan and/or IRS regulations usually limit the percentage of salary deferral contributions. There are also restrictions on how and when employees can withdraw these assets, and penalties may apply if the amount is withdrawn while an employee is under the retirement age as defined by the plan. Plans that allow participants to direct their own investments provide a core group of investment products from which participants may choose. Otherwise, professionals hired by the employer direct and manage the employees' investments (www.investopedia.com, 28.03.2014).

Table 1.1 History of auditing

Period	Stated audit objectives	Extent of verifications	Importance of internal controls
Ancient to 1500	Detection of fraud	Detailed	Not recognized
1500–1850	Detection of fraud	Detailed	Not recognized
1851–1905	Detection of fraud Detection of clerical error	Primarily detailed, samplings seen, some tests	Its existence among standard systems of accounting is recognized, but somehow neglected
1906–1933	Determination of fairness of reported financial position Detection of fraud and errors	Detailed and testing	Slightly recognized and gains importance
1934–1940	Determination of fairness of reported financial position Detection of fraud and errors	Sampling, development of new techniques	Awakening interest
1941–1960	Determination of fairness of reported financial position	Sampling, development of new techniques	Substantial emphasis
1961–1970	Identification of the truthfulness of financial statements and to ensuring that financial statements were fairly presented	Methods resembling previous era	Substantial emphasis
1971–1980	Affirmation of the truthfulness of financial statements and ensuring that financial statements were fairly presented	The more internal control of the company became effective, detailed substance testing abandoned, confidence in the system	Substantial emphasis
1981–1990	Financial table audit, advisory services to audit client	Testing, detailed substance testing, analytical procedures, risk-based auditing	Substantial emphasis
1991–2000	Business risk approach: a broad range of client's business risks are relevant to the audit Corporate governance ability of the client	Testing, detailed substance testing, analytical procedures	Substantial emphasis

(continued)

Table 1.1 (continued)

Period	Stated audit objectives	Extent of verifications	Importance of internal controls
2001–2010	Obtaining reasonable assurance whether financial tables are prepared in accordance with applicable financial reporting framework, express an opinion about financial tables	Testing, detailed substance testing, analytical procedures	Substantial emphasis
2011–	Determining and reporting the degree of relationship of the financial information with predefined criteria	Control testing, independent tests of transactions, analytic procedures, detailed examination of balances	The efficiency of internal control over financial reporting is reported

Source Until 1960 organized partly from Brown (1962)
Years between 1960 and 2000 summarized from Lee and Azham (2008)
From 1989 on organized partly from American Institute of Certified Public Accountants. Research. Standards. Audit & Attest Standards. AU Sect. 329, Analytical Procedures http://www.aicpa.org/research/standards/auditattest/pages/sas.aspx#SAS43, 10.05.2012
From 2011 on organized partly from Arens et al. (2012)

plan[4] accounts with money invested in the markets; this makes accounting and auditing vital to the integrity of the capital markets and to the infrastructure the entire financial system (Harris 20.03.2014). The process of business world becoming without frontiers, the rapid integration of capital markets, changes parallel to tax domain, transparency, the more frequent usage of concepts like corporate governance, and a whole raft of many other factors caused financial tables' importance to increase and widened the usage area. According to Hegarty (2007) basic components resting under a sound financial reporting system might be listed as follows (as cited by Parlakkaya et al. 2014: 1666): (1) Accounting Standards, (2) Legal Structure, (3) Oversight and Impositions, (4) Education, (5) Professional Ethics, and (6) Auditing Standards. These basic components are handled from several aspects in this book.

[4]Thrift savings plan (TSP): Congress established the TSP in 1986 and it offers the same types of tax benefits and savings as a 401(k). Each pay period, the agency the employee works for deposits 1% of the employee's basic pay into the employee's TSP. On top of that, the employee has the option of making additional contributions, which the agency will match (up to 4% of employee pay). These extra contributions are tax-deferred and administered by the Federal Retirement Thrift Investment Board. Just like a 401(k), you can choose how these funds are invested. Upon setting up the TSP, you will be given a list of fund choices. Since TSP does not function as a pension like the Basic Benefit Plan and Social Security, employee's earnings in future would be based on the funds chosen, the amount of money contributed above the amount what the employer deposits and market conditions that are outside of control. http://www.investopedia.com/articles/personal-finance/062513/what-federal-employees-retirement-system-fers-and-how-does-it-work.asp, 28.03.2014.

Operations research/management science (OR/MS) as a scientific and systematic approach in decision making needs information at the firsthand besides other elements, in order to achieve healthy results. A systems approach best equips the decision maker to determine which alternative actually will maximize the realization of the goals of the organization. It is apparent that without correct information, management science, which is expected to serve useful for the public, organizations, and investors, will become dysfunctional and meaningless. An organization's accounting department can be vital in providing the necessary data needed (Cook and Russell 1981: 9, 17).

Investors, who are intending to invest in stocks and debt instruments publicly offered by public companies, employ several analyses. Fundamental analysis among these; along with economic analysis and industry analysis comprises business analysis as well. Along with qualitative factors like product features, firm management, markets—the firm takes place, the characteristics of these markets, and the level of adaptation of the firm to these features; quantitative factors also take place in these analyses. Quantitative analysis is directed to examination of the historic performance of the firm, through financial tables like balance sheet, income statement, flow of funds statement, etc. Trustworthiness of the information displayed through financial tables is among significant issues of securities investors. For example, inventory evaluation method and profit share disclosures are quite critical information (Başoğlu et al. 2009: 453–460). According to both International Accounting Standards (IAS 1) and Turkish Accounting Standards about Presentation of Financial Tables (TAS 1), a complete set of financial tables includes sections listed below (www.kgk.gov.tr, 02.01.2015; www.iasplus.com, 19.02.2017):

(1) A statement of financial position (balance sheet) at the end of the period.

- A statement of profit or loss and other comprehensive income for the period (presented as a single statement, or by presenting the profit or loss section in a separate statement of profit or loss, immediately followed by a statement presenting comprehensive income beginning with profit or loss).
- A statement of changes in equity for the period.
- A statement of cash flows for the period.
- Notes, comprising a summary of significant accounting policies and other explanatory notes.
- Comparative information prescribed by the standard.
- A statement of financial position (balance sheet) as at the beginning of the earliest comparative period, if an entity applies an accounting policy retrospectively or makes a retrospective restatement of items in its financial statements, or when it reclassifies items in its financial statements.

In order to enable the decision makers to utilize the information taking place in financial tables the best and swiftly way, these tables have to be understandable, fulfilling the need, reliable, comparable, and prepared on time. Financial tables are the formalized presentation of an entity's financial position and financial performance. According to TAS 1 the objective of general purpose financial statements is: (1) to provide information about the financial position, financial performance, and cash flows of an entity that is useful to a wide range of users in making economic decisions, (2) to display how efficiently the managers utilize the sources entrusted to them.

The wide user group of financial tables encompasses investors, creditor institutions, rating agencies, other-related parties, and the public in general. Both specific characteristics of financial tables, and the existence of standards inhold the factors would be impacting the quality of audits finally. Some of the specific characteristics of financial tables are mentioned below. Financial tables demonstrate the administrative performance of managers; namely, the level of accountability of themselves about the usage of sources entrusted to them (www.kgk.gov.tr, 06.01.2015, KOBI TFRS, p. 3). Nonetheless; it should not be forgotten that, skills, talents, and ethics of managers; loyalty of the employees; reputability of the firm, and far too numerous positive and negative factors do not find a place in financial tables due to the fact that it is not possible to put these in numbers (Usta 2005: 63–64).

Management's identification of transactions, events, and conditions that give rise to the need for accounting estimates is likely to be based on: (1) management's knowledge of the entity's business and the industry in which it operates, (2) management's knowledge of the implementation of business strategies in the current period, and (3) management's cumulative experience of preparing the entity's financial statements in prior periods (www.kgk.gov.tr, TSA 540, 2014: 18). The experiences and ethical values of management, responsible from preparation of financial tables, add subjectivity into determination of income and expenses. For example, differences in evaluation of inventory, dissimilarities in methods for calculating amortization, and similar reasons cause variations in calculation of end of period income (Usta 2005: 63–64).

One of the reasons why financial table information is not gospel truth is the presence of inflation. The impact of inflation on corporate finance has to be assessed under the titles listed below (https://financenmoney.com, 06.01.2015): (1) inflation and asset revaluation, (2) inflation and firm value, (3) inflation and financial returns, (4) inflation and innovation in the financial markets, (5) inflation and financial analysis, and (6) inflation and capital budgeting. Besides, the assumption that the value of money stays constant would cause the analyses and interpretations to become unhealthy (Usta 2005: 63–64). Along with the specific characteristics of financial tables, standards have impact on audit quality. Financial reporting practice under a given set of standards is sensitive to the incentives of the managers and auditors responsible for financial statement preparation. Preparer incentives depend on the interplay between market and political forces in the reporting jurisdiction (Ball et al. 2003: 1) as displayed in Fig. 1.4. Ball, Robin, and Wu, who analyzed the quality of accounting in the East Asian countries, found out that, incentives dominate accounting standards as a determinant of financial reporting in Hong Kong, Malaysia, Singapore, and Thailand. They say, for countries seeking higher financial reporting quality, changing manager, and auditor incentives become more

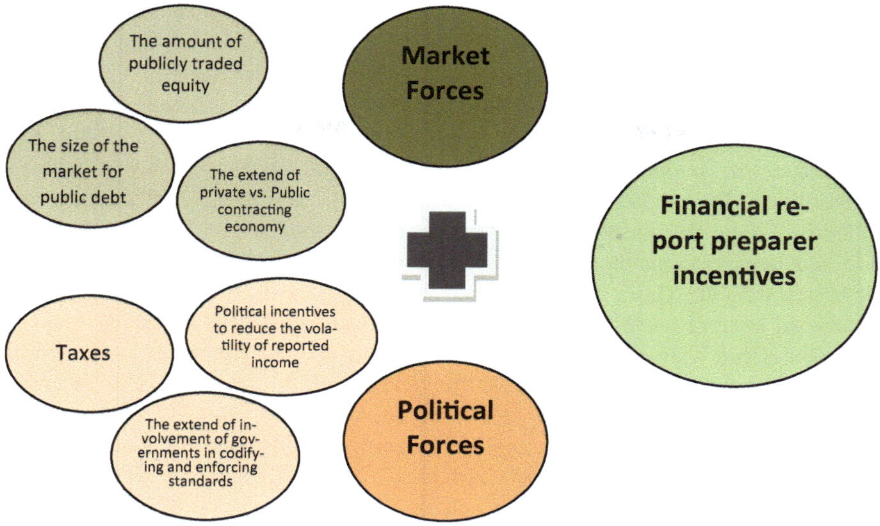

Fig. 1.4 The interplay between market and political forces impacting financial statement preparer incentives. *Source* Ball et al. 2003. "Incentives versus standards: Properties of accounting income

important than mandating foreign accounting standards. A study supporting Ball and other's findings is done by Christensen, Lee, and Walker in 2008.

As Lee et al. put forth, existing studies at that time documented improvements in accounting quality following voluntary International Financial Reporting Standards (IFRS) adoption. Since adopting IFRS became mandatory in 2005, and between 1998 and 2005 German firms could voluntarily adopt IFRS, the authors benefited from this setting in comparing the effects of mandatory and voluntary adoption of IFRS on audit quality. They categorized the data set as voluntary IFRS adopting firms and resisting firms and examined earnings management and timely loss recognition, most often accepted as two dimensions of accounting quality. They observed accounting quality improvement in firms adopting IFRS voluntarily, where this kind of observation lacks in mandatory adoption. Upon this observation, they concluded that unless the firms comprehend the benefits of IFRS adoption, an improvement in accounting quality is not absolute (Christensen et al. 2008: 1, 28).

Ashbaugh conducted a study on annual reports of 211 non-US firms listed with London Stock Exchange to determine firms' accounting standard choices; and found a positive association between firms' disclosures of International Accounting Standards (IAS) financial information and the number of foreign equity markets in which their shares trade. Besides, firms were more likely to disclose IAS financial information, when IAS requires more financial disclosure and restricts the accounting method choice relative to the firm's domestic GAAP. The third finding is that, at the times of participating in seasoned equity offerings, the non-US firms become more likely to disclose IAS financial information. The author points to Leutz and Verrecchia study (2001) and concludes that these efforts are directed to lowering the information asymmetry component of the firms' own costs of capital (Ashbaugh 2001: 131–132).

At the International Organization of Securities Commissions (IOSCO) roundtable in Paris on July 1, 2007, panelist Michael Cook[5] uses a sports analogy and says the *defense part* of financial reporting has grown stronger, and this part includes all the factors designed to protect the reliability and credibility of financial information. These factors are internal control, auditing, certification, and whistleblowing. The reason of the defense bring so strong is that, financial reporting side had been playing the defense for a long period of time. As a result, Cook diagnoses that the value, relevance, and usefulness of the financial information, which had been protected so much, is rapidly declining (Cook 2007: 7).

Auditors are viewed as a component of the web of assurance surrounding financial institutions, and they have the responsibility to ensure that financial statements prepared by the management present a *true and fair view*. As the value, relevancy, and usefulness of financial information is brought up for discussion, the Treasury Committee of House of Commons—United Kingdom (UK), parallelly stated that they received evidence alleging that auditors failed to fulfill the responsibility stated above by approving banks' financial statements shortly before they failed during 2007–2008 financial crises (House of Commons 2009: 76). This assessment further opens the contemporary role and relevancy of audit function (Humphrey et al. 2011: 432). According to Cook, companies are making increasing efforts to provide financial information that does make a real difference to the marketplace. However, most of this information is being delivered outside the basic, regulated financial system. While the need for such information grows, the ability to respond to these needs from within the defense system continues to decline. The *offensive information* described above would include business performance matrices and pro-forma net income information and could enhance the utility and relevance of financial reporting in broad sense (Cook 2007: 7). The main reason in giving wide coverage to Cook's words in the panel is—prior to discussing the quality of audit—to remark what really is the information audited, and probably what is meant primarily with financial reporting, and the need to change and organize what is presented in order to fulfill today's necessities.

As a result of the study on 2004 annual reports and 2005 financial statements of 1039 companies in 14 EU countries plus Norway; Macías an Muiño found evidence that accounting systems in IFRS adopting countries are directed toward investors' and creditors' demands, and accounting systems in partially IFRS adopting countries are more oriented toward satisfying regulatory needs, like calculating taxes (Macías and Muiño 2011: 74–75).

Within the scope of the studies mentioned here, it can be assumed that IFRS would have accounting quality enhancing effects in general, which in turn will

---

[5]**J. Michael Cook**: Chaired the audit committees at Burt's Bees, International Flavors & Fragrances, Comcast Corporation and Eli Lilly & Co. Chairman and CEO of Deloitte Haskins & Sells. Retired Chairman and CEO of the Deloitte & Touche in 1989.

improve the quality of financial reporting; thus, we can conclude that IFRS will have positive impacts on audit quality as well. Though the IFRS are not the core of this book, the support of standards to auditing in overcoming confidence issues in financial reporting brings IFRS into agenda. As well known, accounting data as the basis of financial information is the main audit input. Even though IFRS gained international recognition, and are being adopted in many countries following legislative arrangements, there are both supporters and opponents.

Kaymaz and Karaibrahimoğlu address the issue in their paper and advocate that IFRS may provide cost savings despite obstacles regarding practices (2011: 27). Psaros and Trotman explain that Australian reporting standards are principles-based standards set providing minimum level of guidance; and as the result of the experiment they conducted, they drive attention of the regulators and standard setters to the fact that, management as financial statement preparer, appear to vary their assessments of case-specific information to fit with their judgments (2004: 77, 90). There are also researchers who believe that the quality of accounting will diminish under circumstances, where IFRS adoption is compulsory, but practice mechanisms are loose (Barth et al. 2006: 9).

Cameran, Campa and Pettinicchio believe that the quality of the earnings reported is still an important issue, due to the fact that privately held companies' owners/managers who are in charge of preparing financial statements, have conflicts of interest with lending banks and fiscal authorities. Besides, they also verify that IFRS adoption on, e.g., earnings quality is still an open issue for public companies, and there are conflicting research results considering this issue (Cameran et al. 2014: 281).

Even though there is no single measure of financial reports' quality; less earnings management, more timely loss recognition, and higher value relevance of earnings and equity book value are implications of higher accounting quality (Barth et al. 2006: 10). Based on legal and ethical grounds, company *clawback provisions* (www.cambridge.org, 06.01.2015) would force executives who commit fraud to return bonuses and pay. Clawback provisions are functional not only in fraud cases, but it may also be beneficial to obviate earnings management and the like. As a result of their study about voluntary clawback provision and its effects on financial statements' quality; Dehaan et al. conclude that under voluntary clawback provision quality reducing behaviors are receded (Dehaan et al. 2013: 1028). Barth et al. (2006) compared attributes of accounting amounts resulting from applying domestic GAAP to those resulting from applying IAS for 411 firms across 24 countries. They found evidence that accounting amounts for firms applying IAS are of higher quality than those applying domestic GAAP (quoted by Barth et al. 2006: 7).

In her dissertation Li Dang states that perceived audit quality is based on perceptions of financial statements users, while actual audit quality refers to the auditor's ability to detect and report accounting misstatements (2004: 2). She defines the audits where materially misstated financial statements receive unqualified audit opinions, as apparent audit failure; and obtains audit failure data from the Web site of American SEC (Dang 2004: 6). In order to use in comparative analyses, she also compiled earnings management data from three different sources, and compared audit failure cases determined for the period 1980–2000, against non-audit failure cases states as control group. As a result of her study on 419 companies at a yearly average, she found positive meaningful relation between earnings management and audit failure. Thus, she concluded that poor actual audit quality is associated with higher levels of earnings management (Dang 2004: ix).

1.2.3 The Relation Between Audit and Fraud

Fraudulent financial reporting and corrupt business practices go back to the beginning of the public corporation. Regarding its history, as a case to be considered relatively new is the British East India Company; which was taken public with approximately 125 shareholders and operated between 1600 and 1874. Due to management abuse and fraud, both in 1698 and also in the late 1700s, the company caused this page to be opened (Rezaee and Riley 2009: 16). At the core of the issue of trust lies the burden taken by companies, states, and consequential losses for citizens. Thus, handling the issue of trust in a broad way is possible. Such a huge burden can be assessed both quantitatively and qualitatively.

As Roman Tomasic quotes from Crenshaw (1990), it has been suggested that fraud and other criminal conduct played an important role in the collapse of about 40% of the savings and loan institutions, which had been taken over by the US government's Resolution Trust Corporation (Tomasic 1992: 44). The savings and loan crisis (the S&L crisis) of the 1980s and 1990s was the failure of 1043 out of the 3234 savings and loan associations in the USA from 1986 to 1995, the Federal Savings and Loan Insurance Corporation (FSLIC) closed or otherwise resolved 296 institutions from 1986 to 1989, and the Resolution Trust Corporation (RTC) closed or otherwise resolved 747 institutions from 1989 to 1995 (law.lexisnexis.com, 31.01.2013; en.wikipedia.org, 31.01.2013).

As an anti-fraud organization and provider of anti-fraud training and education the Association of Certified Fraud Examiners (ACFE) in its reports defines occupational fraud as; the use of one's occupation for personal enrichment through the deliberate misuse or misapplication of the employing organization's resources or assets (www.acfe.com, 12.11.2012). Colby as a Certified Fraud Examiner (CFE) defines *financial statement fraud* as the deliberate misrepresentation of the financial condition of an enterprise accomplished through the intentional misstatement or omission of amounts or disclosures in the financial statements in order to deceive financial statement users (www.cga-pdnet.org, 07.01.2015; Colby 2004: 1).

According to Rezaee and Riley (2009: 7), financial statement fraud in USA is commonly caused by management manipulation of earnings to deceive dispersed investors, while it is committed in Europe to benefit controlling shareholders at the expense of minority shareholders. As Coffee states in the dispersed ownership structure characterizing the United States (US) and the United Kingdom (UK), controlling shareholders or controlling blocks are uncommon, and since managers sell their shares at the market price they are more concerned with maximizing it.

However, in concentrated ownership systems as it is in Europe, there is normally a controlling shareholder who can directly monitor the firm's management. Thus, European managers have less incentive to cook the books (Coffee 2004: 43). These differences present challenges to the board of directors, audit committees, external auditors, and regulators in three ways (Rezaee and Riley 2009: 7): (1) Fraud prevention and detection methods that are effective in USA in minimizing financial statement fraud may not work well in the other countries. (2) The primary focus in USA is on earnings manipulations, which happen less frequently in other countries. (3) Laws, regulations, and SOX-like standards designed to prevent and detect financial statement fraud may not be effective in other countries to protect investors from fraud.

Loebbecke and Willingham (1988) hypothesized that the probability of a material irregularity is a function of the extent to which three factors exist in a particular business situation. These factors are (1) conditions allowing the commission of an irregularity, (2) motivation for the commission of an irregularity, and (3) personal attitudes allowing the commission of an irregularity. If all three factors are present, there is a high probability that material management fraud will occur. If any of the three factors is missing, then there is less likelihood that a management fraud will occur (quoted by Green and Calderon 1994: 253).

Having started publishing the first report in 1996, ACFE releases *Report to the Nations on Occupational Fraud and Abuse* biennially since 2002. Table 1.2 is a comparison of data compiled from these reports. While the general purpose of the table is delivering financial impact of occupational fraud, the core is emphasizing the share of financial statement fraud within the financial loss. As stated in the "Analysis Methodology" of 2012 Report, average losses are heavily skewed by a limited number of very high-dollar frauds; therefore all loss amounts are calculated using median loss rather than average. This way it is believed to provide a more conservative and more accurate picture of typical impact of occupational fraud schemes (ACFE 2012 Report to the Nations on Occupational Fraud and Abuse, 2012: 65).

Throughout the years, reports of ACFE evolved; thus, reports of 2010, 2012, and 2014 give place to frauds reported by non-US residing CFEs. Even though the continuously developed report serial loses its comparability, it draws attention to specific issues, which are crucial for our book. One of these is, financial statement fraud being the least common among other fraud cases, but the most costly form of fraud. Among ACFE reports, only 2010 Report gives place to the total amount of loss caused by financial statement fraud. According to the report, combined total loss estimated by CFEs for USA is \$18 billion, and 68% of the schemes, i.e., \$12.24 billion, are caused by financial statement fraud (www.acfe.com/rttn-archive.aspx, 12.11.2012). According to CFEs estimates for cases all over the world, the total loss caused by 2016 cases in the last study exceeds \$6.3 billion. The losses in the previous reports were \$3.7 billion in 2014 and \$3.5 billion in 2013. In case 2010 estimate for USA for financial statement fraud is adapted to 2016 loss data for the world; it can be put forth that financial statement fraud costs \$4.28 billion in countries CFEs report from.

Table 1.2 Synopsis of occupational fraud and abuse pointing to the importance of trust in financial reporting

$ (USD)	2014	2012	2010	2008	2006	2004	2002	1996
Asset misappropriation rate (%)	85.0	86.7	86.3	88.7	91.5	92.7	85.7	81.1
Median loss of asset misappropriation ($)	130,000	120,000	135,000	150,000	150,000	93,000	80,000	65,000
Financial statement fraud rate (%)	9.0	7.6	4.8	10.3	10.6	7.9	5.1	4.1
Median loss of financial statement fraud ($)	1 million	1 million	4.1 million	2 million	2 million	1 million	4.25 million	4 million
Rate of corruption (%)	37.0	33.4	32.8	27.4	30.77	30.1	12.8	14.8
Median loss of corruption ($)	200,000	250,000	250,000	375,000	538,000	250,000	530,000	440,000

Source Organized from ACFE reports of 1996–2002–2004–2006–2008–2010–2012 and 2014. “Report to the Nations on Occupational Fraud and Abuse.” http://www.acfe.com/rttn-archive.aspx. Accessed 12 Nov 2012 and http://www.acfe.com/rttn-download-2014.aspx. Accessed 25 May 2014

As it is extremely hard to detect fraud and the impacts of it, starting from this point, determination of the monetary magnitude is so hard as well. Lene Bjørn Serpa, one of the keynote speakers of the third conference on corporate governance (2013) organized by Copenhagen Business School and De Montfort University, stated that even at Maersk[6] Group, which is perceived as having good corporate governance practices, fraud and corruption do not always go public. She also emphasized its necessity for prestigious companies, not to reveal even few fraud cases, and handle them within the company for the sake of the reputation of them. Having in mind the attitude of the business world under similar circumstances, it is not complex to comprehend that ACFE data do not provide all information about the size of fraud.

As stated before, financial reporting implicates asymmetric information infirmity, thus confidence issue. The function of auditing mitigates asymmetric information problem (Dang 2004: 23).This is a big problem to be overcome and is to be resolved urgently and perennially for the sake of a healthy economic life. Audited financial statements compose the basic source for investors to evaluate public companies. Since the financial reporting crisis of 2001/2002, society, securities regulators, and institutional investors alike paid more attention to the role of auditors in the capital markets. Securities regulators **started** monitoring the credibility of financial reporting—paying attention to the enhancement of audit quality, the accessibility of audit service, and its delivery (Abma, 10.12.2009: 1; IOSCO Consultation Report, Sep 2009: 1). As Wellink stresses, high-quality audits of banks complement supervisory processes and increase supervisory efficiency (14.01.2010: 1; IOSCO Consultation Report, Sep 2009: 1).

1.2.4 Twentieth Century Notable Accounting Scandals and the Thirst for High-Quality Audits

There are many accounting scandals witnessed during twentieth century; but Kreuger & Toll and McKesson & Robbins cases are scandals lived at the very beginning of the century and are infamous frauds, which put stamp on history by causing lots of investors to lose money. The instigator of Kreuger & Toll case the industrialist Ivar Kreuger; born to an industrialist family, graduated from college at age 16 and began studies at the Royal Institute of Technology in Stockholm, earned combined master's degrees covering both the faculties of mechanical and civil engineering, at the age of 20, is an entrepreneurial personality. The construction firm Kreuger & Toll formed in Sweden in 1908 put its signature under important buildings like Stockholm Olympic Stadium. Besides his own enterprises, Kreuger

[6]**Maersk Group**: Integrated transport and logistics company with multiple brands and is a global company in container shipping and ports. Including a stand-alone energy division, the company employs roughly 88,000 employees across operations in 130 countries (www.maersk.com).

laid his hands on Kreuger family match factories until then run by his father, brother, and uncle, which encountered financial problems and from 1911 on his story continued as being called the *Match King* (http://en.wikipedia.org, 04.11. 2012). According to Clikeman, after the World War I, many European countries were in need for funds to rebuild their economies. Kreuger & Toll offered loans of up to $125 million to governments in return for receiving the exclusive right to sell matches within the countries' borders. Prices were set by contract and the loans were repaid through an excise tax on matches. This strategy enabled Kreuger & Toll to obtain absolute monopolies in 15 countries and dominate the match market in 19 others. To raise the funds he needed to lend to the European governments, Kreuger organized an American subsidiary to sell stocks and bonds to US investors by paying dividends of up to 20% annually. Next phase was his plans to dominate the world match market start deteriorating into an enormous *Ponzi Scheme*[7]. At the time, funds from new investors and lenders were interrupted due to Big Depression, Kreuger gave himself away (Clikeman 2003: 2–3).

The mastermind of McKesson & Robbins scandal is Philip Musica, also known as F. Donald Coster, born in Napoli in 1877, was an Italian swindler whose criminal career spanned parts of three decades and the person who turned down an offer to run for president in 1936 on the Republican ticket out of fear of being unmasked. His various crimes included tax fraud, bank fraud, and bootlegging. He wanted to become a major player on Wall Street, and when McKesson & Robbins, a well-respected drug maker and distributor, was up for sale he got his chance. In 1926, he merged Girard & Co., which he had set up in 1923, with McKesson for $1 million. While McKesson was the surviving company, Coster became the merged company's president. With the assistance of his brothers his machine continued to roll through the Great Depression until by 1937; McKesson was the third-largest drug company in the world then. When McKesson's board ordered him to convert $2 million of his crude drugs into cash to build up profits and reduce outstanding debt; Musica/Coster responded with a demand that the firm should obtain a $3 million loan for improvements. The company's treasurer on a hunch discovered Coster had stolen $3 million from McKesson over the years (http://en.wikipedia.org , 06.11.2012).

The intense collective complaints of investors about their losses due to recent scandals helped build political support for passage of the US securities acts in 1933 and 1934. In a few months following McKesson & Robbins scandal, American Institute of Accountants[8] brought significant advices for auditor assignment and alterations considering auditing test procedures. Both acts required companies to publish audited financial statements before selling securities to the public and

[7]**Ponzi Scheme**: is a fraudulent investing scam promising high rates of return with little risk to investors. Returns for older investors are paid by acquiring new investors. Eventually, there is not enough money to go around, and the schemes unravel (www.investopedia.com, 10.03.2012).

[8]**AICPA**: Founded in 1887 as American Association of Public Accountants (AAPA), the AICPA represents the CPA profession, is renamed a few of times. 1917–1957 was the era of American Institute of Accountants (www.aicpa.org, 04.11.2012).

established the Securities and Exchange Commission (SEC) to oversee corporate financial reporting (Clikeman 2003: 1, 3). The first major endorsement for the establishment of audit committees came from the New York Stock Exchange (NYSE) in 1939, also as a result of the McKesson and Robbins case. The Exchange's report stated, "...where practicable, the selection of the auditors by a special committee of the board of directors composed of directors who are not officers of the company appears desirable" (Birkett 1986: 4). NYSE also recommended the auditors address their report to the shareholders. In the summer of 1939, the American Institute of Accountants appointed its first standing committee on auditing procedures. The committee's first standard, Statements on Auditing Procedure No. 1, *Extensions of Auditing Procedure*, made observing inventory and confirming accounts receivable standard audit procedures. These two procedures would have helped detect the McKesson & Robbins fraud (Clikeman 2003: 1, 3, 6). According to Clikeman, these reforms shaped the accounting profession's next six decades.

Along with the prominent accounting scandals at the beginning of the twentieth century, the plots at the last 20 years of the century did also played a role in substantial changes in audit process. Some of them lived between 1980 and 2014 are shown in Table 1.3 date sorted from latest to earliest. As the table is examined, it is clearly seen that there are 55 scandals, which caused financial and emotional damages to the countries they are hosted by; incited losses to governments and investors, and resulted in irreversible dramatic changes in shareholders' lives. The column "Year" shows the year the scandal went public. "Data about Fraud" column supplies data compiled from several sources within the reach; about the material size of the fraud, prison sentence or criminal fine given by authorized bodies, whichever is appropriate. The methods used in perpetrating fraud are explained in the "Course of Fraud" column; some footnotes are given for jargon. As mentioned before, the table starting with Nugan Hand Bank (1980) case from bottom up, ending with Autonomy Corporation (2012) case displays 55 scandals about each some search is made. Visits are paid to their Web sites if any, court decisions are read, news in the press are followed, and several academic papers are reviewed. During this phase, at the first place it is observed that company managers implement their fraud plans in accordance with the idiom *devil looks after his own*. The second observation is that, whatever the top managers/groups do, come to the attention of the very next followers or close subordinates, where the witnessing people mostly try to urge the perpetrator to stop the misconduct, and frequently fail in inducing their bosses. There are cases, where the witness who fails to do so, becomes the collaborator.

Any deeper search to understand the scandals, within a specific time span, helped to find out which accounting firm audited which scandalous company. This in turn helped to start the discussion about the responsibilities of the assigned accounting firms in these scandals. In order to better understand the scandals tabulated, there is a need for some definitions. Course of fraud in Enron case is creative accounting. Creative accounting is also called as *aggressive accounting* or *innovative accounting* (www.investopedia.com, 31.01.2014); though deviating from what those standards intend to accomplish, consists of accounting practices that

Table 1.3 Prominent accounting scandals between 1980 and 2014

Company	Year	Data about fraud	Auditing firm	Country	Course of fraud
1. Autonomy Corporation	2012	$8.847 billion (HP reported 2013 1st quarter results)	Deloitte & Touche	USA	Accounting improprieties, misrepresentations and disclosure failures by the previous management before Hewlett-Packard (HP) acquired the company (Norris, 30.11.2012)
2. Olympus Corporation	2011	>$1.7 billion	Ernst & Young	Japan	Tobashi[a] using acquisitions
3. Sino-Forest Corporation	2011	>$3.05 billion	Ernst & Young	Canada–China	Inflation of assets and investments, overstating revenues, Ponzi Scheme, forgery
4. Lehman Brothers	2010	≈$175 billion	Ernst & Young	USA	Failure to disclose Repo 105 transactions to investors. Non-disclosure of debt payment with the money aroused from this failure to investors
5. Satyam Computer Services	2009	$1 billion	PricewaterhouseCoopers	India	Falsified accounts
6. Anglo Irish Bank	2008	€87 million	Ernst & Young	Ireland	Hidden loans controversy: by circular transactions hiding the loans granted to managers
7. Bernard L. Madoff Investment Securities LLC	2008	$18 billion	Friehling & Horowitz	USA	Massive Ponzi scheme
8. AIG (American International Group, Inc.)	2004	$122.8 billion	PricewaterhouseCoopers	USA	Accounting of structured financial deals
9. Chiquita Brands International	2004	Fine: $25 million	Ernst & Young	USA	Illegal payments to paramilitary groups
10. Nortel	2003	$3 billion false revenue	Deloitte & Touche	Canada	Distributed ill-advised corporate bonuses to top 43 managers

(continued)

Table 1.3 (continued)

Company	Year	Data about fraud	Auditing firm	Country	Course of fraud
11. HealthSouth Corporation	2003	CEO is paid unearned salary, bonus and profits from sale of shares	Ernst & Young	USA	Revenues are overstated by $1.4 billion, assets by $800 million between 1999 and 2003
12. Parmalat	2003	€14 billion or £7 billion hole in accounts/10 year prison term	Grant Thornton SpA and Deloitte & Touche (Reece, 12.01.2004)	Italy	Falsified accounting documents
13. Royal Ahold	2003	Overstatement of revenue by $24 billion, and profit by >$1 billion	Deloitte & Touche	Holland	Inflating promotional allowances: $800 million
14. Sunbeam	2002	$19 million	Arthur Andersen	USA	Overstated sales and revenues. 1996: inflating reorganization expenditures, 1997: inflating revenue
15. Merrill Lynch	2002	Fine: $100 million	Deloitte & Touche	USA	Conflict of interest. Publishing misleading survey results
16. ImClone Systems	2002	Fine: 7 years 3 months	KPMG	USA	Insider trading
17. Vivendi Universal	2002	Loss: €23.3 billion	Arthur Andersen	France	Financial reshuffling. As a response to the loss, supporting media holdings by selling shares in portfolio of small companies
18. Freddie Mac	2002	Fine: $125 million	PricewaterhouseCoopers	USA	Deflating revenue by $5 billion
19. Adelphia	2002	$100 million	Deloitte & Touche	USA	With complicated cash management, moving funds to family companies
20. Kmart	2002	End of 2001 bank loans: $970 million	PricewaterhouseCoopers	USA	Misleading accounting practices. Pretending company has losses, making luxurious spending
21. Homestore.com	2002	$100 million	PricewaterhouseCoopers	USA	Recording barter transactions as sales
22. CMS Energy	2002	Deal: $123 million + interest	Arthur Andersen	USA	By round trip trades inflating revenue by more than $5.2 billion

(continued)

Table 1.3 (continued)

Company	Year	Data about fraud	Auditing firm	Country	Course of fraud
23. Bristol-Myers Squibb	2002	Fine: $150 million & $50 billion worth of shareholders' fund	PricewaterhouseCoopers	USA	(1) By channel stuffing; inventory shown on customers, thus revenues are inflated by $1.5 billion (2) Cookie jar[b] accounting
24. Merck & Co.	2002	$12.4 billion	PricewaterhouseCoopers	USA	Recorded co-payments that were not collected
25. Peregrine Systems	2002		KPMG	USA	Overstated $100 million in sales by improperly recognizing revenue from third-party resellers
26. Duke Energy	2002		Deloitte & Touche	USA	Round trip trades
27. AOL (America Online)	2002		Ernst & Young	USA	Overstated revenue by $49 million
28. Global Crossing	2002		Arthur Andersen	Bermuda	Network capacity swaps to inflate revenues
29. Halliburton	2002		Arthur Andersen	USA	Improperly booked $100 million in annual construction cost overruns before customers agreed to pay for them
30. El Paso Corporation	2002		Deloitte & Touche	USA	Round trip trades
31. Dynegy	2002		Arthur Andersen	USA	Round trip trades
32. Mirant	2002	Revenue overstated by $1.1 billion	KPMG	USA	Overstated assets and liabilities
33. Nicor	2002		Arthur Andersen	USA	Overstated assets, understated liabilities
34. Reliant Energy	2002		Deloitte & Touche	USA	Round trip trades
35. Qwest Communications	2002		1999, 2000, 2001 Arthur Andersen; 2002 Oct KPMG	USA	Inflated revenues
36. Tyco International	2002		PricewaterhouseCoopers	Bermuda	Improper accounting
37. WorldCom	2002	$161 billion	Arthur Andersen	USA	Overstated cash flows
38. Enron	2001	$67 billion	Arthur Andersen	USA	Scamming by creative accounting

(continued)

Table 1.3 (continued)

Company	Year	Data about fraud	Auditing firm	Country	Course of fraud
39. One.Tel	2001		Ernst & Young	Australia	Via pump and dump[c] method defraud investors. Through misselling defrauding the supplying partner
40. Xerox	2000		KPMG	USA	Falsified financial results
41. Computer Associates	2000	Compensation: $225 million Fine: 12.5 years prison term	KPMG	USA	Inappropriate recording of 1998–1999 revenue
42. Unify Corporation	2000		Deloitte & Touche	USA	Security fraud and conspiracy
43. MicroStrategy	2000	Deal: $10 million	PricewaterhouseCoopers	USA	Showing losses as profit
44. Lernout & Hauspie	2000		KPMG	Belgium	Fictitious transaction in Korea; improper accounting methods elsewhere
45. Waste Management, Inc.	1999		Arthur Andersen	USA	Misleading financial statements
46. Cendant	1998	Loss: $14 million Fine: 12 tears prison term	Ernst & Young	USA	Inflating revenue by $500 million in three years
47. Sybase	1997		Ernst & Young	Japan, USA	Three managers of the company's Japanese division inflate profits of their operations
48. Informix	1996		Ernst & Young	USA	Improper booking of $278 million in revenues
49. Phar-Mor	1992	Fine: $1 million and 235 months imprisonment	Coopers & Lybrand	USA	Mail fraud, wire fraud, bank fraud, and transportation of funds obtained by theft or fraud
50. Bank of Credit and Commerce International (BCCI)	1991	Immense amount	Ernst & Young and Pricewaterhouse	England	All kinds of international financial crimes

(continued)

Table 1.3 (continued)

Company	Year	Data about fraud	Auditing firm	Country	Course of fraud
51. Polly Peck	1990	£550 million	BDO, Stoy Hayward	England	CEO A. Nadir moved funds between a complex network of offshore companies based in Switzerland and the Bahamas to benefit himself, family & associates (Croft 23.01.2012)
52. MiniScribe	1989	$171 million Fine: $568 million	Coopers & Lybrand	USA	Inflated inventory count, breaking into the accountant's lockboxes, replacing independent count to match the newly inflated numbers (Green and Calderon 1994: 266)
53. Barlow Clowes	1988	£17 million Fine: 10-year imprisonment	Deloitte & Touche	England	Gilts management service. £110 million missing (www.sfo.gov.uk, 11.03.2012). 16 customers committed suicide
54. ZZZZ Best	1986	$100 million	Ernst & Whinney (today partially Ernst & Young)	USA	Barry Minkow Ponzi Scheme
55. Nugan Hand Bank	1980		Pollard and Heuschkel	Australia	Money laundering (www.aic.gov.au, 10.03.2012)

Source Inspired by Wikipedia, Accounting Scandals. Notable Accounting Scandals (http://en.wikipedia.org/wiki/Accounting_scandals, Accessed 10 Mar 2012) Missing data collected from several sources listed in References, and organized

[a]*Tobashi* is Japanese for "flying away" and is a financial fraud where a client's losses are hidden by an investment firm by shifting them between the portfolios of other (genuine or fake) clients. Any real client with portfolio losses can therefore have their accounts flattered by this process. This cycling cannot continue indefinitely and so the investment firm itself ends up picking up the cost. As it is ultimately expensive, there must be a strong incentive for the investment firm to pursue this activity on behalf of their clients (www.wikipedia.com, 10.03.2012)

[b]*Cookie Jar Accounting* A disingenuous accounting practice in which periods of good financial results are used to create reserves that shore up profits in lean years. Used by a company to smooth out volatility in its financial results, thus giving investors the misleading impression that it is consistently meeting earnings targets (www.investopedia.com, 10.03.2012)

[c]*Pump and dump* Pump and dump is a scheme that attempts to boost the price of a stock through recommendations based on false, misleading, or greatly exaggerated statements. The perpetrators of this scheme, who already have an established position in the company's stock, sell their positions after the hype has led to a higher share price. This practice is illegal based on securities law and can lead to heavy fines (www.investopedia.com, 10.03.2012)

follow required laws and regulations. The aim of creative accounting is to falsely portray a better image of the company by capitalizing on loopholes in the accounting standards. Although creative accounting practices are legal, the loopholes they exploit are often reformed to prevent such behaviors. As Enron had no qualms to engage in financial shenanigans, companies have numerous avenues of fraud if they so desire. In most instances of far-reaching and complex fraud, financial shenanigans were not detected even by a company's auditors and accountants. Financial shenanigans include (www.investopedia.com, 31.01.2014):

(1) recognizing revenues prematurely;
(2) Recording sales made to an affiliate or;
(3) Recording sales of unshipped items;
(4) Capitalizing rather than expensing research and development costs;
(5) Reclassifying balance sheet items to create income;
(6) Amortizing costs or depreciating assets at a slower pace;
(7) Setting up special-purpose vehicles (SPV) to hide debt or mask ownership, and so on.

With the intention of deflating debt load, and inflating shareholders' equity, Enron utilized SPVs. As Platt and Kawa (2012) explain, an SPV is a legal entity typically used to serve as a counterparty with the main corporation. In finance it is often used for securitization, but it has also been used to hide risky corporate behavior or transactions and conceal corporate relationships. Not only Enron, but also WorldCom cooked their books to improve their financial figures. *Cook the books* is an idiom describing fraudulent activities performed by corporations in order to falsify their financial statements. Typically, cooking the books involves augmenting financial data to yield previously nonexistent earnings (www.investopedia.com, 31.01.2014). Enron accelerated revenues, delayed expenses, manipulated pension plans, and implemented synthetic leases.

The acts being tried to be characterized are the proof of how crucial internal and external audit both are, and must be integral and constant parts of business life. Auditing process is anticipated to detect inferior and/or imprudent management and inform-related parties. From this standpoint, it can be assumed that auditing has a role in extending the enterprises' lifespan, thus impacts sustainability.

1.2.5 Responsibilities of Auditing Firms in Frauds

Analyzing Table 1.4 that is derived from Table 1.3 and displays the distribution of prominent accounting scandals on country basis, it is seen that there are 55 scandals; where 39, namely 72.22% of them happened in USA. The headquarters of Sybase, which is on the 46th line of the main table, is in USA; therefore, the scandal is counted for USA. However, when the case is analyzed, it is understood that five managers of Japanese division caused the fraud; the company itself revealed the fraud; and the responsible people were fired following the trials (www.sybase.com, 12.03.2012).

Table 1.4 Distribution of prominent accounting scandals on country basis (1980–2014)

Country	Number of scandals	% share in total
USA	39	70.91
England	3	5.45
Bermuda	2	3.64
Australia	2	3.64
Holland	1	1.82
Japan	1	1.82
Italy	1	1.82
Ireland	1	1.82
India	1	1.82
Canada	1	1.82
Canada–China	1	1.82
France	1	1.82
Belgium	1	1.82
Total	55	100.00

Source Derived from Table 1.3

Analyzing Table 1.5, that is derived from Table 1.3 and displays the distribution of prominent accounting scandals on auditing firm basis, it is seen that out of 55 scandals, the auditing firm in 12 cases is Ernst & Young, which is one of Big Four auditing firms. Deloitte & Touche and Arthur Andersen are in the second line with eleven scandals each. The auditor of ten scandalous companies on the list is PricewaterhouseCoopers. The share of KPMG's audit clients with seven accounting scandals makes up 12.07%. Ernst & Young and PricewaterhouseCoopers are listed twice in BCCI case due to their alternating and/or concurrent roles as auditors. This is clarified beneath the table. The auditing firms Grant Thornton SpA and Deloitte & Touche are associated with Parmalat case. Since they take place twice in the table, this is also clarified in the lines beneath the table. The same correction is done for duplicate entries of auditing firms Arthur Andersen and KPMG for their roles in Qwest Communications case.

As the table displaying the distribution of prominent accounting scandals on yearly basis; it is observed that in three decennaries, with 24 scandals—42.59%—year 2002 is at the top line. SOX being enacted in 2002 is not a coincidence (Table 1.6).

From Table 1.3 it is apparently seen that nine out of 11 scandals auditing firm Arthur Andersen is associated with, happened in USA. Six out of 12 scandals auditing firm Ernst & Young is associated with, happened in USA as well. While nine out of ten scandals auditing firm PricewaterhouseCoopers involved came to light in USA; the host of six out of seven scandals KPMG is involved then as auditor, is also the same country.

One of the outstanding details in Hewlett-Packard (HP)—Autonomy case is that, before acquisition, autonomy was audited by the auditing firm Deloitte's British branch (Garside 24.08.2014), and Hewlett-Packard (HP) was audited by auditing firm Ernst & Young (Economist 08.12.2012) and hired another auditing firm KPMG, for it to determine the state of Autonomy before acquiring it (Jones and

Table 1.5 Distribution of prominent accounting scandals on auditing firm basis (1980–2014)

Auditing firm	Scandals	Share (%)
Ernst & Young	12	20.69
Deloitte & Touche	11	18.97
Arthur Andersen	11	18.97
PricewaterhouseCoopers	10	17.24
KPMG	7	12.07
Coopers & Lybrand	2	3.45
BDO, Stoy Hayward	1	1.72
Ernst & Whinney (today partially Ernst & Young)	1	1.72
Friehling & Horowitz	1	1.72
Grant Thornton SpA	1	1.72
Pollard and Heuschkel	1	1.72
Total	**58**	**100.00**
Ernst & Young and PricewaterhouseCoopers rotating	−1	
Grant Thornton SpA and Deloitte & Touche together	−1	
Arthur Andersen KPMG consecutively	−1	
Total	**55**	

Source Derived from Table 1.3

Binham 29.11.2012) and KPMG delivered an opinion stating there isn't any significant problem in the books of Autonomy. Norris, sarcastically states that if three of the four big auditing firms are involved, it should be no surprise that the final one would be brought into the issue. Hence, HP chose another global audit firm, PricewaterhouseCoopers, as an independent forensic consultant to investigate the claims of a whistleblower (McKenna 20.11.2012), investigation found serious accounting improprieties, misrepresentation and disclosure failures (Norris 29.11.2012). This one and other similar cases brought into light cause the quality of auditing or expectations from audits to be questioned.

Another finding supporting the concerns regarding audit quality is a fact that is being stated in the reports of ACFE. Biennial ACFE Reports which are issued nine times since 1996 give wide coverage to 16 fraud preventing tools to be utilized, and the success of each tool in preventing fraud. Independent audits of the organization's internal controls over financial reporting have been compared to external audit on financial tables. While external audits of financial statements—the most commonly implemented control among the victim organizations in ACFE studies—shows the least impact on the median loss suffered, with an associated reduction of 3.4%; independent audits of the organization's internal controls over financial reporting reduces median loss suffered by 35.8%. Similarly, independent audits of the organization's internal controls over financial reporting are able to reduce the duration of fraud by 50%; the ratio of external audits of financial statements to reduce the duration of fraud is 29.2% (www.acfe.com, 12.11.2012). When

Table 1.6 Distribution of prominent accounting scandals on yearly basis (1980–2014)

Year	Number of scandals	% share in total
2002	24	43.64
2000	5	9.09
2003	4	7.27
2008	2	3.64
2004	2	3.64
2001	2	3.64
2011	2	3.64
2012	1	1.82
2010	1	1.82
2009	1	1.82
1999	1	1.82
1998	1	1.82
1997	1	1.82
1996	1	1.82
1992	1	1.82
1991	1	1.82
1990	1	1.82
1989	1	1.82
1988	1	1.82
1986	1	1.82
1980	1	1.82
Total	55	100.00

Source Derived from Table 1.3

Table 1.2 where financial statement fraud rate is compared to other types of fraud, it is observed that the median loss mentioned hit record high in 2002 and reached 4.25 million dollars.

An analysis handling a real-life audit failure, and conducted based on auditor deposition testimony and audit working papers shows that; *understanding the client's business*[9] or *business understanding approach* in other words, will help in preventing audit failures. Auditor has to gather and utilize information about the business of the client, the industry it is operating in, and economical forces impacting the industry/business (Erickson et al. 2000: 168). Critics (Erickson et al. 2000) have contended that many prior financial frauds could have been detected had auditors considered the consistency between reported financial performance and non-financial information, such as economic and industry trends (quoted by Cohen et al. 2009: 3).

[9]**Understanding the client's business**: knowledge of a client's business enables the auditor to evaluate the reasonableness of client transactions. Not limited to these: information regarding client's organizational structure, business strategy, product markets, operating philosophy, and contractual relationships (Erickson et al. 2000).

1.2.6 A Milestone in Audit History: Sarbanes–Oxley Act and Quality

Investors lost their faith in stock markets due to their huge losses caused by Enron and WorldCom scandals. Stock market dropped by more than 22% between April and July 2002. At the very first hearing of the Senate Banking Committee, Chairman Sarbanes, who spent considerable efforts to enact the act (SOX), outlined the main issues he wished to focus on (Harris 20.03.2014):

- Inadequate oversight of accountants;
- Lack of auditor independence;
- Weak corporate governance procedures;
- Stock analysts' conflicts of interest;
- Inadequate disclosure provisions;
- Grossly inadequate funding of the (SEC).

Leaving aside the degree of fulfillment of the above-mentioned initial purposes, SOX is a mandatory act no matter small or big all organizations must comply, and introduced major changes to the regulation of financial practices and corporate governance. Named after Senator Paul Sarbanes and Representative Michael Oxley, who were its main architects, it also set a number of deadlines for compliance (www.soxlaw.com). The bill was passed into law on July 30, 2002. Chapter 98—Public Company Accounting Reform and Corporate Responsibility under US Code Title 15—Commerce and Trade is about this act (www.uscode.house.gov, 12.12.2011, United States House of Representatives). Frame Plan of the Act, which induces and organizes new bodies; defines auditing and related parties of audit in detail; establishes rules concerning each manager at every level of management of public companies; and brings regulations regarding inspection of auditors is tabulated in Appendix A. The Act has eleven titles about which it is believed that the most important ones are 302, 401, 404, 409, 802, and 906 numbered sections (www.soxlaw.com, 09.03.2012, Sarbanes-Oxley Forum). These sections mentioned and the titles they belong are given below (www.taft.law.uc.edu, 09.03.2012, University of Cincinnati):

TITLE III: *Corporate responsibility*

Section 302: Corporate responsibility for financial reports;

TITLE IV: *Disclosures in periodic reports*

Section 401: Disclosures in periodic reports;
Section 404: Management assessment of internal controls;
Section 409: Real Time Issuer Disclosures.

TITLE VIII: *Corporate and Criminal Fraud Accountability*

Section 802: Criminal Penalties for Altering Documents.

TITLE IX: *White-Collar Crime Penalty Enhancements*

Section 906: Corporate Responsibility for Financial Reports.

Occupying a considerable place in auditing literature SOX became the target of several comments, discussions, and criticism, while being considered as a turning/starting point. According to Rezaee and Riley, many sections of SOX only have probably symbolic effects, and through signaling effect s, influence market participants' confidence in securities market (Rezaee and Riley 2009: 18).

Before the formal evaluation of control systems is mandated, auditors had largely moved away from extensive testing of internal control systems precisely because it is unclear how to interpret the implication of a control weakness for the accuracy of the client's financial statements (Francis, 2011: 136). With Section 404 of the SOX, evaluation of control systems has become mandated. Despite the SOX mandated this and significantly higher audit fees has been created, this is still the case. Since 2001, audit fees have increased more than 50%. According to Francis, it is unclear if audit quality has been positively affected by this effort, because there is still no basic understanding of how internal control systems map to financial statement reliability (*ibid.*).

DeFond, Mingyi, Carr and Zhang address the issue in their article that, SOX might have an unintentional but decreasing effect on corporate bondholder value, namely earnings quality. The authors state that the findings of previous studies are conflicting; while Zhang (2007) finds that stock prices decline in response to the passage of SOX, Rezaee and Jain (2006), and Li et al. (2008) find that the stock market reacts favorably to the passage of SOX (quoted by DeFond et al. 2011: 466). DeFond et al. further the study of Zhang, by examining the effects of 17 events on

Table 1.7 Assessment of SOX from bondholders' perspective

Positive effects	Negative effects
Stockholders are likely to bear the bulk of the costs of implementing SOX	Corporate governance systems are primarily designed for the benefit of stockholders. Therefore, management focuses on stockholders. This leads in wealth transfers from bondholders to shareholders
Ceteris paribus[a], if any of the changes under SOX benefit bondholders, then bondholders may be better off, as long as the implementation costs are reasonably low	If the expected costs of implementing SOX impose costs on bondholders, then the costs associated with SOX may swamp any potential benefits to bondholders
SOX may also benefit bondholders by reducing management's propensity to make risky investments	SOX may also harm bondholders because it reduces future cash flows, both in terms of implementation costs and in distracting management from productive activities

(continued)

Table 1.7 (continued)

Positive effects	Negative effects
R&D expenditures and capital investment decline following SOX, but corporate cash holdings increase	SOX may harm bondholders by more closely aligning the interests of managers and stockholders
If decreased risk taking reduces the variation of expected future cash flows, without reducing mean expected cash flows, then bondholders are expected to benefit	The ban on non-audit services under SOX may impair audit quality by eliminating the knowledge spillovers that auditors potentially derive from doing both audit and consulting work
SOX may reduce corporate fraud, which would decrease the risk of bond default	SOX is likely to cause managers to pay less attention to "value creation"
The quality of financial reporting may increase; this should improve the ability of bondholders to assess default risk	SOX banning incumbent auditors from providing non-audit services may unintentionally reduce financial reporting quality

Source Tabulated from DeFond et al. (2011)
[a]*Ceteris paribus* With all other factors or things remaining the same

debt instruments, the events, which are disclosed in media from January 2002 until the date SOX passed and are previously studied by Zhang. Their initial sample is composed by 2671 US straight corporate bonds issued by 847 corporations, and reduced to 769 bonds issued by 229 corporations that satisfy data requirements for their regression analysis (2011: 468–69). Their event study results show that the negative bond market reaction found in the primary analysis is significantly more negative among non-investment grade bonds that are likely to undergo the greatest changes under SOX. Thus, DeFond et al. conclude; endogenous changes imposed by SOX do not favor corporate bondholders. The positive and negative effects of SOX discussed in the above-summarized paper are tabulated in Table 1.7.

Chapter 2
External Audit in USA, European Union, and Turkey

Abstract This Chapter explains legal forms, ownership and management structures of external auditing firms in USA, EU, and Turkey. It also gives organizational structure of auditing firms in these countries. The profile of the auditing firms in Turkey from organizational structure, number of partners, ownership, audit staff, and licence aggreements with foreign auditing firms is drawn. The term, leverage is introduced in this Chapter. External audit regulations, as the third part of this Chapter, covers CMB's TCC's and POA's comtemporary legislations in Turkey from a historical view.

Keywords Auditing firms · Regulations · Organizations · USA
EU · Turkey

This section is about the course of proceeding of external audit and corporate organizations of auditing firms in Turkey, USA, EU countries like England, Germany, and France. In the first place, information is given about external audit in USA, and the organizational structure of auditing firms in USA is covered. Subsequently, courses of proceeding of external audit in some of the EU countries are touched on, and legal structures are mentioned about. In the third place, auditing firms in Turkey are examined, and based on observations about radical changes in audit field and data compiled since 2012; the profile of auditing firms is depicted. Following these, external audit regulations in Turkey are addressed by covering the activities and operations of Capital Markets Board of Turkey (CMB) in the first place; Turkish Code of Commerce (TCC) in the second place; and in the last place the operations, practices, and arrangements of the Public Oversight Authority (POA) regarding auditing, which became the sole body within the frame of regulations. Afterward, POA's operations, practices, arrangements, and broad authority are compared to its American counterpart Public Company Accounting Oversight Board's (PCAOB) functioning.

I. Kesimli, *External Auditing and Quality*, Accounting, Finance, Sustainability, Governance & Fraud: Theory and Application,
https://doi.org/10.1007/978-981-13-0526-9_2

2.1 Auditing Firms in USA and European Union

There is no room in this book about full detail and comparison of auditing firms, but course of proceeding of external audit and corporate organizations of auditing firms in USA and some of the EU countries are discussed under this title. Further audit quality assessment takes place in the following section.

Basically, auditing firms' activities are auditing, consultancy, tax consultancy, and other operations besides these. Auditing activity by itself comprises administrative audit, financial audit, audit of management, performance audit, systems audit, and audit of several other factors.

Auditing firms primarily compete on the basis of reputation, size, industry know-how, and audit fees. Audit quality would be added as another subject of competition; however, as mentioned in the 2009 Consultation Report *Transparency of Firms that Audit Public Companies* of International Organization of Securities Commissions (IOSCO), lack of transparency of audit firms retains investor confidence in financial reporting and disables providing additional information when market participants make decisions, including investors' decisions about whether to invest in companies or ratify the appointments of issuers. Jere Francis supports this opinion by resembling accounting firms to a black box (Francis 2006: 7).

CPA firms vary according to the range of services offered and due to the nature of these services, which affect the firms' organizations and structures. Three factors impacting all accounting firms' organizational structure are as follows (Arens et al. 2012: 47):

(1) *The need for independence from clients*. Independence permits auditors to remain unbiased in drawing conclusions about the financial statements.
(2) *The importance of a structure to encourage competence*. Competence permits auditors to conduct audits and perform other services efficiently and effectively.
(3) *The increased litigation risk faced by auditors*. Audit firms continue to experience increases in litigation-related costs. Some organizational structures afford a degree of protection to individual firm members.

2.1.1 External Auditing Firms in USA

Being a CPA is required in order to become an external auditor in USA. Those willing to become a CPA have to fulfill the educational requirements independently determined by each state, and take the Uniform CPA Examination, and fulfill the probation requirements of each state or territory, which are again determined independently by each state. State and territory requirements for licensure keep in sight the below-listed factors (www.aicpa.org, 16.01.2015):

- *Age*: e.g., for New York state minimum age is 21.
- *Citizenship*: e.g., New York State doesn't require citizenship.
- *Residency*: e.g., New York State doesn't require residency.

- *Social Security Number*: e.g., New York State asks for it.
- *Education Requirement for Licensure*: e.g., New York State requires 150 h including B.A. for candidates having graduated after 08/09 or 120 h including B.A. for those who graduated before 08/09. Fifteen years of public accounting experience acceptable to the State Board for Public Accountancy may be substituted for education for the admission to the examination.
- *Participation in International Examination Program*: e.g., is compulsory in New York State.
- *Hours in accounting courses*: the accounting board of the related state announces the accounting courses to be taken, the levels and the hours required.
- *Exam sitting requirements*: e.g., in New York State; B.A. (120 h) including a course in each of the following is required: Financial accounting, Cost or management accounting, Taxation, and Audit and attestation.
- *Experience requirements*: e.g., in New York State; one-year experience gained in employment in a public accounting firm, government, private industry or an educational institution is required.
- *Ethics exam*: e.g., there is no ethics exam in New York State.

SOX rules that accounting firms must register with the PCAOB to prepare or issue an audit report for a public company or another issuer, or a broker-dealer, or to play certain roles in those audits. Non-American accounting firms are also subject to PCAOB regulation (www.pcaobus.org, 16.01.2015).

Accounting firms intending to register with the Board have to make an initial payment, announced by the Board based on the number and qualifications of issuer audit clients of the preceding year. The current application fee schedule starts from $500 and is up to $390,000. The annual fee is due by July 31 of each year and must be paid by each firm that is registered as of March 31 of that year. The annual fee for the firms with more than 500 issuer audit clients and more than 10,000 personnel is $100,000; firms with more than 200 issuer audit clients and more than 1,000 personnel have to pay $25,000 annually, and annual fee for all other firms is $500 (www.pcaobus.org, 16.01.2015 and 01.06.2017).

The auditing firms those registered with the PCOAB are displayed in the Web site of PCAOB. As of June 2017, there are 1966 auditing firms registered with PCAOB, where 1063 are American firms. Among 903 non-American auditing firms, there are 19 Turkish firms. For example, there are 69 Indian firms, 53 British firms, 43 Chinese firms, 41 Australian firms, and 35 auditing firms represent Hong Kong among non-American auditing firms. Registered auditing firms are currently categorized as (www.pcaobus.org, 16.01.2015):

- Category A—Audit report for at least one issuer.
- Category B—No audit reports for issuers but played a substantial role in the audit of at least one issuer.
- Category C—Audit reports for at least one broker-dealer.
- Category D—No audit reports for broker-dealers, but substantial role in audit of at least one broker-dealer,
- Category E—None of the above,

- Category F—No Form 2 filed

The descriptions of Category A and B did not change from 2015 to 2017; whereas, Category C, D and E shifted one level down; and a new Category C was created—*Audit reports for at least one broker-dealer*. As of June 2017, there are 535 firms under Category A (638 in 2015); 103 firms under Category B (122 in 2015); and the newly created Category C comprises 293 auditing firms. Only three firms are under Category D, but 962 firms are categorized as E and those, which did not file Form 2, are 70 auditing firms.

Regarding all categories; out of 1063 (1265 in 2015; 1455 in 2012) registered American auditing firms 342 (439 in 2015; 536 in 2012) are under Category A. There are eight American firms under Category B, 287 under Category C, three under Category D; 962 are categorized as E, and Category F comprises 37 American firms. Assessment of Category A in 2017 reveals that 49 out of 342, namely 14.33% of registered American auditing firms are from New York. California follows with 12.28 and Texas with 9.36% (Table 2.1).

The comparison of data throughout the years shows that the number of PCAOB registered auditing firms dropped by 13.06% from year 2012 to 2015, and another decrease of 9.48% is lived from 2015 to 2017. Similarly, Category A lost 18.10% of firms from year 2012 to 2015; and it decreased by 16.14% from year 2015 to 2017. This may be another issue for research in the future.

The Organizational Structure of CPA Firms Authorized to Exercise Audits in USA The nature and range of services offered by CPA firms vary and affect the organization and structure of the firms. According to Arens et al. there are three main factors influencing the organizational structure of all firms. The first one is the need for independence from clients. Independence permits auditors to remain unbiased in drawing conclusions about the financial statements. The second one is the importance of a structure to encourage competence. Competence permits auditors to conduct audits and perform other services efficiently and effectively. The third one is the increased litigation risk faced by auditors. As the auditing firms continue to experience increases in litigation-related costs, the organizational structures affording a degree of protection to individual firm members are to be preferred (2012: 46).

The relations between the central office and branches, or as seen in international auditing firms, relations between local office partners impact the audit and audit outcomes. Auditing firm structural attributes that may affect the audit quality are listed below (Francis 2006: 7):

(1) The degree of centralization of the auditing firm's management control system.

    - Local office partners have to oblige to the advice of the central office about clients.
    - Local office partners do not have to oblige to the advice of the central office about clients.

(2) The structure of the partners' incentives/payment agreements and the impact of this on the attitude and behavior of the partner.

Table 2.1 State-wise distribution of PCAOB category A registered American auditing firms in 2015 and 2017

		2015		2017	
	Total	439	%	342	%
1	New York	60	13.67	49	14.33
2	California	53	12.07	42	12.28
3	Florida	41	9.34	27	7.89
4	Texas	37	8.43	32	9.36
5	New Jersey	22	5.01	14	4.09
6	Illinois	17	3.87	17	4.97
7	Pennsylvania	17	3.87	15	4.39
8	Ohio	15	3.42	12	3.51
9	Georgia	14	3.19	11	3.22
10	Utah	14	3.19	10	2.92
11	Colorado	11	2.51	9	2.63
12	Maryland	10	2.28	9	2.63
13	Nevada	10	2.28	4	1.17
14	Massachusetts	10	2.28	7	2.05
15	Michigan	9	2.05	8	2.34
16	Connecticut	8	1.82	6	1.75
17	Missouri	8	1.82	7	2.05
18	Tennessee	8	1.82	3	0.88
19	Virginia	7	1.59	8	2.34
20	Washington	7	1.59	6	1.75
21	Louisiana	6	1.37	4	1.17
22	Minnesota	6	1.37	5	1.46
23	North Carolina	5	1.14	4	1.17
24	Wisconsin	5	1.14	4	1.17
25	Alabama	5	1.14	3	0.88
26	Indiana	4	0.91	3	0.88
27	West Virginia	3	0.68	2	0.58
28	Arizona	3	0.68	1	0.29
29	Delaware	2	0.46	2	0.58
30	Maine	2	0.46	2	0.58
31	Mississippi	2	0.46	2	0.58
32	North Dakota	2	0.46	2	0.58
33	Oregon	2	0.46	2	0.58
34	Rhode Island	2	0.46	1	0.29
35	South Carolina	2	0.46	1	0.29
36	Arkansas	1	0.23	1	0.29
37	Hawaii	1	0.23	1	0.29
38	Iowa	1	0.23	1	0.29

(continued)

Table 2.1 (continued)

		2015		2017	
	Total	439	%	342	%
39	Kansas	1	0.23	0	0.00
40	Kentucky	1	0.23	1	0.29
41	New Mexico	1	0.23	1	0.29
42	Oklahoma	1	0.23	1	0.29
43	Vermont	1	0.23	1	0.29
44	District of Columbia	1	0.23	0	0.00
45	New Hampshire	1	0.23	1	0.29

Source Public Company Accounting Oversight Board (PCOAB). Registration and Reporting. Registered Firms. Organized based on the published data at http://pcaobus.org/Registration/Firms/Pages/RegisteredFirms.aspx. Accessed 04 Jun 2017 and 12 Jan 2015

- Payment is bound to partner's client portfolio.
- Payment is bound to the office's client portfolio.
- Profit sharing pools are used all over the firm, and the distribution is based on the partner's personal portfolio or on the performance of the engagement office.
- Payment is bound to the accounting firm's overall performance.

For example, it had been brought forward that the model—distributed control system—adopted by Arthur Andersen, where local office partners are not obliged to conform to the advice of the central office about clients, has an important role on Enron audit (Francis 2011: 138). There are six organizational structures available to CPA firms.

Proprietorship A business owned by a single individual is called a sole proprietorship. The owner of a sole proprietorship is personally liable on all business obligations since there is no legal separation between the owner and the business. From a legal perspective, there are no formalities. There is no separate entity, thus the firm is taxed on personal income (www.wcl.american.edu, 16.01.2015).

General Partnership This is a standard form of partnership, where all of the partners are equally responsible for the business's debts and liabilities and are allowed to be involved in the management of the company. Any obligation made by one partner is legally binding on all partners, whether or not they have been informed (http://definitions.uslegal.com, 16.01.2015).

General Corporation A partnership formed by two or more persons and having one or more general partners and one or more limited partners, or their equivalents under any name (www.leginfo.legislature.ca.gov, 05.06.2017 and 17.01.2015).

Professional Corporation A professional limited liability company (PLLC) is a business entity designed for licensed professionals of the same profession. While many businesses choose to form a limited liability company (LLC) because of the tax, limited liability, and other benefits, some states do not allow LLCs to be owned by professionals whose occupation requires a license. In these states, licensed professionals who want the benefits of an LLC must form a PLLC instead. This kind of company helps licensed professionals to protect their personal property from litigation risks. Partners are not protected from their personal liabilities, but from the misconduct of the other partners of the company (www.incorporate.com, 16.01.2015).

Limited Liability Company A limited liability company (LLC) combines the most favorable attributes of a general corporation and a general partnership. An LLC is typically structured and taxed like a general partnership, but its owners have limited personal liability similar to that of a general corporation. All of the states have LLC laws, and most also allow accounting firms to operate as LLCs (Arens et al. 2012: 47).

Limited Liability Partnership (LLP) Sometimes called a registered limited liability partnership (RLLP), it provides all of its owners with limited personal liability. LLPs are particularly well-suited to professional groups, such as lawyers and accountants. In fact, in some states LLPs are only available to professionals. An LLP protects each partner from debts against the partnership arising from professional malpractice lawsuits against another partner (www.nolo.com, 16.01.2015.). It is not surprising that all of the Big Four firms and many smaller firms now operate as LLPs (Arens et al. 2012: 47).

As explained above there are six organizational structures available to CPA firms. Except for the proprietorship, each structure results in an entity separate from the CPA personally, which helps promote auditor independence. The last four organizational structures provide some protection from litigation loss (Arens et al. 2012: 47). As of June 2017, out of 1063 (1265 in January 2015) PCAOB registered American accounting firms, company names of 925 (1081 in January 2015) firms contain an abbreviated extension. Based on this data, companies in the legal form of limited liability partnership (LLP) make up 31.24% (29.05% in January 2015); professional corporations (PC) 19.35% (23.50% in January 2015); and limited liability companies are 14.92% (13.69% in Jan 2015) of these. It is apparently observed that professional corporations decrease in percentage, while LLP and LLC forms gain weight. This trend supports the comments of Arens et al.

Evolving duties and responsibilities accelerate the advancement in CPA firms. Additionally, diversity of client engagements equips audit staff members with sectoral experience. Assuming that beginning assistants on the audit have deeper knowledge in computer and audit technology, they are given greater responsibility and challenges in very shorter periods of time. In addition, competence is promoted, due to the hierarchical nature of CPA firms. New staff assistants are supervised directly by the senior or in-charge auditor. The staff assistant's work is then reviewed by the in-charge as well as by the manager and partner. Individuals at each level of the audit supervise and review the work of others at the level just below them in the organizational structure. The experience and responsibilities of each classification level within CPA firms are summarized in the table below (Arens et al. 2012: 47) (Table 2.2).

Table 2.2 Staff levels and responsibilities

Staff level	Average experience (years)	Typical responsibilities
Staff assistant	0–2	Performs most of the detailed audit work
Senior or in-charge auditor	2–5	Coordinates and is responsible for the audit fieldwork, including supervising and reviewing staff work
Manager	5–10	Helps the in-charge plan and manage the audit, reviews in-charge's work, and manages relations with the client. A manager may be responsible for more than one engagement at the same time
Partner	10+	Reviews the overall audit work and is involved in significant audit decisions. A partner is an owner of the firm and therefore has the ultimate responsibility for conducting the audit and serving the client

Source Arens et al. 2012

The positions and responsibilities displayed in the table have value as guidance; they will be handled under several headlines throughout the book. Moreover, it is to be kept in the minds that concepts/definitions in the USA and EU literature differ.

2.1.2 External Auditing Firms in European Union Countries

In order to become an auditor in EU, it is initially required to have attained university entrance level, then completed a course of theoretical instruction, undergone practical training and passed an examination of professional competence of university, final examination level organized or recognized by the state (8th Directive Article 4, 1984). Among other requirements, there is a minimum of three years' practical training in inter alia the auditing of annual accounts or similar financial statements. Article 8 of 8th Directive says that at least two-thirds of such practical training must be completed under a person approved under the law of the Member State in accordance with the Directive.

There is considerable uniformity among EU Member States with respect to the specific rules on ownership and composition of the management board in terms of minimum requirements. All countries require a majority of voting rights in audit firms to be held by qualified auditors, as required by 8th Directive from 1984. However, some Member States require 75% or more of the owners of auditing firms to be qualified auditors. It is thought that slightly relaxing the rules would create opportunity for new investments and new entries to the market (www.ec.europa.eu,

12.03.2012, EuropeanCommission, oxera_report_en.pdf, 2007: 48). European Commission commissioned the above-quoted report from Oxera[1] The report aims to provide insight into the interactions between ownership and concentration, and to stimulate further policy debate. Even though the fact that policy-oriented reports commissioned to other parties largely ignore the extant research literature is verbalized by academics like Francis (2011: 139–140), Francis et al. (2013), this book refers to Oxera Report with the intention to shed light on this research. According to the report the question, to what extent the corporate structure adopted by audit firms —whether driven by the rules or by commercial factors—affect the market's ability to deliver a more open configuration that would reduce some of the concerns expressed about concentration and choice in the audit market, comes forth (www.ec.europa.eu, 12.03.2012, European Commission, oxera_report_en.pdf, Oxera Report 2007: Executive Summary, iii).

Currently, the corporate structure of auditing firms is employee-owned corporate form. The cost of capital for auditing firms—including the international networks—may be higher than that of multinational companies of similar size, as auditing firms tend to raise capital at the national rather than global level. The auditor makes a personal financial investment in the auditing firm, where the ownership stakes are illiquid. Due to lack of diversification, in return for the risk undertaken, audit partners are likely to require additional return. The new structures, which auditing firms may adopt, have to combine the opportunity of finding low-cost capital from diversified external investors and securing human capital (www.ec.europa.eu, 12.03.2012, European Commission, oxera_report_en.pdf, Oxera Report 2007: 155).

As mentioned in the Oxera Report, a profitable business depends on professional management. For example, a health center lacking professional management would not provide sustainable profitability; or despite their experience, a company founded by engineers may be deprived from competitive advantages regarding several aspects. Analogically what is needed by auditing firms is also professional approach and management. The market success of auditing firms which solely make audits—those providing consultancy service are exempt—is also in question.

Following auditing firm mergers, increasing concentration has been observed in global audit market. The process regarding mergers is summarized schematically in Fig. 2.1. In the wake of concentration, auditing firm choices of audit clients diminished to Deloitte & Touche, Ernst & Young, KPMG and PricewaterhouseCoopers being mentioned as Big Four, and these are also individually the biggest auditing firms in some of the countries. Audit of big public companies is being provided by international network of Big Four. Table 2.3 shows 2011, 2012, 2013 and 2014 summarized data of Big Four, sorted according to revenue. Big Four is followed by relatively smaller firms

[1]**Oxera Consulting Ltd** is registered in England No. 2589629 and in Belgium No. 0883.432.547 and is not licensed in the conduct of investment business as defined in the Financial Services and Markets Accountability 2000.

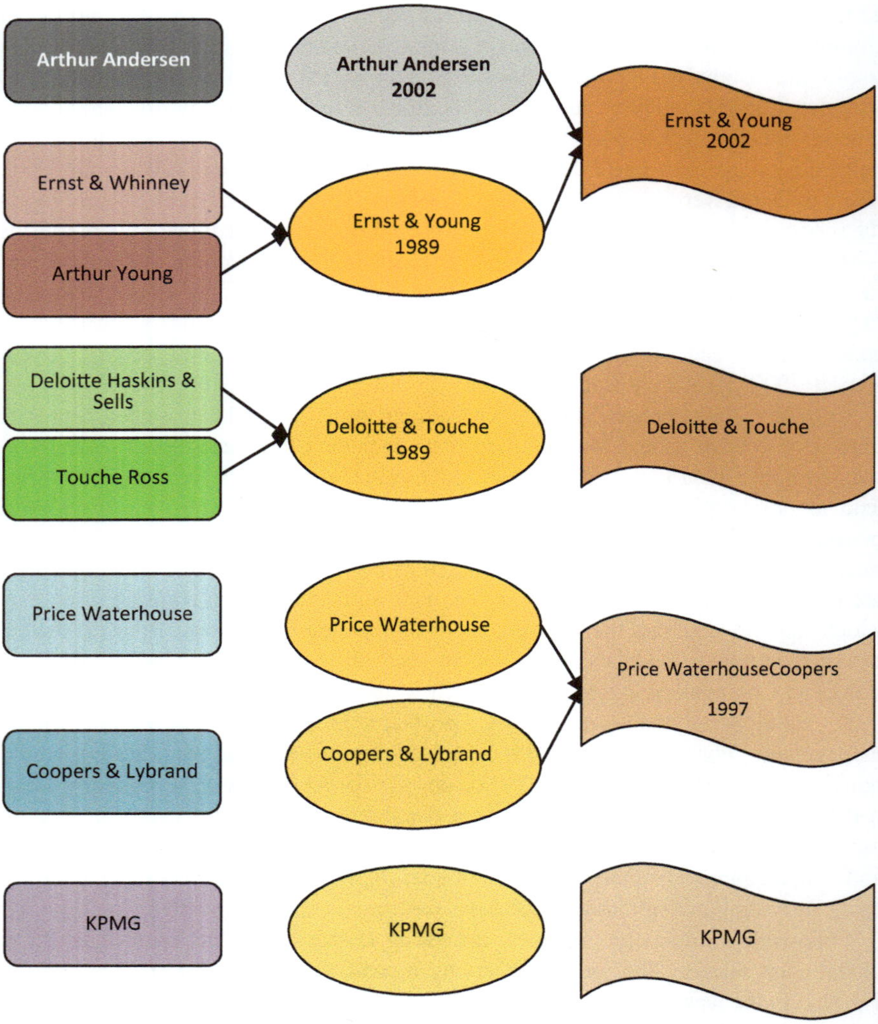

Fig. 2.1 Mergers from Big Eight to Big Four during 1989–2002. *Source* (1) European Commission 2007. (2) http://www.ey.com/GL/en/About-us/Our-people-and-culture/Our-history/About-EY—Key-Facts-and-Figures—History—Timeline. Accessed 31 Jan 2015. (3) http://www2.deloitte.com/global/en/pages/about-deloitte/articles/about-deloitte.html. Accessed 31 Jan 2015. (4) http://www.pwc.com/gx/en/careers/our-history.jhtml. Accessed 31 Jan 2015

named mid-size, which have remarkable international networks. The systemic concerns about the broader impact of the lack of choice on the soundness of major financial markets naturally relate more to the larger listed companies (www.ec.europa.eu, 12.03.2012, European Commission, oxera_report_en.pdf, Oxera Report 2007: 2).

Table 2.3 Summarized data of Big Four regarding size

Auditing firm	2014 revenue	#of employees	#of countries having operations
Deloitte Touche Tohmatsu	34.20 billion $	210,400	>150
PricewaterhouseCoopers	33.95 billion $	195,433	157
Ernst & Young	27.40 billion $	190,000	>150
KPMG	24.82 billion $	162,031	155
Auditing firm	2013 revenue	#of employees	#of countries having operations
Deloitte Touche Tohmatsu	32.40 billion $	>200,000	>150
PricewaterhouseCoopers	32.10 billion $	184,235	157
Ernst & Young	25.80 billion $	174,808	>150
KPMG	23.42 billion $	155,180	155
Auditing firm	2012 revenue	#of employees	#of countries having operations
PricewaterhouseCoopers	31.50 billion $	180,529	158
Deloitte Touche Tohmatsu	31.30 billion $	193,000	>150
Ernst & Young	24.40 billion $	167,225	>140
KPMG	23.03 billion $	145,000	153
Auditing firm	2011 revenue	#of employees	#of countries having operations
PricewaterhouseCoopers	29.20 billion $	168,710	158
Deloitte Touche Tohmatsu	28.80 billion $	182,000	>150
Ernst & Young	22.90 billion $	152,000	>140
KPMG	22.70 billion $	145,000	153

Source Data gathered from auditing firms' Web sites

Deloitte. About. Facts and Figures. http://www.deloitte.com/view/en_GX/global/press/facts-figures/index.htm. Accessed 06 May 2012. http://www2.deloitte.com/global/en/pages/about-deloitte/articles/about-deloitte.html. Accessed 22 Dec 2013. http://www2.deloitte.com/global/en/pages/about-deloitte/articles/about-deloitte.html. Accessed 26 Jan 2015

PricewaterhouseCoopers. Press Room. Facts and Figures. http://www.pwc.com/en_GX/gx/press-room/pdf/2011_fact_sheet.pdf. Accessed 06 May 2012. http://www.pwc.com/en_GX/gx/annual-review/2012/assets/pwc-global-annual-review-2012.pdf. Accessed 22 Dec 2013. http://www.pwc.com/gx/en/annual-review/2013/assets/pwc-global-annual-review-2013.pdf. Accessed 22 Dec 2013. http://www.pwc.com/gx/en/global-annual-review/assets/pwc-global-annual-review-2014.pdf. Accessed 26 Jan 2015

Ernst & Young. Newsroom. Facts and Figures. http://www.ey.com/GL/en/Newsroom/Facts-and-figures, 06.05.2012. http://www.ey.com/GL/en/About-us/Our-global-approach/Global-review/global-review-2013-facts-and-figures#page1, 22.12.2013. http://www.ey.com/US/en/Newsroom/Facts-and-figures. Accessed 22 Dec 2013 and 26 Jan 2015

KPMG. Who we are. http://www.kpmg.com/global/en/whoweare/Pages/default.aspx. Accessed 06 May 2012. http://www.kpmg.com/global/en/about/international-annual-review/financials-organization/pages/default.aspx. Accessed 22 Dec 2013. http://www.kpmg.com/Global/en/about/international-annual-review/financials-organization/Documents/2014/kpmg-by-the-numbers-2014.pdf. Accessed 26 Jan 2015

Explanations of International Organization of Securities Commissions (IOSCO) Paris Roundtable (2007) panelist Daniel Bouton[2] at the third panel—"Audit Firm Concentration—Potential Effects on Audit Quality"—gives idea about French auditing market. Bouton states that French companies must comply with several specific regulations, issued either by the EC or by the French Parliament, and many of these regulations have contributed to the solidification and maintenance of this oligopoly. He also reminds the existence of an ancient French regulation, which is excellent in theory, requiring every large listed company to be audited by two auditors (Bouton 2007: 29). Vincent Baillot[3] reminds that this rule had been implemented since 1966 (Baillot 2007: 31). Panelist Bouton admits that such a four eyes rule might have prevented the Enron debacle. However, when companies are required to select two auditors out of a choice of four, it is like beginning a tennis tournament with only two players (Bouton 2007: 29). Against this commentary, Michel Prada[4] says he witnessed a significant case in which problematic issues were raised following a disagreement between the two auditors. This, make him believe that in case it is well organized; the joint audit may be valuable (Prada 2007: 31). Again from Bouton's statement, it is understood that another excellent French rule forbids a company's statutory auditor from serving as the advisor for another mission, in order to keep the two tasks clearly separated. Another rule forbidding the selection of an auditing firm, which has performed any advisory mission for a firm as its auditor, rounds up the aforementioned rule (Bouton 2007: 29–30). It can be presumed that French regulation has created an unhealthy situation that penalizes the international expansion of auditing firms, to the benefit of the Big Four, thus accelerating concentration. It is apparent that such a concentration would push audit service prices up. Bouton boldly proposes to apply anti-concentration rules to the Big Four and backs up his opinion by saying that Société Générale's[5] audit expenses have increased by 3.6 times while net banking revenues of the bank increased only by 2.4 over the past decade (Bouton 2007: 30).

The Subcommittee on Concentration and Competition established by United States Treasury Department's Advisory Committee on the Auditing Profession (ACAP) recommends reduction of barriers to the growth of smaller auditing firms consistent with an overall policy goal of promoting audit quality. Due to the fact that smaller auditing firms are likely to become significant competitors in the market for larger company audits only in the long term, the Committee recognizes that monitoring potential sources of catastrophic risk faced by public company auditing firms and creating a mechanism for the preservation and rehabilitation of troubled larger public

[2]**Daniel Bouton**: CEO of Société Générale.

[3]**Vincent Baillot**: President, La Compagnie nationale des commissaires aux comptes (CNCC).

[4]**Michel Prada**: The Chairman of the IOSCO Technical Committee.

[5]**Société Générale S.A.** is a French multinational banking and financial services company headquartered in Paris. It is France's third-largest bank by total assets, sixth largest in Europe or seventeenth by market capitalization.

company auditing firms have a higher priority in the near term (United States Treasury, www.treasury.gov, 03.01.2013, ACAP, Final Report 2008: VIII: 4, 9). Along with these, the Committee recommends adopting annual shareholder ratification of public company auditors by all public companies (*ibid.*, VIII: 20).

Concerns caused by concentration are not new; instead, they go back to 1989. Due to mergers among auditing firms, the number of the most effective auditing firms of the world, called as Big Eight until then, dropped to six, thus becoming called as Big Six. Then, following the merger in 1997 Big Five, and in the aftermath of the collapse of Arthur Andersen in 2002, the Big Four became dominant. These mergers are displayed historically and schematically in Fig. 2.1.

It seems that, during merger and acquisition era, mergers are not limited to the former big eight firms. Synergy resulting in greater productivity is often presented as justification for mergers and acquisitions. Combining two firms may result in substantial savings of fixed costs for knowledge and support personnel. In addition, the merged firm may be better able to exploit opportunities to generate additional revenues because of its size, blend of professional skills, and experience. Merger activities among accounting firms may create scale economies due to these savings (Banker et al. 2003: 256–273). In, a market where mergers and acquisitions result in decreased number of players, due precautions are not taken, and due regulations not brought may result in concentration.

It is explicit that concentration will cause stress on audit client companies that are served by auditing firms. Under such a picture, it is not hard to guess the consequences of any of Big Four leaving the market. How an important problem will be faced due to concentration in audit market and lack of choice in relation to this is well understood as the data, the results of a study implemented in April 2006, is looked below:

- Big Four serves 99% of the companies listed in FTSE[6] 100 Index.
- Big Four stand for 99% of total revenue earned from companies listed FTSE 350 Index.
- Financial sector companies listed in FTSE 100 Index have hardly any chance of alternative selection.
- Concentration caused high audit prices.

The networks of four big auditing firms dominate the audit service varieties and providence of services large public companies need to hire. These four big auditing firms audited 98 percent of the largest 1500 public companies in USA with revenues more than one million dollars (www.gao.gov, GAO 2006: 19) and as of February 2008 (https://frc.org.uk, FRC 2008: 22) audited 96.2% of the FTSE 250 companies (www.iasplus.com/iosco/0909transparency.pdf, 12.03.2012, IOSCO Consultation Report, Sep 2009: 4).

[6]**FTSE**: Financial Times Stock Exchange—an indexing corporation as an entity of FTSE Group, a British provider of stock market indices.

Following their foundations, globally operating auditing firms lived several mergers and their number showed variabilities. More specifically, the transition from Big Eight to Big Four during 1989–2002 is plotted in Fig 2.1.

When it comes to regulations, the factors to be taken into consideration are as shown in Fig. 2.2. As seen from the figure they are as follows:

1. Concentration and Choice
2. Auditor Independence and Ownership Rules;
3. Auditor Liability;
4. Audit Quality.

As seen in the figure, each factor has a reciprocal impact on each and every other factor. James Cox, the panelist at the International Organization of Securities Commissions (IOSCO) roundtable in Paris on July 1, 2007, lists the progress and causes of mergers and acquisitions apparently seen in Fig. 2.1; by underlining the fact that official guidelines actually favored concentration, provided it led to better quality, but disregarding the fact that this will end up with oligopoly (Cox 2007: 26). Providing auditing services enabled them to get a foot in the door, and compete against companies such as McKinsey[7]. The global criterion of the profitability of accounting firms is the revenue per partner. One of the facts enabling the most profitable firms to earn the money is; the ratio of audit professionals to audit partners, namely leverage (PCAOB 2013; Deltas and Doogar 2004; Doogar and Easley 1998; Kinney 1986). The fewer owners it is needed to service a given amount of client revenue, the more the firms will earn per partner (Adamson, http://www.adamsonadvisory.com/, 31.01.2015). By bringing the question why the small and mid-level auditing firms did not become larger; Cox answers that the biggest hurdle documented was the reputation effect. According to Adamson's evaluation, it is understood that profitability would be another answer to this. According to Cox, there seems to be a halo effect[8] being audited by a Big Four firm and the market does not believe smaller firms possess the necessary skill package (Cox 2007: 26).

Jason Karaian, the global finance and economics editor at Quartz—the digitally native news outlet with a founding team including veterans of some of the world's highest-quality news organizations who report in 115 countries and speak 19 languages—published data supporting the issue. The article states that, firms outside of the Big Four audit only 15 of the UK's 350 largest listed firms; all but two of the S&P 500[9] use a Big Four bookkeeper. Globally, the Big Four collect two-thirds of

[7]**McKinsey**: is a global management consulting firm that serves businesses, governments, non-governmental organizations, and not-for-profits (www.mckinsey.com).

[8]**Halo effect**: is a cognitive bias in which an observer's overall impression of a person, company, brand, or product influences the observer's feelings and thoughts about that entity's character or properties (Kağıtçıbaşı 2010: 270).

[9]**S&P 500**: is an American stock market index based on the market capitalizations of 500 large companies having common stock listed on the NYSE or NASDAQ. The S&P 500 index components and their weightings are determined by S&P Dow Jones Indices.

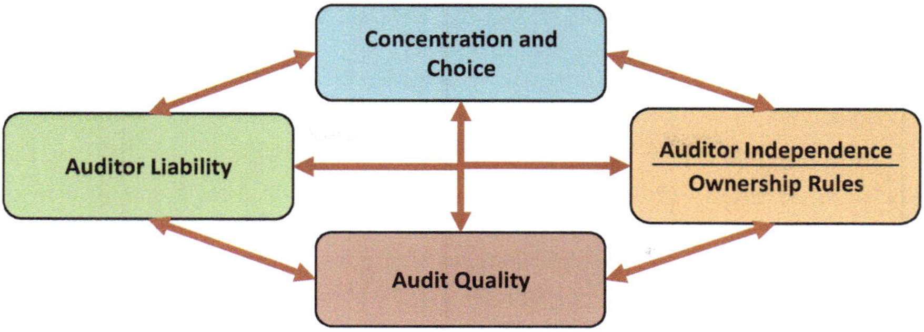

Fig. 2.2 Policy context of the audit market. *Source* European Commission 2007

the accounting industry's $165 billion in annual fees. Karaian points the fact, Enron's accounting scandal brought down Arthur Andersen in 2002, but since then the Big Four firms have weathered the collapse of clients like Lehman Brothers along with plenty of other legal missteps that happened on their watch without suffering too much damage.

Specifically, financial institutions suffered during and after the year 2007, when the global financial crisis was triggered, and it is not a secret that they had been rescued by governments in Anglo-Saxon countries. It is understood that financial system and the economy felt discomfort from this situation; however, inspecting the ligament of auditing firms to the crisis had then been postponed during such a period when taking measurements to get over the crisis with least damage had priority.

European Commission's 2010 Green Paper on "Audit Policy: Lessons from the Crisis" raises important issues like regulatory oversight, competition in the audit market, the dangers of having very few firms with the capacity to audit global transnational corporations, professional judgment, innovative audit practices, and social responsibility (Humphrey et al. 2011: 431). Apparently, compulsory rotation of auditing firms raised by the 2010 Green Paper had not been realized (European Commission 2010: 11). According to Karaian, notwithstanding numerous attempts in UK, neither rotation periods became 5–7 years, nor the oligopolistic structure is demolished, and Britain is not alone in its inability to shake things up (Karaian 17.10.2013).

The Organizational Structure of CPA Firms Authorized to Exercise Audits in EU: Legal Forms, Ownership, and Management Structures The structures of auditing firms are to be discussed under three headings as ownership, corporate governance and management structure. The adopted ownership, corporate governance, and management structures impact decision taking processes and therefore have effects on the independence of the individual audit decisions. The relations of these three structures are illustrated at Fig. 2.3. Along with the legal structure, the ownership structure defines the legal owners of the firm and typically also defines the distribution of both voting rights as well as the cash flow rights among shareholders.

The legal forms generally adopted by auditing firms in Germany, France, UK, and Poland are as follows (www.ec.europa.eu, 12.03.2012, European Commission, oxera_report_en.pdf, Oxera Report, 2007: 89–91):

Stock Corporation/Public Limited Company This legal form requiring a minimum capital of €50,000 is equivalent to Aktien Gesellschaft (AG) in Germany, and Société Anonyme (SA) or Société Anonyme Simplifiée (SAS) in France. All companies must have a supervisory (Vorstand), as well as a management board (Aufsichtsrat) to monitor the directors. However, individuals are prohibited from sitting on both boards at the same time (http://de.wikipedia.org/wiki/Aufsichtsrat,10.08.2012; http://de.thefreedictionary.com, Free Online Dictionary, 10.08.2012).

Limited Liability Company This legal form of a company requires minimum €25,000 capital and is broadly equivalent of Gesellschaften mit beschränkter Haftung (GmbH) in Germany, and société a responsabilité limitée (SARL) in France. Only firms with more than 500 employees are required to have a supervisory board. Auditing firms in Ireland are not permitted to organize under this legal form; therefore, auditors in Ireland are either individually working accountants or partnerships formed by accountants.

General Partnership This legal form requires at least two partners, where all partners have unlimited liability. In Germany, this is Offene Handelsgesellschaften (OHG), equivalent to the unlimited liability company or the general partnership in the UK and société en nom collectif (SNC) in France, though auditing firms cannot be organized as such in France.

Limited Partnership in Germany, this is Kommanditgesellschaften (KG), equivalent to a limited partnership in UK. In France, the most close legal form to this is société en commandite simple (SCS). It must have at least two partners, where at least one partner has liability limited to his/her individual capital contribution and at least one partner has unlimited liability.

Professional Partnership This legal form, where all partners have limited personal liability is recognized as Partnerschaft Gesellschaften in Germany, broadly equivalent to the Limited Liability Partnership (LLP). This legal form is not allowed to auditing firms in Ireland (www.ec.europa.eu, 12.03.2012, European Commission, oxera_report_en.pdf, Oxera Report, 2007: 90). As asked from all of the limited liability partnerships, UK regulation requires auditing firms organized under this legal form to publish their audited financial statements (MacKenzie–Grant Thornton[10], 15.01.2010: 6).

---

[10]**Grant Thornton International (GTIL)** is an umbrella organization that does not provide services to clients and is a private company limited by guarantee, incorporated in England and Wales. GTIL and the member firms are not a worldwide partnership. Each member firm is a separate legal entity. Membership in the global organization does not make any firm responsible

Association Limited by Shares This legal form is a limited partnership with shares called as Kommanditgesellschaften auf Aktien (KgaA) in Germany and Spolka Komandytowa in Poland, where it is adopted by some of the smaller professional services firms.

In UK, auditors are able to adopt any legal form. An individual or a firm can be assigned as the auditor. The firm can be a corporation or partnership.

In their comment letter to IOSCO Consulting Report, Eumedion, Corporate Governance Forum states that the prevailing ownership and governance rules within auditing firms stimulate conservatism. According to their opinion, it is a question of time before the private partnership model will no longer be tolerated by the users of audit service, as many audit partners—also those without extraordinary performance—became rich, while the governance of some of these firms is relatively poor (Abma 09.12.2009: 3). IOSCO Consultation Report received contribution from 21 institutions, organizations, and persons. The fact that contributors represent a variety of stakeholders like service providers, regulators, and those benefitting from the services rendered, assists important issues to rise to the surface. With the eighteenth question, which is directed under the assumption that transparency will have a positive impact on audit quality, it is tried to be understood whether increased transparency will increase the trust in financial reporting or not. Opposite to the dignified approach and comments of the Eumedion representing European investors—emphasizing the usefulness of the coverage of nonbinding auditor's advices—*Fédération des Experts comptables Européens* (FEE) contents itself with a short comment stating that the answer of this question doesn't have any applicability (Damme 13.01.2010: 14). *Financial Reporting Council* (FRC), the center of which is based in London, shared an opinion supporting Eumedion's one in the same medium; and drove attention to the contradiction of auditors, who undertake the role of intermediating the financial table users in accessing the desired transparency, being least transparent (Haddrill 22.12.2009: 1). Even though it is definitely natural of diversified stakeholders having conflicting opinions, it is also understood that it is a necessity to be in continuous communication for the sake of common path.

As seen from the above-given data, the legal form adopted by auditing firms differs among traditionally employee–ownership prevailing EU countries. Notwithstanding this variety, in all EU countries except for Austria where only the auditing firm is liable to the audit client and UK, where auditing firm is the statutory auditor, the auditor who signs the audit report is liable to the audit client (www.ec.europa.eu, 12.03.2012, European Commission, oxera_report_en.pdf, Oxera Report, 2007: 92) (Table 2.4).

Corporate governance arrangements define the relations between the firm's owners and its managers. Effectively, corporate governance describes the mechanisms for the firm's owners to exercise control over the firm (www.ec.europa.eu, 12.03.2012, Oxera Report, 2007: 95). Legal restrictions at national and EU level

---

for the services or activities of other member firms (https://www.grantthornton.global/en/about/governance-and-management/. Accessed 31 Jul 2017).

Table 2.4 Legal partners, partnership, and members of audit firms in EU countries

Partner	
Member	Partner
Equity partner	Non-equity partner
Legal partner (Ownership rights)	Senior employee salaried
Have voting rights	Don't have voting rights

Source European Commission Oct 2007

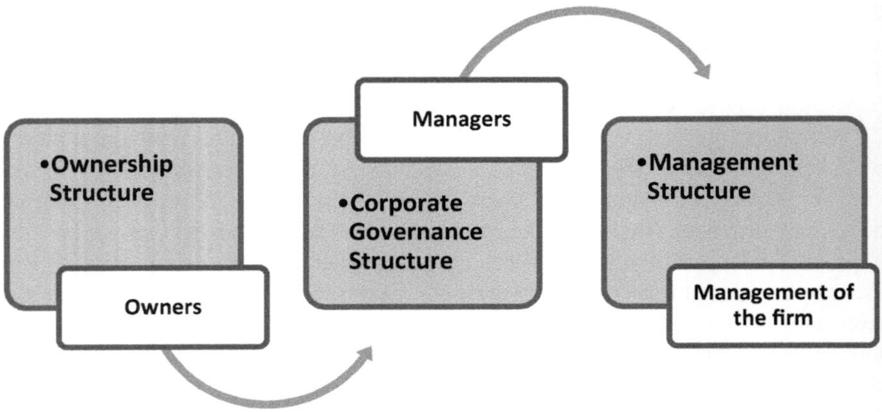

Fig. 2.3 Relationships between ownership, corporate governance, and management structures. *Source* European Commission 2007

govern the ownership composition of auditing firms. The composition of management bodies of auditing firms is also restricted by legal restrictions. Even though significant differences persist, corporate governance arrangements of auditing firms echo the corporate governance structure s of investor-owned corporations.

As seen from Fig. 2.3, the third structure interwoven with the other two is management structure. Management structures represent mechanisms via which agents on behalf of the owners—i.e., managers—manage the firms on a day to day basis. These structures also govern the process of strategic decisions making of the firm that are within the realm of managerial discretion (*ibid.*).

2.2 Auditing Firms in Turkey

As happened in developed countries in the world, in the post-SOX era, there had been numerous regulations made in Turkey; considerable efforts had been spent by regulators, regulating institutions, and professional organizations. The underlying reason of all these efforts is to establish and safeguard the trust of stakeholders, especially investors in securities markets. Fulfilling this aim by solely making arrangements in regulations is beside the point. Regrettably, monitoring and oversight are imperative in order to secure the abidance to the regulations and legislations. The expensive audit mechanism is a bitter pill to be swallowed by the society for the sake of thwarting probable overcosting and irreversible failures.

Fundamentally, the primary concern being tried to be defined will never be a matter of discussion in societies composed of individuals who interiorize ethical values. Companies, which are managed by executives, who comprehend the meaning and significance of stakeholders of the organization, will volunteeringly abide the rules and regulations and operate in cooperation with generally agreed standards anyway.

2.2.1 The Profile of Auditing Firms in Turkey

This title is allocated for developing the profile of auditing firms carrying service in Turkey. Auditing firms are handled from many aspects; organizational structure, legal form, capital and capital structure, number of partners, number of auditors, licensing agreements with foreign institutions if any, the share of income earned from different activities in total revenue, the existence of their Web sites and similar aspects. Comments and suggestions follow determination of situation. Bearing the whole of the research in mind, connections are built among the profile revealed and several opinions mentioned.

2.2.1.1 Organizational Structure

In its broad meaning, organization is a social system among individuals. In the narrow sense tough, organization is a patterned group of relations, namely a structure. The process or the act of establishing this structure is also defined as organizing. Raison d'être of the organization is that the realization of specific objectives needs the efforts of a group instead of one person's. Organizational structure is a tool, and this human-related tool needs to be adjusted according to the individuals' personalities, who are to coordinate the activities; to the nature of the business, and surrounding environmental conditions (Koçel 2001: 22). As all kinds of business entities do, auditing firms also need the most appropriate organizational structure.

Firms hire and train audit personnel, and incentivize auditors through compensation and other organizational policies; therefore, in understanding audit quality, firms become crucial. Moreover, firms devise the audit programs and testing procedures that guide the evidence collection process, and have internal administrative structures to assure quality and compliance with their firm's audit policies (Francis 2011: 137).

Auditing firms' organizational structures that have critical impacts on audit quality are handled in this section. It is not uncommon that these kinds of data are collected by surveys or interviews; however, it is always possible that some part of data is available in the Web sites of related parties. In this section, the purpose of which is exploring the organizational structure of auditing firms, for the collection of desired data the publically accessible Web sites of auditing firms and other-related organizations had been preferred. To accomplish this objective of this section; auditing firms' organizational structures, legal forms, capital and capital structures, numbers of partners, numbers of auditors, licensing agreements with foreign institutions if any, the shares of income earned from several activities in total revenue, the existence and status of their Web sites and similar aspects are determined here. Samples of organizational structure of auditing firms operating in Turkey are given below. The first illustration belongs to an auditing firm, which has a license agreement with a foreign institution (Fig. 2.4).

The second one shows the organizational schema of an auditing firm, which does not have any such licensing agreement with a foreign institution (Fig. 2.5).

The data used in the study, which has the objective of exploring the profile of the auditing firms having operations in Turkey, are compiled through a lengthy process. The beginning of the studies is in the early months of 2012. At those times, all of the data about auditing firms were collected from the Web site of CMB. During the research process, regulating bodies and/or institutions that have a voice in audit-related issues, were exposed to considerable and radical changes. While accessing some data became easier, some were no more published on the related Web sites. Therefore, even tough sources benefited from in profile analysis are the exact ones, the basic structure was not kept as it was before. The data, which are no more available, are kept as they were, assuming that they will no longer be updated, thus will be unchanged, and these data had been used in comments.

Even though an increase in the number of the auditing firms publishing their transparency reports within the frame of Independent Audit By-Law (IAbL) is observed; some of the details of data available pre-POA era are no more preserved. Moreover, some of the auditing firms, which were active at the time the research started, and at the times when whole data in some areas were fully accessible, became inactive as of May 2014. Transparency reports on the other hand caused loss of data, even though they enabled more access to some information regarding some issues. The repeated search revealed that there are 114 auditing firms on the list in POA Web site as of May 3–25, 2014 (www.kgk.gov.tr/dk/index.aspx, 16.05. 2014). Some of these do not audit Public Interest Entities[11] (PIEs), thus these are excluded from the research.

[11]**Public Interest Entities**: are entities governed by the law whose transferable securities are admitted to trading on a regulated market. Credit institutions, insurance undertakings, or entities designated by the government as public-interest entities, for instance, undertakings that are of significant public relevance because of the nature of their business, their size or the number of their employees.

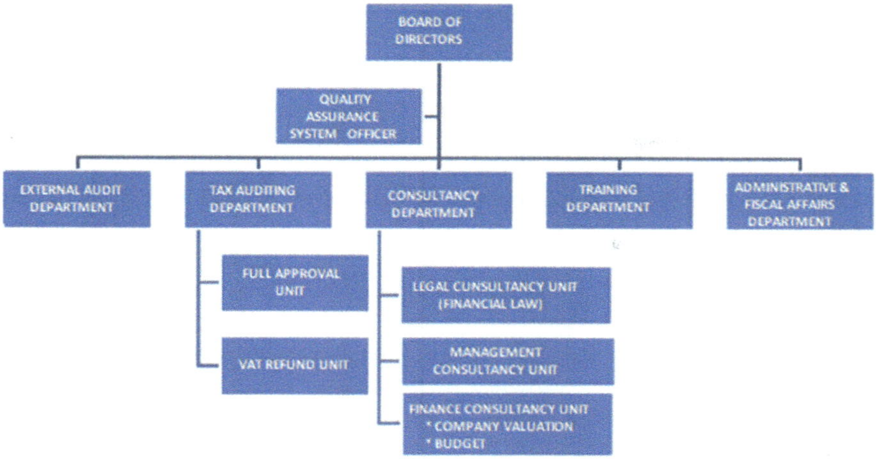

Fig. 2.4 Organization structure sample—National CPA Firm Having License Agreement with a Foreign Institution. *Source* Translated and re-illustrated from Itimat Bağımsız Denetim (Itimat CPA) Web site. http://www.itimat-ymm.com/Detail.aspx?pageID=51. Accessed 16 Oct 2013

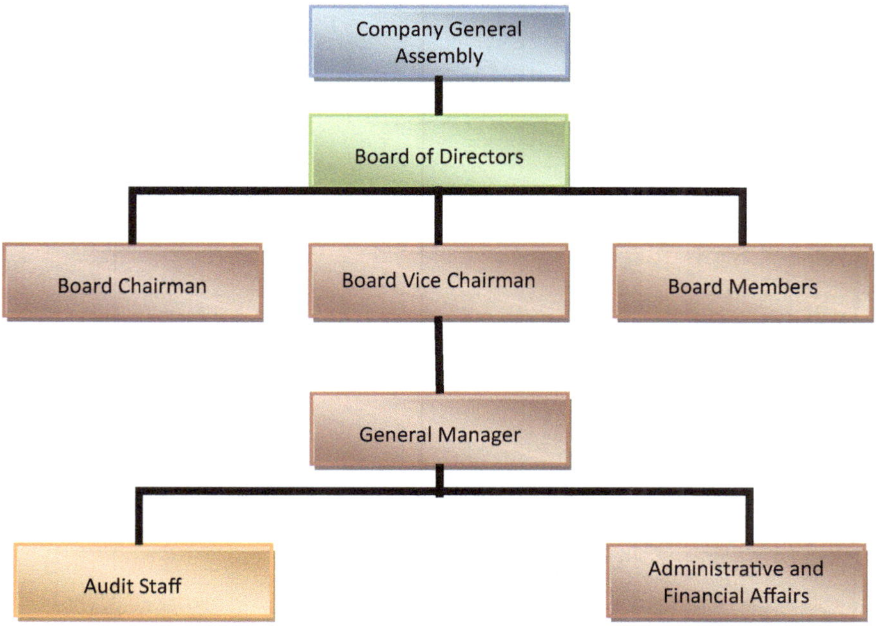

Fig. 2.5 Organization structure sample—National CPA Firm Having No License Agreement with a Foreign Institution. *Source* Translated and re-illustrated from Mod Denetim (Mod CPA) Web site. http://www.moddenetim.com.tr/2010-yili-seffaflik-raporu.pdf. Accessed 16 Oct 2013

2.2.1.2 Number of Partners, Their Shares and Capital Ownership

As of the number of the partners and their distribution in the 2012–2013 era, 94 auditing firms have 847 partners. Average number of partners in this era is 9.01 (Table 2.5).

When it comes to the 2013–2014 era, while there are 87 auditing firms performing PIEs auditing, only 85 of them the data of which had been accessed are taken into consideration. These firms have 780 partners in total. Average number of partners in this era is 9.18. The frequency distribution of partners is displayed in the above-given table.

The distribution of the number of partners of auditing firms is shown in the graphic below. As seen from the graphic, the largest groups are made up by auditing firms that have five, eight, and six partners consequently. The total of these three groups is 54.12%, namely 46 out of 85 auditing firms. The remaining 45.88% is composed of auditing firms, the numbers of partners ranging between four to thirty (Graphic 2.1).

Table 2.5 Number of partners of audit firms in Turkey

Number of partners	Frequency 2013–2014	Frequency 2012–2013	Weight % 2013–2014	Weight % 2012–2013
30	1	1	1.18	1.06
29	1	1	1.18	1.06
23	0	2	0	2.13
20	1	1	1.18	1.06
19	2	2	2.35	2.13
18	1	0	1.18	0
17	2	0	2.35	0
15	2	2	2.35	2.13
14	5	4	5.88	4.26
13	3	4	3.53	4.26
12	0	2	0	2.13
11	7	8	8.24	8.51
10	4	6	4.71	6.38
9	1	3	1.18	3.19
8	15	7	17.65	7.45
7	7	8	8.24	8.51
6	14	20	16.47	21.28
5	17	23	20.00	24.47
4	2	0	2.35	0
			100.00	100.00

Source Table created based on the data compiled from transparency reports and Web sites of regulating institutions

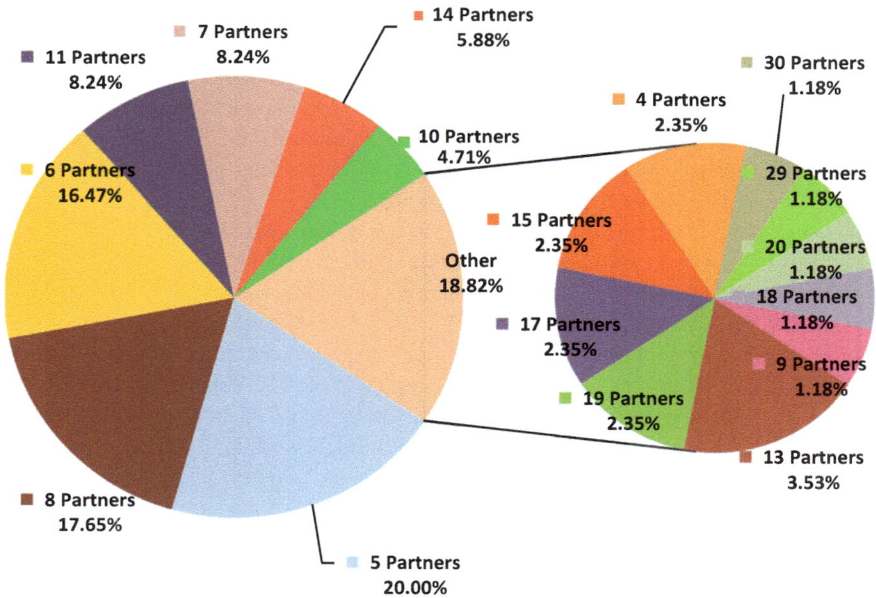

Graphic 2.1 Distribution of number of partners of auditing firms performing in Turkey. *Source* Prepared based on the transparency reports of auditing firms

It is thought; the more the number of partners is, the more evenly capital ownership will be distributed. However, analysis revealed otherwise. At the first-hand 2012–2013 era is evaluated. Among 94 auditing firms; the average share the biggest shareholding partner holds is 52.52% of the capital; the maximum is 99.86% and the minimum is 7.14%. When the second biggest shareholder is considered; the average share the second biggest shareholding partner holds is 22.84% of the capital; and it is observed that the share of the second biggest shareholder ownership changes from 0.10 to 50% of the capital. At the auditing firm with 30 partners—this is the auditing firm with topmost number of partners—the biggest shareholder owns 48.77% of the of the capital and the second biggest one holds 8.40% of the shares. At the auditing firm with five partners—this is the auditing firm with least number of partners—the biggest shareholder owns 57.56% of the of the capital and the second biggest one holds 29.88% of the shares.

Considering the time span of the research, the same evaluation is done for the 2013–2014 data as follows. Among 85 auditing firms; the average share the biggest shareholding partner holds is 52.98% of the capital; the maximum is 99.99% and the minimum is unchanged—7.14%. When the second biggest shareholder is considered, the average share the second biggest shareholding partner holds is 22.06% of the capital; and the share of the second biggest shareholder ownership changes from 0.00016 to 49.90% of the capital. The auditing firm with 30 partners, which has maximum numbers of partners, did not issue its 2013 transparency report as of May 17,

2014. Due to this fact, previous year's data had been used, which reminds us that the biggest shareholder owns 48.77% of the capital and the second biggest one holds 8.40% of the shares. At the two auditing firms with four partners both—these two are the auditing firms with least number of partners in this era—the biggest shareholder owns 99.60% of the of the capital in one of the auditing firms and 33.33% of the shares in the other four-partner firm. The second biggest shareholding partners at these firms hold 0.20 and 33.33% of the shares consequently.

As the capital of the auditing firms is examined, it is seen that on the average 94 auditing firms have a capital of 110,403 Turkish liras (≈\$57,295.66) during 2012–2013 era, and 20 auditing firms have a capital above the average. Where the highest capital is 820,000 Turkish liras, the minimum is 50,000 Turkish liras, which is the capital of 50 auditing firms. The total capital of the representatives of Big Four in Turkey is 240,100 and the average of their capital is 60,025 Turkish liras. When the data of the 2013–2014 era is considered, on the average 85 auditing firms have a capital of 132,264 Turkish liras (≈\$62,294.65), and 21 auditing firms have a capital above the average. While the highest capital rises to 1,000,000 Turkish liras, there is not any change considering the minimum capital, which the capital of 39 auditing firms in this era. In dollar terms, the rise in the maximum capital is 10.68%. On the side of the Big Four party, there is no change recorded. On the contrary, of their superiority in the number of their audit staff, it is observed that Big Four does not have a prominent capital position in Turkey. Since the quality of the services sector heavily depends on the human capital, which is far more critical than the tangible capital; this issue is to be kept in mind while assessing the quality of audit.

2.2.1.3 Audit Staff: Numbers, Distribution, and Leverage

As the audit teams of auditing firms are considered, in the 2012–2013 era 94 auditing firms have 2425 auditors as their staff. As mentioned before, one of the deformed data is about audit teams of auditing firms. Formerly all the data derived and used were available on the CMB Web site; however, determination or this situation for 2013–2014 era became bound to and is constricted by transparency reports. The titles and the degrees of auditors employed by auditing firms during the 2012–2013 era is in the below-given graphic (Graphic 2.2).

An auditing firm's staff consists of 26 auditors on the average, and the number of auditing firms employing 26 or more auditors is 13. Among 94 auditing firms, Başaran Nas CPA has the most crowded audit staff. The smallest audit staff consists of four auditors. With a total of 989 auditors as staff, the auditing firms having license agreements with Deloitte & Touche, Ernst & Young, KPMG and PricewaterhouseCoopers make up 40.78% of auditors of 94 auditing firms in Turkey. When we focus on Big Four, it is observed that staff assistants build 72.30% of audit staff. As all auditing firms are examined, auditors make up 16.08% of the staff, where this ratio drops to 11.73% for Big Four in Turkey. Similarly, the share of the managing auditors within the staff drops to 7.18%. As auditing firms besides Big Four are considered; auditors make up 19.08%, staff assistants 32.66, and partners responsible for leading audits 22.01% of the staff consequently.

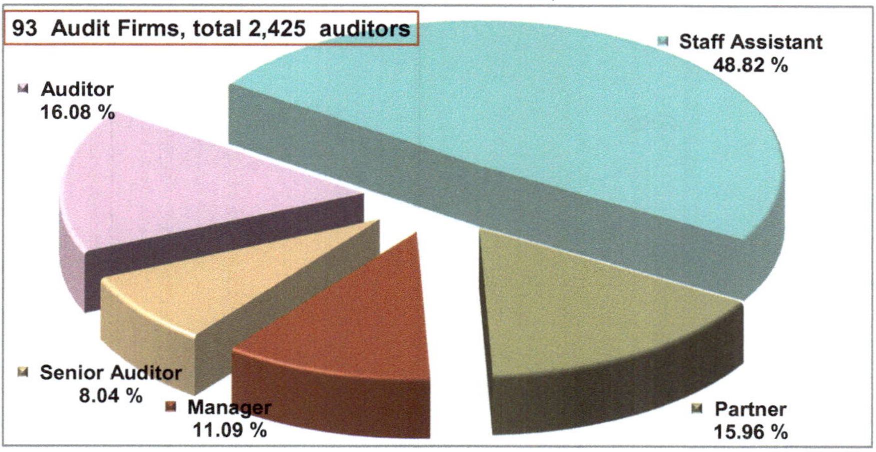

Graphic 2.2 Distribution of the staff of the auditing firms performing in Turkey during 2012–2013 Era. *Source* Prepared based on the transparency reports of auditing firms

Data related to auditing firms performing in Turkey had been downloaded again as of June 2015. As displayed at the graph given below; at this time period the number of auditing firms is 95, and the total of the audit staff of all auditing firms is 3148. Thus, the growth rate of audit staff became 29.81% (Graphic 2.3).

The average number of auditors employed by auditing firms at this time is 33, and auditing firms employing 33 auditors or more is ten. Among 95 auditing firms, Başaran Nas CPA is again the most crowded staff owning auditing firm. The smallest staff is made up of six and this is valid only for one firm. With a total of 1563 auditors as staff, the auditing firms having license agreements with Deloitte & Touche, Ernst & Young, KPMG and PricewaterhouseCoopers make up 49.65% of auditors of 95 auditing firms in Turkey. When we focus on Big Four, it is observed that staff assistants build 86.50% of audit staff. As all auditing firms are examined, auditors make up 11.31% of the staff, where this ratio drops to 3.39% for Big Four in Turkey. The share of the managing auditors within the staff drops to almost one third and becomes 4.73. As auditing firms besides Big Four are considered; auditors make up 19.12%, staff assistants 35.14, and partners responsible for leading audits 20.95% of the staff consequently. Even though this is an issue to be handled later in detail, shortly we can comment that while the situation for the Big Four in Turkey worsens, it is somehow stable for the rest of the auditing firms performing in Turkey. The comparison of the audit staff structure and staff distribution of auditing firms for the two eras—2012–2013 and 2015—the detailed data of which had already been given above, are tabulated (Table 2.6).

As apparently seen from the table, within the time period given, audit staff grew by 29.81%; on the contrary the number of partners and managers, and their shares in audit teams dropped drastically. The highest rise is observed in staff assistants. Their number increased by 725 fellows, the rate of increase is 61.23%.

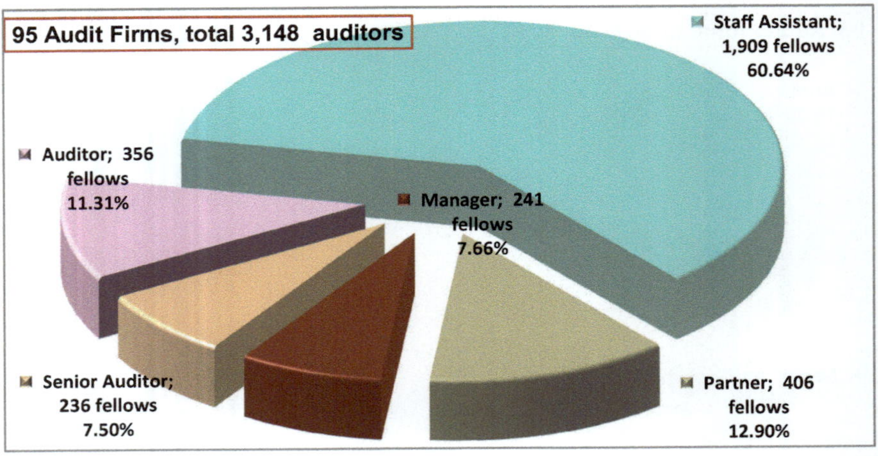

Graphic 2.3 Distribution of the staff of the auditing firms performing in Turkey (2015). *Source* Prepared based on the transparency reports of auditing firms

Table 2.6 Comparison of the audit staff structure and staff distribution of auditing firms (2012–2013 and 2015)

	Total number of auditors	Partner	Manager	Senior auditor	Auditor	Staff assistant
2015	3148	406	241	236	356	1909
Share in the staff	100.00%	12.90%	7.66%	7.50%	11.31%	60.64%
2012–2013	2425	387	269	195	390	1184
Share in the staff	100.00%	22.01%	16.43%	9.82%	19.08%	32.66%
Change between two periods	723	19	−28	41	−34	725
Change between two periods	29.81%	4.91%	−10.41%	21.03%	−8.72%	61.23%

The comparison of audit staff of the auditing firms having license agreements with Deloitte & Touche, Ernst & Young, KPMG and PricewaterhouseCoopers and others is given in Table 2.7.

The ratio of audit professionals to partners is defined as ***leverage*** (PCAOB 2013; Deltas and Doogar 2004; Doogar and Easley 1998; Kinney 1986). When calculations are done for all of the auditing firms performing in Turkey, the leverages come out as given below:

$$\text{Leverage} = \frac{\text{Number of Non} - \text{Partner Audit Staff}}{\text{Number of Partners}}$$

$$2012{-}2013\ \textit{era}\ \text{Leverage}_{\text{All Firms}} = \frac{2,038}{387} = 5.27$$

Table 2.7 The audit staff of the Big Four and other auditing firms (2015 vs. 2012–2013 Era)

		Total number of auditors	Partner	Manager	Senior auditor	Auditor	Staff assistant
All Firms	2015	3148	406	241	236	356	1909
	2012–2013	2425	387	269	195	390	1184
All Firms	2015	100.00%	12.90%	7.66%	7.50%	11.31%	60.64%
	2012–2013	100.00%	15.96%	11.09%	8.04%	16.08%	48.82%
Big Four	2015	1563	74	23	61	53	1352
	2012–2013	989	71	33	54	116	715
Big Four	2015	100.00%	4.73%	1.47%	3.90%	3.39%	86.50%
	2012–2013	100.00%	7.18%	3.34%	5.46%	11.73%	72.30%
Other Firms	2015	1585	332	218	175	303	557
	2012–2013	1436	316	236	141	274	469
Other Firms	2015	100.00%	20.95%	13.75%	11.04%	19.12%	35.14%
	2012–2013	100.00%	22.01%	16.43%	9.82%	19.08%	32.66%

$$2012-2013\ era\ \mathrm{Leverage}_{\mathrm{Big\ Four}} = \frac{918}{71} = 12.93$$

$$2012-2013\ era\ \mathrm{Leverage}_{90\ \mathrm{Firms}} = \frac{1,120}{316} = 3.54$$

$$2015\ \mathrm{Leverage}_{\mathrm{All\ Firms}} = \frac{2,742}{406} = 6.75$$

$$2015\ \mathrm{Leverage}_{\mathrm{Big\ Four}} = \frac{1,489}{74} = 20.12$$

$$2015\ \mathrm{Leverage}_{91\ \mathrm{Firms}} = \frac{1,253}{332} = 3.77$$

As seen from the calculations, the leverage of Big Four is 12.93 in 2012–2013 era and is almost four times of the leverage of the remaining auditing firms. The gap enlarged in 2015 and Big Four leverage reached 20.12, which is almost 5.34 times of the leverage of the remaining 91 auditing firms. The leverages for the two time periods are comparatively tabulated (Table 2.8).

Among Big Four Akis CPA has the highest leverage—23.85. The lowest leverage among all auditing firms is 0.25, and belongs to BD CPA, the audit staff of which consists eight partners and two staff assistants.

Auditors and/or auditing firms with a higher proportion of Non-Audit Services (NAS) in their product mix are expected to have higher leverage (Deltas and Doogar 2004: 13). The average of the leverages of all audit firms is 5.27 in 2012–2013 era, and 6.75 in 2015. It is and will be emphasized throughout the text that, the composition of the audit team has an effect on audit quality. Nonetheless,

Table 2.8 Leverages of the auditing firms performing in Turkey

	Increase rate (%)	2015	2012–2013
All firms	28.08	6.75	5.27
Big four	55.61	20.12	12.93
Other auditing firms	6.50	3.77	3.54

quantitative criteria solely do not become an indicator; they act as determinants in assessing the audit quality. According to Robert Conway, a depressed leverage is one of the factors positively impacting audit quality (Conway 25.11.2009: 11). Most probably, the education, age and experience of the audit team members have impacts on audit quality. However, by alleging their workload, professional secrecy, client's secrecy, firm's secrecy, etc., auditing firms do not cooperate enough with researchers in revealing the quality of audit. Gönen and Uzay stated the difficulties encountered during their research at a conference (2009: 5).

2.2.1.4 Transparency of Auditing Firms and Distribution of the Revenue

As of their Web sites in the 2012–2013 era, it is observed that while some of the auditing firms have user-friendly Web sites, some do not even have one. Out of 94 auditing firms, 80 have Web sites; three have a Web site under construction, the Web sites of two auditing firms have malicious content, which deterred us from continuing our visit, and the remaining nine auditing firms do not have a Web site. In fact, the existence of a Web site does not mean much either. According to IAbL Article 36, all auditing firms having performed a PIE audit in a calendar year, should send/upload their previous year's transparency reports to POA next year, and publish it in their own Web sites as well. Those who have a special accounting period should do so until the end of the fourth month following the closing of their accounting period. Out of 94 auditing firms, which are the object of the study, 58 performed at least one audit of a company listed in Borsa Istanbul during 2012. Being listed in Borsa Istanbul makes the audit client a PIE according to Article 36. Logically during 2012–2013 era, there must have been issued at least 58 transparency reports by 58 auditing firms. However, only 24 auditing firms out of 80, which have a Web site, issued a transparency report or annual report. According to the Provision (j) of the Paragraph 2 of Article 36, financial information indicating the weight of audit activities such as the distribution of total revenues by the audit of financial statements, other audits, and non-audit services should take place in the transparency report. Nonetheless, only five out of 24 auditing firms having issued transparency report for the 2012–2013 era indicated the required financial information in detail. Of a great number of financial information data listed in the "Contents" of transparency reports have been clipped and not published. It is observed that some of the auditing firms inscribed the phrase "Financial data is sent to the Prime Ministry Undersecretariat of Treasury" and omitted the data mentioned. In addition, there are some auditing firms, which redirect the visitors to the Web site or annual report of their licensing foreign institutions.

As of May 2014, 81 auditing firms out of POA listed 85 auditing firms have Web sites; and 67 published 2013 transparency report. It is seen that some reports had been published not earlier than end of May; and ironically, most of the transparency reports were hidden under irrelevant places such that they are untraceable. This undesired situation is not concordant to the principle of transparency. Two auditing firms out of Big Four had already published the transparency report before May 17, 2014, while the other two did so toward the end of the month. As of January 2015, the number of auditing firms having a Web site rose to 83; the number of transparency report publishing auditing firms rose to 71, and it is observed that lots of auditing firms revised and republished their transparency reports.

As stated throughout the book, for a long-time income statue of auditing firms remained puzzle and been shared only with related authorities. The proficiency thesis of Pirgaip, an assistant expert at CMB, without indicating the source, touches upon the distribution of revenue of auditing firms in Turkey. According to this thesis, 69.80% of 2001 revenue of auditing firms is from auditing; the income earned from other professional services makes up 20.86%, and a slice of 9.33% stands for miscellaneous services (2004: 30). Even though the distribution of the revenue is undetermined at a study of Gönen and Uzay (2009: 14), they identified the services rendered by auditing firms in Turkey.

The services rendered by auditing firms are as follows according to their proclaims:

- Auditing;
- Finance Consultancy;
- Tax Consultancy;
- Law Consultancy;
- Training;
- Assertion and certified councillorship (CPA);
- Management Consultancy;
- Other Consultancy.

Other consultancy is also to be detailed further as follows:

1. *Accounting Services;*
2. *Internal Audit;*
3. *Outsourcing;*
4. *Change Management;*
5. *Investment Consultancy;*
6. *Human Resources;*
7. *Tourism Consultancy;*
8. *Information Technology Consultancy;*
9. *Customs Advisor.*

POA's power of sanction is mentioned before. As soon as it is noticed that the essential data/information is not concordant to POA legislation; or some transparency reports or some parts of the reports are missing; the researcher corresponded with POA, and demanded the missing information. Even though the reply was not promising, and in fact stating that information not shared with the public is not available with the third parties either; this alerted POA, and via its own Web site the authority reminded auditing firms to complete the information required and asked them to upload their income statements until May 31, 2014. Respecting auditing firms' Web sites and transparency reports, the sanction power of POA comes into play in the second half of 2014. Toward last phases of the research, transparency reports became published on POA Web site, and there are 71 auditing firms listed.

As the links given at POA Web site are traced, it is seen that two auditing firms published their transparency reports in the name of other auditing firms, and three of them do not have any report file to be downloaded at the traced address. Some auditing firms state their revenue in Turkish lira, some in percentages; there are auditing firms as well which have revenue displayed both in monetary terms and in percentages. To conclude, 71 out of 85 auditing firms published 2013 transparency report, and 64 of them stated the revenue in monetary terms. The revenue of only two auditing firms is composed of income generated solely from auditing, and there is one auditing firm, the audit service revenue is null. The distribution of the reported revenue generated from all activities of auditing firms is plotted in the graph below.

As stated before, some reported in Turkish lira, others in percentages, therefore, the slices in the pie graph shows the average of the income generated from each activity; and summing them up is nonsense. According to transparency reports, on the average 40.80% of the revenue of auditing firms in Turkey is generated from auditing, and 23.99% is earned from services within the Law No. 3568. Full confirmation activity generated 9.11% on the average, where consultancy services brought 6.58% (Graphic 2.4).

Again, as understood from the graph, information systems audit makes up 0.19% of the revenue, tax audit 11.26%, and other activities generated 8.47% on the average.

The total revenue of 64 auditing firms, which stated their income in monetary terms, is 416,812,482 Turkish liras in 2013. External audit revenue of these firms is 246,539,413 Turkish liras. Thus, a meaningful average is to be calculated. On the average, the external audit revenue of 64 auditing firms is 59.15%; the related graph is given below; (Graphic 2.5).

The total revenue of the auditing firms having license agreements with Deloitte & Touche, Ernst & Young, KPMG, and PricewaterhouseCoopers generated from external audit makes up 76.61% of their total revenue. In order to get a healthy rate, it is essential to consolidate the income of all firms that are related to each auditing firm and are involved in bookkeeping, tax audit, and consultancy to audit clients of the related auditing firms. This is also required for the assessment of the principle of independence. The external audit revenue total of the first ten auditing firms as of 2013 is 225,522,737 Turkish liras. The below-given graph displays the distribution of this revenue among first ten. As seen from the graph, DRT CPA, one of the Big Four representatives in Turkey, earned 29.83% of the revenue of the first ten. The representative of the Pricewaterhouse Coopers, Başaran Nas CPA has a share of

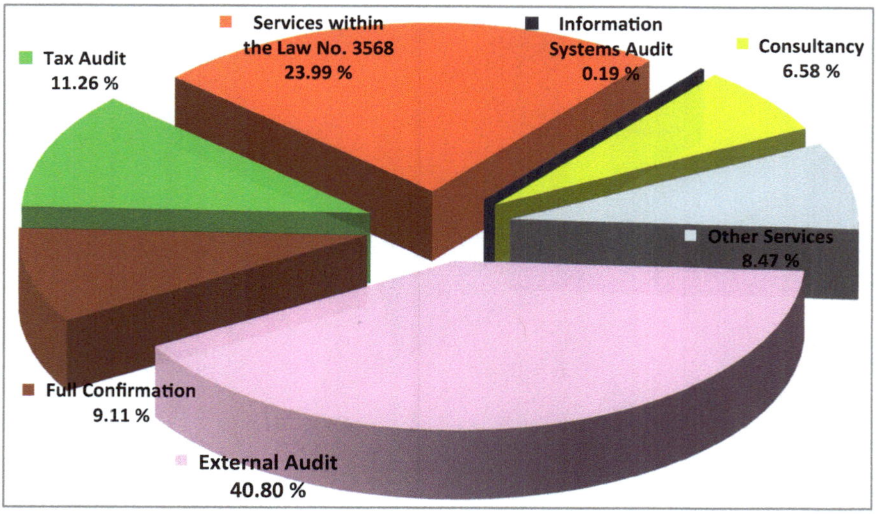

Graphic 2.4 Distribution of 2013 revenue of auditing firms reported in percentages. *Source* Prepared based on the transparency reports of auditing firms. *Note* Since transparency reports have missing data, summation of slice values is meaningless

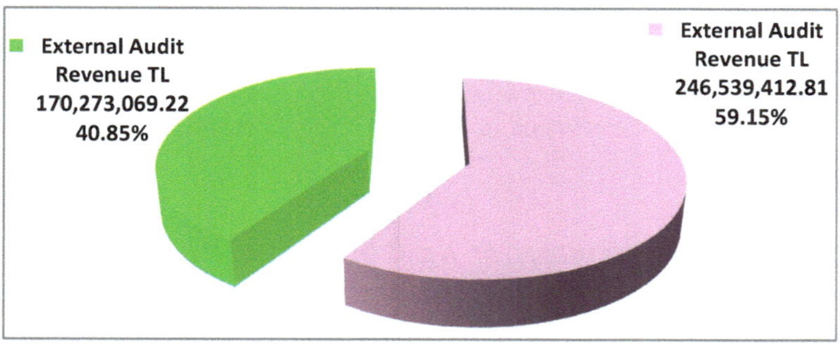

Graphic 2.5 Distribution of 2013 revenue of auditing firms reported in monetary terms. *Source* Prepared based on the transparency reports of auditing firms. *Note* The graph is based on the data of 64 auditing firms, those having displayed their revenue in monetary terms

23.65%, Akis CPA representing KPMG earned 17.06%, and Ernst&Young Global Limited representative Güney CPA got 16.48% of this revenue. Thus, while the share of Big Four in Turkey became 87.02%; remaining six auditing firms got 12.98% of the revenue of the first ten. For convenience, instead of using the full trade name, the term "CPA" substitutes "Bağımsız Denetim ve SMMM/YMM A. Ş." (Graphic 2.6).

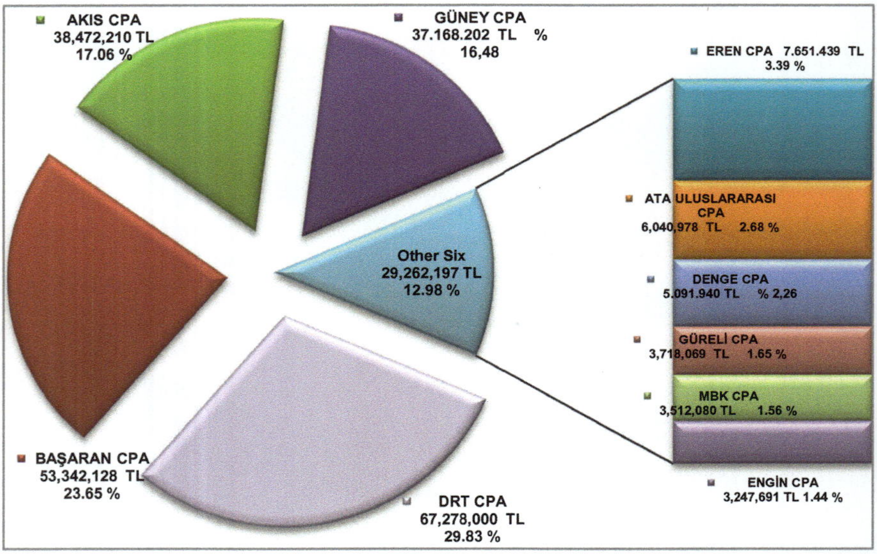

Graphic 2.6 First ten firms as of 2013 external audit revenue. *Source* Prepared based on transparency reports

The total external audit revenue of auditing firms ranking among top ten makes up 91.48% of the aggregate external audit revenue of all auditing firms performing in Turkey. The external audit revenue of Big Four, which are among this group, represents 79.61% of the revenue of the Turkish audit market.

2.2.2 License Agreements of Auditing Firms Performing in Turkey and Their Activities Before PCAOB

Inevitably, auditing firms performing in Turkey also have licensing agreements with global institutions as their counterparts in other countries do. Regarding 2012–2013 era when the study had started, 55 out of 94 auditing firms active then, did have a licensing agreement with a foreign institution, and remaining 39 did not have any. In the below-given table, auditing firms are matched with their foreign licensing institutions or solution partners as of 2013–2014 era. It is observed that, some foreign institutions became solution partner or have a licensing agreement with more than one auditing firm in Turkey. In fact, a detailed research revealed that some of the auditing firms under different trade names have the same postal address and/or telephone number. As seen from the table, the transparency reports of 49 auditing firms are timely, and 54 of them have relation with a foreign institution. For convenience, instead of using the full trade name, the term "CPA" substitutes "Bağımsız Denetim ve SMMM/YMM A.Ş." (Table 2.9).

Table 2.9 Foreign institutions or solution partners the auditing firms have licensing agreements

Trade name	Foreign institution or solution partner the auditing firm has licensing agreement	Transparency report
Total: 54 auditing firms		49
Köker CPA	Agn International	2013
Bilgili CPA	Agn International Ltd	2013
Rehber CPA	Antea Alliance of Independent Firms	2013
Güreli CPA	Baker Tilly International	2013
BDO Denet CPA	Bdo International	2013
Işık CPA	Bkr International	2013
Ege CPA	Ch International	2013
Elit CPA	Cpa Associates International Inc.-USA	2013
Crowe Horwath Olgu CPA	Crowe Horwath	2013
Kavram CPA	Crowe Horwath International	2013
Drt CPA	Deloitte Touche Tohmatsu International	2013
Ser-Berker CPA	Dfk International	2013
Değer CPA	Ecovis Europe	2013
Ac İstanbul Uluslararası CPA	Enterprise Network Worldwide	2013
Güney CPA	Ernst&Young Global Limited	2013
Rasyonel CPA	Euraudit Int	NA
İtimat CPA	Fidunion International	2013
Engin CPA	Grant Thornton	2013
Eren CPA	Grant Thornton	2013
Güncel CPA	Groupe Laviale Sohaco	2013
Birleşim CPA	Hazlems Fenton	2013
Hlb Saygın CPA	Hlb International	2013
Çağdaş CPA	Iapa International	2013
Güçbir CPA	Iapa International	2013
Consulta CPA	Inaa Group	2013
Detay CPA	International Experts and Consultants Iecnet	2013
Türkmen CPA	International Practice Group	2013
Bakış CPA	Ipg International Pratice Group	2012
Mega Global Uluslar Arası Anonim Şirketi	Jeffreys Henry International	2013
Artı Değer Uluslararası CPA	Jhi Jeffreys Henry International	2013
Arkan Ergin Uluslararası CPA	Jpa International	2013
Ihy CPA	Kingston Sorel International	2013
Akis CPA	KPMG	2013
Ata Uluslararası CPA	Kreston International	2013

(continued)

Table 2.9 (continued)

Trade name	Foreign institution or solution partner the auditing firm has licensing agreement	Transparency report
Total: 54 auditing firms		49
Dmr CPA	Kudos International Network	2013
Legal Yönet CPA	Lea Global	2013
Denge CPA	Mazars Société Coopérative À Responsabilité Limitée	2013
Mgı CPA	Mgi Business Solutions Worldwide	2013
Mbk CPA	Moore Stephens International Ltd	2013
Arılar CPA	Nexia International	2013
Oluşum CPA	Nexia International	NA
Yöntem CPA	Nexia International	2013
As CPA	Nexia International Ltd	2013
Karma CPA	Parker Randall International	2013
Sun CPA	Pkf Worldwide	2013
Yeditepe CPA	Praxity-Global Alliance Ltd.	2013
Türkerler CPA	Premier International Associates	2013
Başaran Nas A.Ş	Pricewaterhouse Coopers	2013
Birleşik Uzmanlar CPA	Primeglobal	2013
Med CPA	Rg Treuhand Müth and Partner Gmbh	NA
Kapital Karden CPA	Rsm International	2013
Dmf Sistem U.a. CPA	Russell Bedford International	NA
Ulusal CPA	The International Accounting Group	2013
Uzman CPA	Uhy Urbach Hacker Young International Ltd.	2013

Source Prepared based on transparency reports

Recently, one of the objectives of regulation of authorities is to enable integration with the global financial markets. Such integration necessitates usage of foreign licenses. Creating demand for the services supplied by auditing firms performing in Turkey and sustaining this are important. As 94 auditing firms active during 2012–2013 era are considered, 18 are registered with PCAOB. In 2012–2013 era, firms registered with PCAOB were categorized as follows:

A—Audit report for at least one issuer;
B—No audit reports for issuers but played a substantial role in the audit of at least one issuer;
C—No audit reports, not played a role in an audit, but prepared financial tables for at least one broker-dealer;
D—None of the above;
E—No Form 2 filed.

As seen from the table, during 2012–2013 era, four Turkish auditing firms prepared audit reports for at least one issuer; one auditing firm prepared not any audit reports for issuers but played a substantial role in the audit of at least one issuer. One out of remaining 13 auditing firms prepared financial tables for at least one broker-dealer; two did not yet filed for Form 2; and the rest did not prepare any reports, nor did they take place in an audit (Table 2.10).

As of end of 2014; number of auditing firms in Category A dropped to two; did not change in Category B, though the auditing firm changed; and no single auditing firm is categorized in C and E anymore. Three auditing firms formerly on the list do not take place on the list anymore, while three new auditing firms from Turkey entered the list. Most of the data interpreted in this section is available in Appendix A.

Table 2.10 PCAOB registered auditing firms performing in Turkey

Trade name	PCOAB registration category	
	2012–2013	2015
DRT BAĞIMSIZ DENETIM VE SMMM A.Ş.	B	A
TÜRKMEN BAĞIMSIZ DENETIM VE YMM A.Ş.	A	A
AKIS BAĞIMSIZ DENETIM VE SMMM A.Ş.	A	B
BAŞARAN NAS BAĞIMSIZ DENETIM VE SMMM A.Ş.	D	D
BILGILI BAĞIMSIZ DENETIM VE YMM A.Ş.	A	D
DENET BAĞIMSIZ DENETIM YMM A.Ş.	D	D
DENGE BAĞIMSIZ DENETIM SMMM A.Ş.	D	D
ENGIN BAĞIMSIZ DENETIM ve SMMM A.Ş.	–	D
GÜNEY BAĞIMSIZ DENETIM VE SMMM A.Ş.	D	D
IHY BAĞIMSIZ DENETIM VE YMM A.Ş.	D	D
IŞIK YMM ve BAĞIMSIZ DENETIM A.Ş.	D	D
IRFAN BAĞIMSIZ DENETIM VE YMM A.Ş.	D	D
ITIMAT BAĞIMSIZ DENETIM VE YMM A.Ş.	D	D
MED YMM A.Ş.	–	D
MERCEK BAĞIMSIZ DENETIM VE YMM A.Ş.	D	D
SAMDEN-SAMSON BAĞIMSIZ DENETIM A.Ş.	–	D
ULUSAL BAĞIMSIZ DENETIM VE YMM A.Ş.	C	D
YILDIZLAR BAĞIMSIZ DENETIM VE YMM ANONIM ŞIRKETI	E	D
BAYLAN BAĞIMSIZ DENETIM VE SMMM A.Ş.	D	–
CAN ULUSLARARASI BAĞIMSIZ DENETIM ve SMMM A.Ş.	E	–
DETAY BAĞIMSIZ DENETIM VE DANIŞMANLIK A.Ş.	A	–
TOTAL	18	18

Source http://pcaobus.org/Registration/Firms/Pages/RegisteredFirms.aspx. Accessed 04 Jan 2015 and 06 May 2012. Based on the information published on PCAOB Web site

With few alterations, firms registered with PCAOB are currently categorized as follows:

A—Audit report for at least one issuer;
B—No audit reports for issuers but played a substantial role in the audit of at least one issuer;
C—Audit reports for at least one broker-dealer;
D—No audit reports for broker-dealers, but substantial role in audit of at least one broker-dealer;
E—None of the above;
F—No Form 2 filed.

2.3 External Audit Regulations in Turkey

The title external audit regulations in Turkey covers some important points in the history of audit-related legislation, the oversight and supervision of auditing firms by POA, and CMB beforehand, external audit within the scope of TCC, and POA in detail.

The audit dimension of accounting profession in Turkey started with acting as court expert, and between 1926–1934 high-profile members of accounting profession were authorized to perform tax audit according to tax legislation. In the following periods, legislative actions continued, while professional organization activities took place on the other hand (Masum Türker, February 2006; quoted by Uzay, Tanç, and Erciyes, *Türkiye'de Muhasebe…*, July 2008).

Before legislative efforts regarding external audit in Turkey; there was external audit of joint-stock company accounts performed by a Supervisory Board as an inspecting body established in accordance with the TCC; and statutory audit of joint-stock company performed by governmental bodies according to TCC, Joint-stock Company Audit Code dated 1972, and Inspection Board Code (Gücenme and Arsoy, 2006; quoted by Uzay, Tanç, and Erciyes, *Türkiye'de Muhasebe…*, July 2008).

The first steps considering audit were taken following the obstacles Turkish companies faced in the 1970s at the time they wanted to benefit from foreign financial sources necessitating audited accounts. Developments in external audit in Turkey started following the flow of foreign capital, the requirements of foreign capital enterprises for consolidation of accounts, exploration of international financial facilities, investment incentives, the desire to advise on joint ventures and the like causing audit requirements. Along with enhancements in financial markets, from 1987 on external audit became an issue of interest for regulating bodies (Uzay *et al. Türkiye'de Muhasebe…*, July 2008).

Energy Market Regulatory Authority (EMRA) and Banking Regulation and Supervision Agency (BRSA) external audit legislations are left outside the research. Legislative arrangements of EMRA ended in 2011. The last by-law dates July 4, 2011, the latest communiqué dates November 29, 2011, and the last auditing firms board resolution dates August 11, 2011. Moreover, whoever wants to perform an audit of a company in the energy market is obliged to get authorization of POA. Therefore, EMRA legislation is excluded from the research.

The BRSA list *Auditing Firms Authorized to Perform an Audit of Banks in 2013* published on November 13, 2013, has 49 banks and seven auditing firms. Some of the banks auditor's responsibility inactive, and some are not public. In fact, in case it is needed for the assessment of audit quality, these seven auditing firms are handled in this study anyway. Out of 49 banks on this list, 93.88%, namely 46 are audited by Big Four in Turkey, and the remaining three are audited by three different auditing firms. BRSA adopted POA's Independent Audit By-Law numbered 28509 and dated December 12, 2012. Therefore, BRSA legislation is also excluded from the study.

2.3.1 Capital Markets Board of Turkey and External Audit

External audit arrangements in Turkey had been started by CMB from 1987 on. In the aftermath of approximately 19-year period, the arrangements continued again with a communiqué of CMB in 2006. The *Communiqué Regarding Independent Auditing in Capital Markets (Communiqué)* is to a great extent accordant with International Standards on Auditing (ISAs). Besides, in 2013 the related articles of the Communiqué were made compatible with the Capital Market Law No. 6362, and POA legislation. Nonetheless, parts of the Communiqué from two to 34 remained in force since the publication of TSAs was not completed by POA then (www.spk.gov.tr, 11.04.2014). For the time being, the Communiqué establishes a basis for quality control studies of CMB. Due to this fact, and since the Communiqué served as guidance for the Turkish audit market more than 25 years, some parts of the Communiqué are discussed in this book.

With the Communiqué Regarding Independent Auditing in Capital Markets Serial: X, No. 22, external audit, auditing firms and external auditor are defined. According to the Communiqué, external audit is the auditor issuing a written report expressing an opinion about whether the yearly financial statements and other financial information to be disclosed or asked by CMB are fairly stated in accordance with the applicable financial reporting standards, by accumulating evidence about information to provide reasonable assurance, and by doing such that evidence gathered from books, records, and documents by applying all external auditing techniques pursuant to external audit standards (www.spk.gov.tr, Communiqué Serial: X, No. 22, 18.02.2012).

The external audit of PIEs and companies determined by POA as of their field of activity, size, number of employees, and criteria like that, are only performed by auditing firms.[12] The audits of rest of the entities are done by auditing firms and auditors. Public interest entities (PIE) are listed below (IAbL: Part 1, Art. 4(d)):

[12]**Audit firm**: means an equity capital company that is authorized by the Authority to carry out statutory audits and the partners of which are the members of the profession, who acquired certified public accountant or sworn in certified public accountant license (www.kgk.gov.tr).

(1) publicly held companies;
(2) banks;
(3) insurance, reassurance and pension companies;
(4) factoring companies;
(5) financing companies;
(6) financial lease companies;
(7) asset management companies;
(8) pension funds;
(9) issuers as defined by the Capital Markets Law dated 28/7/1981 and numbered 2499; and
(10) the entities, which are evaluated in this scope by the Authority since they significantly concern the public interest regarding their fields of activity, trading volumes, number of personnel they employ.

Auditing firms are entities, that are qualified according to the Communiqué Regarding Independent Auditing in Capital Markets Serial: X, No. 22, are eligible according to the Law— Capital Market Law No. 6362—, and which are authorized to perform audits of financial tables of publicly traded companies (www.spk.gov.tr, Communiqué Serial: X, No. 22, 18.02.2012).

Audit Network means a structure for cooperation that aims at profit or cost sharing or shares common ownership, control or management, common quality control policies and procedures, a common business strategy, the use of a common brand or trade name or a significant part of professional resources regardless of the fact that if there is a legal connection between audit firms or statutory auditors (www.kgk.gov.tr, IAbL: Part 1, Art. 4).

Statutory auditor means the natural persons assigned by auditing firm at all levels to perform external audit. According to seniority from top to down the titles auditors can get are partner, manager, senior auditor, auditor, and staff assistant. The ***senior auditor***, who can be an outsider or insider of the auditing firm, is a person who has knowledge about external audit processes, laws, legislations, and regulations applicable, the business environment of the audit client, and is experienced in external audit and financial reporting specific to the audit client's sector (www.spk.gov.tr, Communiqué Serial: X, No. 22, 18.02.2012). Figure 2.6 displays the titles auditors can get in auditing firms in Turkey, and Fig. 2.7 exhibits audit team members and their duties.

The purpose of external audit is to provide an opinion to be issued by a statutory auditor, about whether financial tables prepared in accordance with financial reporting standards are disclosing the true financial position and results of activities of the company with all due aspects and in all its important parts. Even though external auditor opinion upgrades the confidence level of financial tables, this opinion is not to be assessed as information about the future position of the company and that activities of the company audited will be effectively and productively managed in the future as well (www.spk.gov.tr, 18.02.2012).

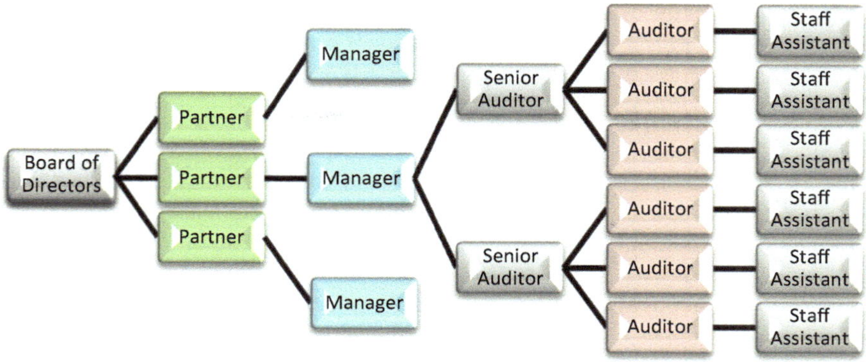

Fig. 2.6 Titles auditors can get in auditing firms in Turkey. *Source* Illustrated based on CMB Communiqué Serial: X, No. 22

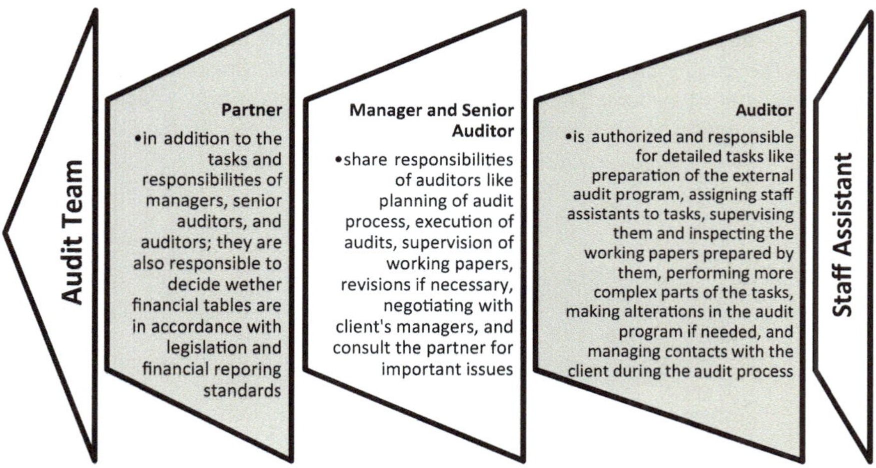

Fig. 2.7 Audit team members and their duties. *Source* Illustrated based on CMB Communiqué Serial: X, No. 22

Carrying out audit has been arranged in the Communiqué from the 10th Article on. According to this, the partner auditor during the audit process where the audit has to be carried out pursuant to regulations and standards on auditing is responsible from issues related to staffing and directing, supervision and productivity, and also from preparation of the auditor report to reflect the reality. The partner auditor manages the audit process by informing the audit team about their (1) responsibilities, (2) the nature of the business' activities, (3) risk-related issues, (4) problems that may arise, (5) details about how to carry out the audit.

The responsibility of auditors who take part in audit team is to perform their duties with an objective perspective, professional skepticism, and paying ultimate attention to principles of ethics. This is illustrated in Fig. 2.8.

Other duties, authorities, and responsibilities of auditing firms and auditors are organized with the 19th Article of the Communiqué. According to this; for any audit, an audit team composed of three official and three reserve members has to be established. Thus, each audit is to be performed by an audit team composed of at least three auditors fulfilling the requirements specific to the audit from number and expediency perspective. The distribution of the authority and responsibility in the teams that are composed of a manager, a senior auditor, and auditor and which are under the supervision of a partner auditor, are done according to pre-set criteria (www.spk.gov.tr, Communiqué Serial: X, No. 22, 18.02.2012).

Monitoring and Coordination With the objective of providing the required quality in external audit and establishing public confidence in external audit; there is ***quality assurance system*** in Turkey in order to ensure the work done by auditing firms or auditors is in accordance with predetermined standards and principles. The relation between quality control assurance committee and external audit team is shown in Fig. 2.9. The quality assurance system established by POA determines the frame of the quality control system. The monitoring and coordination title, which is directly related to the quality control policies and procedures, is covered in the Communiqué Article 20 (www.spk.gov.tr, Communiqué Serial: X, No. 22, 18.02.2012) (Fig. 2.9).

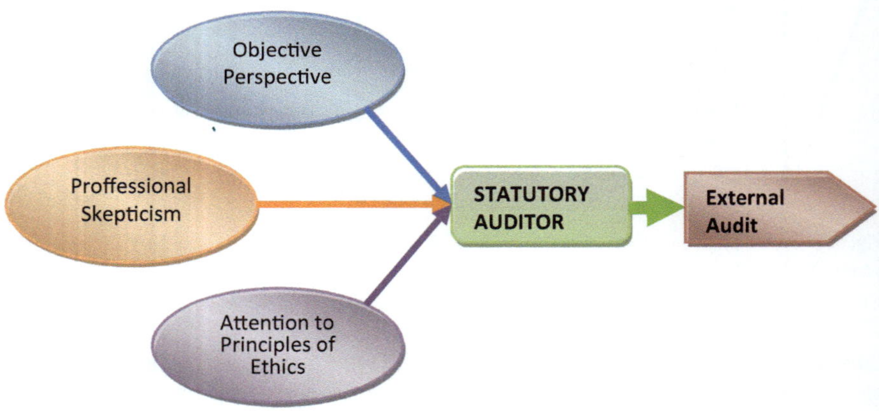

Fig. 2.8 The expected attitude of statutory auditor during audits. *Source* Illustrated based on CMB Communiqué Serial: X, No. 22

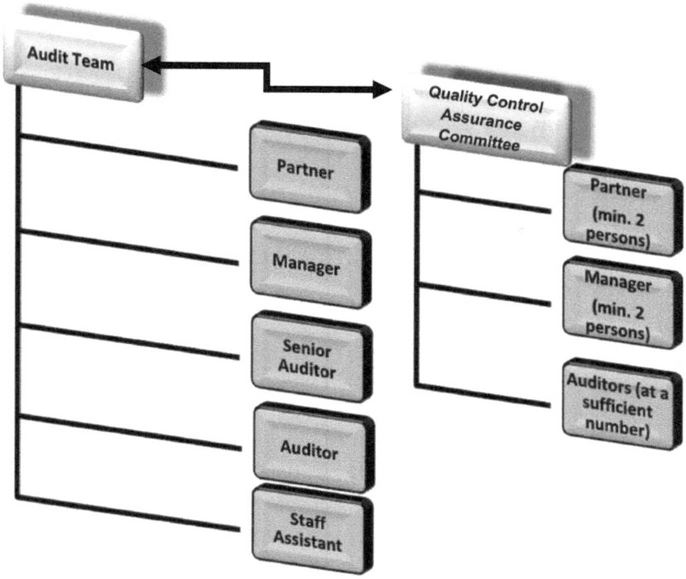

Fig. 2.9 Quality control assurance committee and audit team. *Source* Illustrated based on CMB Communiqué Serial: X, No. 22. *Note* Whatever the title an auditor carries within the auditing firm, there cannot be more than one partner auditor in an audit team

2.3.2 External Audit and Turkish Code of Commerce, Law No. 6102

New resettlements are witnessed with the publishment of the Turkish Code of Commerce No. 6102 (TCC) in 2011; while there were regulations established and organized since 1987 and were still valid at the time the new TCC was published. In addition to the companies where external audit is compulsory, the new TCC prescribes external audit for a wide range of further companies and especially for small and medium-sized companies as well. The third chapter of TCC No. 6102 handles audit. As described in TCC, audit is performed to state and explain; whether financial tables of the company and the annual report of the board of directors, the consolidated financial tables and the annual report of the board of directors related to consolidation comply with the information gathered by the auditor during the act of audit (www.resmigazete.gov.tr, 03.08.2011).

Even though TCC No. 6102 had been published on 13 February 2011, articles regarding public company audits enacted on January 1, 2013. The Act No. 6335 amending TCC, TCC's enforcement and the manner of its application was published on June 29, 2012, and enacted on June 1, 2012. TCC No. 6102 also stated how audit-related regulations would follow during the time until POA was established. According to the amendment; the Temporary Article 2 organizes it such that, Union of Chambers of Certified Public Accountants of Turkey (TÜRMOB) together with a related body, would determine the Turkish Standards on Auditing (TSAs) in coordination with ISAs. The Temporary Article 3 organizes it such that, auditors will be inspected by the Ministry of Industry and Trade[13] (www.resmi-gazete.gov.tr, 03.08.2011). This topic is covered below in detail under the title Public Oversight—Accounting and Auditing Standards Authority Public Oversight and Audit. Audit-related articles of TCC No. 6102 are summarized in the below-given table (Table 2.11).

As seen from the table confidentiality obligation of auditors is enacted by Article 404. Auditors would have shared the information and observations they gathered during audits over an open source of database with other auditors, if there had not been confidentiality obligation. Such mutuality would be expected to have a positive impact on audit quality. However, as in Turkey, there is confidentiality obligation of auditors all over the world. This apparently is valid for US, as well. As Francis regrets, the auditing profession does not have good base rate data to help the auditor determine if there is a significant probability of a material error or irregularity in the financial statements when auditor observes a particular set of diagnostic cues from the control system. For example, National Transportation Safety Board in USA collects data on accidents with a view to identifying and correcting systemic safety threats. Analogous to this, continues Francis, there has long been—since 1978—a call for auditors to publicly share this kind of information in a national database. Francis concludes that the litigation risk of the auditor hinders him/her from sharing this kind of information (Francis 2011: 136).

Similar to Francis' suggestion, the Subcommittee on Firm Structure and Finances, established by the United States Treasury Department's Advisory Committee on the Auditing Profession (ACAP), recommends PCAOB to create a national center to facilitate audit firms' and other market participants' sharing experiences and developing best practices regarding fraud prevention and detection (United States Treasury, www.treasury.gov, 03.01.2013, ACAP, Final Report, 2008: VII: 1).

2.3.3 *Public Oversight—Accounting and Auditing Standards Authority*

Public Oversight—Accounting and Auditing Standards Authority was established in Turkey in accordance with *Public Oversight, Accounting and Auditing Standards Authority's Organization and Responsibilities Statutory Decree* Law No. 660, issued on November 2, 2011. The POA is a governmental, non-profit, regulatory body and the sole supreme authority in determining accounting and auditing standards and ethical rules, authorization and registration of independent auditors and audit firms under a public oversight system and monitoring their activities

[13]**Ministry of Industry and Trade**: currently Ministry of Customs and Trade

Table 2.11 Audit-related Articles of TCC No. 6102

Article No.	TCC article
Article 397	*Audit in general*
	Financial tables of public company and enterprise are audited by an auditor according to POA published TSAs that are congruent to ISAs
	The fact whether the financial information, that are involved in the annual report of the board of directors, are consistent with the audited financial tables and reflect the truth or not, is within the scope of an audit
	Entities subject to audit are obliged to declare whether their financial tables prepared are audited or not, and if audited, the auditor opinion is to be stated on the financial table title. This provision is also applied to the annual report of the board of directors. Though subject to audit; financial tables and the annual report of the board of directors, which are not audited, are disregarded
	In case financial tables of public company and enterprise, and the annual report of the board of directors are changed in the aftermath of publication of the auditor report, and the changes are capable to affect the audit reports; then financial tables and the annual report of the board of directors are re-audited. The re-audit and the résumé are specifically explained in the report. The appropriate attachments reflecting the need of re-audit are enclosed with the auditor opinion
	The audit of the financial tables of public company and enterprise, and the annual report of the board of directors is the audit of the inventory, accounting, the internal audit of the company pursuant to TSAs, the reports presented, and the audit of the annual report of the board of directors. This audit also consists of inspection of the fact, whether everything is in compliance to Turkish Accounting Standards (TASs), TCC, and financial table-related articles of incorporation or not. Audit is conscientiously performed within the scope of the principles determined by POA according to the requirements of the profession, and in compliance with the ethical codes
Article 515	*Fair presentation*
	Financial tables of public companies are prepared in accordance with TASs by showing the company assets, debt and liabilities, equity and operational results; in a way they are true, comprehensible, comparable, fulfilling the needs and the qualifications of the entity, transparent and reliable, adhering to and reflecting the truth as it is. Audit is performed to find out whether the company's and enterprise's assets and financial position are reflected according to the fair presentation principle or not; and if not, the causes are to be stated fairly
Article 398	*The object and scope of audit*
	The auditor assigned to audit the entity's financial tables, inspects the financial tables of the companies included in the consolidated financial tables, especially focuses on implementations and eliminations according to the fair presentation principle. In case the company apt to consolidation had already been audited voluntarily or pursuant to regulations, or the company having the headquarters abroad had already been audited congruent to the audit foreseen by law; the auditor does not inspect these companies
	Prepared separately by the auditor, the auditor along with the auditor report presents another report to the board of directors. A report, about whether the board of directors established the system as foreseen in TCC, to timely detect risks threatening or possibly will threat the company, and manage these risks, and established the authorized committee to handle risks or not; and in case such a system exists, the structure of it, and the implementations of the committee

(continued)

Table 2.11 (continued)

Article No.	TCC article
Article 399	*Choice of auditor, dismission of auditor and termination of contract*
	Companies choose the auditor by the general assembly, and the auditor of an enterprise is chosen by the parent company general assembly. The auditor must to be chosen for each and every period, and no matter what prior to the end of the period auditor is to be assigned. Following the selection, without any delay board of directors has to get the name of the auditor chosen recorded to the trade registry, declared at both Turkish Trade Registry Gazette, and its Web site. Unless another auditor is chosen, the auditor chosen to audit the financial tables of the parent company that is included in consolidation is accepted as the auditor of the entity's financial tables as well
	An auditor may be removed from the assignment; in case another auditor had been assigned. Besides, upon the request of the general assembly or 10% of the shareholders—five percent of the shareholders of public companies—after hearing-related persons and the assigned auditor, and only if there are valid causes, especially upon existence of suspicion of biased auditor behavior, another auditor may be assigned by the Commercial Court of First Instance
	In case an auditor had not yet been chosen until the fourth month of the accounting period, an auditor is assigned by the Commercial Court of First Instance upon the request of the general assembly, any member of the general assembly, or any of the stockholders
	The above procedures are applicable in case of rejection of the assignment by the auditor who is chosen, the auditor annulling the agreement, cancelation of assignment decree, the decree falling into abeyance, auditor being unable to perform the duty due to legal reasons, and auditor being precluded from performing the duty. The court decree is flat
	The auditor is only allowed to annul the agreement upon a valid reason or if he/she had been sued for being precluded from performing the duty. Having disagreements about the content of the opinion letter, and the audit being limited by the audit client or avoiding the delivery of the opinion are not counted as valid reasons. The annulment of the agreement by the auditor has to be written and reasoned. The auditor is obliged to present the results obtained until the annulment time to the general assembly. These results are to be prepared as a report. In case the auditor notifies about the annulment, the board of directors immediately chooses a temporary auditor and presents the annulment notice to general assembly, and submits the temporary auditor to the general assembly
Article 400	*Who can be assigned as the auditor*
	According to TCC; persons who got a license pursuant to the Law dated 1/6/1989 and Numbered 3568 on Certified Public Accountancy and Sworn-in Certified Public Accountancy, earned the title Certified Public Accountant or Sworn-in Certified Public Accountant, and authorized by POA; or their partners and/or an equity company established by such persons may become an auditor In case any of the below-listed circumstances are in question for the persons described above; CPA, Sworn-in Certified Public Accountant (SiCPA), and/or the equity company and any of the partners of these, and persons employed by these or persons performing the profession together with persons mentioned here are not allowed to perform an audit for the related company. *If any persons mentioned above*:

(continued)

Table 2.11 (continued)

Article No.	TCC article
	(a) Has equity of the audit client company, (b) Is a manager or employee of the audit client company; or had been at such a position within three years prior to the assignment as the auditor, (c) .... • Is the representative or the legal representative, • Is a member of the board of directors, • Is a manager or the owner, • Has equity more than 20%, • Is a relative or relative in law up to third ascend/descend or spouse of the audit client company's managers, or of any members of the board of directors, of a legal entity which has relations with the audit client company, (d) Works at an entity in relation to the audit client company, or is employed by a company, which has more than 20% stake of such a company, or in any way serves a natural person, who has more than 20% of the shares of the audit client company, (e) Did contribute in bookkeeping or preparation of the financial tables of the company to be audited except for the audit, (f) Since contributed in bookkeeping or preparation of the financial tables of the company to be audited except for the audit; is by him/herself the person who cannot be the auditor mentioned in (e), is the owner/partner of such a firm, is the legal representative, representative of a natural person/legal corporation, member of board of directors of such a firm, (g) Is employed in the service of an auditor, who cannot be the auditor since he/she fits the conditions mentioned in (a) through (f), (h) More than 30% of the revenue generated from professional activities over the last five years are earned from audit and consultancy services given to the company to be audited, or to companies having more than 20% of the shares of the audited company and is expected to earn such way in the current year *cannot be the auditor*
	An auditor having served for seven years of the last ten years cannot be re-chosen as the auditor, unless three years pass. POA is authorized to shorten these periods. Auditor cannot give consultancy or any other service to the audit client company, except for tax consultancy and tax audit; and is not allowed to do so via a subsidiary firm
Article 401	*Obligation of submission and the right to demand information*
	Without any delay, the board of directors gets the financial tables and annual report prepared, approves them, and hands to the auditor. The board of directors provides all the means to the auditor in order to enable him/her to inspect the books, correspondence, documents, assets, liabilities, cash, commercial papers, and inventory and perform the audit. The auditor and the transaction auditor within the scope of the audit ask the board of directors for all kind of information necessary for a statutory and diligent audit and ask for the submission of documents forming a basis. In case it is essential for preparations of a year-end audit, auditor has presumed authority ahead of financial table issuance. For a diligent audit, auditor may use his/her authorities upon subsidies and parent company
	The board of directors who is responsible for preparation of the consolidated financial tables, is obliged to hand the financial tables of the entity, annual report of the entity, financial tables of each of the group companies, board of directors'

(continued)

Table 2.11 (continued)

Article No.	TCC article
	annual reports of each of the group companies, and in case an audit had already been performed, the audit report of the subsidies and the parent company to the auditor, who is going to audit the consolidated financial table.
Article 402	*Audit report*
	About the type of the audit performed, the scope of it, the nature of it, and the results of it the auditor prepares a clear, understandable, simply written, and comparable to the previous year report; the subject matter of which is financial tables. Besides, in a separate report, the auditor assesses the board of directors' examinations in the annual report about the position of the company or the entity regarding consistency with financial tables and conformance to reality
	While assessing, the auditor takes the financial tables of the parent company and entity as the basis. The report first states the opinion about the assessment of the board of directors' examinations about the financial position of the company end the entity. Along with the analysis of the company and the entity regarding going concern principle and their enhancement in the future within the context of financial table audit; this opinion discusses the financial position of the company to the extent board of directors' report, the annual report of the entity and documents alike allow
	In the main body of the audit report, it is clearly stated whether the bookkeeping system, and both the financial tables and entity's financial tables are conforming to the financial reporting related decrees of the law, and of the articles of incorporation or not; and whether the board of directors made required explanations and gave the documents asked by the auditor within the scope of the audit or not. Besides, it is stated whether the financial tables and the books, as the basis of these, are kept in concordance with the accounting plan foreseen or not; and reflect the assets of the company, the financial position and profitability of it are fairly and truly presented within the frame of TASs or not. In case an assessment during audit had been done pursuant to Article 398 of TCC, the conclusion of this is reported separately. The auditor signs his/her report and submits to the board of directors
Article 403	*Opinion letters*
	Auditor expresses the results of the audit in his/her opinion letter. Along with the type of the audit performed, the scope of it, the nature of it, this letter also comprises the assessments of the auditor. In case the auditor issues an unqualified report; he/she states in the letter that there is no inconsistency encountered during the audit, performed according to Article 398 and TSAs, with respect to TASs and other requirements; that according to the information gathered through the audit, the financial tables of the company/entity are true, and presentations of assets and financial position, and returns are true and fairly presented in the financial tables
	In the opinion letter, it is pointed that there is no reason for the board of directors to take the responsibility of issues related to the financial tables; and on the contrary, if there is need for any responsibility to be undertaken, this is to be emphasized. The opinion is written in the way POA determines and is understandable by everybody. In case the auditor has any drawbacks, he/she can put reservations to his/her opinion, or issue a qualified opinion. Unqualified report with an explanatory paragraph or modified wording is issued in cases, where financial tables contain inconsistencies, which are correctible by authorized boards of the company, and these inconsistencies do not have massive and capital

(continued)

Table 2.11 (continued)

Article No.	TCC article
	effects on the results published in tables. The subject of reservation, the scope of it, and the way how the correction will be done are shown explicitly in the unqualified report with reservation
	In case there are uncertainties in the books of the company to the extent preventing an audit pursuant to related audit regulation, and blocking an opinion to be reached; or limitations are set by the audit client; however the auditor doesn't have evidence to prove these, he/she is allowed to disclaim from issuing an opinion following required explanations. **Disclaim** bears the consequences of an adverse opinion. With a decree, POA regulates the causes, procedures, and the reasoning regarding disclaim
	In case there is a **qualified report** issued; in four working days following the date the opinion delivered to itself, the board of directors calls the general assembly to a meeting, and general assembly elects a new board of directors. Unless stated otherwise in the articles of incorporation, the previous board of directors may be re-elected. Within six months, the new board of directors gets financial tables prepared pursuant to law, articles of incorporation and the standards, and presents these to the general assembly along with the auditor report. In case it is an **unqualified report with an explanatory paragraph** (limited opinion) issued, then, general assembly settles the required precautions and corrections
Article 404	*Confidentiality obligation of auditors*
	The auditor, transaction auditor, the special auditor and assistants of these, and the representatives of the audit firms, who assist them in auditing are obliged to perform the audit in a fair and objective manner and have the obligation of confidentiality. They cannot without permission take advantage of company and business secrets they acquainted during their audit activities. Those who willfully neglect their obligations are responsible to subsidiaries as well. In case causing harm is more than one person, responsibility becomes consecutive. Delinquent persons may be sentenced to pay indemnification for the loss they caused per audit they performed. The restrictions for persons causing loss, is also valid in case there are several persons included in the audit, or in case more than one incident bearing responsibility, and also in cases when some persons may have acted intentionally
	In case the auditor is an equity company assigned to perform an audit, obligation of confidentiality comprises the board of directors of this firm, the members of it, and the employees of it. Indemnity obligation born by these provisions is neither eliminable nor constricted. Claims about the confidentiality obligation laps in five years starting from the date of report. Nevertheless, in case the negligent act constitutes a crime and period of limitation is longer pursuant to Turkish Code of Crime, then the same lapse is applied to indemnity case as well. Denouncement provisions of crime regulation are preserved
Article 405	*Opinion dissidences between the client and auditor*
	Upon request of the board of directors or auditor, based on the file Commercial Court of First Instance of the district of the audit client headquarters brings a verdict; if there are opinion dissidences between the audit client and the auditor about year-end accounts of the company and the entity, financial tables and the board of directors' annual report, from applications of the provisions of the related law, administrative authority, and articles of incorporation. The decision is final. Litigation expenses are undertaken by the audit client company

Source Turkish Code of Commerce (TCC). Law No. 6102 /13/01/2011, 14 February 2011 Monday Official Gazette No. 27846. Retrieved from http://www.resmigazete.gov.tr/main.aspx?home=http://www.resmiga-zete.gov.tr/eskiler/2011/02/20110214.htm&main=http://www.resmigazete.gov.tr/eskiler/2011/02/20110214.htm. Accessed 12 Feb 2013

within the frame of quality assurance. The POA is responsible for setting standards that ensure the preparation and auditing of financial statements in compliance with international standards. The POA is also responsible for achieving an effective public oversight in Turkey (www.kgk.gov.tr/content_detail-219-516-teskilat-ve-gorevleri-hakkinda-yonetmelik.html, 03.03.2012) and has four main functions:

- Setting accounting standards;
- Setting auditing standards;
- Authorizing and registering auditors and audit firms;
- Overseeing, inspecting and applying legal enforcement to auditors and audit firms.

Essentially, POA adopted the functions foreseen by EU Directives for the public oversight bodies. In the EU countries the oversight of auditors and audit firms comprises (Directive 2014/56/EU, Article 18, 2014); (1) authorization and register of auditors and audit firms, (2) professional ethics, quality control system of audit firms, and adoption of audit-related standards (3) continuous education and quality control systems (4) investigation of auditors and audit firms, and enforcements.

The Board of POA, which is connected to the Prime Ministry, is composed of nine members appointed by the Council of Ministers among people with at least ten years of experience in one of the fields of accounting, finance, tax, auditing and law after receiving undergraduate degree or academicians in one of above mentioned disciplines having worked in academia not less than ten years. Not a person or an authority can give orders or instructions to influence POA's decisions. POA Board members are non-practitioners of the audit profession and shall not engage in any public or private institutions operating in areas regulated and supervised by POA; academic activities like lectures and conferences are exempt. Neither shall they undertake freelance activities nor have shares in entities operating in a sector or area regulated and supervised by POA; they shall not engage in trade, either. POA's revenue is made up by treasury grants, revenues earned from copyrights of accounting and auditing standards, and other income (www.resmigazete.gov.tr. Official Gazette No. 28103: IAbL 660).

POA in Turkey and Public Company Accounting Oversight Board (PCAOB) are two authorities whose names are almost identical, by all appearances resembling each other; however, on the basis of establishment and functions they perform two institutions quite different than each other. In order to show the differences, this section handles institutions related to POA and PCAOB; their organizational structures and functions are evaluated and displayed on charts and tables. The organizational chart of POA as foreseen in the IAbL 660 is given first.

Figure 2.10 is important as it shows the initial intentions on the authority. As apparently seen from the figure, including the chair, there are nine board members foreseen; however, as of October 2015 would be board members who would have been the nominees of Turkish SEC and TÜRMOB are missing (http://www.kgk.gov.tr/UnitMembers/3/1/KURUL-U%CC%88YELERI%CC%87, 15.10.2017). Besides, instead of six service units, there are nine departments serving. Moreover, opposite to the initial chart, there are three deputy chairpersons to be assigned. The current organizational chart is given in Fig. 2.11.

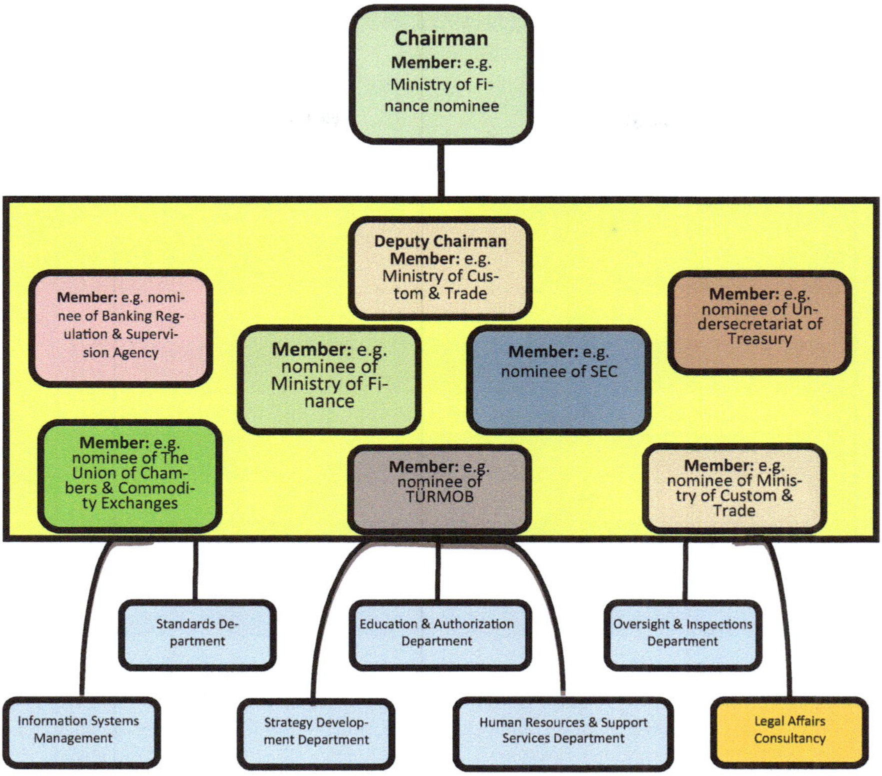

Fig. 2.10 The organizational chart of Public Oversight—Accounting and Auditing Standards Authority in Turkey (2012). *Source* Illustrated based on Statutory Decree dated 26/9/2011 and numbered 660 on the Organization and Duties of Public Oversight, Accounting, and Auditing Standards Authority (the Independent Audit By-Law—IAbL 660)

POA's audit-related activities, operations, and regulations are compared to its American counterpart PCAOB's functioning. The role undertaken by POA being distributed among various bodies, the autonomous bodies being established totally independent from political power, and these bodies synchronizing their operations in harmony are the initial and striking results. Contrary to expectations, the number of members from accounting/audit profession in PCAOB and its subcommittees is restricted. As PCAOB Web site is searched for biographies of members, it is observed that two out of five members of PCAOB are CPAs; out of 19 members of Investor Advisory Group (IAG) only one member is a CPA; and none of 40 members of the Standard Advisory Group (SAG) is a CPA (www.pcaob.org, 11.01.2015). In addition, the 8th Directive of EU shows a similar approach and remarks that public oversight has to be supervised by persons who are not a member of the accounting profession (www.worldbank.org, 2010: 6; http://eur-lex.europa.eu/, 2006: Ar. 20).

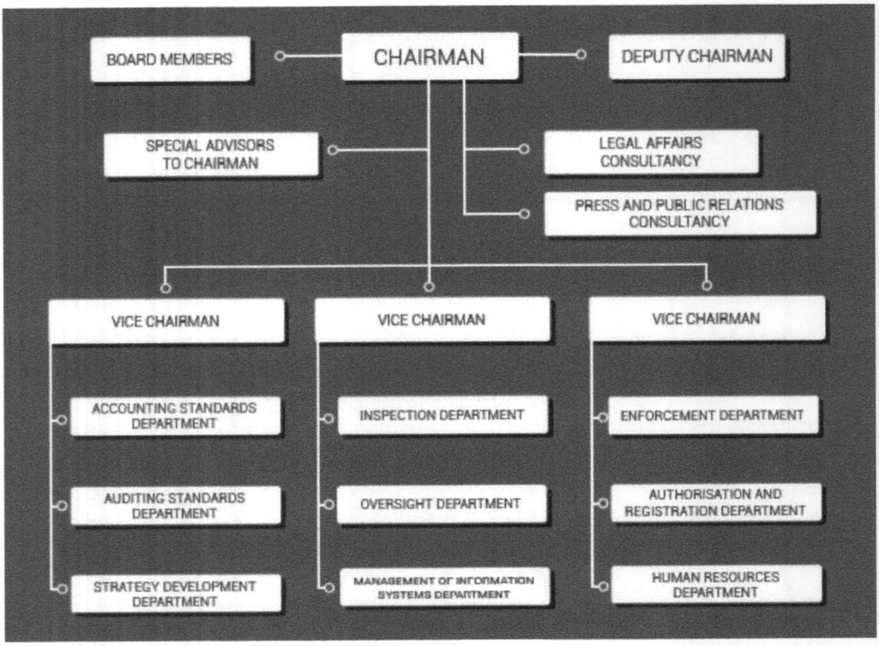

Fig. 2.11 The organizational chart of Public Oversight—Accounting and Auditing Standards Authority in Turkey (2014). *Source* Public Oversight—Accounting and Auditing Standards Authority. Institutional. http://www.kgk.gov.tr/content_detail-178-733-kgk-teskilat.html. Accessed 30 May 2014

Differences between POA and PCAOB are also observed concerning the way member assignments as well. In Turkey, the board members are assigned upon Council of Ministers decision, whereas the American board members are assigned by Securities and Exchange Commission (SEC). In US to keep the political independence, the President appoints SEC members by fulfilling the requirement that not more than three members are from the same political party. However, in Turkey like POA members, the SEC members are also appointed by Council of Ministers. Whether Turkish practice will guard political independence or not, is to be seen in periods to come; or it will be understood whether guarding political independence is an objective, or not.

Another discriminating feature is the duties assumed by the authority. Table 2.12 displays these differences in a comparative and explanatory way. As followed from the table, when compared to the American counterpart, POA is designed to undertake many and varied tasks each requiring concentration and specialization. It is not possible to foresee what will happen in the future and whether the institute will be organized in a similar way, as it is in United States parallel to the needs arising. Another contrast is the fact that PCAOB regulations at the firsthand being presented to Securities and Exchange Commission (SEC), whereas in Turkey POA

Table 2.12 The comparison of Oversight Authorities in Turkey and USA

	Public oversight—Accounting and Auditing standards authority—POA	Public company accounting oversight board—PCAOB
Duty	Setting and issuing Turkish Accounting Standards	It is a duty of: Financial Accounting Standards Board—**FASB**
	Making secondary legislations regarding the implementations of the standards, and approving the regulations/adjustments done by other authorities, which have the authority to make necessary regulations regarding their fields	No observations
	Setting and issuing the Turkish Standards on Auditing consonant to international standards	It is a duty of: International Auditing and Assurance Standards Board—**IAASB** under International Federation of Accountants—**IFAC**
	Setting the rules of establishment and operating principles of audit firms and auditors	It is a duty of: American Institute of Certified Public Accountants—**AICPA**
	To oversee the regulatory compliance of auditors and audit firms according to their declarations, explanations, and activities, and to monitor the compliance of transparency reports with legislation and timely publication	Safeguarding the rights of investors by overseeing the audit of public companies
	Suspension or decertification the operating licenses of auditors and audit firms not conforming to the rules and regulations	It is a duty of: American Institute of Certified Public Accountants—**AICPA**
	To make relevant operations related to authorization of the audit firms and auditors, to record them in the official registry, to carry out examination and continuing education of auditors, conducting disciplinary actions, determining the standards of continuous education, and professional ethic codes, and establishing the quality control system for these	It is a duty of: American Institute of Certified Public Accountants—**AICPA**
	Making regulations toward providing independence and objectivity of audit, and improving the quality of audit	
	To contribute in establishment of public conscience	Further the public interest in the preparation of informative, accurate, and independent audit reports

(continued)

Table 2.12 (continued)

	Public oversight—Accounting and Auditing standards authority—POA	Public company accounting oversight board—PCAOB
# of board members	Nine members, including the Chairman	Five members, including the Chairman
Duration of membership	6 years	5 years
Frequency of meeting	min. weekly	min. trimonthly - possible to attend via teleconference or telephone
Prerequisite of membership	Members are not allowed to have shares in areas and sectors the Authority is to regulate and audit; are not allowed to become an arbitrator and become a referee, and not allowed to engage in trade	Two members at most are allowed to be a CPA, inactive for at least five years regarding the accounting profession before appointment
	Members should not have made an audit in the last three years, not have a seat in the board of directors of an audit firm or not have been employed by an audit firm and should not have a direct/indirect partnership of an audit firm	
Assignment	Council of Ministers	The five members of the Board, including the Chairman, are appointed to staggered five-year terms by the SEC, after consultation with the Chair of the Board of Governors of the Federal Reserve System and the Secretary of the Treasury
Subcommittees	Not established yet	1) Investor Advisory Group (IAG)—19 members* 2) Standard Advisory Group(SAG)—40 members*

*number of members as of 11 January 2015

Source (1) Independent Audit By-Law No. 660, 02 Nov 2011 Wednesday Official Gazette: 28103; (2) PCAOB. Public Company Accounting Oversight Board (PCOAB). Rules. http://pcaobus.org/Rules/PCAOBRules/Documents/Bylaws.pdf, http://pcaobus.org/About/Pages/default.aspx, 06.02.2013; (3) Arens et al. 2012

has been announced as the sole agent. At the time SOX foreseen the establishment of PCAOB, subcommittees had also been included in the act, only their titles had not been determined at that time. Below, the institutions mentioned in the table are shortly explained respectively:

PCAOB is a non-profit institution foreseen by SOX and established by the Congress with the objective of safeguarding the rights of investors by overseeing the audit of public companies and bankers. The Board's decisions, standards, and budget are under surveillance of SEC. The five members of the Board, including the chairman, are appointed to staggered five-year terms by the SEC, after consultation with the Chair of the Board of Governors of the Federal Reserve System (FED) and the Secretary of the Treasury. Maximum two members are allowed to be a CPA, inactive for at least five years regarding the accounting profession before appointment. Within the body, the institution nestles the Investor Advisory Group (IAG) composed of 19 members and the Standard Advisory Group (SAG), which has 40 members (http://pcaobus.org/About/Board/Pages/default.aspx, 11.01.2015).

Even though setting audit standards, determining the rules of establishment and operating principles of audit firms and auditors, and registry, examinations and disciplinary actions against audit firms and auditors, and the like are seemingly the duties of several institutions besides PCAOB according to Table 2.12, the core responsibilities of PCAOB foreseen by SOX are as follows (Hanson 24 Oct 2014):

- Registration of public accounting firms that audit public companies or broker-dealers;
- Inspections of registered public accounting firms;
- Setting of auditing standards for the audits of public companies and broker-dealers; and
- Investigations and disciplinary proceedings in cases where auditors may have violated certain provisions of the securities laws or applicable standards or rules.

From this perspective, the functions undertaken by POA are parallel to its American counterpart's.

FASB With full time serving seven board members appointed by the Financial Accounting Foundation (FAF) Board of Trustees generally twice for five-year terms; and 60 staff members supporting, the Financial Accounting Standards Board (FASB), established in 1973, is an independent, private-sector, not-for-profit organization; establishing financial accounting and reporting standards for public and private companies and not-for-profit organizations that follow Generally Accepted Accounting Principles (GAAP). The FASB is recognized by SEC as the designated accounting standard setter for public companies. FASB standards are recognized as authoritative by many other organizations, including state Boards of Accountancy and AICPA. Accounting and reporting standards regarding public companies fall in jurisdiction of SEC. Since allocation of resources depend on esteemed, accurate and comprehensible financial data; standards gain importance for the economy to function effectively. While setting the standards SEC will confide in the private sector as long as public interest is looked after. As stated in its Web site; the collective mission of the FASB, the Governmental Accounting Standards Board (GASB) and the FAF is to establish and improve financial accounting and reporting standards to provide useful information to investors and other users of financial reports and educate stakeholders on how to most effectively understand and implement those standards. The FAF Trustees, who have different work experiences and areas of expertise, bring a unique perspective, and are responsible for providing oversight and promoting an independent and effective standard-setting process. FASB Advisory Groups are standing resources to the

FASB and its staff, and as of mid 2013 include GASB, Financial Accounting Standards Advisory Council (FASAC), and Governmental Accounting Standards Advisory Council (GASAC) (www.fasb.org, 06.07.2013). As of Oct 2017, FASB Advisory Groups are Investor Advisory Committee (IAC), which provides advice, from the investors' perspective, on current and potential FASB agenda projects; Not-for-Profit Advisory Committee (NAC), which provides advice on existing guidance, current and proposed technical agenda projects, and longer-term issues related to the not-for-profit sector; Small Business Advisory Committee (SBAC), which provides advice on FASB projects related to the operationality and the anticipated costs, complexities, and benefits of potential solutions principally from a small public company perspective; and The Financial Accounting Standards Advisory Council (FASAC) (www.fasb.org, 25.10.2017). FASAC *the Council* for short, formed in 1973 concurrent with the establishment of the FASB has members drawn from the ranks of CEOs, CFOs, senior partners of public accounting firms, executive directors of professional organizations, and senior members of the academic and analyst communities, all with an interest in the integrity of full and complete financial reporting and disclosure. The primary function of FASAC is to advise the FASB (the Board) on issues related to projects on the Board's agenda, possible new agenda items, project priorities, procedural matters that may require the attention of the FASB, and other matters as requested by the chairman of the FASB.

IFAC The International Federation of Accountants (IFAC) was founded on October 7, 1977, in Munich, Germany, at the 11th World Congress of Accountants by 63 founding members from 51 countries to strengthen the worldwide accountancy profession in the public interest. As of November 2016, IFAC's membership includes over 175 members and associates in more than 135 countries and jurisdictions worldwide. Table 2.13 displays the boards and committees established to develop international standards and guidance and to focus on specific sectors of the profession. Developing high-quality international standards in auditing and assurance, public sector accounting, ethics, and education for professional accountants and supporting their adoption and use; facilitating collaboration and cooperation among its member bodies; collaborating and cooperating with other international organizations; and serving as the international spokesperson for the accountancy profession are the mission of the Federation (http://www.ifac.org/about-ifac/organization-overview/history, 06.02.2013; 08.02.2015; 04.11.2017).

IAASB International Auditing and Assurance Standards Board (IAASB), which is a subcommittee of IFAC was founded in March 1978, and was previously known as the International Auditing Practices Committee (IAPC). Members of the IAASB can be nominated by any stakeholder, including IFAC member organization, the Forum of Firms, international organizations, government institutions, and the general public. As of November 2017, the Board has 18 members from 13 countries; four public members, five non-practitioner members, and nine practitioner members. Besides, the board has two observers and 17 technical advisers from 11 countries (http://www.iaasb.org/about-iaasb/members, 08.11.2013).

Table 2.13 Several boards and committees affiliated to International Federation of Accountants IFAC

Description	Short name	Establishment date
International Auditing and Assurance Standards Board (formerly the International Auditing Practices Committee)	IAASB	March 1978
International Accounting Education Standards Board (formerly the Education Committee)	IAESB	October 1977
International Ethics Standards Board for Accountants (formerly the Ethics Committee)	IESBA	October 1977
Professional Accountants in Business Committee (formerly the Financial and Management Accounting Committee; originally established as the Management Accounting Committee)	PABC	October 1977
International Public Sector Accounting Standards Board (formerly the Public Sector Committee)	IPSASB	May 1987
Transnational Auditors Committee	TAC	May 2000
Compliance Advisory Panel	CAP	November 2003
Professional Accountancy Organization Development Committee (formerly Developing Nations Committee)	PAODC	November 2005
Small and Medium Practices Committee	SMPC	November 2005

Source Organized based on Web page of International Federation of Accountants (IFAC). About IFAC. http://www.ifac.org/about-ifac/organization-overview/history. Accessed 06 Feb 2013

AICPA Founded in 1887, the AICPA represents the CPA profession nationally regarding rule-making and standard-setting and serves as an advocate before legislative bodies, public interest groups and other professional organizations. The AICPA develops standards for audits of private companies and other services by CPAs; provides educational guidance materials to its members; develops and grades the Uniform CPA Examination; and monitors and enforces compliance with the profession's technical and ethical standards. The AICPA Council determines Institute programs and policies. The Council is made up of elected and appointed members from each of the 50 states, the District of Columbia, Puerto Rico, the US Virgin Islands and Guam. The composition of the Council is detailed in Table 2.14. The board of directors acting as the executive body of the Council has to meet at least five times a year, and twice a year report to the Council. As it was on February 8, 2013, the board of directors is composed by 23 persons; the chair of the meeting, vice chair of the meeting, deputy chair of the meeting, the chairman, who is the CEO, and members on Nov 9, 2017 (www.aicpa.org, 08.02.2013).

SEC The mission of the Securities and Exchange Commission (SEC) is to protect investors; maintain fair, orderly, and efficient markets; and facilitate capital formation. The SEC strives to promote a market environment that is worthy of the public's trust. The Commission's responsibilities are: (1) interpret and enforce

Table 2.14 The composition of the American Institute of CPAs (AICPA) Council

Composition	Number of members	Term of seat
Members elected by membership in each state with an equitable allocation for each state based on AICPA membership	139	3 years
One member designated by each state society	54	1 years
Members at large	21	3 years
Members of the Board of Directors	23	varies
AICPA past presidents and chairs of the board	28	permanent
Total	265	

Source American Institute of CPAs (www.aicpa.org). Accessed 06 Feb 2013 and 09 Nov 2017

federal securities laws; (2) issue new rules and amend existing rules; (3) oversee the inspection of securities firms, brokers, investment advisers, and ratings agencies; (4) oversee private regulatory organizations in the securities, accounting, and auditing fields; and (5) coordinate US securities regulation with federal, state, and foreign authorities. The Commission's meetings are open to the public and the news media unless the discussion pertains to confidential subjects, such as whether to bring an enforcement action.

The five SEC commissioners are appointed by the president with staggered five-year terms. By law, no more than three of the Commissioners may belong to the same political party, ensuring non-partisanship. The agency's functional responsibilities are organized into five divisions and 23 offices, each of which is headquartered in Washington, DC. The Commission's approximately 4600 staff are located in Washington and in 11 Regional Offices throughout the country. The SEC organization chart is given as a list and in Fig. 2.12 as well (http://www.sec.gov, secorg.pdf, 08.02.2013, 17.11.2017).

The Commission consists of four Commissioners and one Chairman with the following staff support structure.

- Divisions and Offices reporting to the Office of the Chairman
    - Five Divisions
        1. Corporation Finance;
        2. Enforcement;
        3. Investment Management;
        4. Economic and Risk Analysis;
        5. Trading and Markets.
    - Twenty-three Offices;
        1. Administrative Law Judges;
        2. Chief Accountant;

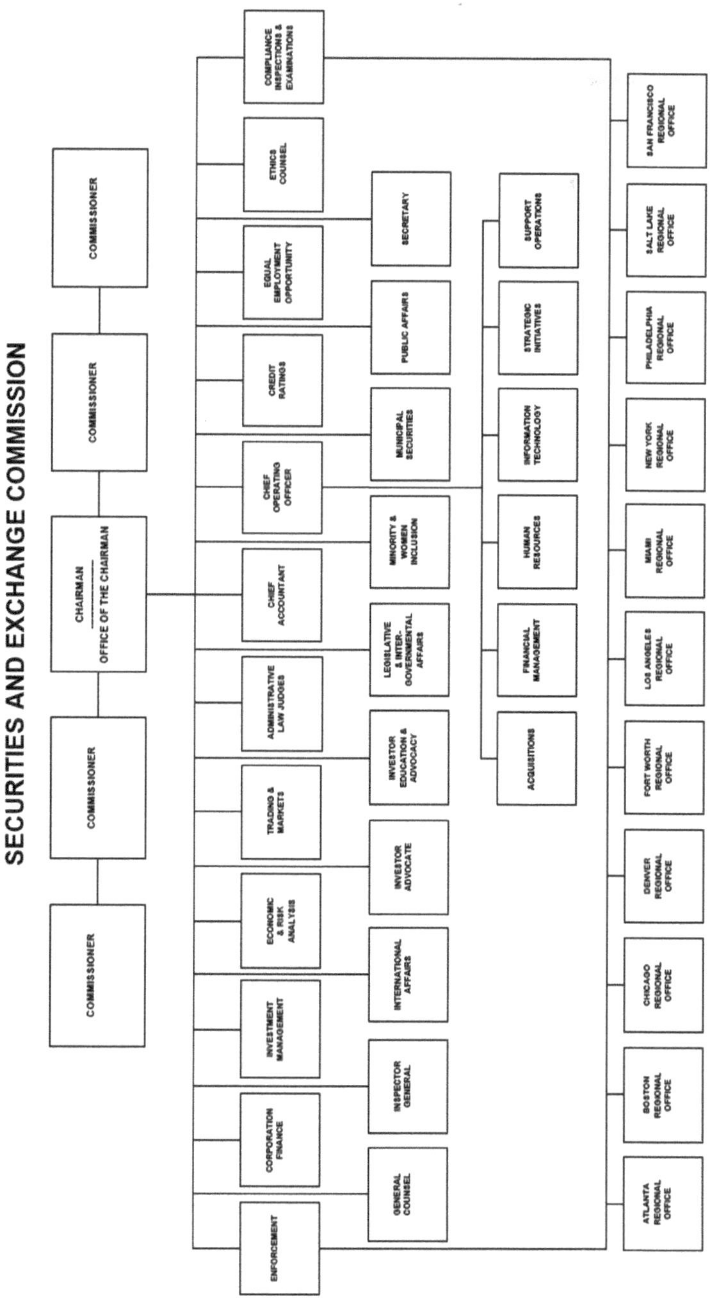

Fig. 2.12 Securities and Exchange Commission (SEC) organization chart. *Source* U.S. Securities and Exchange Commission (SEC). About Us. What We Do. http://www.sec.gov/images/secorg.pdf. Accessed 17 Nov 2017

3. Chief Operating Officer;
    1. Acquisitions;
    2. Financial Management;
    3. Human Resources;
    4. Information Technology;
    5. Strategic Initiatives;
    6. Support Operations;
4. Compliance Inspections and Examinations;
5. Credit Ratings;
6. Equal Employment Opportunity;
7. Ethics Counsel;
8. General Counsel;
9. Inspector General;
10. International Affairs;
11. Investor Advocate;
12. Investor Education and Advocacy;
13. Legislative and Intergovernmental Affairs;
14. Minority and Women Inclusion;
15. Municipal Securities;
16. Public Affairs;
17. Secretary.

- Regional Offices reporting to both Division of Enforcement and Office of Compliance Inspections and Examinations;
    - New York Regional Office;
    - Boston Regional Office;
    - Philadelphia Regional Office;
    - Atlanta Regional Office;
    - Miami Regional Office;
    - Chicago Regional Office;
    - Fort Worth Regional Office;
    - Denver Regional Office;
    - Salt Lake City Regional Office;
    - Los Angeles Regional Office;
    - San Francisco Regional Office.

CMB As the regulatory and supervisory authority in charge of the securities markets in Turkey, Capital Markets Board of Turkey (CMB) is established and empowered by the Capital Markets Law (CML) Law No. 2499, which was enacted in 1981, with the objectives of taking the necessary measures for fostering the development of capital markets, and hence contributing to the efficient allocation of financial resources in the country while ensuring investor protection. CMB makes detailed regulations for organizing the markets and developing capital market instruments and institutions in Turkey. Within the scope of its mission the CMB's main strategic objectives are (www.cmb.gov.tr,17.11.2017): (1) enhancing investor protection, (2) adopting the norms of the international capital markets and fully integrate them into regulations, (3) promoting and enhancing the effectiveness of both the supply and the demand side of the markets, (4) promoting transparency and fairness in the capital markets, (5) facilitating modernization of the market structure, (6) enhancing the infrastructure of the capital markets, and (7) enhancing the quality of the work products and staff members of the Board.

The Executive Board of CMB consists of seven members/commissioners. The Council of Ministers appoints two members from four nominations by the Ministry of State—Responsible for the Economy. The other five members are appointed from the nominations of the Ministry of Finance, the Ministry of Industry and Commerce, the Banking Regulatory and Supervisory Board, the Association of Trade Chambers and Exchanges, and the Association of Capital Markets Intermediary Institutions. Each of these institutions nominates two candidates, one of whom is to be elected. All Commissioners are appointed by the Council of Ministers for a six-year period. The Council of Ministers appoints one of the members as the Chairman and the Board elects one member as the Vice Chairman. The Executive Board is proclaimed by law to be at the highest level within the decision-making mechanism of the CMB and is empowered to decide on any issue within the authority of the CMB (www.cmb.gov.tr, 17.11.2017).

The CMB organization chart is displayed in Figs. 2.13 and 2.14.

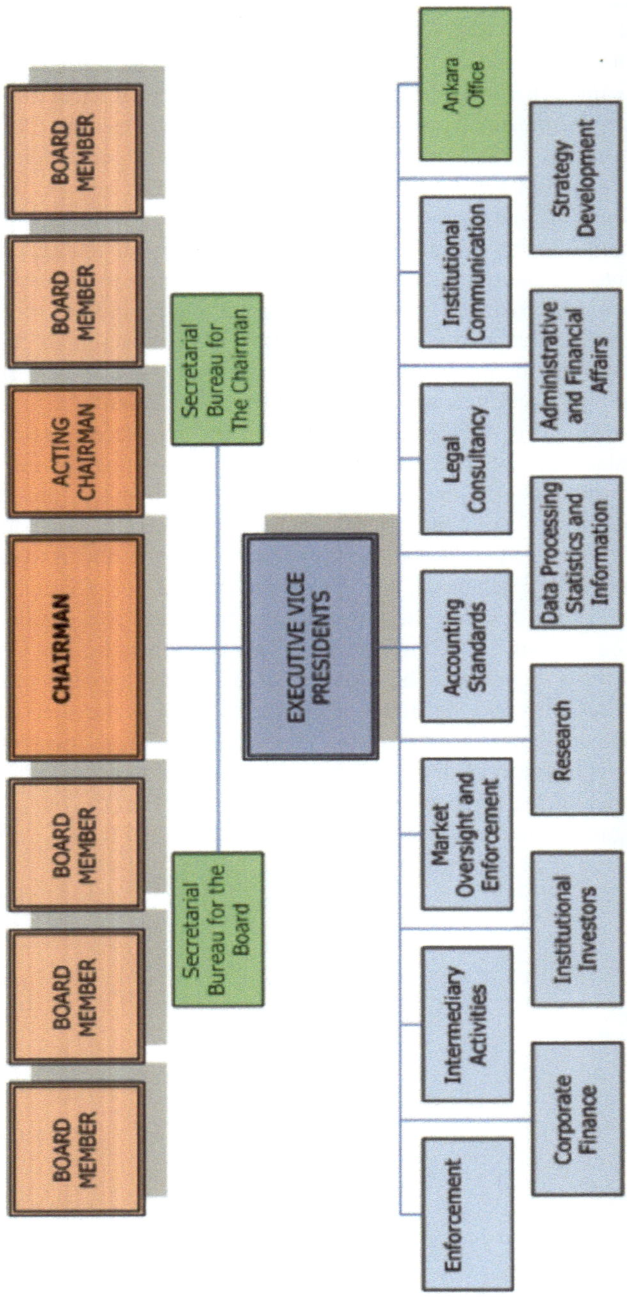

Fig. 2.13 Capital Markets Board of Turkey—Organization chart. *Source* Capital Markets Board of Turkey. About us. Organization. CMB Introductory Booklet, p 7. http://www.cmb.gov.tr/Sayfa/Index/0/5. Accessed 17 Nov 2017

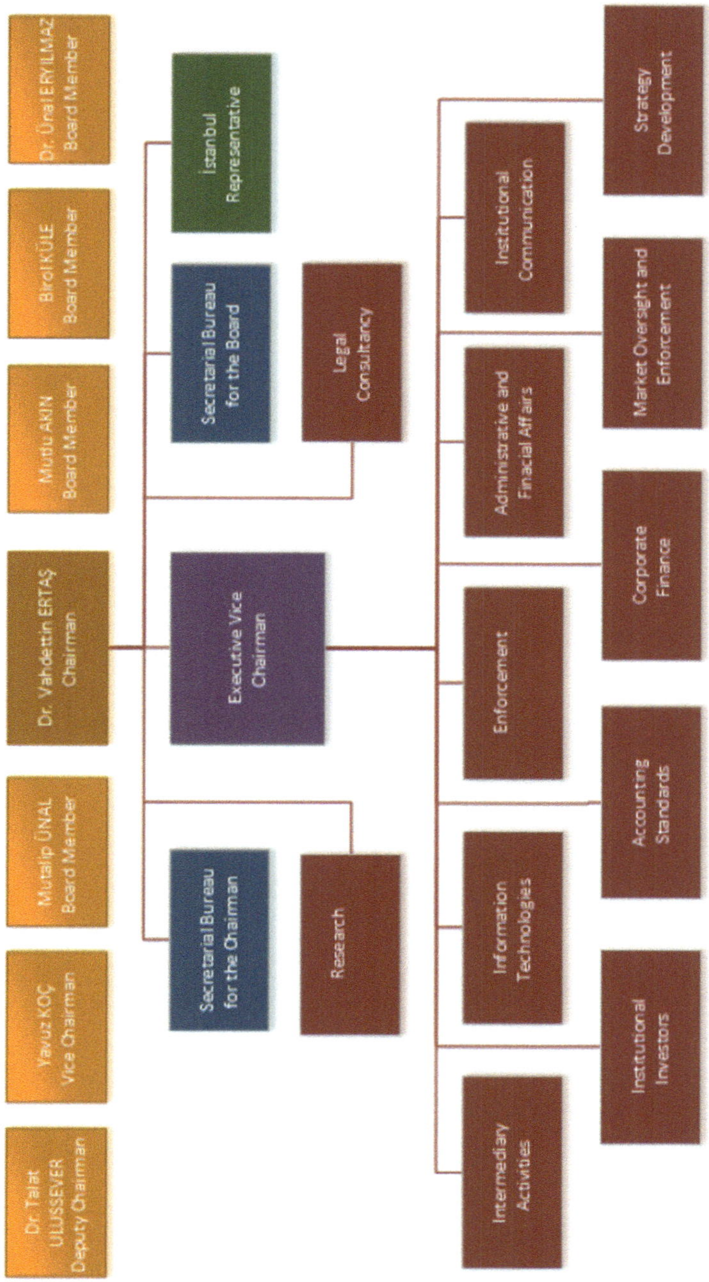

Fig. 2.14 Capital Markets Board of Turkey—Organization Chart Nov 2017. *Source* Capital Markets Board of Turkey. About us. Organization. http://www.cmb.gov.tr/Sayfa/AltSayfa/49#. Accessed 17 Nov 2017

Chapter 3
External Audit from Process and Quality Perspective

Abstract This Chapter focuses on the quality of audit, which has many determinants. One of them is the audit process itself. Acceptance of an audit engagement, the planning of an audit, the audit team, consultations and communications during an audit are important issues handled in this Chapter. Next comes independence of the auditor, audit firm, and audit team. Transparency issue follows. Since the audit client as an input has influence on audit quality, this is also explained here. The last part of this Chapter is about regulating authorities, oversight function, and sanction of them. The outlook of audit firms in Turkey follows.

Keywords Audit process · Independence · Transparency · Quality Oversight

3.1 The Impact of Audit Process on Audit Quality

This section, where audit is more particularly handled from process and quality perspective, assesses the specific process, which starts with strategy determination and ends up with quality control of audit. The process of audit is approached in detail, how audit client companies impact the quality is scrutinized, and the importance of independence and transparency which are at utmost consequence is emphasized.

The foundation of business science lies in the input-process-output triad. This triad in the independent audit framework is shown in Fig. 3.1.

In terms of the service sector, the audit process in which the audit client is involved remains extremely critical and determines the quality of service. According to Knechel (2010), while the quality of the audit is affected by the auditing process, regulatory authorities' efforts to standardize the audit process reduce the quality of audit outputs (quoted by Humphrey 2011: 433). In this section, the audit process is dealt within the context of the impact on audit quality.

I. Kesimli, *External Auditing and Quality*, Accounting, Finance, Sustainability, Governance & Fraud: Theory and Application,
https://doi.org/10.1007/978-981-13-0526-9_3

3.1.1 *The Impact of the Audit Strategy on the Quality of Audit*

The word strategy borrowed from French means a path held to achieve a predetermined purpose (www.tdk.gov.tr, 21.11.2014). The root word is based on the Greek word *stratēgía*, which means a long-term prominent plan or method to achieve success in the business world (www.thefreedictionary.com, Free Online Dictionary, 21.11.2014). Strategies need to be determined with precision when the audit function is fulfilled. The strategy chosen will have a critical role in achieving the objectives of the audit. The planning of the audit includes the establishment of a general audit strategy for the audit and the development of the audit plan. Adequate planning contributes in various ways to the control of financial statements (www.kgk.gov.tr, TSA 300, 2014: 6). Figure 3.2 displays the planning of audit.

In case the audit is not an audit of an already client company and is an audit of a new client, the auditor is obliged to implement the acceptance of the client and the audit agreement-related audit procedures mandated by TSA 220; in cases where the

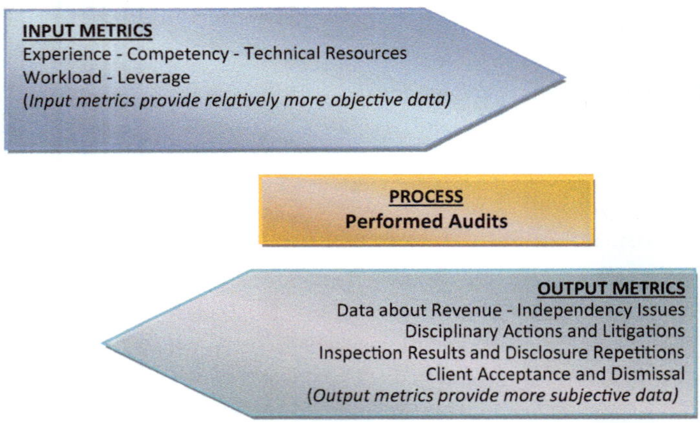

Fig. 3.1 Triad in the independent audit framework. *Source* International Organization of Securities Commissions—IOSCO (2009). Technical Committee. Transparency of Firms that Audit Public Companies: Consultation Report. Illustrated based on text pp. 14–17. http://www.iosco.org/library/pubdocs/pdf/IOSCOPD302.pdf, Accessed 05 May 2012

Fig. 3.2 Scope of audit planning. *Source* Figured from p. 6, TSA 300

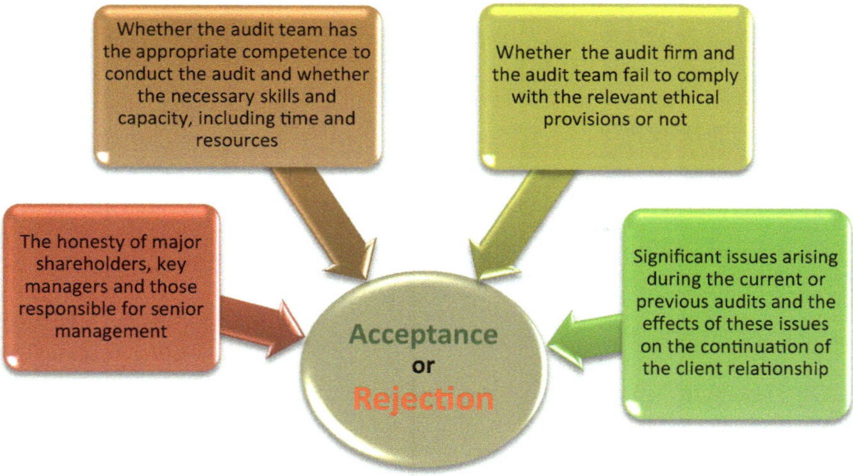

Fig. 3.3 Information to be taken into consideration during the acceptance and resumption of the client relationship and the audit contract. *Source* Figured from p. 15, TSA 220

auditor changes, it is necessary to communicate with the previous auditor in accordance with the relevant ethical provisions (www.kgk.gov.tr, TSA 300, 2014: 8).

Quality Control Standard 1 obliges an audit firm to obtain any kind of information deemed necessary according to the circumstances: (1) before establishing an audit relationship with a new client, (2) while continuing to provide audit service to an existing customer, and (3) while considering a new audit job from an existing audit client (www.kgk.gov.tr, TSA 220, 2014: 15). For example, the following information in Fig. 3.3 is helpful to the in-charge auditor in determining whether the results reached in terms of accepting and maintaining the client relationship and the audit agreement were appropriate (www.kgk.gov.tr, TSA 220, 2014: 15):

For each external audit to be undertaken, an external audit strategy should be established that determines the scope, timing, and orientation of the external audit. The strategy established provides guidance on the development of a detailed and thorough external audit plan (www.kgk.gov.tr, TSA 300, 2014: 7). As stated in TSA 300 the schedule which is to be followed in establishing the audit strategy for recurrent audits is summarized below (Fig. 3.4):

3.1.2 Planning Audits and the Impacts of Planning upon Audit Quality

Once the strategy is established, a more detailed external audit plan can begin to be developed. TSA 300 "Planning an Audit of Financial Statements" works through the planning of external audit. A plan that is an orderly or step-by-step conception or proposal for accomplishing an objective according to Turkish Language

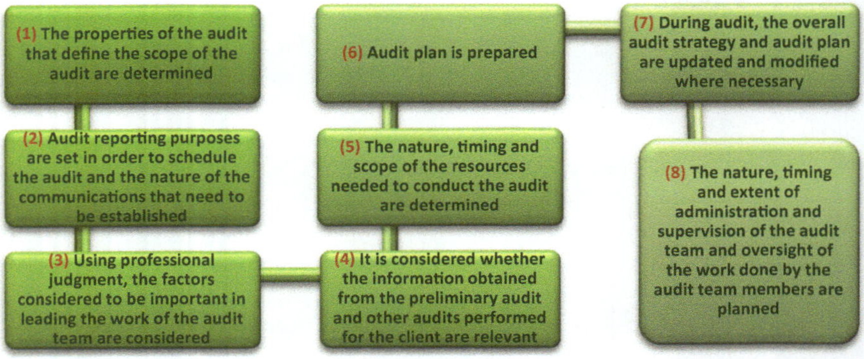

Fig. 3.4 Process to be followed in the formation of the audit strategy. *Source* Figured from pp. 7–8, TSA 300

Association (www.tdk.gov.tr, 21.11.2014) is designed to achieve external audit objectives through the effective use of resources, when external audit is the concern. The external audit relation of the auditor with the audit client is an utmost important issue influencing audit quality, and Turkish Standards on Auditing stand on the issue sensitively. International Standard on Quality Control 1 in Appendices—that is translated in Turkish by POA—handles the issue in detail.

The use of appropriate audit techniques for business operations and the timely execution of audit practices improve the quality and reliability of audit activity and processes. Conducting the audit plan or programs prepared for the audit activity in accordance with the importance of the job with professional expertise will shorten and improve the quality of audit conducted in the business (Tanç and Uzay 2013: 12). Once the strategy is established, the auditor should prepare the more detailed audit plan. In the audit plan, the auditor defines the nature, timing, and extent of the planned risk assessment procedures, as defined by TSA 315 "Identifying and Assessing the Risks of Material Misstatement through Understanding the Entity and Its Environment." Later on, as stated in TSA 330 "The Auditor's Responses to Assessed Risks" determines the nature, timing, and extent of the audit procedures applied after the planned risk assessment at the management statement level. The auditor also defines other planned audit procedures that should be applied in order to ensure compliance of the audit to the TSAs (TSA 300, 7). After providing the necessary preliminary information, the auditor divides the operation into audit areas[1]. Taking into consideration the costs and necessity, and taking into account the procurement–production–sales processes of the enterprise, he/she shall determine the new audit areas by merging the related accounts. The audit plan can be viewed as the time, personnel, and audit technique allocation process to the audit areas during the audit (Kaval 2008: 68).

[1]**Audit area**: They are account units that need to get opinions about. Each of the financial statement items is a separate audit area (Kaval 2008: 68).

During the audit, the auditor updates and changes the overall audit strategy and audit plan as necessary. The nature, timing, and extent of administration and supervision of the audit team and oversight of the work done by the audit team members are planned by the auditor. The auditor includes any changes and the reasons of these changes in the working papers in case there are changes/modifications in (a) general audit strategy, (b) audit plan, (c) any significant changes made during the audit, in the general audit strategy or in the audit plan (TSA 300, 8). The acquisition of the information mentioned in Fig. 3.3 helps building assurance about the features of the audit work planned by the auditor. There are three basic reasons why the auditor should make appropriate planning within the framework of the agreement: (1) ensuring that the auditor obtains adequate and appropriate evidence in order to minimize the legal liability in the future and to preserve the respectability of the business environment, (2) in order to ensure competitiveness, keeping the cost of audit at reasonable levels, and (3) avoiding misconceptions with the client in order to be able to perform good customer relationships and high-quality work at a reasonable cost level (Arens 2012: 184).

Participation of the in-charge auditor and other key members of the audit team in the audit planning process enables them to benefit from their experience and intuitions and thus improves the effectiveness and efficiency of the planning process. Factors influencing the structure and scope of planning activities are summarized in Fig. 3.5.

Planning is not a separate phase of the audit, but usually begins immediately after the completion of the previous audit or in connection with the previous audit, and continues until the completion of the current audit. It is a recurring process. Planning, however, also includes taking into account the timing of specific activities and audit procedures that must be completed before the subsequent audit procedures are applied (TSA 300, A2). In this context, the auditor takes into consideration the issues set out in Fig. 3.6.

It has already been emphasized in the book that, in discovering financial frauds, non-financial information is also important along with financial information. Within this context, when taking audit planning decisions, it is important to seriously consider the non-financial information and the importance of integrating such information into financial data (Cohen et al. 2009: 3).

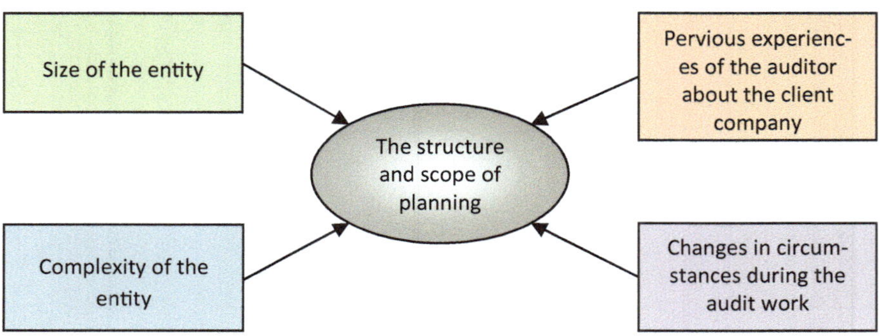

Fig. 3.5 Structure and scope of planning activities. *Source* Figured from TSA 300

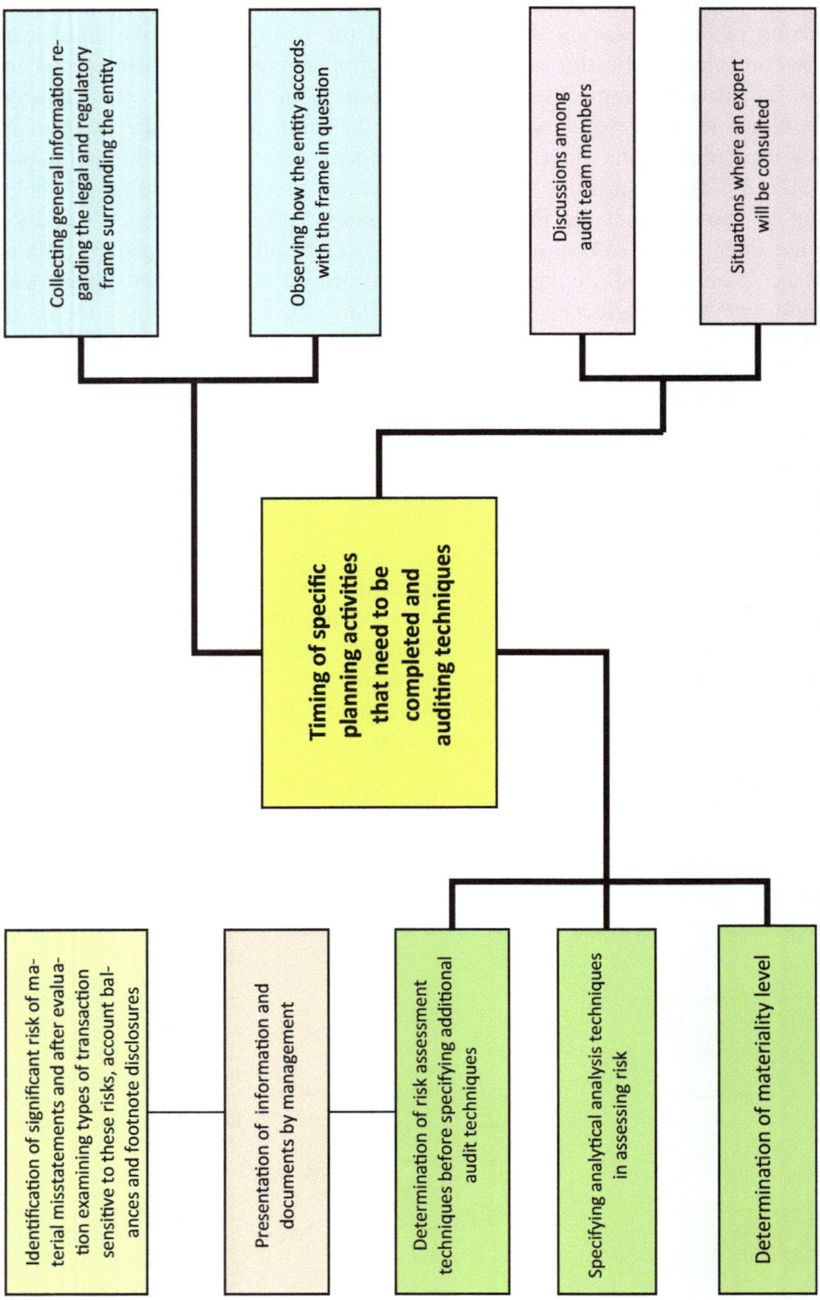

Fig. 3.6 Specific planning activities that are to be completed at the time of planning and the timing of audit techniques. *Source* Figured from TSA 300

Factors affecting the auditor's planning decisions include the level of competence of the computer assurance specialist (CAS) and the expertise of the auditor in the field of accounting information systems (AISs). As a result of a semi-experimental case study with auditors in a complicated accounting information system environment, it is observed that CAS competence and AIS expertise influence the auditor's risk assessment to a great extent. Furthermore, it is seen that in cases where there is a lack of expertise in AIS, competency in CAS plays a very significant role (Brazel and Agoglia 2004: 1, 16).

3.1.3 Acceptance and Continuance of External Audit Service

The acceptance and continuance of audit service are addressed between 26th and 28th paragraphs of Standard on Quality Control 1 (SQC 1). The capacity of the audit firm along with its recourses, the competency of its staff, as well as their capabilities comes at the first line. The second headline is the integrity of the client. Continuance of the client relation and withdrawal from the engagement are the other topics covered in this group (SQC 1, 26–28).

The integrity of those who are active in management of the audit client's entity, the integrity of the individuals responsible for the management and the main partners, the adequacy of the audit team along with the sufficiency of the recourses and time required to fulfill the work, and audit firm's and audit team's commitment to ethical principles are utmost important factors and impact the audit quality. TSA 210 "Agreeing the Terms of Audit Engagements" and TSA 220 "Quality Control for an Audit of Financial Statements" deal with these issues (www.kgk.gov.tr, 12.07.2014). For example, since a switch of the audit client's business to another field, where the audit firm does not have knowledge and expertise, would have a negative impact on the quality of the audit, the in-charge auditor must notify the audit firm without delay, and the necessary actions are to be taken.

The number of auditors to be allocated to audit areas should be determined. Inventory counts at key points should be considered when determining the number of auditors. TSA 500 "Audit Evidence" and TSA 501 "Audit Evidence—Specific Considerations for Selected Items" comprise details regarding inventory (www.kgk.gov.tr, 12.07.2014). When an audit of a group of financial statements is in question, the scope of the review of the work of other auditors is also a factor in determining the number of auditors and is covered under TSA 600 "Special Considerations—Audits of Group Financial Statements (Including the Work of Component Auditors)" (www.kgk.gov.tr, 12.07.2014). At the time the audit budget is being prepared, the hours required to be spent by the auditors to the audit will be determined. The designated working hours will take into account the high-risk areas. The budget allocated may not meet the required budget. This may put stress on determination of the number of the auditors. The quality of an audit that is not carried out by adequate and appropriate auditors may not reach the desired levels.

3.1.3.1 The Audit Team and Its Impacts on Audit Quality

The audit team having the ability and the competence required to perform audit tasks undertaken is important for the sake of the audit quality. Besides, the audit team performing the audit work according to audit standards and in accordance with legislative regulations is also an agent. If it is the case that financial statements reflect the truth, as expected from a high-quality audit, following the audit work the financial table users are not anticipated to face any loss. An audit team meeting all these expectations will be established in case the following points are taken into consideration carefully. The below listed factors are conformant to TSA 220:

- Signing on with the auditors who received relevant education;
- Teaming up the auditors, who gained experience by attending audit works enough, with the audit team;
- Teaming up the auditors, who have adequate knowledge about audit standards, with the audit team;
- The audit team members having enough knowledge about legislative regulations;
- The audit team members having a good grasp of information technologies;
- The audit team members having enough knowledge of the sector in which the audit client has business;
- Teaming up the auditors, who have professional decision-making ability, with the audit team; and
- The audit team members having the ability to comprehend the audit firm's quality control policy and procedures.

Even though the titles of the audit team members are displayed in Fig. 2.9, it is not stated how many persons will be from which title. According to CMB Communiqué Art. 19, for each audit work, an audit team of six, composed at least of three full members and three associate members, is to be established (www.spk.gov.tr, Communiqué Serial: X, No. 22, 18.02.2012). However, it is to be kept in mind, that whatever the title of an auditor within the audit firm he/she is associated with is, according to TSA 210, there cannot be more than one in-charge auditor in any audit team.

Audit Engagement Agreements in Turkey and Audit Team Survey

On the basis of the sample engagement agreement concordant to TCC, a survey is designed to explore the real audit team at work in Turkey as perceived by the managers of the audit clients. The questionnaire is designed in the aftermath of the main survey of this study, by regarding the leverage mentioned before, and the results are assessed here. In the first part of the questionnaire, there are three questions to explore the age, experience, and the tenure of the respondent in the current audit client company, and three questions directed to find out the department and the position of the respondent within the company, and the sector of the company. Besides, there are eight yes/no questions to be evaluated by the respondent regarding the audit engagement agreement signed with the audit firm chosen, and four yes/no questions regarding the auditing in general. Even though it would be the research question of another survey, regarding the audit quality the managers of the audit clients are also asked the maximum acceptable ratio of assistant staff within an audit team. The survey design enables the respondents to write their opinions in boxes under relevant questions.

The questionnaire is sent to the same addresses, which belong to the respondents of the survey explained in detail in the fourth section of the book. It is answered by 56 audit client managers from 21 different sectors, where 48.21% work at accounting department, 28.57% at management department, and 17.86% at finance department. The remaining three managers are employed at internal control, R&D, and sales departments. As positions are examined, it is seen that 42.86% are the managers of the departments they are assigned, 23.21% are chief financial officers, and 8.93% are finance managers. With an average of 45, their age range is 30–70. Their tenure at the current company starts from five months and has an average of approximately 13 years, and the maximum is 35 years. The total years of respondents' professional experience range between five years, three months, and 43 years—the average is 23 years.

While the percentage of the managers stating that the titles of the audit team members are explicitly written in the audit engagement agreement is 96.43, 92.86% say that the names of the audit team members are explicitly included in the agreement. According to the 76.79% of the respondents, the working hours of each audit team member are explicitly stated in the agreement, and 80.36% state that hourly rate of each audit team member is plainly written in the engagement. IAbL Art. 29 sets forth that audit engagement agreement should in detail state the names and titles, the working hours, and hourly rates of each member of the audit team along with the total audit fee (www.kgk.gov.tr, 01.01.2015). As assessed within Independent Audit By-Law, there seems distress regarding hourly fares and working hours.

The rate of managers, who say that it is explicitly stated in the audit engagement agreement, how many audit staff will take part in the audit team, is 82.14. The audit clients, who compare the team stated in audit engagement agreement and the team, which actually comes for auditing, from title, name, and number perspective, make up 76.79%. However, those who penalize a considerable deviation from audit engagement agreement drops to 26.79%. Furthermore, only 19.64% declare that such an enforcement clause is added in the agreement. The questions directed to explore the personal opinions of managers follow this set of questions targeting determination of the situation.

While the ratio of managers believing that too many staff assistants involved in an audit team negatively impacts audit quality is 44.64%, the ratio of those considering this situation as a cost-reducing fact is 35.71%. As the company, the managers are currently working is taken into consideration, 10.71% state that cost is more crucial than audit quality for their companies. The managers sharing the opinion "*we would not get audit service, if it were not a legal requirement,*" which is the question asked in order to be related to the cost of audit, is 14.29%. The graph shows the distribution of the opinions of the managers about the maximum percentages of staff assistants found acceptable within an audit team (Graphic 3.1).

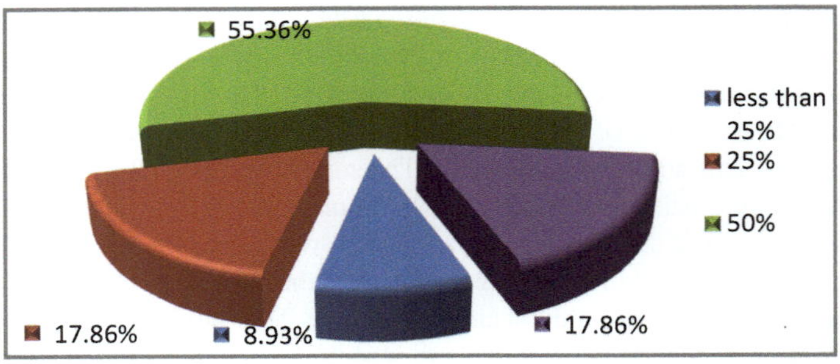

Graphic 3.1 Maximum percentages of staff assistants found acceptable within an audit team according to survey results

The ratio of managers approving staff assistants building half of the audit team is 55.36%. Those thinking that 25% is appropriate and those approving 75% are the same, 17.86%. Managers having a relatively marginal opinion that staff assistants' ratio in an audit team should not exceed 25% make up 8.93% of respondents. The views of managers about audit quality shared via the above-mentioned questionnaire are summarized as follows:

- High levels of sectoral information of auditors and staff assistants would increase audit quality;
- On the job training for staff assistants is good;
- The audit team being experienced and well informed will make an addition to audit quality;
- Rotation causing price decreases, thus causing a decrease in audit hours spent, which would end up by skipping some of the audit procedures and some issues being left unnoticed; and
- Giving importance to team leadership.

These observations deserve attention for the sake of audit quality.

3.1.3.2 Interactions Between the Responsibilities of the Audit Team, Oversight, Review, and Audit Quality

The audit team meticulously fulfilling its responsibilities would positively impact audit quality. For the sake of audit quality, it is very important that the engagement partner informs auditors in the audit team about their responsibilities, the essence of the business operations, risk-related matters, problems that would arise during auditing, and the details of duties related to the execution of the audit activity. The engagement partner oversees the compliance of auditors in the audit team with ethical principles. The *basic ethical principles* are integrity, objectivity, professional competence, professional due diligence, reliability, and professional conduct. According to regulations of POA, the responsibilities of the audit team and the in-charge auditor are listed below:

- Within the scope of the audit company's quality control system, audit teams are responsible of applying valid quality control procedures for the audit in question and are responsible of presenting required information to ensure the functioning of the chapters of the quality control system of the audit firm on independence are effective (TSA 220, 3).
- In-charge auditor is responsible of the quality of any and every audit he/she is assigned for (TSA 220, 8).
- By observations during the audit and by making inquiries in necessary cases, in-charge auditor shall always be cautious about situations which indicate that members of the audit team do not comply with the relevant ethical provisions. With the help of the quality control system of the audit firm or in another way, whenever his/her attention is drawn to instances implying that the members of the audit team are not in compliance with the relevant ethical provisions, the in-charge auditor decides, in consultation with other persons in the audit firm, on the steps to be taken (TSA 220, 9–10).
- In-charge auditor will make sure that the audit team and the experts, the auditor who is not an audit team member consulted, have the necessary competence and skill to perform an audit in accordance with the current legislative provisions and the auditor report to be in accordance with the conditions prevailing (TSA 220, 14).
- In-charge auditor takes the responsibility of the audit team conducting necessary consultations on difficult or controversial issues. He/she makes sure that the audit team makes necessary consultations during the audit in an appropriate manner within the team and outside itself with other parties at the appropriate level (TSA 220, 18).
- In case there are differences of opinion among team members, with persons consulted, or under appropriate conditions, with the in-charge auditor and supervisor of the audit quality, the audit team applies the audit firm's policies and procedures related to handling these differences and resolution setting (TSA 220, 22).
- While taking steps to undertake the responsibility for the overall quality of each audit, the in-charge auditor emphasizes the importance of carrying out the audit work in accordance with the professional standards and the provisions of the current legislation, adhering to the quality control policies and procedures of the audit firm, preparing the auditor's report in accordance with the prevailing conditions, and the audit team expressing its concerns without any fear and pressure in terms of quality of audit while giving messages to the other members of the audit team, (TSA 220, A3).

Leading and supervision of audit include (1) the follow-up of the progress of the audit, (2) the assessment of (a) the competence and ability of the audit team members, (b) whether they have enough time to do their work, (c) whether they understand the directives or not, and (d) whether the work in question is in accordance with the planned approach, (3) handling the issues that arise during the performance of the audit, (4) the assessment of the importance of these, and adaptation of the planned approach in an appropriate way, and (5) determination of the issues to be evaluated or consulted by the senior members of the audit team during the audit (TSA 220, A15).

The fact that the independent auditors of the audit team undertake the responsibility of carrying out the duty they are assigned for with objectivity, professional skepticism, and due diligence, while taking into account the ethical principles, also affects the audit quality positively. It is crucial that all auditors on the team understand the purpose of the audit. The audit performed as a teamwork and fellowship enables the junior staff in the team to comprehend the purpose of the work assigned to them. According to Standard on Quality Control 1 (SQC 1), the audit firm policies and procedures related to the responsibility to review are determined on the basis of senior staff reviewing the work of the less-experienced ones in the team. Though it is not compulsory, the in-charge auditor may review all of the working papers. What a sample review process may contain is listed below (TSA 220, A16–18):

(1) The assessment of whether the audit is performed in accordance with the current legislative provisions and according to professional standards;
(2) Evaluation of whether any important issue that needs further assessment arose or not;
(3) Understanding whether adequate consultations are done, whether the conclusions are documented, and whether the requisites of these results are done;
(4) Determining the need to make revisions, if there is any, regarding the specifications, timing, and the scope of the audit performed;
(5) Assessment of whether the work done supports the results obtained, and whether it is documented properly;
(6) Evaluation of whether the evidences obtained are enough and relevant to support the report; and
(7) The assessment whether audit procedures objectives are met or not.

The review regarding the audit quality is a process, designed to objectively assess the important judgments the team passed before or after the report date and the results the team reached while composing the audit report. This process is applied to independent audits of the financial tables of companies determined by POA and publically traded companies, and to those audits, the quality of which the audit firm decides is necessary to be reviewed. The engagement partner being sure of having gathered satisfactory evidence capable to support the audit report is also important. Reviews and interpretations of the open-ended critical issues of the external audit, which are identified during the audit, particularly difficult and subtle areas, significant risks, and other areas where the engagement partner is deemed important, are defined as ***peer review*** and are directed to enhance audit quality. Peer review is supported by the Communiqué (www.spk.gov.tr) and TSAs of POA (www.kgk.gov.tr).

Most research reveals positive effects of good quality control and review on the quality of the audit. On the other hand, a small number of studies have identified that some aspects of the quality control and review process may lead to undesirable adverse effects on the quality of auditor judgments. The adverse effects can be listed as follows (Knechel et al. 2013: 396–397):

(1) When they are informed about the preferences of the person who is going to review before commencing the inspection tasks, the judges of the auditors are often prone to preferences of the person.
(2) Overconfidence of partners in predicting their subordinates' abilities affects staff allocation decisions adversely.
(3) Auditors' performance reputations and the congruency of this with reviewer's initial opinion may cause reviewer judgments of a preparer's work to be biased.

According to Knechel et al., higher levels of audit review, including concurring partner reviews, help to reduce these biases. The review being conducted on electronic medium and the timeliness of reviews are also found to influence the quality of audit work (2013: 397). The role of the auditor is based on complex-structured standards. It is unlikely that this duty will be counter-controlled through a simple structured checklist (Delespaul[2], 2005). Even though it is a difficult task, yet there is a need for quality control of independent audit. Statement on Quality Control Standards (SQCS 8) points to audit firms establishing and maintaining a system for quality control of accounting and auditing practices. Audit firm should establish a quality control system that will provide reasonable assurance that the firm and its employees adhere to professional standards, regulatory provisions and laws, and that the reports prepared by the firm or its contractual partners are in accordance with the requirements (Hayes et al. 2005: 424).

Engagement quality control review is a process designed to provide an objective evaluation, before the report is released, of the significant judgments the engagement team made and the conclusions it reached in formulating the report (www.aicpa.org, SQCS No. 8[13], 13.06.2015). Engagement quality control reviewer would be a partner, other person in the firm, suitably qualified external person, or team made up of such individuals, none of whom is part of the engagement team, with sufficient and appropriate experience and authority (*ibid.*). Within the framework of the update service of *Generally Accepted Auditing Standards* (GAAS) 2011 issue features six elements of quality control (Georgiades 2011: 1). These are the ones touched by Arens et al. Quality control system of the audit firm has to involve the policies and procedures directed to the elements mentioned. The elements are listed below:

(1) Leadership responsibilities for quality within the firm—the tone at the top;
(2) Relevant ethical requirements;
(3) Acceptance and continuance of client relationships and specific engagements;
(4) Human resources;
(5) Engagement performance; and
(6) Monitoring.

[2]**Jean-Claude Delespaul**: Technical advisor to IFAC Board. La Compagnie nationale des commissaires aux comptes. La Délégation internationale pour l'audit et la comptabilité (DIPAC) founder (www.ifac.org).

The firm should establish a monitoring process designed to provide it with reasonable assurance that the policies and procedures relating to the system of quality control are relevant, adequate, and operating effectively (ISQC 1, 52). Each firm must certify its own quality control policies and procedures. The procedures should depend on the size of the firm, the number of offices in operation, and the nature of the activity. The quality control procedures of a multinational company with complicated customers and functioning in 150 international offices should be significantly different from a five-employee company specialized in small inspections in one or two industries. The quality control system includes policies and procedures that point to six elements. These are listed in Table 3.1 with brief descriptions and procedural examples that firms might use to satisfy the requirement (Arens et al. 2012: 54).

Though it is mentioned in detail in the fourth chapter of the book dedicated to the survey conducted, here it will be appropriate to mention the opinions of audit team members in Turkey about quality control policy and procedures and quality control department.

Table 3.1 Elements of quality control

Element	Summary of requirements	Example of a procedure
Leadership responsibilities for quality within the firm ("tone at the top")	The firm should promote a culture that quality is essential in performing engagements and should establish policies and procedures that support that culture	The firm's training programs emphasize the importance of quality work, and this is enforced in performance evaluation and compensation decisions
Relevant ethical requirements	All personnel on engagements should maintain independence in fact and in appearance, perform all professional responsibilities with integrity, and maintain objectivity in performing their professional responsibilities	Each partner and employee must answer an "independence questionnaire" annually, dealing with such things as stock ownership and membership on the boards of directors
Acceptance and continuation of clients and engagements	Policies and procedures should be established for deciding whether to accept or continue a client relationship. These policies and procedures should minimize the risk of associating with a client whose management lacks integrity. The firm should also only undertake the engagements that can be completed with professional competence	A client evaluation form, dealing with such matters as predecessor auditor comments and evaluation of management, must be prepared for every new client before acceptance

(continued)

Table 3.1 (continued)

Element	Summary of requirements	Example of a procedure
Human resources	Policies and procedures should be established to provide the firm with reasonable assurance that	Each professional must be evaluated on every engagement using the firm's individual engagement evaluation report
	All new personnel should be qualified to perform their work competently	
	Work is assigned to personnel who have adequate technical training and proficiency	
	All personnel should participate in continuing professional education and professional development activities that enable them to fulfil their assigned responsibilities.	
	Personnel selected for advancement have the qualifications necessary for the fulfillment of their assigned responsibilities	
Engagement performance	Policies and procedures should exist to ensure that the work performed by engagement personnel meets applicable professional standards, regulatory requirements, and the firm's standards of quality	The firm's director of accounting and auditing is available for consultation and must approve all engagements before their completion
Monitoring	Policies and procedures should exist to ensure that the other quality control elements are being effectively applied	The quality control partner must test the quality control procedures at least annually to ensure the firm is in compliance

Source Arens, A. A., Elder, R. J., and Beasley M. S. (2012). *Auditing and Assurance Services.* 14th Edition. Boston, Prentice p. 54

- Regarding the quality control department, 37.63% of auditors and 33.33% of audit firms' managers state that quality control department exists and operates effectively.
- The percentage of auditors believing that quality control department exists, however would operate more effectively, is 25.81, where the managers' is 41.67.
- Managers at 37.5% and auditors at 45.65% think that audit firms are not at the desired level in establishing quality control policy and procedures and informing their staff about these, written and oral.

3.1.3.3 Consultation, Differences of Opinion, Communication with Appropriate Individuals

It is important the engagement partner comes to the conclusion that the audit team member auditors received necessary consultancy in difficult and sensitive matters; and during auditing, from within the team and from outside the team, if necessary from outside the audit firm organization, consulted with individuals having the required knowledge in an appropriate way. The counseling described above has to satisfy the engagement partner from content and extent perspective. Conclusions being put into writing and settled with the person consulted and also the matter upon which settling parties agreed on being put into practice will produce positive effects on audit quality.

It is natural that not all external audit firms have the same size, the same facilities, or the same capabilities. In case the audit firm does not have sufficient internal resources, the firm getting consulting services from professional organizations, regulatory agencies, and other companies is vital for the consistency of the audit quality. The firm establishing and implementing policies and procedures for addressing and resolving differences of opinion within the engagement team; with those consulted; and, when applicable, between the engagement partner and the engagement quality control reviewer positively effects audit quality. For a high-quality audit, it is also essential of the engagement team members feel free and without being uneasy to communicate the opinion differences to the engagement partner and/or to the other members of the team whenever required.

TSA 260 organizes the communication with those charged with governance, namely the top management. Mutual and effective communication is essential for assisting the auditors, and those responsible for the senior management understand the issues related to the audit and for developing a constructive business relationship among themselves. It is also vital for the senior management to fulfill their responsibilities of supervising the financial reporting period. These help to reduce the risk of material misstatement in the financial statements.

External Audit Matters Interesting the Management That Need to be Communicated

Below is a compilation of the paragraphs of TSAs and SQC 1 that are applied in the external audit of financial statements, and are imperative that certain matters be communicated to those charged with governance:

- The audit firm assigns the responsibility of each audit to an in-charge auditor and establishes policies and procedures that force, the identity and duty of the in-charge auditor, to be communicated to key managers and the senior-level management (SQC 1, 30[a]).
- In cases where not all those charged with governance are involved in business management, the auditor understands the processes followed by the management in determining the risks of fraud, and how those who are responsible for

senior management perform monitoring the internal controls created by the management to reduce these risks (TSA 240, 20).

- In case facing exceptional circumstances as a result of an error that is fraudulent or suspected of being fraudulent cause questioning the continuance of the engagement, the auditor negotiates the withdrawal if he/she effectuates and reasons of it with the appropriate level managers and senior-level managers (TSA 240, 38[c][i]).
- In case detecting fraud or obtaining information pointing to the possibility of fraud, the auditor timely reports to the persons at appropriate levels of management, in order to inform the individuals mainly responsible of detecting and preventing fraud (TSA 240, 40).
- In instances where the auditor detects a fraud by (a) the management, (b) employees that have important tasks in internal control, or (c) other persons that are at a position enabling them deceit that may cause a significant effect on financial statements, or suspects such as fraud, report the matter to the senior management on time under circumstances where not all those charged with governance are involved in business management. If the auditor suspects a fraud the management is involved, then reports his/her doubts to the senior management and negotiates with them the nature, the timing, and the scope of the audit procedures required to complete the audit (TSA 240, 41).
- In order to help identify other contraventions that may have significant effects on the financial statements, the auditor applies audit procedures of (a) interrogation of the management and those responsible for the senior management about the compliance with the other legislation, and (b) examination of correspondence with licensors or regulatory bodies, if any (TSA 250, 14).
- When the auditor suspects about contraventions, he/she negotiates the matter with the management and under appropriate conditions with those who are responsible for senior management. In case management and under appropriate conditions those who are responsible for senior management do not provide satisfactory information about the compliance of the business with regulations, and when auditor concludes that the impacts of contraventions would be crucial for the financial statements, he/she considers getting legal consultancy (TSA 250, 19).
- Due to the reason that not all those charged with governance are involved in business management, consequently them not being aware of detected or suspected contraventions that the auditor reported afore, the auditor reports the contraventions that aroused his/her attention, detected, or suspected during the audit letting aside the explicitly trivial ones to the senior management. If he/she comes to judge that the contravention stated is deliberate and material, he/she reports the matter to the senior management in the shortest possible time. If auditor speculates the management or senior managers have participation in contravention, then he/she reports the matter to an upper level like audit committee or supervisory board. In case such an upper level does not exist, or the auditor believes they will not take action upon auditor notification, or the auditor

not being sure who is to be reported, then the auditor considers the need to get legal consultation (TSA 250, 22–24).

- The auditor reports the material internal control deficiencies detected during the audit to those charged with governance written and on time (TSA 265, 9).
- As long as not forbidden by legislation, the auditor reports the uncorrected mistakes and the possible solitary or collective impacts of these on the auditor report opinion, to those charged with governance. In his/her notification, the auditor describes material mistakes separately. Auditor demands the correction of uncorrected mistakes (TSA 450, 12).
- Additionally, the auditor reports the impact of previous periods' uncorrected mistakes regarding transaction classes, account balances, and explanations as a whole on the financial statements to those charged with governance (TSA 450, 13).
- In case the rejection of confirmation request by management is not found reasonable by the auditor or at the end of alternative audit procedures the auditor not being able to find relevant and reliable evidence, the auditor communicates those charged with governance in compliance with TSA 260. At the same time according to TSA 705, the auditor decides on the impacts of this fact upon the audit and auditor opinion (TSA 505, 13).
- In case the auditor gets audit evidence that opening balances involve mistakes that would materially affect current period's financial statements, the auditor applies additional relevant audit procedures under current circumstances to determine the effect of the mistakes mentioned on the current period's financial statements. If he/she decides current period's financial statements involve these kinds of mistakes, according to TSA 450 the auditor reports the mistakes mentioned to the appropriate level of management and those charged with governance (TSA 510, 7).
- In cases where not all those charged with governance are involved in business management, the auditor communicates about significant matters that arouse associated to related parties, with those charged with governance (TSA 550, 27).
- The auditor applies audit procedures designed to get relevant and efficient evidence that all events that happened between financial statements report date and auditor report date that necessitate corrections or explanations in financial statements are detected. He/she applies these procedures comprising the period between financial statements date and auditor report date, and the period between financial statements date and the closest date to the auditor report's date. While determining the essence and the scope of these kinds of procedures, the auditor takes into consideration the risk evaluation he/she did (TSA 560, 7)
  - For example, interrogation of the management and those charged with governance about whether an event, that would affect the financial statements following the balance sheet date, happened or not (TSA 560, 7[b]).
  - For example, scrutinizing the minutes of meetings done by the company partners, management, and those charged with governance after the financial

statements' date if there is any, and interrogation of these people about the issues discussed in those meetings but the minutes of which are not yet written (TSA 560, 7[c]).

- In the aftermath of the auditor report, the auditor does not have an obligation to perform any audit procedure related to the financial statements. However, in case there is a situation about which the auditor gets informed after the auditor report and before the issuance of the financial statements and that had he/she known about, might cause him/her to make alterations in the auditor report, the auditor negotiates the matter with the management and in appropriate circumstances with those charged with governance (TSA 560, 10[a]).
- Sometimes, it might be the case that legislation and financial reporting frame do not oblige the issuance of the altered financial statements by management; therefore, the auditor is not required to present a restated or new auditor report. Nevertheless, in cases where auditor finds it necessary to make alterations in financial statements and the management does not make changes, if the report is already presented to the client, the auditor (TSA 560, 13) notifies the management and in cases where not all those charged with governance are involved in business management, to those charged with governance, not to release the financial statements without required changes are done. If the financial statements are released against this notice without required changes are done, the auditor takes relevant steps to block the faith in the auditor report (TSA 560, 13[b]).
- In the aftermath of the issuance of the financial statements, the auditor does not have an obligation to perform any audit procedure related to these financial statements. However, in case there is a situation about which the auditor gets informed after the issuance of the financial statements and that had he/she known about, might cause him/her to make alterations in the auditor report, the auditor negotiates the matter with the management and in appropriate circumstances with those charged with governance (TSA 560, 14[a]).
- In cases where auditor finds it necessary that alterations to be made in financial statements, and the management does not make changes, and neither takes necessary steps to inform the persons, whom the formerly issued financial statements reached, the auditor notifies the management and in cases where not all those charged with governance are involved in business management, to those charged with governance, that he/she will take relevant steps in the future to block the faith in the auditor report. If the management and those charged with governance do not take necessary steps against this notice, the auditor takes relevant steps to block the faith in auditor report (TSA 560, 17).
- In cases where not all those charged with governance are involved in business management, the auditor communicates those charged with governance about the events and circumstances detected, which may seriously cause doubts about going concern of the business. This communication that is to be established with those charged with governance covers the below-stated issues: (a) Whether the events and circumstances generate significant uncertainties, (b) whether it is

appropriate to use going-concern assumption in preparation of financial statements, and (c) the sufficiency of the explanations related to the matter in financial statements (TSA 570, 23).

- Group audit team notifies those charged with governance of the group about the below-listed matters in addition to the matters mandatory according to TSA 260 and other TSAs (TSA 600, 49): (a) general information about the types of work to be carried out in relation to the units' financial information, (b) general information about the work to be carried out by unit auditors in relation to the critical units' financial information, and general information about the type of planned contribution of the group audit team, (c) the instances where the assessment of the group audit team about the work of the unit auditor provokes concerns about the quality of the work in question, (d) all restrictions on group audit, for example the group audit team's access to information being restricted, (e) instances where the group management, unit management, the employees who have critical roles in controls overall the group are involved in fraud, or there is fraud hinted, or other person's involvement in fraud where fraud causes material mistake in group financial statements.
- In auditing the external auditor makes all the judgements and in order to avoid over usage of the work of internal audit function does plan using the work of internal audit lesser and more direct work when the following happens (TSA 610, 18): (a) (i) in the planning and implementation of the relevant audit procedures, and (ii) as the weight of the judgment increases in assessment of the audit evidence gathered, (b) taking consideration specifically the risks identified as serious, the risk of "material misstatement" assessed at the management statement level increases, (c) as the institutional stance of the internal audit function and related policies and procedures' sufficiency of backing the impartiality of internal auditors diminishes, and (d) when the level of competency of the internal audit function falls.
- In case the auditor finds out that the management has been limiting the scope of the audit as likely to lead to a qualified opinion or disclaimer about financial statements, he/she asks the management to lift the limitation. If the management refuses lifting the limitation, the auditor communicates to those charged with governance, in cases where not all those charged with governance are involved in business management, and decides whether it is possible to apply alternative procedures to obtain sufficient appropriate audit evidence (TSA 705, 11–12).
- When the auditor concludes that the effects of the undetected misstatements, if there is any, on the financial statements are possibly material and widespread, thus a qualified opinion would not be sufficient to adequately communicate the seriousness of the situation and therefore withdraws from the audit and communicates the facts about misstatements causing the qualified opinion, to the those charged with governance (TSA 705, 13–14).
- In case, there is significant misstatement in disclosing information that is required to be disclosed in financial statements, the auditor negotiates the facts about nondisclosure to those charged with governance (TSA 705, 19[a]).

- When the auditor considers issuing an opinion other than unqualified opinion in his/her report, he/she communicates the circumstances leading him/her to issue this opinion to those charged with governance (TSA 705, 28).
- In case the auditor considers adding an *Emphasis of Matter* paragraph or *Other Matter* paragraph, he/she communicates this consideration and the proposed text to those charged with governance (TSA 706, 9).
- If the auditor concludes that there is a material misstatement regarding the previous period's financial statements, audited by the predecessor auditor and been issued an unqualified opinion, communicates this misstatement to the appropriate level of management and in cases where not all those charged with governance are involved in business management to those charged with governance and demands the previous period's auditor to be informed. If the prior period financial statements are amended and the predecessor auditor agrees to issue a new auditor's report on the amended financial statements of the prior period, the auditor shall report only on the current period (TSA 710, 18).
- In cases when the other information need to be corrected and the management does not accept making this correction, in cases where not all those charged with governance are involved in business management, the auditor communicates this issue to those charged with governance, and (a) according to TSA 706, the auditor adds the Other Matter paragraph explaining the material inconsistency or (b) does not present the auditor report or (c) withdraws from the engagement, where it is possible under the applicable law or regulation (TSA 720, 10).
- In cases when the other information need to be corrected and the management does not accept making this correction, in cases where not all those charged with governance are involved in business management, the auditor communicates his/her concerns about other information to those charged with governance and takes necessary steps (TSA 720, 13).
- In cases when the auditor concludes there is existence of a material misexplanation in the other information, in cases where not all those charged with governance are involved in business management, the auditor communicates his/her concerns about the other information to those charged with governance and takes necessary steps (TSA 720, 16).

The auditor notifying those charged with governance about of the issues, which are composed of information not corrected and are misleading, the issues that solely would not impact, but collectively may have significant effects on financial statements, is important in terms of quality of audit. Apart from this, it is also important that the audit issues observed during the audit process, that are of interest of the management, are notified to those charged with governance. Notifying those charged with governance should not be ignored about the fact that the external audit may not be designed to detect all kinds of issues interesting those charged with governance. Auditing issues that concern management should be communicated to those charged with governance in due time to enable the responsible persons to take the necessary precautions. The communication with those charged with governance would be oral or written. The decision to communicate oral or in writing depends on the nature, size, operational structure, legal structure, and communication processes of the audited entity, as well as on the characteristics, sensitivity, and importance of the audit issues that must be communicated. Furthermore, frequency of reporting or communication among those charged with governance and the external auditor are also factors in determining the type of communication. In case the communication about audit issues concerning the management is oral, the auditor documents the issues negotiated and the answers received through working papers. Depending on the characteristics, sensitivity, and importance of the audit issues that are communicated with those charged with governance, it might be preferred oral communication to be approved in written form.

In USA where applications are similar to Turkish ones regarding this issue, AS 1301—formerly PCAOB Auditing Standard No. 16—organizes the communication to the audit committee for the audits having been performed since December 15, 2012. The auditor should establish an understanding of the terms of the audit engagement with the audit committee. This understanding includes communicating to the audit committee the following:

1. The objective of the audit:
    a. Integrated audit[3],
    b. Audit of financial statements;
2. The responsibilities of the auditor; and
3. The responsibilities of management.

The auditor should record the understanding of the terms of the audit engagement in an engagement letter and provide the engagement letter to the audit committee annually. The auditor should have the engagement letter executed by the appropriate party or parties on behalf of the company (Appendix C: C1, www.pcaobus.org, 19.01.2013; https://pcaobus.org/Standards/Auditing/Pages/AS1301.aspx#_AppC, 21.01.2018). Communicate to, as used in this standard, is meant to encourage effective two-way communication between the auditor and the audit committee throughout the audit to assist in understanding matters relevant to the audit. It is well understood that such a communication about the audit matters probably will promote the transparency and enhance audit quality.

Confirmation Letters of Business Management and Communication

The auditor receives written explanation from the persons responsible for the management and those charged with governance that they accept their responsibilities regarding the design, implementation, and maintenance of internal control for prevention and detection of fraud. On the second hand, the auditor receives written explanation that management explained the results of their assessment of the

[3]**Integrated Audit**: combines a financial statement audit with an audit of internal controls.

risk that the financial statements may contain material misstatements due to fraud. Third, the auditor shall receive written explanation that the management shared the information they have about the realized or suspected frauds where the management, the employees who have important duties in the internal control, or other persons who may be able to conduct a fraud which may have significant impact on the financial statements. Lastly, the auditor gets written explanation that the management has already explained all the information they have about allegations issued by the employees, former employees, analysts, regulatory agencies, or others regarding fraud realized or suspected, those affecting financial statements of the entity (TSA 240, 39). Due to the nature of the fraud and irregularity and because of the existence of the difficulties encountered by the external auditor in determining the material mistakes in the financial statements caused by fraud and irregularities, obtaining confirmation is important.

Whenever the auditor has determined that there is evidence that fraud may exist, that matter should be brought to the attention of an appropriate level of management. This is appropriate even if the matter might be considered inconsequential, such as a minor defalcation by an employee at a low level in the entity's organization. Fraud involving senior management and fraud—whether caused by senior management or other employees—that causes a material misstatement of the financial statements should be reported directly to the audit committee in a timely manner and prior to the issuance of the auditor's report. In addition, the auditor should reach an understanding with the audit committee regarding the nature and extent of communications with the committee about misappropriations perpetrated by lower-level employees (TSA 240 and AS 2401).

The auditor, who is suspicious of the integrity or truthfulness of the management or those charged with governance, may seek legal counseling to determine the appropriate course of action. Around the beginning of the audit, there will be a mutual agreement about the nature and scope of the communication to be established, regarding the fraud and irregularities caused by people other than the management of the entity, not causing a material misstatement of the financial statements, with those charged with governance. In the possible shortest time, the auditor informs the management or those charged with governance of the entity about the considerable weaknesses in internal control conduct and establishment of internal controls that are related to the irregularity and fraud to be detected and prevented, which drive his/her attention (TSA 240). If the auditor believes that there is weakness in risk assessment process of the management of the entity, or detects a material misstatement in financial statements due to lack of necessary controls to be done by the management or because of insufficiency of the controls required, then he/she shares these matters with those charged with governance. The auditor evaluates whether there is any other issue related to fraud and irregularity to be negotiated with those charged with governance. The scope of such an evaluation is summarized in Fig. 3.7 as below (TSA 240, A64).

According to Arens et al., the first course of action when an illegal act has been identified is to consider the effects on the financial statements, including the adequacy of disclosures. These effects may be complex and difficult to resolve.

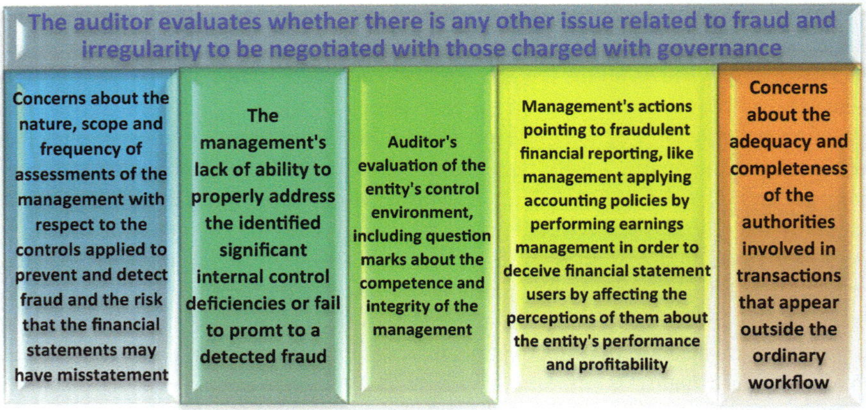

Fig. 3.7 Issues the auditor can discuss with those charged with governance about fraud and irregularities. *Source* Figured from TSA 240, A64

A violation of civil rights laws, as an example, could involve significant fines, but it could also result in the loss of customers or key employees. These losses could materially impact revenues and expenses in future. In case the auditor concludes that the disclosures relative to an illegal act are inadequate, the auditor should modify the audit report accordingly (2012: 136).

Prior to the final audit report, the auditors will usually discuss their findings with the audit committee especially irregularities, illegal acts, and reportable conditions (Hayes et al. 2005: 424). The auditor should also consider the effect of such illegal acts on the CPA firm's relationship with management. If management knew of the illegal act and failed to inform the auditor, it becomes questionable whether management can be believed in other discussions (Arens et al. 2012: 136). The auditor's professional obligation to protect the confidentiality of customer information may prevent a fraudulent user from being reported to a party outside the customer. However, the statutory responsibilities of the auditor differ from case to case, and in certain circumstances, the obligation to keep confidentiality can be removed by legislation or court decisions. In some cases, it may be a legal obligation for an auditor who audits a financial institution to report the fraud to an authority. In addition, in some cases it may be necessary for the auditor to report the errors to related authorities, when the management and those charged with governance do not take the necessary corrective steps. The confidentiality obligation of auditors makes it generally impossible to report fraud and error to third parties. However, in some cases communiqués or laws make this obligation null and void (TSA 240, A65). As Hayes et al. summarize (2005: 523); (1) in the USA, the auditor is required to report fraud or error by financial institutions to the supervisory authorities, and (2) in the Netherlands, if sufficiently corrective measures are not taken by the directors and the fraud is considered material, the auditors have to withdraw from the engagement. In statutory audits, the auditor must report such a withdrawal to the Ministry of Justice; (3) in France, auditors must report illegal acts and fraud; (4) German auditors have to report fraud to the boards of directors in their auditor's report; this is also indicated in the tax return of the company, and, therefore, indirectly, it is also a report to the authorities.

In written or oral, the auditor should communicate with the audit committee or others of equivalent authority to make sure that they know of the illegal act. In cases when the communication is oral, the nature of the communication and discussion should be documented in the audit files. If the client either refuses to accept the auditor's modified report or fails to take appropriate remedial action concerning the illegal act, the auditor may find it necessary to withdraw from the engagement. If the audit client is a publicly held company, the auditor must also report the matter directly to the American SEC. Such decisions are complex and normally involve consultation by the auditor with the auditor's legal counsel (Arens et al. 2012: 136).

3.1.4 Audit Report and Its Impacts on Audit Quality

The purpose of the independent expert opinion is to lend credibility to the financial statements. The communication of the auditor's opinion is called attestation, or the attest function. In an audit, this attestation is called the *audit report* (Hayes et al. 2005: 12). Nick Land[4] finds it surprising that the audit report, which is the only truly independent voice in a set of accounts, is the one part of the financial statements that there is normally no point in reading. Audit report has not fundamentally changed for 80 years in USA and for about 150 years in the UK (Land 2014; 86).

The users of financial statements of either public companies or private companies are primarily shareholders and investors, followed by other stakeholders. Therefore, the opinion of Eumedion[5] Corporate Governance Forum, which is one of the institutions representing the European investors, matters. Eumedion's comment letter sent to International Organization of Securities Commissions (IOSCO) Consultation Report states that (1) the current form and the language of the audit report are highly standardized, (2) the report does not allow too much comment other than pass/fail, and (3) the financial statements users becoming inure with the wording forces the informational value of the audit report close to zero. The Forum proposes the report to be reorganized such that it becomes an important form of

[4]**Nick Land**: Chairman, Audit and Assurance Council, UK Financial Reporting Council. The Financial Reporting Council (FRC). The FRC is the UK's independent regulator responsible for promoting high-quality corporate governance and reporting to foster investment. Public company board member.

[5]**Eumedion**: operates as a representative of the interests of institutional investors in the field of corporate governance and sustainability. The name "Eumedion" means "Good Guardian" in Greek. http://www.eumedion.nl/en/abouteumedion. Accessed 14 Sept 2012.

communication between auditors and investors. For example, the report would include the judgments of the auditor throughout the audit process (Abma, 10.12.2009: 5).

Increasing the value of the audit report is on the agenda of International Auditing and Assurance Standards Board (IAASB), and some of the ISAs are under revision. New ISAs are proposed, and ISAs reviewed are developed and accepted by IAASB. One of these, ISA 701[6] establishes requirements and guidance for the auditor's determination and communication of key audit matters (KAM). KAM, which are selected from matters communicated with those charged with governance, are required to be communicated in auditor's reports for audits of financial statements of listed entities (www.ifac.org, Complete Exposure Draft, Reporting on Audited Financial Statements, 08.09.2013). At the Public Company Accounting Oversight Board's Public Meeting on the Auditor's Reporting Model, Sven Gentner[7] representing EU states that all initiatives taken have the objective of achieving greater transparency and summarizes the decisions taken by EU Commission. There will be a statement that indicates by whom or by which body the auditor was appointed, another statement indicating the date of the appointment and the period of total uninterrupted engagement, including previous renewals and reappointments of the auditor. Other precautions are the obligation to report on any material uncertainty related to events or conditions that may cause significant doubt about the entity's ability to continue as a going concern, and the obligation to describe the most significant assessed risks of material misstatements, as well as a summary of the auditor's response to those risks, and, finally and where relevant, key observations arising with respect to those risks (Gentner 2014: 80–83).

3.2 Basic Determinants of Audit Quality

The fact that the prospects for the auditing profession are directly related to the quality and effectiveness, as well as the perceived value, of independent audits has once more been recognized at the end of twelve-month works of United States Treasury Department's Advisory Committee on the Auditing Profession (ACAP). Ultimately, it is a combination of transparency and trust that enables financial markets to function efficiently. A strong and vibrant auditing profession is a critical element of that regime and especially important to the US capital markets where more than 100 million people invest their savings and retirement assets (United States Treasury, www.treasury.gov, 03.01.2013, ACAP, Final Report, 2008: II: 1). According to Goetsch and Davis, ***quality*** is a concept related with products,

[6]**ISA 701**: International Standard on Auditing (ISA) 701, *Communicating Key Audit Matters in the Independent Auditor's Report.*

[7]**Sven Gentner**: Counselor, Economic and Financial Affairs Section, Delegation of the European Union to the United States.

services, people, processes that meet or exceed existing expectations, and the environment (quoted by Durukan and Ikiz 2007: 41). Zeithaml et al. state that ***service quality*** encompasses both the "output" produced and "how the service is provided" or "the style how it is delivered" (*ibid.*).

As Redmayne states, over the past 20 years a number of researchers have tried to research and define audit quality. However, there is still no consensus on what audit quality is or how to measure it. That is because audit quality relies on perceptions and those perceptions depend on whose views are taken into consideration. Given how difficult it is to define audit quality, researchers, regulators, and professionals often refer to audit quality by negation, much like when one tries to define independence, as what is "not" audit quality (www.nzica.com, 2013). Knechel et al. share this opinion. While it would be ideal to define audit quality for what it "is," the reality is that researchers, regulators, and professionals can often do no more than describe what high audit quality "is not," i.e., in terms of errors or deficiencies that reduce audit quality (Knechel et al. 2013: 386).

According to Suseno, audit quality has three aspects. These are inputs, processes, and context. The input comprises of two dimensions, (1) personal attributes of auditor with indicators (i) expertise, (ii) ethical values, (iii) mindset, and (2) auditing process with the indicators (i) auditing method reliability, (ii) the effectiveness of audit tools, and (iii) availability of technical support. Output in audit quality has two dimensions: (1) public auditor report and (2) public auditor communication. Context factor consists of two factors: (1) governance and (2) law and regulation (Suseno 2013: 82–83).

According to Jere R. Francis, audit standards imply that audit quality is achieved by the issuance of the *appropriate* audit report on the client's compliance with generally accepted accounting principles. However, audit quality is a complex concept and cannot be reduced to a simple definition. Francis (2011: 127) argues that there are gradations of audit quality across a continuum from low-quality to high-quality audits, and that quality is affected by each element of the framework in Fig. 3.8. The audit report, which is one of the two primary observable outcomes of the audit process, is directly under the auditor's control. The other outcome, the client's audited financial statements, is also affected by the audit process even though it is under the responsibility of the client (*ibid.*, 129). When the audit quality drivers as put forth by Francis are evaluated for Turkish case, at first sight there are not big differences. However, the institutions having effects on audit industry[8] at the first hand, and on economic behavior on the second hand seem to be differing. Figure 3.8 shows the audit firms composing the audit industry in a scatter way

[8]**Audit Industry**: Even though industry has connotations with manufacturing, etymologically the word comes from Latin *industria* meaning diligence and from an uncertain origin *industrius* meaning active. This is followed by the French usage "systematic work or labor" around 1475. In the aftermath of Industrial Revolution, with the increased use of men's labor in making of goods and services for sale, the word bore the attribute of "systematic work and continuous employment" (www.thefreedictionary.com, 29.10.2013). Therefore, this book prefers usage of audit industry.

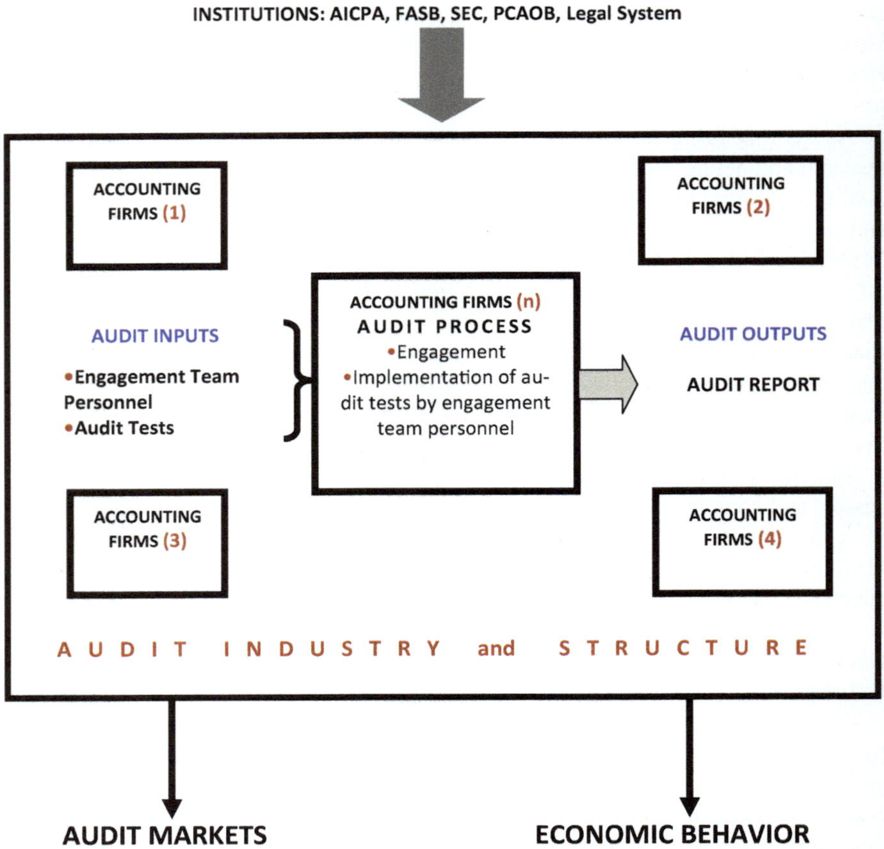

Fig. 3.8 Multiple drivers of audit quality. *Source* Francis, J. R. (2011). A Framework for Understanding and Researching Audit Quality. Auditing, 30(2), 125–152. doi: 10.2308/ajpt-50006. Organized from pp. 126–127

around the figure. The input/output process is the same for each one. The audit inputs are of course not only the engagement team personnel and the audit tests performed. For simplicity, only the two are mentioned briefly. When it says "quality is affected by each element of the framework in the figure," it has to be understood that regulatory bodies, oversight mechanism, audit firms, the ways the audit firms work, auditors, the industry the business is in, and many other factors impact the audit quality. All of these directly affect the audit markets and economic behavior.

There are similarities in the names of institutions in different countries. However, when it comes to Turkey, there are considerable differences in the operations and authorities contrary to the similarities in titles. As it was compared in Table 2.12, the duties undertaken by POA in Turkey are done by Financial Accounting

Standards Board (FASB), International Auditing and Assurance Standards Board (IAASB), and American Institute of CPAs (AICPA). Even though these bodies have organic bonds to each other, they keep their autonomy. The AICPA, the FASB, SEC, PCAOB, and the legal system displayed in Fig. 3.8 are the POA and the legal system in Turkey.

3.2.1 *The Factors Impacting the Audit Quality: Independence, Transparency, and Other Factors*

Under this title, the factors researched under subtitles along with the main factors like independence and transparency will be discussed. The title transparency comprises the transparency of the quality indicators, the transparency of the governance of the audit firm, and the transparency of the financial statements of the audit firm itself. Under other factors, human resource policy and procedures, local office or partner, quality control systems and the like are discussed.

3.2.1.1 Independence

Even though the factors mentioned in the opening paragraph do have influence on audit quality, as the interest of all stakeholders is taken into consideration, the most outstanding factor impacting the audit quality is **independence**. The core of this book is about independence. Independence is to be defined as being not influenced by others; being impartial; being free from outside control; not subject to another's authority; etc. The Turkish definition can be looked up from TLA. In the auditing context, simply it is the independence of external auditors from parties that might have a financial interest in the business being audited. It is characterized by integrity and an objective approach to the audit process. The concept requires the auditor to carry out his/her work freely and in an objective manner.

As Kinney states, in 1997 AICPA proposed a definition of independence, which focuses on the auditor's independence from the information itself rather than from the registrant as preparer of the information (1999: 73). According to the definition of the Communiqué, which served as the primary guide in Turkish audit market until POA took over the flag, independence regarding the audit profession is the set of behaviors and understandings that will ensure the honest and impartial conduct of professional activity. External audit firms and external auditors have to be independent during their audit work. Apart from being honest and impartial, external auditors should also not have special circumstances that could undermine their independence (www.spk.gov.tr, Communiqué Serial: X, No. 22, 18.02.2012). Another definition says independence is being objective and unbiased while performing professional services, being independent in fact and in appearance (Rittenberg et al. 2012: 26). DeAngelo brings a new attribute and explains the *level of auditor independence* as the conditional probability that, given a breach has been discovered, the auditor will report the breach (1981a: 116). As stated in the Handbook of the Code of Ethics for Professional Accountants, which is translated, adopted, and published among TSAs by POA, independence comprises the independence of mind as well as independence in appearance (2012: 46). (1) Independence of mind is the state of mind that permits the expression of a conclusion without being affected by influences that compromise professional judgment, thereby allowing an individual to act with integrity and exercise objectivity and professional skepticism. (2) Independence in appearance is the avoidance of facts and circumstances that are so significant that a reasonable and informed third party would be likely to conclude, weighing all the specific facts and circumstances, that a firm's, or a member of the audit team's, integrity, objectivity, or professional skepticism have been compromised (TSA, Code of Ethics for Professional Accountants 2015: 130).

The value of audit depends heavily on public perception of the independence of auditors. The reason for the desire of the majority of different users to rely on the reports of the CPAs is the expectation of an unbiased opinion. Arens et al. state that where auditors are truly independent, but the financial statements users believe auditors are the voice of their clients, then a significant portion of the value of the audit function is lost (2012: 90). The benefits of ensuring the independence of the auditor extend to the full effectiveness of a whole of capital markets (Hayes et al. 2005: 83). Within the framework of the definitions of independence made and the applicable rules, auditors have a number of responsibilities for this. The engagement partner at the head of the audit team must reach a conclusion that independence has been achieved. To this end, the responsible engagement partner shall perform the activities indicated in the Fig. 3.9 (Kishalı et al. 2013: 8):

When the engagement partner identifies a condition threatening the independence that cannot be eliminated or reduced to an acceptable level, he/she should discuss it with the audit firm. At the end of discussions, precautions like giving start to actions like the cancelation of the activity or transaction or withdrawal from engagement are to be taken, and all discussions and conclusions reached are to be written down. Lynn E. Turner[9] who made a dissenting statement to the Final Report of the United States Treasury Department's Advisory Committee on the Auditing Profession (ACAP) in 2008, states that conflicts and questions of independence arise from the auditor being paid by the very company they audit. Turner believes that this continues to be the *elephant in the room* people chose to ignore (2008: IX: 2). The direct payment of the auditor's fee by the audit client leads to conflicts of interest. As argued by ET Bureau, a better way could be for companies to pay audit fees into a fund maintained by stock exchanges, for listed companies, or with the registrar of companies, for non-listed ones. Auditors should be paid

[9]**Lynn E. Turner:** served as the Chief Accountant at the SEC from 1998 to 2001. He serves as a senior advisor to Kroll Zolfo Copper and is a member of the Standards Advisory Group of the Public Company Accounting Oversight Board and the Financial Accounting Standards Board Investor Technical Advisory Committee (2008).

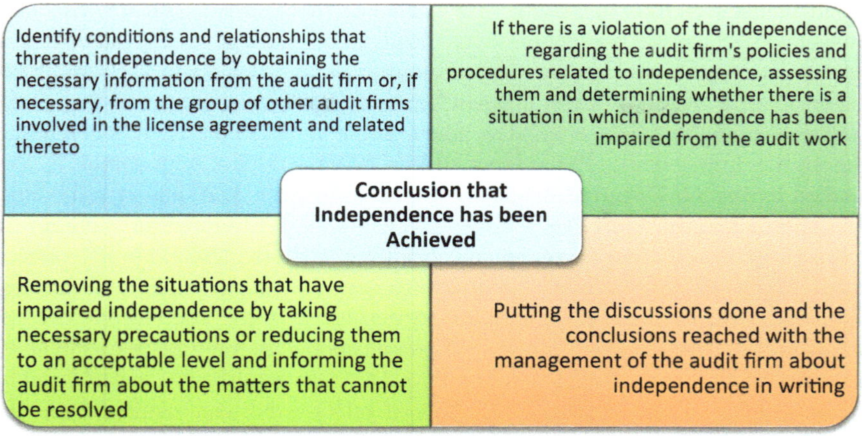

Fig. 3.9 Steps to be taken by the engagement partner in order to conclude that independence has been achieved. *Source* Kishali, Y., Güner, M. F., Pehlivanlı, D. (2013: 8). KGK. Geçiş Dönemi Eğitim Dokümanları. Beykent Üniversitesi. http://www.kgk.gov.tr/content_detail-326-782-.html. Accessed 21 May 2015. "Modül I, Denetim Standartları." Organized from p 8

from this fund, not by any company directly (http://economictimes.indiatimes.com, 03.11.2013). At the end of a two-year study that focused on companies in the Indian state of Gujarat, which requires that industrial plants receive regular audits not only on their financial information but also on levels of pollution generated, auditors were found to be more likely to fudge results when paid directly by the plants then when they were paid from a common pool (Gaetano 18.10.2013). Undertaken with the cooperation of the state government, 233 of 473 industrial plants were audited under a new system where auditors would be assigned to a random plant and be paid a fixed fee from a common pool, while the remaining 240 served as the control group that hired and paid their own auditors (Duflo et al. 2013: 1501, 1515). At the end of the experimental study, it is found that the auditors paid from a common pool reported much higher levels of pollution and were found to be 80% less likely to falsely report that plants were compliant (Gaetano 18.10.2013). This book also has the resolution to payment of audit fee from a pool carefully designed specifically for Turkey.

In a study about audit fees and auditor independence conducted in USA analyzed 1479 financially distressed companies from 2004 to 2006, including 180 with first-time going-concern modified opinion. The analysis indicates that after controlling for other reporting and fee-related factors, auditors issue significantly fewer going-concern modified opinions in the current period to clients that pay higher subsequent total fees. The researchers also found that non-audit services fees in the current year were also significantly negatively associated with going-concern modified audit opinions during the 2004–2006 era (Blay and Geiger 2013: 581, 585).

Independent auditors are obliged to document the elements that threaten their independence, and the prevention mechanisms established against these threats in the working papers, and also are obliged to discuss these issues in the committees responsible for the audit. Each independent auditor should submit a written statement confirming that he/she is independent on the audits to the client's committee responsible from audits. The subject that is addressed by Communiqué is also handled by the 8th Directive Article 42, by PCAOB Rule 3526 and in some other legislation. The 8th Directive requires the auditors (1) to confirm annually in writing to the audit committee their independence from the audited public interest entity; (2) to disclose annually to the audit committee any additional services provided to the audited entity; and (3) to discuss with the audit committee the threats to their independence and the safeguards applied to mitigate those threats as documented by them. With the Rule 3526, PCAOB requires a registered public accounting firm to communicate all kinds of relation that can suppress independence, annual, and written to the issuer's audit committee (IOSCO, www.iasplus.com, 12.03.2012; Consultation Report, Sept 2009: 10, 13).

Another study reminds the regulators to reassess cost/benefit analyses of a truly independent auditor. The researchers introduce a gatekeeper game, which has three players—a manager, an auditor, the investor—by extending the standard ultimatum game to examine their research questions. They explain the three main findings of their study such that: (1) even weak independence leads to effective gatekeeper in that the gatekeeper represents the third party as well as the third party would represent himself/herself in a standard two-player ultimatum game[10], (2) strong independence leads to high levels of rejection, indicating that the gatekeeper is willing to punish the proposer, even if it hurts the third party, (3) in the presence of absolute gatekeeper independence, the duty frame[11] seems to cause the gatekeeper play more attention to the proposer's action (Choy et al. 2008: 23).

The Communiqué of SEC requires the audit firms to write down the precautions, in sequence regarding their importance, to be taken in case there are threats toward independence, and their policies related to independence. According to the Communiqué in case there is a reservation about impairment of independence of the audit firm and/or auditors, it is concluded that the independence has already been impaired. Audit firms and auditors have to be impartial and independent from the audit client entity and by no means have a position in decision-making mechanisms of the audited entity. Additionally according to the Independent Audit By-Law, there must not be exceptions that may impair independence of audit firms and auditors. Art. 22 defines some of the circumstances that impair or cause losing the independence (IAbL: Art. 22):

---

[10]**Ultimatum game**: In the standard ultimatum game, a proposer has the right to divide an economic pie with a second party, the responder. The responder, who represents his/her own interests, can either accept, and receive the proposed transfer, or reject, which results in a zero payoff for both parties (Choy et al. 2008: 6).

[11]**Duty frame**: Wherein the auditor is instructed that he/she represents the interests of the investors (Choy et al. 2008: 5).

(a) If the auditors, the partners of the audit firm, key managers, and the auditors, as well as their spouses—including the divorced ones—their relatives—including the third degree ones, both the blood relatives and the affinities by marriage—entered whether directly or indirectly into debt/credit relationships other than ordinary economic relations, or entered relations to take advantage, by becoming partners, or key manager, and having established business relations;
(b) If the audit fee of previous years has not been paid by the audit client with no valid reason;
(c) The audit fee being bound to the conditions related to audit results, or causing uncertainties regarding the audit quality, or the audit fee being determined by the audit firm taking into consideration the other services provided to the audit client entity; and
(d) Emergence of other circumstances impairing independence.

Art. 22 also defines the course of action under circumstances listed above (*ibid.*):

(a) In case circumstances threatening independence emerge, precautions will be taken.
(b) If it is understood that the precautions taken are insufficient, it is concluded that independence is impaired or lost. Audit firms and auditors are obliged to record in writing and store the threats aroused during their audit activities, the precautions taken against these threats, and all the evaluations regarding these matters.
(c) The instances where independence is impaired or lost are to be notified to POA, and following the permission given by this authority, the engagement will be terminated.

It is explained in IAbL which services provided to the audit client will impair independence (*ibid.*):

(a) The audit firm and the auditors shall not provide services like consultancy and any other service except for those described within the Law No. 3568, which are attestation, tax consultancy, and tax audit.
(b) They shall not do these through firms that are in the same network, or associated audit firm and other firms they own.
(c) Any kind of service given by the natural person partners of the audit firm, the auditors of the audit firm, and key managers are also evaluated within this scope.

The survey as the last chapter of this book discusses the findings of the research. Regarding independence as displayed here, the questionnaire of the survey consists questions directed to audit client entities' managers. Their answers to these questions are really thought provoking. The sum of the ratios of audit client entities' managers who gave answers pro opinion that there would not impose a negative impact on audit quality if consultancy, bookkeeping, external audit, and tax consultancy services are provided by the same accounting firm is 32.43%. This is a considerable ratio. The ratio of audit client entities' managers who are opposing the opinion that the audit client entity receiving consultancy, implementation of the accounting system, and the service alike from the audit firm, which provides the external audit service, puts reservations on audit quality is 23.65%. The survey's another question, targeting codes of ethics, presents the opinion stating that the audit firms **not earning** a considerable portion of their revenue from one client or group of companies has positive impacts on audit quality. However, the ratio of audit client entities' managers who are opposing this opinion is 21.63% in total. As long as there will be managers well disposed to receive these services as described, there will also be audit firms to provide them. Such an actuality deserves close monitoring by public authorities. This is essential for the sake of audit quality.

According to DeAngelo, ceteris paribus, the larger the auditor as measured by the number of current clients and the smaller the client as a fraction of the auditor's total quasi-rents, the less incentive the auditor has to behave opportunistically, and the higher the perceived quality of the audit (1981b: 197). This thesis assists us in understanding what a huge impact, resolving audit firms' dependence on revenues earned from clients, will have on independence.

Turkish Code of Commerce (TCC) and IAbL mention other circumstances threatening independence. The situations causing the self-review threat are also separately covered under Code of Ethics for Professional Accountants (CoEPA) in detail. Some outstanding ones are listed below:

- Auditors shall not take a key position in the audit client entities or their affiliated companies unless two years pass following their leave as auditor where they worked as auditor for the last two years (CoEPA, Art. 26[3]).
- Auditors shall not be a member of the engagement team in case they contributed in bookkeeping or financial statement preparation other than auditing of that entity (TCC, Art. 400 [f]).
- In cases where the audit client is a PIE, the audit firm shall not provide any service including information technology system design or implementation if this system provides a considerable part of the internal control directed to financial reporting, or preparation of financial statements the audit firm is about to issue an opinion, or produces important data for the accounting records (CoEPA).
- Assisting an audit client in developing corporate strategies, identifying possible targets for the audit client to acquire, advising on disposal transactions, assisting finance raising transactions, and providing structuring advice may create advocacy and self-review threat s (CoEPA).
- An audit firm shall not provide the following recruiting services to an audit client that is a public interest entity with respect to a director or officer of the entity or senior management in a position to exert significant influence over the preparation of the client's accounting records or the financial statements on which the firm will express an opinion: (1) searching for or seeking out candidates for such positions and (2) undertaking reference checks of prospective candidates for such positions (CoEPA).
- Litigation Support Services and Legal Services (CoEPA).

- An audit firm's personnel shall not assume a management responsibility when providing internal audit services to an audit client (CoEPA).
- Where the taxation services involve acting as an advocate for an audit client before a public tribunal or court in the resolution of a tax matter and the amounts involved are material to the financial statements on which the firm will express an opinion, the advocacy threat created would be so significant that no safeguards could eliminate or reduce the threat to an acceptable level. Therefore, the firm shall not perform this type of service for an audit client (CoEPA).
- A valuation comprises the making of assumptions with regard to future developments, the application of appropriate methodologies and techniques, and the combination of both to compute a certain value, or range of values, for an asset, a liability or for a business as a whole. Performing valuation services for an audit client may create a self-review threat (CoEPA).

3.2.1.2 Transparency

Currently, audit firms disclose certain information many jurisdictions require. Those jurisdictions have also been evaluating if additional disclosures should be required. This may be defined as transparency. Besides, some audit firms voluntarily disclose information. However, some market participants question the value of the current required and voluntary disclosures as anything more than marketing promotion for audit firms. Enhanced transparency of audit firms may increase investor confidence in financial reporting and provide additional information when market participants make decisions. Examples of these decisions are listed below (IOSCO Consultation Report, Sept 2009: 1);

- Investors decisions about whether to invest in companies;
- Ratify the appointments of issuers audit firms;
- Audit committee decisions related to auditor appointments and fulfillment of their oversight responsibilities; and
- Regulators decisions related to investor protection.

Transparency of Audit Quality Indicators

Among indicators of audit quality, which may also be named as behaviors or attributes are competence, industry expertise of audit personnel, firm culture promoting audit quality, firm-wide quality control system, and auditor oversight to be listed (IOSCO Consultation Report, Sept 2009: 3). Along with repeating these indicators, in their comment letter to the Consultation Report of IOSCO, Abma adds independence, transparency, and communication as additional attributes of audit quality (09.12.2009: 1). Financial Reporting Council (FRC) issued a report in February 2008. Table 3.2 quotes the indicators from the report mentioned (www.frc.org.uk, 05.05.2012).

Table 3.2 Audit quality framework—Audit quality indicators

Driver	Indicators
The culture within an audit firm	The culture of an audit firm is likely to provide a positive contribution to audit quality where the leadership of an audit firm: • Creates an environment where achieving high quality is valued, invested in and rewarded • Emphasizes the importance of "doing the right thing" in the public interest and the effect of doing so on the reputation of both the firm and individual auditors • Ensures partners and staff have sufficient time and resources to deal with difficult issues as they arise • Ensures financial considerations do not drive actions and decisions having a negative effect on audit quality • Promotes the merits of consultation on difficult issues and supporting partners in the exercise of their personal judgement • Ensures robust systems for client acceptance and continuation • Fosters appraisal and reward systems for partners and staff that promote the personal characteristics essential to quality auditing • Ensures audit quality is monitored within firms and across international networks and appropriate consequential action is taken
The skills and personal qualities of audit partners and staff	The skills and personal qualities of audit partners and staff are likely to make a positive contribution to audit quality where: • Partners and staff understand their clients' business and adhere to the principles underlying auditing and ethical standards • Partners and staff exhibit professional skepticism in their work and are robust in dealing with issues identified during the audit • Staff performing detailed "on-site" audit work have sufficient experience and are appropriately supervised by partners and managers • Partners and managers provide junior staff with appropriate "mentoring" and "on-the-job" training • Sufficient training is given to audit personnel in audit, accounting, and industry specialist issues
The effectiveness of the audit process	An audit process is likely to provide a positive contribution to audit quality where: • The audit methodology and tools applied to the audit are well structured and: • Encourage partners and managers to be actively involved in audit planning • Provide a framework and procedures to obtain sufficient appropriate audit evidence effectively and efficiently • Require appropriate audit documentation • Provide for compliance with auditing standards without inhibiting the exercise of judgment • Ensure there is effective review of audit work • Audit quality control procedures are effective, understood, and applied

(continued)

Table 3.2 (continued)

Driver	Indicators
	• High-quality technical support is available when the audit team requires it or encounters a situation it is not familiar with • The objectives of ethical standards are achieved, providing confidence in the integrity, objectivity, and independence of the auditor • The collection of sufficient audit evidence is not inappropriately constrained by financial pressures

The reliability and usefulness of audit reporting	Audit reporting is likely to provide a positive contribution to audit quality where:
	• Audit reports are written in a manner that conveys clearly and unambiguously the auditor's opinion on the financial statements and that addresses the needs of users of financial statements in the context of applicable law and regulations
	• Auditors properly conclude as to the truth and fairness of the financial statements
	• Communications with the audit committee include discussions about:
	  • The scope of the audit
	  • The threats to auditor objectivity
	  • The key risks identified and judgments made in reaching the audit opinion
	  • The qualitative aspects of the entity's accounting and reporting and potential ways of improving financial reporting

Factors outside the control of auditors	Factors outside the control of auditors which are likely to make a positive contribution to audit quality include: • An approach to corporate governance within the reporting entity that attaches importance to corporate and financial reporting and to the audit process • Audit committees that are active, professional, and robust in dealing with issues identified during the audit • Shareholders that support auditors, where appropriate, thereby increasing the likelihood that directors and management will comply with their obligations in relation to the preparation of reliable financial statements • Reporting deadlines that allow the opportunity to carry out an audit without undue reliance on work performed before the end of the reporting period • Appropriate agreed arrangements for any limitation of liability • An audit regulatory environment that focuses on the drivers of audit quality

Source The Financial Reporting Council. Promoting Audit Quality. Audit Quality Framework 2008 policies and procedures 3–7. http://www.frc.org.uk/images/uploaded/documents/Audit%20Quality%20Framework%20for%20web1.pdf. Accessed 05 May 2012

Transparency of Audit Firms' Governance

Currently, in certain jurisdictions audit firms have begun or may begin shortly to disclose governance information as a result of legal and regulatory requirements. As mentioned before, some audit firms voluntarily disclose governance information. Academicians like Francis (2011: 140) state that audit firms reporting to public and become transparent about their activities will be beneficial for the public. Examples of legal requirements for transparency of governance are listed below (IOSCO Consultation Report, Sept 2009: 6):

1. European Union's Directive 2006/43/EC of the European Parliament and of the Council, (8th Company Law Directive);
2. The Japanese Amended Certified Public Accountants Act 1948 (Japan CPA Act);
3. The Canadian Public Accountability Board (CPAB) Rule 212;
4. The US Public Company Accounting Oversight Board's (PCAOB) rules on Periodic Reporting by Registered Public Accounting Firms; and
5. The Department of the Treasury Advisory Committee on the Auditing Profession's (U.S. Treasury Advisory Committee) recommendations to expand transparency of audit firms governance.

The Subcommittee on Firm Structure and Finances established by the United States Treasury Department's Advisory Committee on the Auditing Profession (ACAP) recommends to urge the PCAOB and the SEC, in consultation with other federal and state regulators, auditing firms, investors, other financial statement users, and public companies, to analyze, explore, and enable, as appropriate, the possibility and feasibility of firms appointing independent members with full voting power to firm boards and/or advisory boards with meaningful governance responsibilities to improve governance and transparency of auditing firms (United States Treasury, www.treasury.gov, 03.01.2013, ACAP, Final Report, 2008: VII: 8).

Transparency of Audit Firms' Financial Statements

The audited financial statements of firms provide objective information about the financial stability and dignity of the firm. Financial stability and strength are to be regarded as indicators of audit quality. A firm lacking financial strength makes an impression that the firm is under risk, deprived of sources and understanding that would provide audit quality. In UK, as per legislation non-Big Four audit firms audit Big Four (Brown 15.01.2010: 5). The mentioned implementation contributing to enhancement of transparency of financial statements of audit firms is an expected situation. According to POA CoEPA, audit firms in Turkey shall prepare transparency report and announce it. The audit firms having performed an audit of PIEs within three months shall prepare and on its Web site publish a transparency report signed by the managing body chair. The report should contain the following elements about the audit organization:

- Legal structure and explanation about the partners;
- Explanation on key managers and in-charge auditors;
- Explanation on legal structure and organizational properties of the network the audit firm is a member of;
- Disclosures to associated audit firms and affiliated firms, explanation on the nature of these relationships;
- Explanation on organizational structure;
- The information on most recent inspection date of quality assurance system;
- The list of PIEs audited previous year;
- Explanations on continuing auditor education policies;
- Independence practices and confirmation of independence compliance review;
- Financial information showing the weight of financial table audit fees, distribution of revenue as financial table audit fees, other audits, and non-audit services;
- Partner remuneration policies;
- Description of the auditing firm's quality control system and a statement by firm management on its effectiveness; and
- Other information as required by POA.

The audit firms that did not actually perform an audit of a PIE within a calendar year, though taking place in PIE related lists, disclose this situation in their Web sites on pages related to transparency reports. In case there is an update regarding the transparency report, then both the original and the updated versions shall be available for public access for five years. Even though it is foreseen in IAbL, during the research period, it is observed that in the absence of sanctions, the audit firms do not make necessary disclosures. While there are audit firms publishing their transparency reports easily accessible, there seen transparency reports almost hidden under unexpected menu tabs, such that announcements tab and contact information tab are observed to be used. In some cases it was impossible to find the transparency reports in the audit firm's Web site, and could be discovered when search engines are searched for by matching with the name of the audit firm. Some transparency reports do not have a downloadable file type. The content of the transparency reports are published as embedded in the Web site. Besides, since the details of the transparency reports are not openly stated in the IAbL, there is no standardization of transparency reports. Currently, POA demands the transparency reports by describing the content; however, there seems lack of effective oversight about this matter. As per today, let the errors of facts aside of several transparency reports, two out of Big Four does not even have the transparency reports of year 2017 on their Web sites (www.kgk.gov.tr, 29.01.2018).

3.2.1.3 Other Factors Influencing Audit Quality

As seen from above discussions, transparency and independence are at utmost importance; however, this does not mean that there are no other factors influencing audit quality. In this part, these factors will briefly be handled both in individual and integrated ways.

Network Design

In 2006, the top fifteen auditing networks by revenue, generated over a total of $100.4 billion in revenue (Final Report 2008: V: 10). Network design, as an attribute of the audit quality, is mentioned by several circles, as well as handled in the International Organization of Securities Commissions' Consultation Report. According to the report, a design of network firms may promote the consistency in audits conducted by members of network (Sept 2009: 9). The development of networks grew out of a need to comply with country-specific regulations, which then and now generally mandate that auditing firms be controlled and owned by locally licensed professionals (Final Report 2008: V: 10).

Local Office/Partner

As quoted by Skinner and Srinivasan (2011: 2), local offices are considered as relevant units of analysis for client dependence, industry expertise, and audit quality. Local offices are expected to build a bridge between culture of the hosting country and investing firm. As stated in the Final Report of ACAP, to effectively operate in foreign jurisdictions, auditing firms understood the need to employ individuals familiar with the accounting, legal, cultural, linguistic, and business practices of each relevant jurisdiction (Final Report 2008: V: 10). According to Banker et al., a senior partner in a Big Five firm explained that being in the same city with a client and knowing the client's business more intimately is a quality consideration that reduces exposure to litigation. The authors claim that this may help reduce insurance cost of litigation and may compensate for the lower revenue generation (2003: 281). In a report dated June 2, 2011, the research firm named Muddy Waters LLC, which triggered the Sino-Forest Corporation fraud case, one of the multinational corruption cases of recent years, pointed out two important points for auditors. According to the report, auditors are far less effective in detecting fraud than most investors assume they are. The report states the problem as "fraudsters are willing to forge documents." Another issue with auditors detecting fraud is that when the auditors are based in Canada, and the fraud is in China, the auditors are far less versed in the games fraudsters can play in China (Block 2011: 2).

Nicholas Fraser[12] (2010) emphasizes the importance of the local partner as follows. Transnationality Index assists to grasp the extent of globalization for transnational companies. The Index is calculated as the average of the following three ratios at transnational corporations:

[12]**Nicholas Fraser**: Chair (2011) of the Transnational Auditors' Committee of the International Federation of Accountants (IFAC).

$$1 = \frac{\text{Foreign Assets}}{\text{Total Assets}} \quad 2 = \frac{\text{Foreign Sales}}{\text{Total Sales}} \quad 3 = \frac{\text{Foreign Employment}}{\text{Total Employment}}$$

$$\textbf{Average} = \frac{(1+2+3)}{3}$$

This average in 2008 for the top 100 global non-financial transnational corporations was 62.4% and for 21 of the top 100 that ratio exceeded 80%. According to Fraser, the audit of a company where 80% or more of the assets, sales, and employees are overseas compared to the umbrella entity is obviously not going to be conducted in the same way as a predominantly domestic company. Thus, there is going to need to be heavy reliance on the work of other auditors in those overseas locations. For the top 14 transnational corporations, majority-owned affiliates in overseas host economies range from 62 countries to 111 countries in 2007, and for top 100 the average is 41 countries. Fraser summarizes this issue; today's auditor has no choice but to take a global view in order to issue an opinion on a transnational corporation. The ability for the entire audit team—wherever they are located—to be able to follow the same standards facilitates communications within the team, helps ensure a uniform level of quality, and removes a source of confusion and hence potential non-compliance (2010: 300).

Quality Control System

One of the most influential factors on audit quality is the quality control systems of audit firms. Audit firms have legal and professional requirements to maintain quality control systems. Quality control systems are intended to provide reasonable assurance that the audit firm and its personnel comply with professional, regulatory, and legal requirements and that reports issued by the audit firm or engagement partners are appropriate in the circumstances (IOSCO Consultation Report, Sept 2009: 10, 11).

Human Resource Policies and Procedures

Human resource policies and methods that attach importance to high-quality audit performance and which give priority to the evaluation, compensation, training, and retirement of partners and employees also positively affect audit quality. The aim here is to create incentives for behaviors that lead to improved audit quality.

Ethic Policies and Implementations

As the above-mentioned factors, ethics-related policies and implementations also give clue to decision makers how an audit firm manages audit quality. How audit firms implement and monitor these policies and procedures needs transparency. Even though independence is already discussed previously, it is to be kept in mind that ethics policies and implementations are an integral part of independence. Therefore, disclosures about these need to cover descriptions of these policies and procedures, resources the audit firm allocates for these, how the firm monitors the compliance and disciplinary actions for violations of these policies.

Public Oversight

Fédération des Experts comptables Européens (FEE) (European Federation of Accountants) states in its comment letter to International Organization of Securities Commissions' (IOSCO) Consultation Report that public oversight contributes to enhancing audit quality (Damme 13.01.2010: 2). Subcommittee on Firm Structure and Finances established by United States Treasury Department's Advisory Committee on the Auditing Profession (ACAP) recommends encouraging greater regulatory cooperation and oversight of the public company auditing profession to improve the quality of the audit process and enhance confidence in the auditing profession and financial reporting. Additionally, the Committee stated that regular and formal roundtable meetings of regulators and other governmental enforcement bodies in a cooperative effort to improve regulatory effectiveness and reducing the incidence of duplicative and potentially inconsistent enforcement regimes are prerequisites (Final Report 2008: VII: 3, 6).

Rotation Enforcement

Legislation and implementation regarding rotation are not new in Turkey. The Communiqué decrees that the engagement partner is allowed at a maximum of seven account periods to become part of an audit team in an engagement with a specific client. TCC Article 400 organizes rotation of auditor: (1) Rotation periods shall be calculated over a period of ten years, (2) a retrospective period of ten years shall be considered for each year, and (3) for a total of seven years having undertaken the same audit client engagements, there will be a break of three years. According to EU Commission Statement, PIEs will be required to change their statutory auditors after a maximum engagement period of ten years. Member States can choose to extend the ten-year period up to ten additional years if tenders are carried out, and by up to 14 additional years in case of joint audit, i.e., if the audited company appoints more than one audit firm to carry out its audit. Calibrated transitional periods taking into account the duration of the audit engagement are also foreseen to avoid a cliff effect once the new rules apply (http://europa.eu, 04.02.2015). PIEs will be required to issue a call for tenders when selecting a new auditor, whereby an auditor may inspect a company's books for up to ten years, which may be increased by ten additional years if new tenders are issued (www.europarl.europa.eu, 11.05.2015). As summarized by Soo Young, Youngdeok, and Simnett, advocates of mandatory audit firm rotation argue that auditor independence may be enhanced by increased professional skepticism that comes with fresh eyes. Opponents of this policy argue that incoming auditors may lack industry expertise and detailed knowledge of the client's particular situation, which may result in higher fees for initial engagements and a greater incidence of problem audits in the early years of a new engagement (Soo et al. 2014: 168). In their research Cameran, Prencipe, and Trombetta analyzed lots of academic studies, and found that prior studies mainly focused on how auditor tenure impacts audit quality where audit quality is measured in different ways. The results are mixed. Cameran et al. opens a window for us to learn about Italian legislation. Once appointed, the auditor is retained for the maximum engagement period, i.e., nine years in Italy (2013:7, 11).

According to the survey results of the study given in detail in Chapter 4, 90.32% of auditors, 83.33% of managers of audit firms, and 92.62% of audit client entities' managers believe that practicing rotation has a substantial and positive effect on audit quality.

Restatement of Financial Statements

Fédération des Experts comptables Européens (FEE) reminds in its comment letter to IOSCO Consultation Report that the legislation in various jurisdictions restricts the ability to restate financial statements. Therefore, the number of restatements would not be a relevant indicator of audit quality that contributes to increased transparency about audit quality (Damme 13.01.2010: 9).

The Board of Directors of Audit Client and the Audit Committee

Audit client's board of directors and the audit committee may place a role on the audit quality. The effects of governance on audit quality are examined by Klein (2002); Carcello and Neal (2000, 2003); DeFond et al. (2005); Hoitash and Hoitash (2009); Hoitash et al. (2009) (quoted by Francis 2011: 141). The findings of this literature generally support that companies, the boards of which are seated by more independent directors, and audit committees with accounting and financial expertise hire better quality auditors and are less likely to dismiss auditors following going-concern audit reports (ibid.). Various enforced regulations have focused on enhancing the functions of ineffective executive boards and token audit committees.

Effectiveness of Internal Control System

An effective internal control system is essential for transactions to be recorded timely and correctly, for assets to be protected, and ultimately for a reliable reporting. Then, it would not be wrong to state that the effectiveness of the internal control has impact on audit quality. Since it is for the shareholders interest, companies should invest in internal control in a strong way.

The Structure of the Audit Industry

Along with the attributes listed above, the structure of the audit industry is to be mentioned, too. The accounting firms compose the industry. The structure of the industry is influential upon economic behavior. As quoted by Banker et al. (2003: 256), researchers like Simunic (1980) have argued that the market for the services of CPA firms is competitive. However, since the 1980s lots of things have changed in audit market. When it comes to public companies, the audit market is under hegemony of Big Four. This fact is also stated in the 2007 Oxera Report. The market structure evolving process is also summarized in Fig. 2.1. Such an industry structure is to be called oligopoly. The oligopoly market is a market structure in which there is a lack of competition. In the oligopoly markets, the firms hold each other and negotiate between issues such as supply, price, conditions, and quality. The parties that will suffer in a market, where competition is absent, are primarily the customers and secondly the other stakeholders. In his above-mentioned comment letter to IOSCO Consultation Report, Robert Conway (Conway 25.11.2009: 11) in a very accurate way adds new attributes that impact audit quality according to his experience and observations. He created a pyramid to explain all, where in addition to inputs and outputs of an audit, there are external pressures as well (Fig. 3.10).

Conway's Audit Quality Pyramid has three fundamental levels. Basic inputs, skills and tools, and fortitude are three levels. Much like a real pyramid, each level builds on the foundation of the lower levels. The basic inputs are fundamental to a team of people. In the audit context, basic inputs are: (1) appropriate supervision and review, (2) reasonable partner workloads, (3) reasonable staff workloads, (4) suitably experienced professionals, (5) good audit team continuity, and (6) ongoing continuing education.

Skills and tools, which are the next level up on the Audit Quality Pyramid, are needed to identify auditing and accounting issues and formulate the appropriate corrective action. The skills and tools are: (1) professional skepticism, (2) technical competence, (3) industry expertise, (4) compliance with a sound audit methodology, (5) an environment conducive to seeking consultation, and (6) a vibrant risk management and technical resource function that is independent of audit operations.

The basic inputs, and skills and tools enable the auditor to identify the issues; however, the harder part of the job is meeting the requisites of the fortitude. The fortitude here means resisting to external pressures. As defined by Conway, these are pressures exerted on the walls of the Audit Quality Pyramid and include: (i) retention of the client, (ii) collection of fees, (iii) achieving engagement profit goals, (iv) tight deadlines, and (v) increasing complexity. In order to counter these pressures, various elements are required. These are: (1) a *get it right tone* at the top

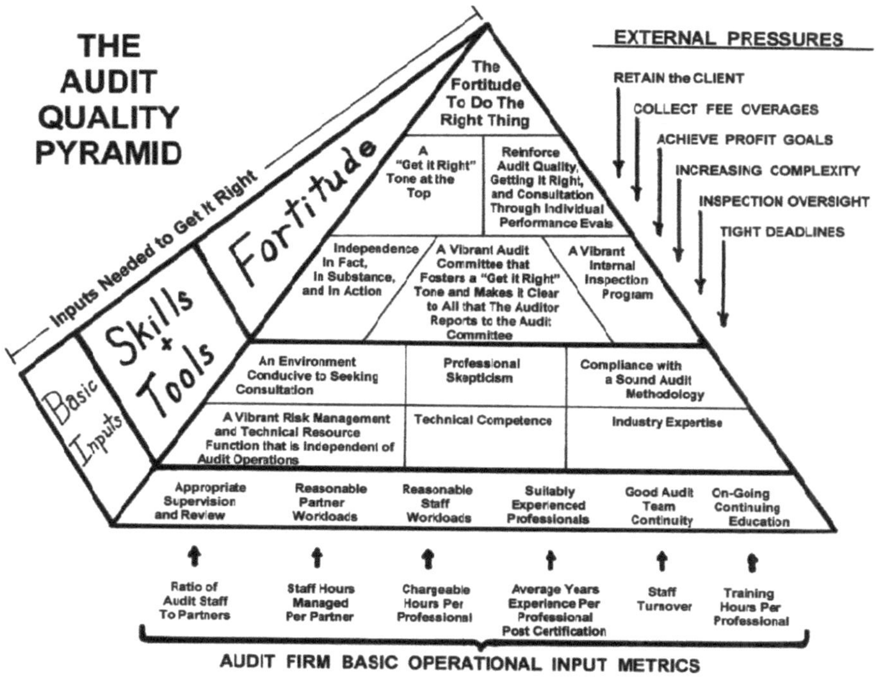

Fig. 3.10 Audit quality pyramid. *Source:* Conway, R. (25.11.2009). *IOSCO Consultation Report Comment Letter*, p. 11. http://www.iosco.org/library/pubdocs/pdf/IOSCOPD339.pdf. Accessed 05 May 2012

of audit firm, (2) a vibrant audit committee that fosters a *get it right tone* and makes it clear to all, that the auditor reports first and foremost to the audit committee, (3) independent in fact, in substance, and in action, (4) a vibrant internal inspection program, and (5) a performance evaluation and compensation process that reinforces audit quality and *getting it right* (Conway 25.11.2009: 28).

Auditor Overconfidence

Along with the above-mentioned attributes, auditor overconfidence is also to be considered in assessing the audit quality. Hunton et al. (2004: 8) examine the risk assessments of 82 information technologies (IT) audit specialists and 83 financial auditors with regard to an experimental case where a client operates either an Enterprise Resource Planning (ERP) or a non-ERP computer system. After reading the cases, participants assessed the following risk categories: (1) business interruption, (2) process interdependency, (3) network security, (4) database security, (5) application security, and (6) overall internal control. In all case scenarios, control weakness is kept same. IT audit specialists assess significantly higher risk across all categories in the ERP, as compared to non-ERP, system condition. The same risks are not identified by financial auditors. Besides, financial auditors did not indicate a greater need to consult with IT specialists in the ERP system environments. Further, they are equally highly confident in the ability of financial audit teams to assess risks in both computing environments. So, Hunton et al. concluded that financial auditors are overconfident in their ability to assess IT-related risks in an ERP computing environment. Even though this study is a specific one, there is always the risk of an auditor to be overconfident; therefore, this is to be considered as an audit quality-impacting factor.

Peer Review

Peer review is also known as practice-monitoring. As Arens et al. (2012) state, CPA firms must be enrolled in an AICPA approve practice-monitoring program for members in the firm to be eligible for membership in the AICPA. Peer review is the review by CPAs, of a CPA firm's compliance with its quality control system. The reviewer determines and reports whether the CPA firm being reviewed has developed adequate quality control policies and procedures and follows them in practice. Arens et al. share the opinion that although there have been several recent high-profile cases involving apparent audit failures, the existing legal exposure of CPAs, peer review requirements, and the potential for interference by the SEC and government have kept audit quality high (*ibid.*). This is an argument that needs further research.

Audit Fee Versus Other Income

The works constituting the revenues of the independent audit firms and their share in the total revenue have an impact on the audit quality. The audit service in general comprises financial statement audit and reporting, statutory audits, and IFRS reporting. Taxes, returns and offsetting services, corporate tax consulting and tax consulting services of real persons are included in tax audit and consultancy. Consultancy services, also known as outsourcing, include audit of accounting and control of declarations, accounting consultancy, and incentive services. Consultancy services for foreign and domestic investors, tax legal counseling, and financial legal counseling can be evaluated within the scope of corporate finance counseling. Management consulting services provided by many audit firms also include strategic planning, corporate performance management, and customer strategies. Access to net revenues of audit firms through public platforms does not seem to be possible at present. However, a close look is to be thrown on the progress of income for years with the help of PCOAB board member Harris' statement. Auditing firms are deriving an increasing share of their revenue from consulting services. Consulting revenue for the Big Four global network firms has increased over the past five years by 33% versus only 6% in audit revenue. Further, each of the Big Four firms is predicting double-digit increases in their consulting and advisory practices over the next ten years, while their audit practices are expected to grow at a slower pace (Harris 20.03.2014). Harris has concerns about the audit quality and points a more careful monitoring, because he believes these diversified lines of activity impact audit quality, auditor independence, conflict of interest, and investor protection.

Audit Client Related Indicators

A number of factors play a determining role in the quality of the audit carried out, including partners, management, employees, other resources they have, the way they work, and the organizational structure, etc. As understood, the number of factors originating from the customer is quite large. In fact, Fig. 3.11 shows the symbiotic relation of the audit firm, the auditor, and the audit client during an audit process. The auditor falling in between his/her firm and the client is illustrated. The proximity of the auditor and the audit client paves the way to many audit quality-damaging relations/incidents.

In the paper "Learning by Doing and Audit Quality," Beck and Wu present a nonstrategic, dynamic Bayesian model in which auditors' learning on the job and their choice of professional services jointly affect audit quality. They admit that the auditor accumulates knowledge by performing NAS, and also claim that the advisory effect of NAS may increase/decrease auditors' engagement risk. By performing NAS, auditors influence their clients' managerial decisions and hence alter their clients' earnings dynamics over time. They explain how the scope of audit has evolved over time and why the boundaries between audit and NAS are constantly shifting. The learning effect and the advisory effect are interdependent and mutually reinforcing (Beck and Wu 2006: 4). According to DeFond et al., the ban on NAS under SOX may impair audit quality by eliminating the knowledge spillovers that auditors potentially derive from doing both audit and consulting work (2011: 466). At the very specific point, we have to recall the times, when audit firms were

Fig. 3.11 Audit firm, auditor, client relationship in the audit service process

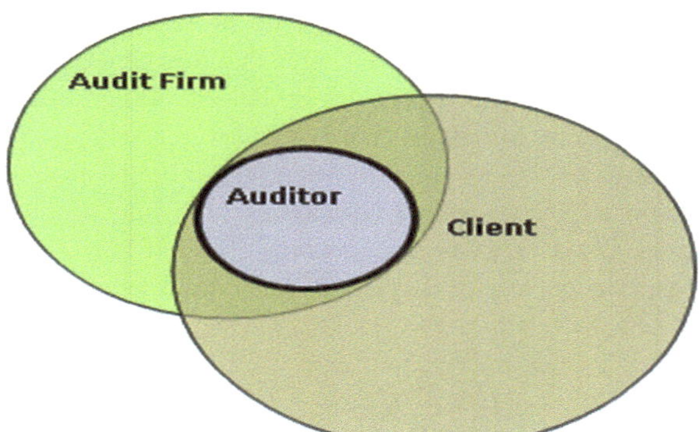

advising their audit client without any restriction. Table 1.3 reminds the tragic denouement of this aspiration. If it had been a perfect practice, the public would not have witnessed all those accounting scandals.

In their paper, Skinner and Srinivasan touch on the forces that motivate the auditors to deliver quality. Under the first motive, if auditors are legally liable for audit failures, they have an incentive to deliver quality to avoid the adverse consequences of litigation. Under the second motive, auditors have reputational incentives to avoid audit failures because audit quality is valuable to clients and so priced in the market for audit services. Under this view, clients defect to other auditors when an audit firm's reputation for quality is called into question. As they summarize, one line of research examines auditor switching around events that signal a decline in an audit firms' quality. A second line of research examines the stock price reaction to events that change market perceptions of audit quality for a given audit firm (2011: 9, 10). Following this introductory literature, the authors conducted their research in Japan, where litigation against auditors is virtually non-existent, meaning that there is effectively no insurance role in Japanese setting. The research started with 2199 firms listed in Tokyo Stock Exchange in 2008 and firms' auditors are identified. Throughout the research, the number of firms fluctuated. The sample is assessed from several aspects being the auditor turnover the basis. They find evidence that a relatively large number of ChuoAoyama's clients left the firm for other auditors as the seriousness of ChuoAoyama's quality problems became evident and after Japanese regulators announced the two-month suspension and PwC formed a new firm. The reputation argument matters more for larger, more prominent firms in Japan. Whenever reputation starts being questioned, audit clients start replacing their audit firms (2011: 30).

The fact of independent auditing at high quality being an indispensable element for well-functioning capital markets is a sufficient motive for auditors to deliver and maintain audit quality. Even if it is not fully valid for Japan, in many developed countries, auditors are likely to encounter litigious cases opened by various stakeholders. The possibility of a lawsuit and consequently the obligation to have occupational insurance constitute a strong justification for maintaining the quality of the audit. At the International Organization of Securities Commissions (IOSCO) roundtable in Paris on July 1, 2007, during the second panel, panelist Gérard De La Martiniere[13] states that there is no professional liability, which cannot be covered by an insurance scheme. He adds that it is generally a question of cost, not capacity; imposing artificial limitations on liability would make the risk analysis, and thereby the insurance coverage, more complex. According to him, increased transparency of audit firms would certainly facilitate external insurance coverage. The high prices proposed by insurance companies take into account the insufficient information level (IOSCO www.iasplus.com, 19.09.2012). The motives behind the auditor's desire to deliver quality audit are figured below (Fig. 3.12).

---

[13]**Gérard De La Martiniere**: Chairman, French Federation of Insurance Companies

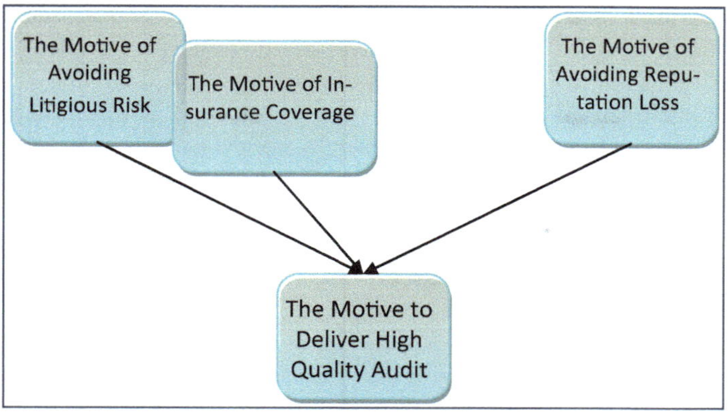

Fig. 3.12 Motives of the auditor to emphasize quality. *Source* Skinner, D. J., Srinivasan, S., (1 July 2011). "Audit Quality and Auditor Reputation: Evidence from Japan". *Chicago Booth Research Paper,* No. 10–15; *Harvard Business School Accounting & Management Unit Working Paper* No. 10–088. Figured from http://ssrn.com/abstract=1557231. Accessed 13 Oct 2011

When audit quality starts being questioned, audit client altering their audit firms is considered necessary for the sake of their own reputation. However, such a situation may mean additional problems and cost to be undertaken. Time lost by the new audit firm in learning client-specific information and developing expertise is to be considered as well. Besides, there will be costs to be undertaken by the successor. These costs are figured below (Fig. 3.13).

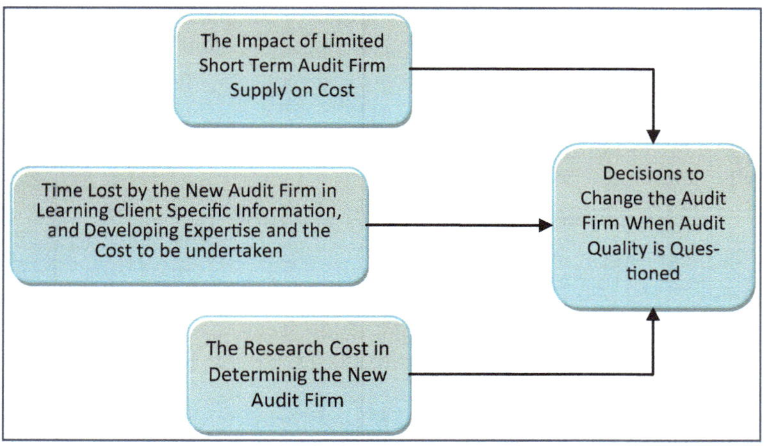

Fig. 3.13 Costs the audit clients face while changing their audit firms. *Source* Skinner, D. J., Srinivasan, S., (1 July 2011). "Audit Quality and Auditor Reputation: Evidence from Japan". *Chicago Booth Research Paper,* No. 10–15; *Harvard Business School Accounting & Management Unit Working Paper* No. 10–088. Figured from p. 2 http://ssrn.com/abstract=1557231. Accessed 13 Oct 2011

When we think that auditing is a service provided by professionals, we can identify a number of features that can affect the quality of audit (Knechel et al.): (1) An audit is an economically motivated response to risk, i.e., *incentives* matter, and (2) the output of an audit is a report but the *outcome* is uncertain and unobservable. While audit quality might be generally believed to be high or low, it is not possible to "know" the residual risk of an engagement (achieved assurance level), i.e., *uncertainty* matters, (3) each engagement is different. The idiosyncratic nature of an audit arises due to variations in client characteristics, audit teams, timing of work, and assessed risk and procedures used, i.e., *uniqueness* matters; (4) the audit is a systematic activity, i.e., *process* matters; (5) the execution of the audit process depends on appropriately leveraging the knowledge and skills of experts, i.e., *professional judgment* matters (2013: 386). In order to increase the audit quality, which is highly subjective and therefore difficult to measure, various institutions open up some proposed debate. When PCAOB considered whether to impose requiring the engagement partner to sign the audit report in addition to, not in place of, the existing requirement for the firm to sign the audit report, believing this could improve audit quality, 30 members of the Standard Advisory Group (SAG) that is composed of auditors, investors, public companies, and the like, in general, supported the proposal and stated that this would enhance audit quality (PCAOB Release No. 2009-005. July 28, 2009, 11.05.2015). In an attempt to identify who would benefit from—and who would pay for—identification of audit engagement partners, Bailey et al. composed an article. They summarized the commentary of responders on this Concept Release, compared these to the requirement under Section 407 of SOX, that companies identify a member of their audit committees a financial expert, examined arguments for and against identifying the audit engagement partner, and summarized the likely impact of adopting the Concept Release. The conclusion states that it is unlikely that audit partner identification would enhance audit quality, and the cost of additional audit and/or quality control procedures associated with implementation will likely be borne by companies and their shareholders (2010: 340).

3.2.2 Auditors' Influence on Audit Quality

The influence of auditors on audit quality has been handled before from several aspects, e.g., under the title 3.1.3.1. The Audit Team and Its Impacts on Audit Quality, the qualifications the auditors have to possess are listed. Here, some other issues will be covered.

Word origin and history for auditor are as follows: in early fourteenth century, "official who receives and examines accounts;" late fourteenth century, "a listener," from Anglo-French *auditour*—Old French *oieor* "listener, court clerk," in thirteenth century; Modern French *auditeur*—, from Latin *auditor* "a hearer," from *auditus*, past participle of *audire* "to hear." Meaning "receiver and examiner of accounts" is because this process formerly was done, and vouched for, orally

(Dictionary.com, 29.06.2015). Another definitions says, an auditor is an official whose job it is to carefully check the accuracy of business records (Investopedia.com, 29.06.2015). According to PCAOB standard, the term "auditor" is intended to include both registered public accounting firms and associated persons (http://pcaobus.org/, AU1, 16.01.2015). In Turkey Art. 4 of IAbL defines the independent auditor as persons authorized by POA to carry out audits, persons who are members of the profession and earned their licenses as Certified Public Accountants or Sworn-in Certified Public Accountants pursuant to the law dated 1/6/1989 and Numbered 3568 on Certified Public Accountancy and Sworn-in Certified Public Accountancy. The work of the auditor is writing the audit report following the completion of the audit, which sets the levels of accuracy and clarity that are under the responsibility of the auditee (e-conomic.com, 29.06.2015).

As stated by Hayes et al., considerable expertise is needed to perform the auditing function. The auditor must be as competent in financial accounting as the most competent of his/her clients. He/she must be an expert in deciding what evidence is necessary to satisfy the assertions of the financial statements. The new auditing environment will demand new skills of auditors if they are to be reporters and assessors of governance and measurements (2005: 4).

The fundamental principles auditors shall comply with are (1) integrity, (2) objectivity, (3) professional competence and due care, (4) confidentiality, and (5) professional behavior. These are among the contents of the Handbook of the Code of Ethics for Professional Accountants. Breach of any of these rules would negatively impact the audit quality. As seen from Fig. 3.8 showing the multiple drivers of audit quality, one of the audit inputs—perhaps the most important—is the auditors. The main determiner of the quality of an audit conducted is employing highly qualified persons. At the International Organization of Securities Commissions (IOSCO) roundtable in Paris on July 1, 2007, panelist Jeremy Jennings[14] stated that there is no problem to attracting talented persons in the accounting profession, but it has become increasingly difficult convince them to work as audit partners. The European Contact Group[15] commissioned a research in 2005, which surveyed 1500 of the group's people across the EU, where 78% of partners and directors surveyed noted that they find the auditing career today less enjoyable and rewarding than they did two years prior to that. Clearly, the liability regime is responsible for some of the concerns audit people have (Jennings 2007: 19).

Another study collected data via a questionnaire from 113 auditors in order to find out factors influencing audit quality. Professional competency, level of education, experience, independence, professionalism, ethical understanding, and problem-solving ability of the auditor highly impact audit quality. It is found out

[14]**Jeremy Jennings**: Ernst & Young European Contact Group Chair

[15]**European Contact Group**: comprises the largest six audit networks—BDO, EY, Grant Thornton, Deloitte, KPMG, and PwC. Primary areas of focus are on public policy matters relating to the EU capital markets.

that the audit quality perceived, legal liability, professional care and due diligence, the audit being performed in a sector where auditor has knowledge are also highly impacting audit quality. Besides, being risk taker or not, working on small samples during auditing, age and gender of the auditor, and the wage expectations are not influencing audit quality as much as expected (Özyurt 2010: 79–80).

The opinions of the auditors, managers of audit firms, and audit client entities' managers about auditor qualifications are discussed in the survey part of this book. These three group members who took part in the survey found—auditor independence, integrity, professionalism, ethical understanding, level of education, experience, professional care and due diligence while auditing, competencies at satisfactory levels, having knowledge about the audit client's entity, conducting audits in sector where the auditor gained expertise—as factors having considerable impacts on audit quality. Neither of these groups found the age, and gender of the auditor, nor did they find auditor's declaration of property to professional chambers regularly as significant factors.

3.2.3 The Influence of Audit Firms on Audit Quality

Formerly, the influence of audit firms on audit quality is discussed from many aspects. Here, their management structures, competition, new client acquisition, leverage, workload, training/education, sustainability, corporate culture, and other factors are covered.

The management structures adopted and applied by audit firms may impact audit quality from several aspects. Therefore, while handling management structures adopted, the facts to take into considerations as defined by EU report are to be as follows (www.ec.europa.eu, 12.03.2012, Oxera Report 2007: 13, 87):

- Existing market structure;
- Existing rules and binding constraints;
- Impact of ownership and management structures on concentration in the audit market;
- Impact of ownership and management structures on entry barriers;
- Impact of ownership and management structures on access to capital;
- Limited availability of liquid assets for the collateral for debt financing; and
- Liability risk involved in large audits.

As mentioned before, audit firms ownership structures in Europe are as employee ownership of senior managers. One of the important benefits of this ownership structure is human capital. Employee ownership creates more economically efficient levels and forms of remuneration for the key employees. As it provides mechanisms for retaining human capital, it also creates incentives for senior employees to mentor junior employees and develops tacit skills that represent an important component of the audit service (www.ec.europa.eu, 12.03.2012, Oxera Report 2007: 87).

Human resource management, handled in various parts of the book, is a sensitive phenomenon that is often overlooked. The relationships with audit clients may sometimes cause stress on the auditors. The reports the audit firms prepare about themselves do not give a hint about how much importance they give on human resource management. One of the suggestions this book is about to urge the audit firms to report in a transparent way about their human capital. Another audit quality-impacting issue regarding the audit firms is adherence to audit engagements. Prolonged audit firm–audit client relations, negligence in adhering the audit engagements, and even acting as if there is no such an engagement, all may harm the quality of audits. Besides, time to time the comradeship between the auditor and the audit client entity causes audit firms getting into trouble with their clients. One of the excellent examples of such a coziness is the palsy-walsy relation of Enron–Arthur Andersen. The consequence of such a breach of friendliness threshold is the auditor loosing his/her objectivity and impartiality.

3.2.3.1 New Client Acquisition and Competition

In USA, many CPA firms developed sophisticated advertisements for the national periodicals and newspapers read by businessmen. Making formal and informal presentations in order to convince the management to alter their CPA firms or to determine potential clients already been served by other CPA firms are common for CPA firms. Bidding for audit and other services is widespread and rather competitive. As a result of these changes compared to past, some companies frequently change their auditors in order to cut costs (Arens et al. 2012: 98). However, according to DeAngelo, clients will change auditors only if they perceive that the present value of incumbent's fees exceeds the present value of a new auditor's fees plus the transaction cost of changing auditors (1981a: 120). The expectation of client-specific quasi-rents to incumbent auditors has two effects. First, it implies that the optimal level of auditor independence is less than perfect independence. In fact, client-specific quasi-rents to incumbency are a necessary condition for lessened independence. Second, competition for the property rights to incumbency forces auditors to "low ball" in the initial period (*ibid.*, 126).

3.2.3.2 Leverage, Workload, and Education/Training

While considering the audit quality indicators, the inputs and outputs summarized in Fig. 3.14 are also worth to take a look. The leverage among inputs is an indicator, about which an idea is to be formed by analyzing the ratio of the time spent by a senior auditor within the audit team on an audit and/or the status of the comparative contribution of more experienced members that take part in an audit team (PCAOB 2013; Deltas and Doogar 2004; Doogar and Easley 1998; Kinney 1986). The fact that the service rendered to the audit client being generated by few numbers of partners and by many less-experienced auditors relative to the number of partners is defined as high leverage; the opposite is low leverage. Regarding audit quality what is desired is the low leverage. As mentioned before, audit firms

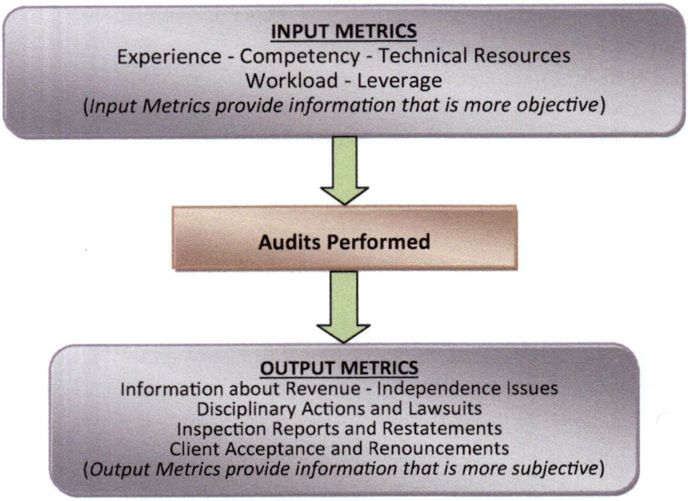

Fig. 3.14 Input and output metrics for audit quality indicators. *Source* International Organization of Securities Commissions—IOSCO (2009). Technical Committee. Transparency of Firms that Audit Public Companies: Consultation Report. Figured from pp. 14–17. http://www.iosco.org/library/pubdocs/pdf/IOSCOPD302.pdf. Accessed 05 May 2012

working with low leverages would have positive impacts on audit quality (Conway 25.11.2009: 11). IOSCO Consulting Report also uses a tone confirming Conway and states avoidance of high leverage would contribute to improving audit quality. According to Rosenberg National MAP Survey conveyed among 425 American CPA firms in 2010, the 54 top firms had a leverage ratio of 7.7 to one, compared to 4.9 to one for all firms in the survey (https://rosenbergassoc.com/; www.adamsonadvisory.com, 31.01.2015).

Under the heading Audit Staff: Numbers, Distribution and Leverage, the leverages of audit firms operating in Turkey are given. According to this, in 2012 Big Four's leverage is 12.41, while the leverage of remaining 90 audit firms' is 3.25, where grand average is 4.86. Moreover under the title 3.1.3.1. The Audit Team and Its Impacts on Audit Quality, leverage is discussed within the survey conducted for this research. Just to remind, the rate of audit client entity's managers believing that audit teams composed of too many audit staff assistants negatively impact the audit quality is 44.64%.

An anonymous CPA with 29 years of experience, and retired Big Four partner in the letter sent to United States Treasury Department's Advisory Committee on the Auditing Profession (ACAP), as personal views states that some of the audit failures originate from excessive workloads, high turnover, and inexperience. According to the anonymous CPA's view, large audit firms do not convey accurate and complete information about themselves. Even though audit quality is not easily measured, there are six drivers of audit quality that can be measured readily and publicly reported by each audit firm annually comparative with the previous year (United States Treasury, 19.09.2012). Among descriptions, the term full-time equivalent (FTE) is mentioned. FTE is a unit to measure employed persons in a way that makes them comparable although they may work a different number of hours per week. The unit is obtained by comparing an employee's average number of hours worked to the average number of hours of a full-time worker. A full-time person is therefore counted as one FTE, while a part-time worker gets a score in proportion to the hours he or she works. For example, a part-time worker employed for 20 h a week where full-time work consists of 40 h is counted as 0.5 FTE (http://ec.europa.eu, 12.06.2015). The six audit quality drivers and a brief description of their importance are quoted below (United States Treasury 19.09.2012):

(1) ***The average years of experience of audit professionals***. Years of experience subsequent to the employee becoming licensed as a CPA are to be counted. This will draw attention to the fact that much of the audit field work in USA is conducted by employees who have not yet become CPAs.

(2) ***Ratio of professional staff to audit partners***. A reasonable ratio will be a good lead in improving the audit quality. FTE[16] will be used in calculations.

$$\textbf{\textit{Leverage}} = \frac{\text{number of audit professionals}}{\text{number of audit partners}}$$

(3) ***Chargeable hours per audit professional***. FTE will be used in calculations. As the workload increases, details will not get the attention they deserve; thus, audit quality will be harmed.

(4) ***Professional chargeable hours managed per audit partner***. FTE will be used in calculations. When the audit partner workloads become excessive, the assurance they would provide for the audit quality will diminish.

(5) ***Annual professional staff retention***. Retention rate is related to staff turnover rate, and staff turnover rate is bound to the rate of working with experienced. There will be positive impacts on audit quality if the result of the formula below is high. However, in case turnover is high, (1) continuity of audit team will get lower from year to year, and (2) experience levels will reduce.

$$\textbf{\textit{Rate}} = \frac{\text{number of audit professionals employed a year ago that are still employed}}{\text{number of audit professionals employed a year ago}}$$

(6) ***Average annual training hours per audit professional***. When workloads become excessive, audit professionals tend to cancel scheduled training because completing existing assignments is seen as a higher priority. This might seem like the right thing to do in the short run, but insufficient training undermines audit quality over the longer term.

---

[16]**Full-time equivalent**: The ratio of the total number of paid hours during a period—part time, full time, contracted—by the number of working hours in that period Mondays through Fridays (www.businessdictionary.com).

The opinions of the anonymous CPA he/she reached as a result of his/her valuable experience, observations, and conversations held with the CFOs of audit client entities and shared publically are concrete advices that are not so hard to apply.

In their comment letter to IOSCO Consulting Report, *Compagnie Nationale des Commissaires aux Comptes* (CNCC), the center of which is in Paris, put forward the fact that audit quality relies mainly on the quality of human resources, hence the importance of initial training that develops general knowledge and open-mindedness, essential qualities for audit quality, that would not be developed via continuing education (Cazes 27.01.2010: 3). In its report, United States Treasury Department's Advisory Committee on the Auditing Profession (ACAP) shares the advices given by the Subcommittee on Human Capital. These advices are quoted below (United States Treasury, ACAP, Final Report 2008: VI: 2—VI: 27):

(1) Implement market-driven, dynamic curricula and content for accounting students that continuously evolve to meet the needs of the auditing profession and help prepare new entrants to the profession to perform high-quality audits.

   (a) Regularly update the accounting certification examinations to reflect changes in the accounting profession, its relevant professional and ethical standards, and the skills and knowledge required to serve increasingly global capital markets.
   (b) Reflect real world changes in the business environment more rapidly in teaching materials.
   (c) Require that schools build into accounting curricula current market developments.

(2) Improve the representation and retention of minorities in the auditing profession so as to enrich the pool of human capital in the profession.

   (a) Recruit minorities into the auditing profession from other disciplines and careers.
   (b) Institute initiatives to increase the retention of minorities in the profession.
   (c) Emphasize the role of community colleges in the recruitment of minorities into the auditing profession.
   (d) Emphasize the utility and effectiveness of cross sabbaticals and internships with faculty and students at Historically Black Colleges and Universities[17].
   (e) Increase the number of minority accounting doctorates through focused efforts.

[17]**Historically Black Colleges and Universities (HBCUs)**: Are institutions of higher education in the United States that were established before 1964 with the intention of primarily serving the African American community. They have always allowed admission to students of all races. Most were created in the aftermath of the American Civil War and are in the former slave states, although a few notable exceptions exist (http://encyclopedia.thefreedictionary.com/Historically+black+colleges+and+universities, Free Online Dictionary, 10.02.2018).

(3) Ensure a sufficiently robust supply of qualified accounting faculty to meet demand for the future and help prepare new entrants to the profession to perform high-quality audits. The private and the public sectors are required to cooperate in this issue.
(4) Develop and maintain consistent demographic and higher education program profile data.
(5) Encourage AICPA and American Accounting Association (AAA) to jointly form a commission to provide a timely study of the possible future structure of higher education for the accounting profession.

Even though some of the advices do not seem to be valid for non-US countries as they are, but can be easily adapted to any country that has minority or ethnicity issues.

Another indicator listed among input metrics is the time audit staff spent on an audit. Input metrics provide relatively objective information as mentioned before. In their comment letter to IOSCO Consulting Report, Deloitte Touche Tohmatsu contributes by stating that the additional time spent, while necessary under the facts and circumstances, would not necessarily make that audit of higher quality than an audit that took fewer hours in a less complex situation (15.01.2010: 7).

3.2.3.3 Sustainability and Corporate Culture

Whether it is sustainability that Enron–Arthur Andersen Case reminds, or sustainability in the context of business administration, when stability in markets is considered, audit firms are required to create a healthy corporate culture and make it a component of sustainability is a requisite. As a definition, sustainability is the way an organization creates value for its shareholders and society by maximizing the positive and minimizing the negative effects of environmental, social, and economic issues. Sustainability has a pragmatic and profound impact on the strategy and operations of companies today. It is not just about being ethically responsible; it is about smart business (www.cimaglobal.com, 25.02.2012). In the Audit Inspection Report published in UK in 2006, the importance of culture in an accounting firm is stressed. According to the Financial Reporting Council, action was needed to reflect more clearly the commitment to quality in the published strategy of the audit practice or the overall objectives of audit firms (www.ifac.org, 01.12.2011; www.frc.org.uk, 25.02.2012).

The penetration of sustainability concept to all bodies of an organization, its strategies, and operations can create value for many dimensions. These would be generating revenue through new products, services, and markets and diminishing costs by efficient resource depletion, decreased energy consumption, and waste minimization as well. Another dimension is the development of brand value, the building of trust through encouragement of positive ambience among employees and other stakeholders. The fourth dimension is providing risk management by abiding rules, avoidance of accidents, and environmental disasters. Sustainability performance management capability provides the information needed/required by decision takers. The discipline and diligence shown in terms of financial information should also be applied to sustainable reporting.

3.2.4 The Influences of the Audit Client to Audit Quality

The influences of the audit client to audit quality have formerly been handled from several aspects, and these aspects are summarized in Table 3.10. Here some additional details will follow.

Of course, the audit of an entity with operations in more than one province, or even countries, will differ from the audit of an entity that does not have operations scattered around. The audit client entities benefitting from several and different computer softwares like SAP, AS400, Logo, Netsis accounting systems, and having Oracle, SQL, DB2, and other databases makes audit service a unique project for each audited entity. As Taşkın states, the fact that the data produced by the systems that generate information coming from different media and that the actual data containing alphanumeric data are among the problems today's auditors have to tackle with. The reason of this is that the data are abstract symbol sequences useful for decision-making and are numerical values, words, or logical values, in short, everything that has the potential to produce information. Direct access to the data, direct retrieval from the database where the information is located, examination of all data in the database, not doing sampling and/or usage of the sampling only for auditing documents will impact audit quality. Rapid analysis of complex and detailed data for a superior audit requires changing strategy when necessary, and data that is unmodified, uncorrupted, and integrated (2011).

One of the factors complicating auditing service is their organizational structures and the fact whether the audit clients are multinationals or not. As emphasized by Block in Sino-Forest Corporation case, the audits where the audit clients' audited entities are at a remote center and the auditors are at another, these audits form a good sample for complicated audits (Block 2011: 2). Being multinational may require the audited audit client to operate under different standards; this may complicate the integration of such audits.

In addition to these, the existence of an efficient corporate-wide management information system and internal control implementation also influence the audit quality. Again, the existence or non-existence of risk culture and a healthily and efficiently operating audit committee are audit quality-impacting factors. The contribution of the top management into strategic audit process is extremely important. The communication between the auditor and top management and the top management adopting an open and supportive attitude will be influential on conducting a high-quality audit. As emphasized in previous sections, governance is very important and the existence of qualitative governance is expected to impact audit quality positively.

As mentioned above, the audit client establishing an efficiently operating audit committee and the efficiency level of it are critical. In the research section of the book, some of the questions directed to the audit client entities' managers are related to the audit committee and its functioning. The very interesting point is the coincidence of the timing of the questionnaire and a change in regulation stating that establishment of audit committee is no more compulsory. Some of the respondents contacted the researcher during 2012–2014, the era during which the survey is conducted, and asked why such questions regarding an abolished rule is asked. Moreover, some of audit client entities' managers declared they will not take the questionnaire just because of these *obsolete* questions. This, exactly this attitude draws the profile of Turkish managers in general. This attitude is the evidence that corporate governance is neither yet understood nor is it interiorized. It is somehow bitter to witness Turkish companies assign managers who do not believe in the necessity of taking initiative in a matter, which is not enforced by law, while western world discusses how to establish more efficient audit committees. Responses regarding audit committee issues are given under the heading Survey of Audit Clients' Managers in detail.

In the earlier sections of the book, reports of Association of Certified Fraud Examiners (ACFE) are covered. In fact, each of these reports is of academic interest. However, the reality revealed is that from structure and the way they transact, to the demographic attributes of managers of audited clients' entities, there are lots of factors resulting in fraud and corruption. Similarly, accounting scandals since the 1980s are also widely covered in previous parts of the book. These two researches are closely knit to each other.

When considered as a whole, the research is about audit quality-impacting factors. The expertise areas of audit client entities' managers, their tenure, and the positions they hold at their current companies, all somehow are related to the quality of the audit. Parallel to these, the structures of the board of directors, their compositions, the number of board members, the board members' areas of expertise, the fact whether any board member had ever been trialed in a court because of practicing his/her profession, and whether he/she had been sentenced or not, are also possibly impact audit quality.

In order to determine the perceptions of both sides of the audit about audit quality Altıntaş conducted a study, where he applied questionnaires to 225 auditors and 140 audit client entities' managers in 2007. The research found that the working conditions in audit firms are hard, and the perception of auditors is not affected by conformity to quality control procedures. Based on findings, Altıntaş concluded that this is due to inefficiency and unproductiveness of the quality control procedures. Besides, he found regulations of chambers of profession regarding the profession inadequate and further concluded that it would enhance the audit quality if chambers of profession emphasize the establishment of professional ethics and code of conduct. Another study conducted in Turkey by Göğer in 2006 found that the auditors put too much emphasis on their clients' opinions and satisfaction with the audit performed, and believe this is the factor impacting the audit quality. According to Göğer, this situation draws a negative picture of audit conducted in Turkey regarding their quality. In case stakeholders like auditors, managers, lenders, rule makers, and investors define non-financial criteria such as, customer satisfaction, employee satisfaction, or increase in the number of retail stores, the inconsistencies resulting from correlations of these criteria with, for example, financial measures like income growth will point to companies with a high likelihood of having fraudulent financial statements (Brazel et al. 2011: C3). This assessment, which means going beyond just commenting on the continuity of the business, is likely to improve the perceived quality of the audit, especially by meeting the expectations of external stakeholders.

Actually, the main customer/consumer of the service supplied by auditors and audit firms ought not to be the audit client itself, but financial table users or decision makers, i.e., mainly the investor. Ultimately, it is the audit client who is responsible with preparing financial statements that are the subject of the audit. Therefore, just taking the audit clients' perceptions as the ground for determining the quality of audit is far from being a prudent approach. In summary, the research that is the core of this book has been carefully designed by taking all these into consideration.

3.2.5 The Influence of Regulating Authorities on Audit Quality

Under this title, the influence of regulating authorities on audit quality is handled with a general perspective and a more detailed discussion about public oversight follows. As mentioned before, there are quite a lot of regulating bodies both in UK and USA, and in Turkey as well. Most of these are already been discussed under several subtitles. European Commission in Europe; SEC and PCAOB in USA; and in Turkey CMB, BRSA, EMRA, and POA are the authorities.

The mission of SEC, one of the regulating authorities in USA, is to protect investors, maintain fair, orderly, and efficient markets, and facilitate capital formation (www.sec.gov). CMB, the Turkish counterpart of it, states its main objective as fair and orderly functioning of the markets and protecting the rights of investors, and its mission, to make innovative regulations, and perform supervision with the aim of ensuring fairness, efficiency, and transparency in Turkish capital markets, and improving their international competitiveness. The goals of CMB are declared as adopting the norms of the international capital markets and fully integrate them into regulations, promoting and enhancing the effectiveness of both the supply and the demand side of the markets, promoting transparency and fairness in the capital markets, facilitating modernization of the market structure, enhancing the infrastructure of the capital markets, and enhancing the quality of the work products and staff members of the Board (www.spk.gov.tr, 09.11.2014). BRSA defines its mission to ensure that the activities of the institutions subject to supervision are carried out safely and firmly within the framework of their duties and authorities, that the credit system works effectively, that the rights and benefits of the savings owners are protected, thus contributing to development of financial markets and financial stability (www.bddk.org.tr, 09.11.2014). EMRA legislation also requires monitoring market performance, establishing and enforcing performance standards, distribution and customer service regulations, and monitoring the activities of market participants (www.epdk.org.tr, 09.11.2014).

PCAOB defines its mission to oversee the audits of public companies in order to protect the interests of investors and further the public interest in the preparation of informative, accurate, and independent audit reports. The PCAOB also oversees the audits of broker-dealers, including compliance reports filed pursuant to federal securities laws, to promote investor protection (www.pcaobus.org, 09.11.2014). The counterpart of the Board in Turkey, POA, defines its mission to set standards to ensure that financial reports are regulated and audited in accordance with international standards and to carry out effective public oversight (www.kgk.gov.tr).

The above-mentioned authorities are the most prominent ones. For the sake of the sustainability, the functioning of these authorities independent from political power is crucial. The expectations of investors and stakeholders, i.e. the public, from these regulatory authorities, must be taken into account by the institutions referred. However, it is important that regulatory and oversight functions are free from power confusion (European Commission 2010: 14). Oversight systems have to be organized, as there will not be any conflict of interest. Clearly written standards will assist the execution function of practitioners. Current rules could be reinforced with a view to ensuring the full independence of the public oversight systems of all Member States from the audit profession (*ibid.*). Besides, cooperation with several stakeholders would possibly enhance audit quality. For example, according to Hanson (24 Oct 2014) audit committees—who share the public oversight's goal of protecting the investors in public companies—provide an important complement to public oversight's work, driving audit quality through their own oversight of auditors and the market incentives they can offer to promote high-quality audits.

3.2.5.1 Oversight of Quality of External Audit

Under this title, a closer look is taken on public oversight systems in EU countries and USA. First comes oversight of external audit quality, Turkish SEC's inspections, and sanctions follow. Later, inspections and public oversight in USA and sanctions of the American SEC are handled.

In quality control inspections realized in USA, EU, UK, Japan, and Canada, it is observed that the organizations follow an operation cycles focused, risk-based examination approach, where organizations' processes and policies developed in almost all fields are under scrutiny and thus the understanding of the activities of the organizations is tried to be fully grasped (Okur 2007: 26). According to Okur, the main objective of quality control inspections is not applying administrative and punitive measures, but trying to understand the environment of the sector, and increasing the quality and reliability of audit function (*ibid.*).

The legislation toward oversight of audits in EU countries shows variations. Public oversight systems are dissimilar in both independence and autonomy, and their functioning. In Löhlein's study, four institutional designs for accounting regulations are distinguished. These are (1) regulation through monitored peer review system, (2) oversight over professional bodies, (3) regulation through independent regulatory agencies, and (4) regulation through governmental agencies (Löhlein 2015: 76–77). The systems mentioned and the EU countries along with

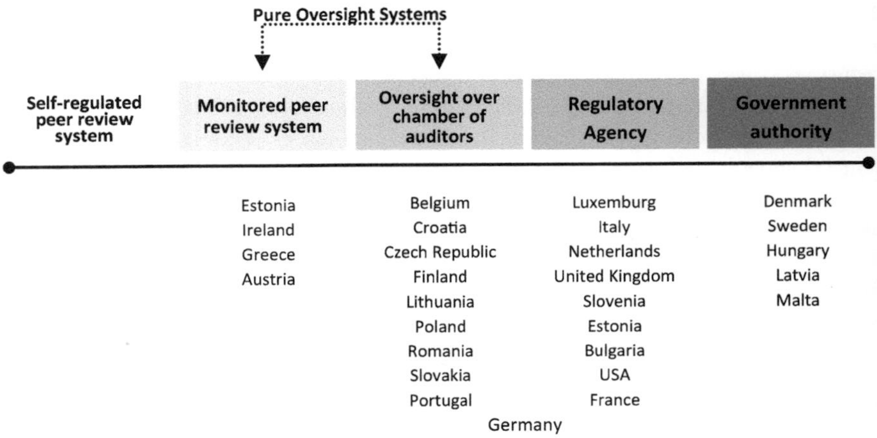

Fig. 3.15 Oversight systems, USA and EU countries adopting them. *Source* Löhlein, L. (2015). "Same but Different—Comparing European Union Audit Oversight Regulation". Audit Financiar, 13(126), 74–80, p 78

USA that adopt them are shown on the continuum shown below (*ibid.*, 78) (Fig. 3.15):

There are two standards established by IFAC to assess the quality of audit of external audit firms.

(1) International Standard on Quality Control 1 (ISQC 1). Quality Control for Firms that Perform Audits and Reviews of Financial Statements, and Other Assurance and Related Services Engagements.
(2) International Standard on Auditing 220 – ISA 220 (Revised). Overall Objectives of the Independent Auditor and the Conduct of an Audit in Accordance with International Standards on Auditing.

Elements of a System of Quality Control according to ISQC 1 are as follows (www.ifac.org, 25.02.2013, isqc-1.pdf):

(a) Leadership responsibilities for quality within the firm;
(b) Relevant ethical requirements;
(c) Acceptance and continuance of client relationships and specific engagements;
(d) Human resources;
(e) Engagement performance; and
(f) Monitoring.

The firm shall establish and maintain a system of quality control that includes policies and procedures that address each of the above elements. With the permission of IFAC, Standard on Quality Control 1 is translated in Turkish and published in 2013.

When it is talked about independence, the first thing coming to mind is independence of auditor. However, independence of the oversight of audit is as important as it is for the auditing process. Establishing the public's faith in the audit mechanism in the aftermath of so many accounting scandals and the financial crisis lies in the independence of oversight. According to the findings of a study done by Löhlein, the oversight of financial reporting is conducted by securities regulators in most of the EU countries. The analysis reveals considerable diversity with regard to the way the various European oversight systems are organized and operate. While Luxemburg, Italy, Latvia, and UK possess relatively independent public oversight systems, Ireland, Portugal, and Slovakia display low levels of independence (Löhlein 2014: 1).

3.2.5.2 Public Oversight Investigations and Sanctions in USA

Section 105 of the SOX grants PCAOB broad investigative and disciplinary authority over registered public accounting firms and persons associated with such firms (http://pcaobus.org, 16.01.2015). The Board may impose disciplinary or remedial sanctions as it determines appropriate, subject to the applicable limitations under Sect. 105(c)(5) of SOX (PCAOB Rulemaking Docket Matter No. 005, 2003: A1–31, A1–32) including:

(1) Temporary suspension or permanent revocation of registration;
(2) Temporary or permanent suspension or bar of a person from further association with any registered public accounting firm;
(3) Temporary or permanent limitation on the activities, functions or operations of such firm or person;
(4) A civil money penalty for each such violation, in an amount equal to–
    (i) Not more than \$100,000 for a natural person or \$2,000,000 for any other person; and
    (ii) In any case to which Sect. 105(c)(5) of SOX applies, not more than \$750,000 for a natural person or \$15,000,000 for any other person;
(5) Censure;
(6) Require additional professional education or training;
(7) Require a registered public accounting firm to engage an independent monitor, subject to the approval of the Board, to observe and report on the firm's compliance with the Act, the Rules of the Board, the provisions of the securities laws relating to the preparation and issuance of audit reports and the obligations and liabilities of accountants with respect thereto, or professional standards;
(8) Require a registered public accounting firm to engage counsel or another consultant to design policies to effectuate compliance with the Act, the Rules of the Board, the provisions of the securities laws relating to the preparation and issuance of audit reports and the obligations and liabilities of accountants with respect thereto, or professional standards;

(9) Require a registered public accounting firm, or a person associated with such a firm, to adopt or implement policies, or to undertake other actions, to improve audit quality or to effectuate compliance with the Act, the Rules of the Board, the provisions of the securities laws relating to the preparation and issuance of audit reports and the obligations and liabilities of accountants with respect thereto, or professional standards; and

(10) Require a registered public accounting firm to obtain an independent review and report on one or more engagements.

The investigations aiming quality control are announced through PCAOB's Web site. Table 3.3 is created by examining these announcements. Starting from the argument that the global audit market is under the hegemony of Big Four, and the data displayed in the table emphasizes Big Four.

As seen from Table 3.3, between 2004 and 2017, PCAOB conducted 2868 quality control inspections of US and non-US audit firms, by disregarding the fact that the audit had been performed within the borders of USA or not. The PCAOB regularly inspects those firms that issue audit reports opining on the financial statements of issuers. In general, the PCAOB inspects each firm in this category either annually or triennially, depending upon whether the firm provides audit reports for more than 100 issuers—annual inspections—or 100 or fewer issuers—triennial inspections. At any time, the PCAOB might also inspect any other registered firm that plays a role in the audit of an issuer, and the PCAOB has a practice

Table 3.3 PCAOB quality control investigations and Big Four. *Source* https://pcaobus.org/Inspections/Pages/InspectedFirms.aspx, Accessed 03 Dec 2017

	# of inspections	Percentage in Year Total	Deloitte Touche	Ernst & Young	KPMG	PwC[a]	Big Four # of inspections on yearly basis	Big Four % of inspections on yearly basis
2004	4	0.14	1	1	1	1	4	100.00
2005	172	6.00	1	1	1	1	4	2.33
2006	206	7.18	1	0	0	1	2	0.97
2007	170	5.93	1	2	4	1	8	4.71
2008	259	9.03	4	5	5	4	18	6.95
2009	214	7.46	2	1	3	3	9	4.21
2010	220	7.67	7	5	7	5	24	10.91
2011	344	11.99	21	13	14	15	63	18.31
2012	257	8.96	5	7	9	12	33	12.84
2013	257	8.96	7	13	9	13	42	16.34
2014	258	9.00	11	9	11	10	41	15.89
2015	218	7.60	7	7	11	10	35	16.06
2016	215	7.50	9	10	10	10	39	18.14
2017[b]	74	2.58	2	2	2	4	10	13.51
Total	2868	100.00	79	76	87	90	332	11.58
Share among Big four %			23.80	22.89	26.20	27.11	100.00	
Share among all investigations %			2.75	2.65	3.03	3.14	11.58	

[a]*PwC* PricewaterhouseCoopers
[b]2017: Incomplete

of inspecting, in each year, some firms in that category. In 2004, the year PCAOB began conducting inspections of registered firms' auditors; there are no inspections other than Big Four. Big Four had 332 inspections in 14 years and thus have 11.58% share of all inspection throughout years. The average of Big Four inspections among others is 15.99%. When Big Four are compared to each other; with 27.11% PricewaterhouseCoopers is the most inspected, and with 22.89% Ernst & Young is the least inspected audit firm for the time period covered in the table. Generally, Big Four have almost equally undergone quality control inspections. With 63 inspections, 2011 is the most stressed year from Big Four side, followed by 2013 and 2014 with 42 and 41 inspections, respectively.

PCAOB inspections are designed to identify and address weaknesses and deficiencies related to how a firm conducts audits. Inspections include evaluation of the firm's performance in selected audit engagements and evaluation of the design and operating effectiveness of a firm's quality control policies and procedures. The inspection staff provides a draft report to the firm. The firm then has an opportunity, but is not required, to provide a written response to the draft report. When the inspection staff has settled on a proposed final version of the report, it recommends the report to the Board for issuance. The Board considers the proposed report and the firm's response to the draft report and discusses details of the inspection and the proposed report with the staff. When the Board is satisfied with the content, it issues a final report and transmits it to the firm. If the firm disagrees with any of the assessments contained in the final report, whether relating to audit deficiencies or quality control criticisms, the firm has the opportunity to seek non-public review by the SEC. After the Board issues an inspection report, the Board promptly transmits a copy of the report to the SEC. It also transmits either a copy of the report or notice of the report's availability to the accountancy board in any US state where the firm is licensed. The Board issues a report on every inspection and makes a portion of the report publicly available. The Board seeks through constructive dialogue to encourage firms to improve their practices and procedures. If, through that evaluation, the Board finds a firm's efforts within that 12-month period to be unsatisfactory concerning any particular criticism, notifies the firm of that determination. The firm then has the option of seeking SEC review of that determination through a process that, under SEC rules, is non-public. If a firm does not request SEC review, or if a firm requests SEC review and the SEC does not object to PCAOB's determination on any particular criticism, PCAOB publicly discloses the portions of the original inspection report that discuss the relevant criticisms. In the past, Deloitte & Touche LLP, in 2008–2009; Ernst & Young LLP, in 2010–2011; KPMG LLP, in 2011–2012; and PricewaterhouseCoopers LLP, in 2009–2010 are disclosed publically since they did not act satisfactorily following inspection reports. The yearly inspected audit firms are listed below (http://pcaobus.org, 17.01.2015):

- BDO USA, LLP;
- Crowe Horwath LLP;
- Deloitte & Touche LLP;
- Ernst & Young LLP;

- Grant Thornton LLP;
- KPMG LLP;
- MaloneBailey, LLP;
- McGladrey LLP; and
- PricewaterhouseCoopers LLP.

Inspection numbers supplied in Table 3.3 do not include 340 audit inspections as of 2015, planned but not have been realized by PCAOB, since the hosting country's legislation did not allow. Out of these, 63.53%, namely 216 audits, are audits performed by Big Four affiliates. Toward the end of 2017, it is 169 audits belonging to 275 audit clients—61.45%. China and Hong Kong lead the way where PCAOB is not allowed to conduct inspections; Belgium, Greece, Poland, Portugal, Italy, Hungary, Ireland, and Luxemburg follow.

Enforcements of SEC in USA

The SEC has the power in certain circumstances to sanction or suspend practitioners from doing audits for SEC companies. The SEC's Rules of Practice permit them to temporarily or permanently deny a CPA or CPA firm from being associated with financial statements of public companies, either because of a lack of appropriate qualifications or having engaged in unethical or improper professional conduct (Arens et al. 2012: 117). In the past, the SEC has temporarily suspended a number of individual CPAs from doing any audits of SEC clients. It has similarly prohibited a number of CPA firms from accepting any new SEC clients for a period, such as six months. In some cases, the SEC has required an extensive review of a major CPA firm's practices by another CPA firm, or made CPA firms make changes in their practices. Individual CPAs and their firms have also been required to participate in continuing education programs. Sanctions such as these are published by the SEC and are often reported in the business press, making them a significant embarrassment to those involved (*ibid.*, 118). The tone Ares et al. uses imply that they somehow criticize the embarrassing part of the action, which to my opinion is just the price of misconduct to be paid by those causing to any size of losses of stakeholders in general.

As mentioned above, sanctions/enforcements regarding CPAs and/or CPA firms are published by the SEC on its Web site. The enforcements are named as Accounting and Auditing Enforcement Releases (AAERs) and are classified in terms of years, quarterly (www.sec.gov, 18.01.2015). Each action is accessible with the help of the online file. Table 3.4 displays the details of SEC releases. As seen from the table, 2007 is the most AAER released year with 232 releases; 2012 is the least AAER released year—85 releases. The average of the last 14 years is 148 releases, and the third quarter is most crowded one among others. Just evaluating the number of releases is not a satisfactory indicator, because for any deficiency the process starts, correspondences follow, and each of the steps are announced. Therefore, the number of releases may be an inflated data about weaknesses.

Table 3.4 SEC Accounting and Auditing Enforcement Releases (2004–2017)

		4th quarter	3rd quarter	2nd quarter	1st quarter
Total	[a]1934	[a]386	589	458	501
%	100.00	18.63%	28.43%	22.10%	24.18%
Year's average	[a]138	[a]28	42	33	36
2017	88	[b]28	19	18	23
2016	110	27	27	25	31
2015	112	21	42	21	28
2014	95	30	28	14	23
2013	87	20	31	21	15
2012	85	20	23	14	28
2011	127	25	27	42	33
2010	129	29	45	26	29
2009	180	39	52	45	44
2008	151	20	51	37	43
2007	232	24	109	41	58
2006	169	40	33	49	47
2005	191	30	57	45	59
2004	178	33	45	60	40

[a]The unpublished data of December 2017 is taken as 18. The last quarter is composed of October and November data, where the assumption for December is added on
[b]December 2017 year average is an assumption

When AAERs are assessed with respect to Big Four, Table 3.5 is the outcome. By all the years, 2.82% of AAERs—54 of them—mention the name of Big Four. The year 2014, when the name of each Big Four audit firm is mentioned five times in AAERs, four of the releases regarding each are related to the same audit performed in China (www.sec.gov, AAER No. 3612, 2014). It is to bear in mind that some of inspections of SEC collide with the ones initiated by PCAOB, and sometimes they are not connected at all.

To summarize, in USA both SEC and PCAOB share the inspection reports with the public. Once the process starts, it is only in the last stage when the authorities make the reports public with all its openness. This is a good practice to be followed by Turkish POA. Sending the inspection/investigation reports to the audit clients' audit committees, and/or sharing the reports with the public will enhance audit quality. In fact, this is the course Financial Reporting Council (FRC) in UK follows (www.frc.org.uk, 05.05.2013, Audit Quality Review).

The effectiveness of public oversight is tied to regular monitoring auditors and audit firms. Peer review is to be promoted. The sanction/enforcements targeting organizations and persons, who do not follow rules and regulations, have to be dissuasive. It has to be provided that audit firms make timely and transparent reporting about themselves. The audit market is to be organized by decreasing the chance of concentration, and the merger of micro-scaled audit firms, which do not have sufficient audit teams, is to be incentivized.

Table 3.5 SEC AAERs regarding Big Four (2004–2017)

		Big Four Share (%)	Big Four Total	Deloitte Touche	Ernst & Young	KPMG	PwC[a]
Total	1916	2.82	54	12	16	15	11
2017	[b]70	1.43	1	0	0	1	0
2016	110	3.64	4	0	3	1	0
2015	112	0.89	1	1	0	0	0
2014	95	21.05	20	5	5	5	5
2013	87	0.00	0	0	0	0	0
2012	85	5.88	5	2	1	1	1
2011	127	3.15	4	1	1	1	1
2010	129	0.78	1	0	0	0	1
2009	180	1.67	3	0	3	0	0
2008	151	0.66	1	0	1	0	0
2007	232	0.86	2	0	2	0	0
2006	169	0.59	1	0	0	1	0
2005	191	4.19	8	3	0	4	1
2004	178	1.69	3	0	0	1	2

[a]*PwC* PricewaterhouseCoopers
[b]December 2017 data not published yet

3.2.5.3 Public Oversight Investigations and Sanctions in Turkey

In Turkey up until POA undertook the responsibility of oversight, public oversight regarding audit firms and audit quality had been done by CMB. The 47th Bulletin of CMB quotes and states that Art. 30 of 8th Directive of European Council foresees the announcement of inspection reports regarding audit firms to the general public. Within this scope, CMB published its compiled report about quality control inspections through 2008–2010 as a statistical data just for one time. CMB inspections last until the conflicts regarding the realm of authority, a power crisis in reality, are resolved. Following the resolution, POA took the absolute authority. However, as of February 2018, there are bulletins published by CMB indicating fines to audit firms regarding their misconduct. Table 3.6 displays quality control inspections of CMB during 2002–2013. The table is created following the analysis of 639 weekly bulletins published by CMB. Among the bulletins, audit-related topics determined are 160. A closer analysis depicted 112 quality control inspections realized by CMB teams.

The cases where auditors are banned first hand, and then the ban is uplifted are not included in the analyses. However, though not covered in Table 3.6, the number of "topics related to audit" includes 28 audit firms voluntarily delisted, a case where auditor's responsibility bore litigious action, and 56 audit firms for the first time included in the list. As observed from the table; 13 audit firms are delisted, they are noticed 59 times to take corrective action, 38 audit firms are sanctioned with an

Table 3.6 CMB quality control inspections (2002–2013). *Source* Created based on the data available at http://www.spk.gov.tr/Bulten. Accessed 18 Feb 2012

	Weekly bulletin	Audit quality control inspection	Topics related to audit	Delisted	Notice/ time given for corrective action	Administrative fine	Following quality control inspection leaving the list voluntarily
	#	#	#	(1)	(2)	(3)	(4)
Total	639	112	160	13	59	38	2
2013	41	1	6	0	0	1	0
2012	48	0	2	0	0	0	0
2011	52	7	15	1	4	2	0
2010	53	19	14	0	12	7	0
2009	57	27	15	2	18	7	0
2008	51	17	20	4	9	4	0
2007	54	1	9	0	0	1	0
2006	55	24	27	2	11	9	2
2005	56	0	9	0	0	0	0
2004	54	3	11	1	0	2	0
2003	63	2	14	2	0	0	0
2002	55	11	18	1	5	5	0

administrative fine, and following a CMB quality control inspection two audit firms informed that they want to be taken out of the list. The graph regarding the analyses of weekly bulletins is given below.

While Graphic 3.2 displays actions in a numeric way, next graph displays the data in percentages (Graphic 3.3).

Yearly data gathered from annual reports published on CMB's Web site, numbers of audit firms listed at CMB at each year, and quality control inspection numbers, are compared and summarized on Table 3.7.

As seen from the table, each year an average of 10.33% of audit firms have undergone a quality control inspection. Thus, the turnover of quality control

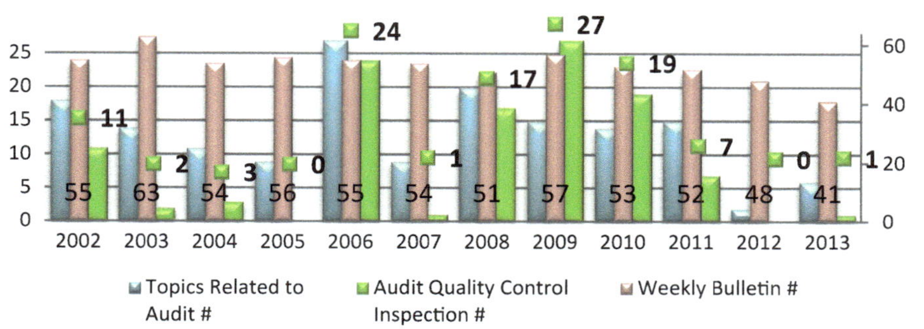

Graphic 3.2 CMB Weekly Bulletins as of audit firms regarding issues (2002–2013). *Source* Created based on the data available at http://www.spk.gov.tr/Bulten. Accessed 18 Feb 2012

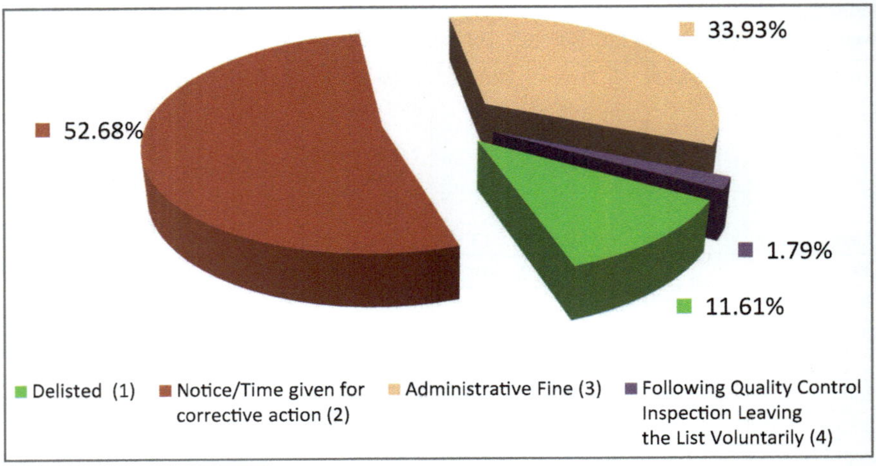

Graphic 3.3 Analysis of CMB Weekly Bulletins (2002–2013). *Source* Created based on the data available at http://www.spk.gov.tr/Bulten. Accessed 18 Feb 2012

Table 3.7 CMB quality control inspections turnover (2002–2013). *Source* Created based on the data available at http://www.spk.gov.tr/Bulten. Accessed 18 Feb 2012

	Audit quality control inspection (QCI) #	Audit firm #	Inspection rate (%)	QCI turnover (yearly)
Total	112	1084	10.33	9.68
2013	1	91	1.10	91.00
2012	0	94	0.00	NA
2011	7	91	7.69	13.00
2010	19	92	20.65	4.84
2009	27	95	28.42	3.52
2008	17	97	17.53	5.71
2007	1	98	1.02	98.00
2006	24	94	25.53	3.92
2005	0	91	0.00	NA
2004	3	83	3.61	27.67
2003	2	80	2.50	40.00
2002	11	78	14.10	7.09

inspections is 9.68 years. This means any of the audit firms listed will undergo an inspection approximately every ten years. These statistics are valid for 2002–2013 period, and the related Graphic 3.4 is given below.

In order to approach quality control assessments from another perspective, analyses are performed based on market share of audit firms listed on CMB, EMRA, BRSA, and the similar institutions, the number of these audit firms' audit clients, and the asset sizes of audit clients. The aim of this analysis is to understand

Graphic 3.4 CMB quality control inspections turnover (2002–2013).
Source Created based on the data available at http://www.spk.gov.tr/Bulten. Accessed 18 Feb 2012

whether the name and the size of the firm and having a license agreement with Big Four influence the choice of audit firm, or not. Once the factors influencing auditor choice are determined, at the second stage, the audit firms that come out of this initial analysis are controlled in order to understand whether these audit firms have ever been subject to enforcements of CMB—administrative fines, notice, delisting, and the like. For this purpose, data of 549 Borsa Istanbul listed public companies are downloaded via dynamic query from Public Disclosure Platform (PDP) as of April 20, 2013. The same analysis is repeated in April 2014 for control purposes and for the sake of the completeness and continuity—there were 604 listed companies then. Only 2012–2013 data are used in quality control analyses.

As mentioned earlier, quality control inspections of CMB are realized with a turnover, where an audit firm would possibly be inspected every ten years. However, Table 3.8 proves why there is no need for inspecting minor audit firms frequently. Big Four affiliates in Turkey audit more than 97% of Borsa Istanbul listed companies based on client asset size, and around 50% based on number of BIST listed companies. In fact, inspecting the first 15 audit firms based on client asset size in 2013–2014 for quality control purposes means having inspected more than 99% of the audit work performed in the market. It is very well known that when it comes to quality control, the benefit 100 percent quality control pales in comparison to the cost of it. Hence, as stated by Okur, in the five developed countries examined in his study, the quality control inspection duty begins with audit firms that undertake most of the financial risk, and the activity plan is established based on the quality and quantity of the work of these audit firms (2007: 26). While CMB quality control inspections regarding 2012–2013 are reviewed, the following are reached. Out of 158 audit regarding topics, 21 are related to the audit firms mentioned. These comprise twelve notices or time allowed for required corrective actions; ten administrative fines; one voluntarily leaving the list of authorized audit firms; and five first-time recognition by

Table 3.8 Market share of audit firms based on client asset size

	Total asset size[a] (million TL)	Listed company #	Share in total TL (%)	Share in total (# of listed companies) (%)
BIST companies (2013–14)	2,419,990	604	100.0000	100.0000
BIST companies (2012–13)	1,944,601	549	100.0000	100.0000
Audit firm known or announced (2013–14)	2,417,949	500	99.9156	85.4305
Audit firm known or announced (2012–13)	1,942,564	458	99.8952	83.4244
Top **15** audit firms serving audit clients with more than 1% market share (2013–14)	2,396,289	419	99.1042	81.2016
Top **13** audit firms serving audit clients with more than 1% market share (2012–13)	1,932,176	375	99.4653	81.8777
Big Four affiliates in Turkey (2013–2014)	**2,358,854**	**304**	**97.4737**	**50.3311**
Big Four affiliates in Turkey (2012–2013)	**1,888,802**	**267**	**97.1306**	**48.6339**

[a]Audit clients'

the authority. Any of the cases may contain more than one action at a time. This is to be interpreted that 20.34% of the notices and 26.31% of administrative fines are reinforcements against first twelve audit firms in audit market—Big Four affiliates in Turkey are among these.

As CMB carry out quality control inspections in Turkey, so does POA. With the enactment of TCC and establishment of the POA, the number of the companies falling in the scope of audit and number of the auditors and audit firms that are subject to oversight have been increased. POA developed an Audit Engagement Portal, an online IT platform where auditors are required to enter details of all of their audit engagements. Auditors are required to upload a copy of all Audit Engagement Letters once signed. They are also required to upload the final audit opinion, thus making available to the audit regulator the key documents at the start and end of the audit process. This portal and the information, which is entered into it by all auditors in relation to all audits, enable POA to perform continuous off-site audit oversight. The data from the platform enables POA to perform analysis of the Turkish audit market, and by linking to the Government's Company and Tax Registries, POA can assess whether all companies that meet the criteria to have an audit are in fact being audited. The Portal also enables POA to monitor audit firms and auditors' engagements. In the future real-time monitoring is planned. The authority inspects audit firms and auditors in the context of sufficient number of selected audit files, notices and documents, and other information within the scope of its quality assurance system. Inspections are carried out in the scope of annual inspection plan prepared by the Board in every year by receiving opinion of relevant authorities. Results of inspections shall be announced to the public opinion every year with a report. Inspections of the audit firms cover (www.kgk.gov.tr): (1) review of audit work performed within the scope of relevant legislations, (2) regulatory compliance of audit firms' activities, (3) quality and quantity of resources spent in audits, (4) audit fees charged, and (5) internal control system of the audit firms. Audit firms which audit PIEs are to be inspected at least once in every three years, and others every six years. POA uses both private and public reporting. The private reports include firm-wide procedures and audit file reviews and reported to audit firms only. Public reporting is done annually to summarize yearlong inspection activities. Enforcements are applied in accordance with the principles and procedures set by POA. POA has authority to investigate and discipline audit firms and auditors for non-compliance with the relevant legislations. In case there are violations found, in addition to fines POA can impose appropriate sanctions that compose of warning, suspension of the approval up to two years, and withdrawal of the approval. In case of repeated violations, aggravated sanctions shall be imposed. As a result of the inspections and investigations carried out by POA and where it is possible to remedy, POA may grant a separate period suitable for remedying the violations and deficiencies detected prior to taking a decision for sanction. Where it is detected that the violations and deficiencies are not remedied by the end of the period so granted, the corresponding administrative sanctions shall apply. In order to assess the quality control systems established by audit firms in Turkey, POA realized quality control system assessment inspections in 2014 and 2015. In 2014 all inspections—63 inspections—were directed to audit firms that perform PIE audits. Following year, 48 audit firms were inspected, where 26 of audit firms have the license to make a PIE audit. Along with quality control system inspections, POA started selected inspections on files. From the annual report of POA, it is seen that in 2016, 26 audit firms and six auditors were inspected, where a total of 29 inspections are based on files. There are 16 PIE audit files among these. The outstanding findings are listed below (www.kgk.gov.tr): (1) 84% of inspections found inadequacies related to understanding the internal control system of the audit client, (2) 80% of findings point to inadequacies regarding determination and assessment of risk of material misstatement, (3) 68% of the findings show that there are insufficiencies regarding audit firms' quality control systems—the most problematic issue is independence, (4) 60% of findings are about problems regarding measurements directed to assessed risks, (5) documentation provisions are not as required in 60% of the inspected audit files, (6) findings pointing to implementation of materiality concept make up 40%, (7) findings related to the usage of sampling methods are 32%, (8) use of external confirmation procedures is another problematic issue in files—28%, (9) findings regarding inventory make up 24%, and (10) group audits are also not as they are desired, 16% of findings are about them.

The POA's 2016 annual revenue is 23,520,431.36 liras. Administrative fines in the same year are 1,329.87 liras, and the share in revenue is 0.0056%. It is possible that same year's fines are not yet reflected to the financial statements. In the same year PCAOB in USA earned $254.7 million, where administrative fines total to $9.5 million. Thus, the share of fines within revenue is 3.73%. Assuming the same percentage is to be provided by POA, POA's revenue based on administrative fines in Turkey has to be 877,283.46 liras. In five years after being established in Turkey, POA is not yet at the desired level regarding effectiveness. Its American counterpart PCAOB precedes POA, and a ten-year gap naturally makes a difference. In the near future, POA is expected to be a more efficiently functioning authority. There is a long way for POA to catch the developed world regarding public oversight.

The Outlook of Audit Firms in Turkey

The outlook of audit firms in Turkey came to light based on the data of the research finalized in 2015. A questionnaire is answered by 93 auditors, who got their certificates from POA in Turkey. Regarding the audit firm they work, those who state that quality control policy and procedures (QCPP) do not exist in their audit firm makes up 7.53%. Those saying that QCPP exists, but auditors are only informed on the duties and responsibilities assigned to them, is 12.9%. Respondents stating that QCPP exists and auditors are only informed verbally about policies and procedures make 6.45%, whereas those saying that auditors are only informed in writing about policies and procedures make 15.05%. The ideal position regarding quality control policy and procedures is that they exist and auditors are informed both in writing and verbally about policies and procedures. Respondents agreeing with this statement make 53.76%. The distribution of the answers is displayed in Graphic 3.5.

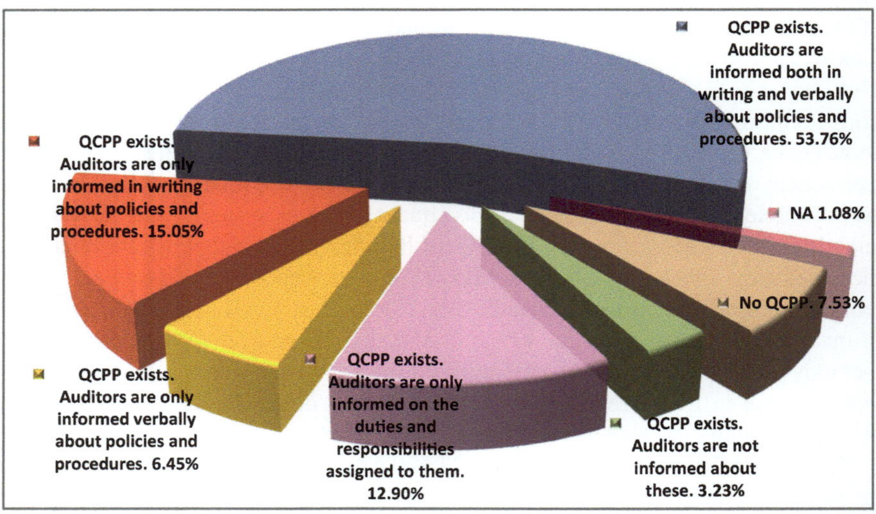

Graphic 3.5 QCPP—quality control policy and procedures in audit firms auditors are employed, or are partners

To talk about quality control policy and procedures, there has to be a quality control department of an audit firm, which is expected to function efficiently and effectively—24.73% of respondents say their audit firms do not have a quality control department. Those stating that their audit firm has a quality control department, but could work more efficiently, make up 25.81% of respondents. While the ratio of respondents saying that they have a quality control department and it functions efficiently is 37.63%, the ratio of those admitting that they have a quality control department (QCD) but not working efficiently is 11.83. The distribution of answers is shown in Graphic 3.6.

The questionnaire is answered not only by the auditors following their certification by POA, but also by the managers of audit firms. This enabled a comparison of responds of employers and employees of audit firms in Turkey. In the following table, opinions of 93 auditors and 24 managers of audit firms in relation to quality control policy and procedures and quality control department are compared.

As followed from Table 3.9, the only opinion of managers of audit firms and auditors close to each other's is that the audit firm they work has a QCD and it functions efficiently. This points to discrepancy of opinions regarding quality control policy and procedures and quality control department. Such a discrepancy in perceptions of two groups would only be an indicator of lack of good governance regarding audit firms. For small-sized audit firms, establishing a quality control department may not be feasible; however, audit firms of an agreeable size are expected to have quality control department and function effectively. Effectively functioning requires quality control policy and procedures to be established and conveyed to the personnel in the most transparent way. Having quality control policy and procedures and an efficient quality control department will definitely enhance audit quality.

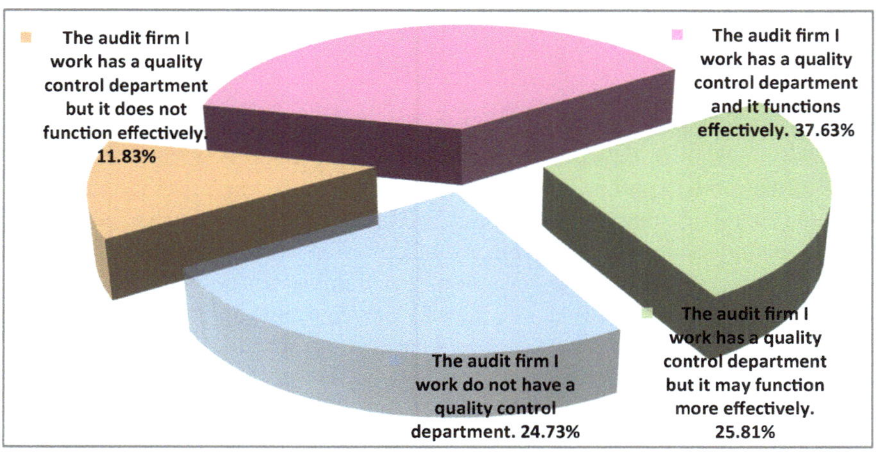

Graphic 3.6 Quality control department in audit firms auditors are employed/partners

Table 3.9 Comparison of opinions of auditors and managers of audit firms regarding QCPP and QCD

Questionnaire's expressions regarding QCPP and QCD				
Select the most appropriate information for your firm's QCPP for independent audit service from the following section!	**Managers of audit firms n = 24**	%	**Auditors n = 93**	%
No QCPP	1	4.17	7	7.61
QCPP exists. Auditors are not informed about these	0	0.00	3	3.26
QCPP exists. Auditors are only informed on the duties and responsibilities assigned to them	5	20.83	12	13.04
QCPP exists. Auditors are only informed verbally about policies and procedures	1	4.17	6	6.52
QCPP exists. Auditors are only informed in writing about policies and procedures	2	8.33	14	15.22
QCPP exists. Auditors are informed both in writing and verbally about policies and procedures	15	62.50	50	54.35
Select the level of impact on the quality of the work of the QCD in your firm, among the options!	**Managers of audit firms *n* = 24**	%	**Auditors *n* = 93**	%
The audit firm I work does not have a quality control department	4	16.67	23	24.73
The audit firm I work has a QCD but it does not function effectively	2	8.33	11	11.83
The audit firm I work has a QCD and it functions effectively	8	33.33	35	37.63
The audit firm I work has a QCD but it may function more effectively	10	41.67	24	25.81
QCD is not necessary	0	0.00	0	0.00

Table 3.10 compiles audit quality-impacting factors mentioned until now.

As summarized in table, there are lots of factors impacting the audit quality. Some of these originate from the audit firm and are in the control of the firm itself. The organizational structure and human resources an audit firm owns are among these. Even though it cannot be evaluated independent from the audit firms he/she is employed, the personality, the education, and training he/she obtained, the environment he/she had been raised, i.e., the auditor as a person affects the quality of an audit. The third factor, in fact a very crucial factor impacting audit quality is the audit client itself. Last but not least comes the public oversight. The last two factors, especially oversight, are factors that are systemic. The first two group of factors are

Table 3.10 Main indicators of audit quality

	Impacting factor	Explanation	
Auditing Firm	Organizational structure	Has to be well designed	1
	Collateral partnerships/indirect partners		2
	Business model	Targets regarding future, mergers, and acquisitions	3
	Diversity of services rendered	Impacts of it upon independence	4
	Implicit shareholders	Tax, accounting, auditing	5
	Regulatory compliance	The degree of it; inspections, warnings, and penalties if relevant	6
	Compliance with the standards of auditing	The degree of it; inspections, warnings, and penalties if relevant	7
	Human resources policy and procedures		8
	Quality control system		9
	The impact of services rendered upon independence		10
	Training policies		11
	Number of companies audited		12
	Average annual training hours per audit professional		13
	Annual professional staff retention		14
	Ethics policies and procedures		15
	Independence	The degree and sustainability	16
	Who pays the audit fee		17
	Satisfactoriness of the fee earned from a client	Price competition	18
	Ratio of professional staff to audit partners—leverage		19
	Time staff spend on an audit		20
	Chargeable hours per audit professional		21
	Professional chargeable hours managed per audit partner		22
	Local bureau/partner		23
	Network design	Network build-up from firms	24

(continued)

Table 3.10 (continued)

	Impacting factor	Explanation	
Auditor	Independence		25
	Regulatory compliance	The degree of it; inspections, warnings, and penalties if relevant	26
	Compliance with the standards of auditing	The degree of it; inspections, warnings, and penalties if relevant	27
	The average years of experience of audit professionals		28
	Number of companies audited		29
	Experience and knowledge about the client and client's industry		30
	Rotation		31
	Restatement of opinion		32
	Professional skepticism		33
	Auditor stress		34
	Over self-confidence		35
Client	Properties of board of directors	Area of specialty, experience, respectability, integrity, etc.	36
	Properties of audit committee		37
	The effectiveness of internal control		38
	Restatement of financial tables		39
	Organizational structure		40
	Corporate governance		41
	Social responsibility		42
	Existence of performance-based incentive premiums	Possibility of management being biased	43
	Abiding by the laws and standards	The degree of it; inspections, warnings, and penalties if relevant	44
Public authority	The effectiveness of public oversight	Continuous monitoring quality	45
	Peer review		46
	Autonomy considering political power		47
	Organizational structure of public authorities related to independent auditing		48
	Effective controls		49
	Penalizing persons and institutions not abiding by laws		50
	The structure of the industry		51

those which are possibly we can manipulate in order to improve audit quality. These factors listed in this table formed the ground of the questionnaires prepared for this research, and three sets of questionnaires are prepared to be answered by auditors, by managers of audit firms, and by audit client entities' managers. Next chapter is about the survey and its findings.

Chapter 4
Survey on Assessment of External Audit Quality in Turkey

Abstract This Chapter gives the details of the main survey of this study, which aims exploring the Turkish audit market, and finding out how the audit firms operate, and what the perceptions and observations of market players are. Some of the outcomes of the survey had already been shared in the previous chapter, whenever appropriate. However, these were just snapshots. This Chapter describes the survey starting from constraints, and methodology, and end with findings. As mentioned before, there are three questionnaires used in this survey. Based on the input–output mechanism of the audit, it is apparent that the audit client is both an input and output as well. The auditor, as the other input, is also the human resource factor of an audit, who actually performs the audit. As the way audit markets operate is considered, there comes the third actor to the scene–the audit firm. The managers of audit firms compose a rich source for information. Due to the importance and effects of these three groups upon the audit quality, this surveys sheds a strong light upon Turkish audit market.

Keywords Survey · Auditor's merits · Opinions · Managers · Auditors

4.1 Constraints

Quality is an issue of every organization from every sector. When sustainability and responsibility of institutionalized organizations are taken into consideration, quality becomes an issue, which cannot be overlooked. Naturally, all corporations operate under several law and legislation; however, this book focuses on quality of audit of public companies. For this reason, the research includes independent auditing firms that are already active in the audit market, performing independent auditing of publicly traded companies. Publicly traded companies here are the public companies listed in Borsa Istanbul, and there are not any constrictions for auditors.

I. Kesimli, *External Auditing and Quality*, Accounting, Finance, Sustainability, Governance & Fraud: Theory and Application,
https://doi.org/10.1007/978-981-13-0526-9_4

4.2 Methodology

Under this title, the model of the research, the population and samples selection for three different groups, data collection, analysis of the data, and interpretations are covered. The whole research presented in this book is planned as a literature survey and a field research made up of three questionnaires. The first-time establishment of POA in Turkey coincides with the schedule of this research. Thus, the research became one that witnessed the role conflicts and stress in audit community in Turkey. For the portion of the study's questionnaire, the research was conducted in three separate groups and the results were integrated when completed. The first questionnaire was designed and implemented for managers of audit firms. The second questionnaire was for auditors, who are not managers in audit firms. Except for partners and board members, all auditors in audit firms were targeted. The third questionnaire was designed for audit client entities' managers. General managers, finance, and accounting department managers, audit committee members, and experts related to audit were the target group for the questionnaire.

Seven point Likert-scaled surveys are designed in accordance with audit quality indicators, determined following literature survey and review of legislation and conducted at the same time interval in the Turkish audit market; to the managers of auditing firms, to auditors, and audit clients. Scales are as follows: (1) strongly disagree, (2) partly disagree, (3) disagree, (4) no opinion, (5) partly agree, (6) agree, (7) strongly agree. Opinions about auditor merits and auditing process are common question groups in surveys.

4.2.1 *Populations and Samples*

As mentioned above, for each of the questionnaires different populations and samples are used. During 2012–2013 CMB in Turkey authorized 93 audit firms to perform external audits. BRSA licensed audit firms are 42, and except for one audit firm, all remaining are on the list of CMB. That single audit firm is not active either. EMRA has 85 audit firms in list, except for on inactive audit firm; all are also on the list of CMB. The 34 audit firms authorized by the Insurance Association of Turkey (IAT) are announced on the Web site of Undersecretariat of Treasury. Except for three of them, the remaining are also in the list of CMB. These three audit firms are either inactive or voluntarily left the list. In summary, audit firm numbers authorized by several institutions in 2012–2013 are as follows:

CMB listed audit firms	93
EMRA listed additional audit firms	1
IAT listed additional audit firms	3
BRSA listed additional audit firms	1
Total	98

During 2013–2014, there are 87 audit firms authorized to perform PIE audits by then newly established POA. These 87 audit firms compose the population of the first questionnaire of the integrated survey.

As mentioned before, the research focuses on BIST listed public companies. For this purpose, data about BIST listed public companies are gathered from Public Disclosure Platform (PDP) via dynamic query. The same data set is once more created in 2014. As of April 12, 2014, there are 604 public companies in BIST, where the names of audit firms of 516 public companies are notified to the requiring institutions. However, financial statements of 16 of these public companies are not available; therefore, these public companies and their audit firms are left aside. For the remaining 500 BIST listed public companies, 59 audit firms are determined, and they are paired. These 59 audit firms authorized by POA to perform PIE audits compose the sample of the first questionnaire of the survey. As mentioned above, 604 BIST listed public companies make the population, and those 500 BIST listed public companies determined as explained above, compose the sample of the second questionnaire of the integrated survey.

Auditors employed by audit firms are the last group of the integrated survey. The third questionnaire is designed for them. The contact details of auditors are listed nowhere. During twelve months, names are compiled from Web sites of audit firms. Another source to collect names of auditors was the POA list where all auditors who earned their licenses from the authority are publicly listed. As of April 6, 2014, there were 6686 persons on the certificate list announced. Based on the real person names gathered from these sources, 1500 e-mail addresses are created. Since POA list contains all names from all over Turkey, the e-mail creation is consciously limited with the names of auditors who are associated with an audit firm. Therefore, the addresses created had a small chance of being a real e-mail address, and the questionnaire being answered was totally hit-or-miss style. As stated by auditors, their year-round workloads are a barrier for them to respond questionnaires. Personal contacts to motivate them to join the survey were not helpful either. In summary, the list derived as described is used to send online questionnaires to auditors, and responses are collected.

4.2.2 Collection of Data

The online questionnaire for managers of audit firms is sent to e-mail addresses of auditors with managerial positions in audit firms via SurveyMonkey. The questionnaire is designed such that it does not allow any unanswered question. There had to be only one answer from each audit firm. Out of 59 audit firms 24 responses are received–40.68% return rate. These 24 auditing firms audit 127 stock exchange quoted companies, namely 27.76% of the market, based on total asset size. The questionnaire contains four sections, 60 questions. The first section collects demographic data of managers of audit firms. The second section directs questions to understand the organizational structure of their audit firms and to determine structural problems. The third section tries to get the opinion of managers of audit firms about merits of auditor impacting the quality of audit. The fourth section of questionnaire is to understand the stance of managers of audit firms toward audit process.

For the second questionnaire designed for audit client entities' managers, initially 516 addresses of BIST listed public companies that are publicly announced on PDP during 2012–2013 are used and sent via SurveyMonkey. The initial return rate was very low. Therefore, in 2013–2014, when PDP started providing much more transparent information about public companies, the Web site of PDP is visited again and contact information of investor contact persons are gathered. In order to do this, pages of 516 public companies are visited one by one, and names of the members of board of directors, executive boards, general managers, coordinators and the like are determined. Following this, 1600 e-mail addresses are derived for 500 public companies. The questionnaire is designed such that it does not allow any unanswered question. Out of 500 public companies 148 responses are received–29.60% return rate. These 148 stock exchange quoted companies from 28 different sectors are audited by 24 different auditing firms. These companies represent 40.41% of total assets and 46.81% of total net worth of 516 Borsa Istanbul stock exchange quoted companies.

The questionnaire of audit client entities' managers with 58 questions is composed of four implicit sections. The first section is about demographic information of respondents, the sector of the company and the structure of the board of directors. The second section is about internal control, audit board, audit committee, choice of audit firm, professions and numbers of any of the above-mentioned board/committee members. The third section of the questionnaire tries to get the opinion of managers of public companies about merits of auditor impacting the quality of audit. The fourth section of questionnaire is to understand the stance of managers of public companies toward audit process.

The process of the questionnaire directed to auditors is already discussed earlier; therefore, it will not be repeated here. At the end of that tough period, 93 responses were available–26 auditing partners and 67 auditors, totally by 93 auditors, where 85 of them are engaged with 35 different auditing firms and eight are anonymous. This questionnaire, which directs 28 questions, is composed of an introductory section aiming to gather demographic data about auditors and of a section trying to get the opinion of auditors about merits of the auditor impacting audit quality. The third section of this questionnaire is to understand the stance of auditors toward the audit process.

4.2.3 *The Analysis and Interpretation of Findings*

The responses are evaluated with the help of statistical methods and results are interpreted. In case there are comments of respondents, these are also quoted.

4.2.3.1 Survey of Auditing Firms' Managers

Auditing firms' managers taking part in the survey are 45 years old, have 16 years of experience, and approximately 11 years of tenure on the average. Except for seven non-partner managers, the average duration of the partnership is ten years.

Table 4.1 Demographics of audit firms' managers

	Average	Minimum	Maximum
Age	45.23	25.63	71.08
Experience as auditor	15.97	0.71	49.71
Tenure with the last audit firm	11.57	0.84	33.01
Worked as partner	9.96	0.13	33.01

Note All data in years

The professional titles they carry are displayed in the graphic below (Graphic 4.1).

The positions the managers of audit firms hold in their current audit firms are shown in the graphic below (Graphic 4.2).

The question whether the auditing firm the manager employed by, has quality control policies and procedures or not, revealed that 4.17% of the firms do not have such policies and procedures (Graphic 4.3).

Out of them, 16.67% have not yet established a quality control department. The percentage of managers agreeing, that auditors are informed about quality control policies and procedures both in written and oral form, is 62.50, and 33.33% of the auditing firms' managers say that there is an effectively functioning quality control department (Graphic 4.4).

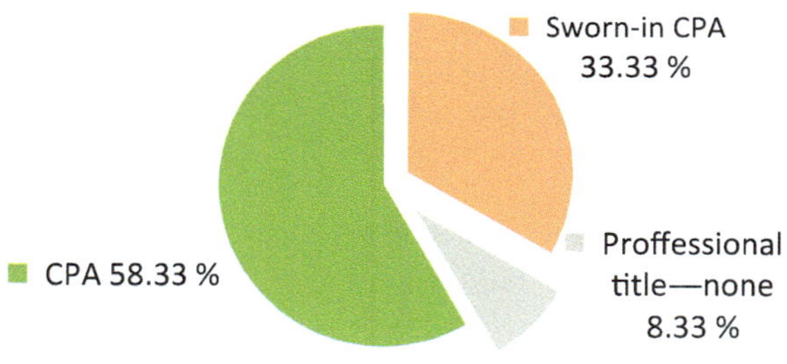

Graphic 4.1 Audit firms' managers' professional titles

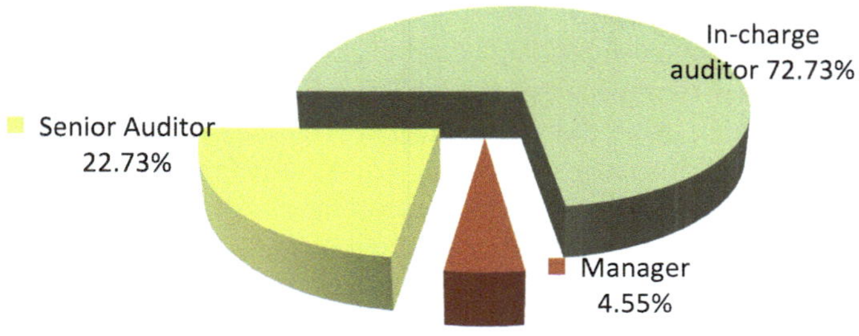

Graphic 4.2 Audit firms' managers' professional positions

Graphic 4.3 QCPP—quality control policy and procedures in audit firms–view of managers of audit firms

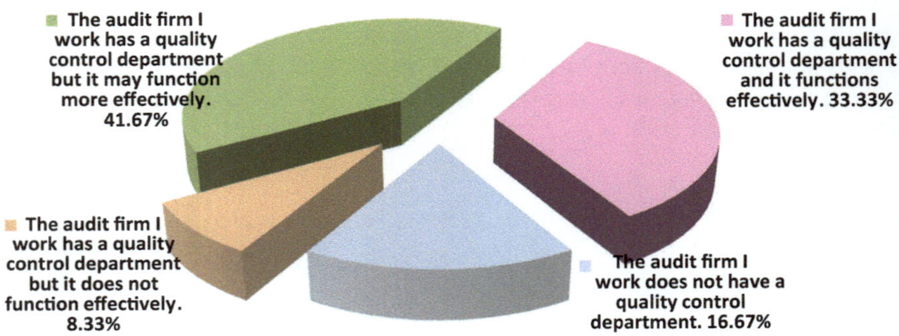

Graphic 4.4 Quality control department in audit firms–view of managers of audit firms

4.2.3.2 Auditing Firms' Managers' Opinions About Auditor's Merits and Demographics

About auditor's age, 45.84% of the respondents do not agree that auditor's age impacts audit quality significantly, and 54.16% of them believe that age is a significant factor. Auditor's gender is not an impacting factor according to 83.34% of the responding auditors. Educational background of the auditor seems to be a significant factor for 79.17% of the auditing firms' managers, whereas 16.67% of them think it is not that important. These are displayed in the Graphic 4.5. As seen from Graphic 4.6, managers of auditing firms, who think that the experience of the auditor absolutely impacts audit quality make up 45.83%, those who partially agree and agree with it make up 53.67% of the respondents. Auditing firms' managers agreeing that professional competence positively counts make up 95.83% of the respondents; same support comes for professionalism, independence, trustworthiness and ethical understanding of the auditor as positively impacting the quality of the audit conducted–Graphic 4.7.

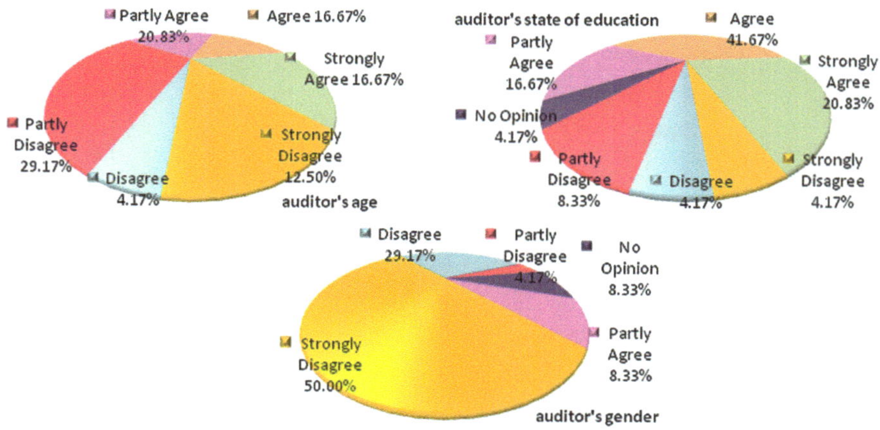

Graphic 4.5 Opinions of managers of audit firms–impacts of auditor's age, education, and gender on audit quality

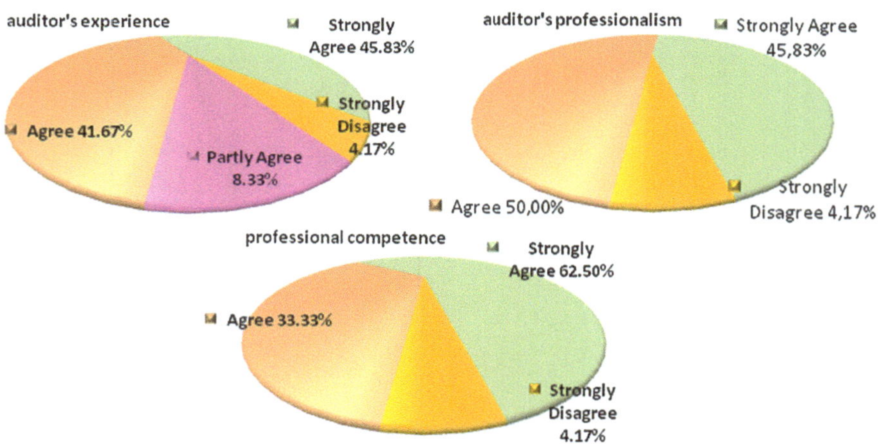

Graphic 4.6 Opinions of managers of audit firms–impacts of auditor's experience, professionalism, and competence on audit quality

Though differing at degree of agreeing; 95.83% of the respondents find professional care and due diligence as an important factor on audit quality, and except for those who say they don't have an opinion—4.17%, the rest believe the audit quality perceived by the auditor significantly impacts the quality of the audit. The statements saying that conducting an audit in a sector where auditor is already specialized, and for a client well known by the auditor would impact audit quality, finds support from 91.87 and 95.83% of respondents, respectively. Statement about auditor's regular declaration of property/wealth is supported only by less than 31% of the respondents Graphic 4.8.

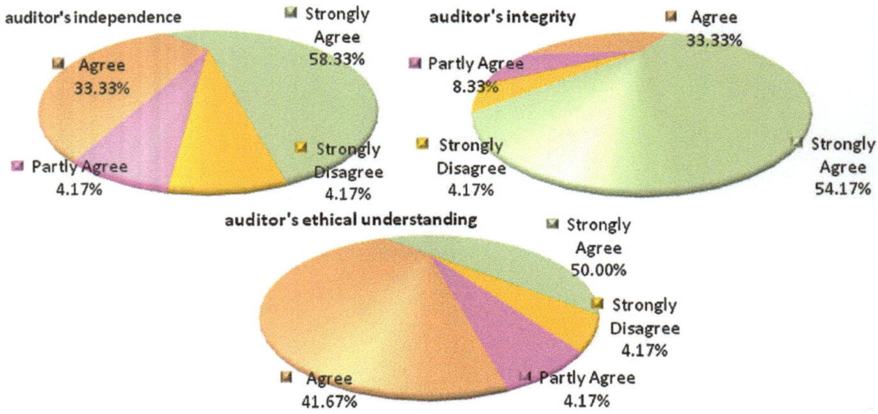

Graphic 4.7 Opinions of managers of audit firms–impacts of auditor's independence, integrity and ethical understanding on audit quality

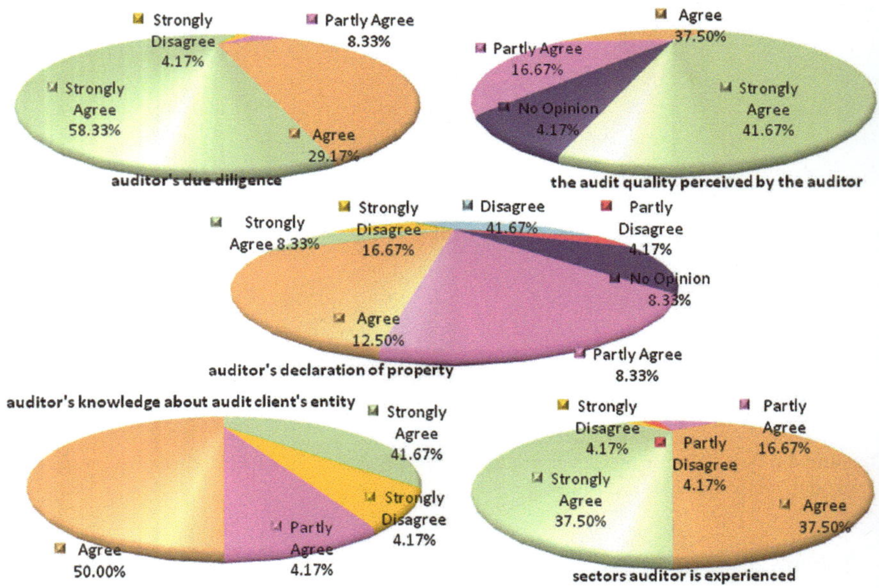

Graphic 4.8 Opinions of managers of audit firms–impacts of auditor's due diligence, perception of audit quality, and sector and client knowledge and declaration of property on audit quality

4.2.3.3 Opinions of Managers of Auditing Firms About the Audit Itself and the Auditing Process

Survey question pointing the positive and significant impact on audit quality of self-created and interiorized additional independence criteria created by the auditing firm, got 87.50% of the respondents' approval. For rotation of the audit team members at certain intervals collected 83.33% of the respondents' agreement (Graphic 4.9).

Managers of auditing firms responding the survey agree that; both a review of the auditor's opinion by a non-audit team member auditor at the completion phase of the audit and review of the working papers at the same phase on the same basis, will enhance the audit quality—95.83% (Graphic 4.10).

The statement that generation of an auditing firm's revenue from a diversity of clients instead of an individual client has positive and significant impact on audit quality received approval from 87.50% of the respondents. The opinion that, "auditing firm having a foreign partner or affiliated to an international network, may have a positive impact on audit quality," finds support from managers of auditing firms by 62.49%; where 53.33% of the agreeing auditing firms' managers are recruited by an auditing firm with a foreign affiliation (Graphic 4.11). Managers of auditing firms who do not agree with this opinion are distributed as follows; 33.33% of them work at an auditing firm with no foreign partner and 55.55% of them work at an auditing firm, which has foreign affiliation. The opinions of managers of auditing firms that have a foreign partner are exclusively displayed in Graphic 4.12.

The following group of questions is prepared to find out the attitude of auditing firms toward independence of the auditor and the auditing firm. Managers of auditing firms saying that all auditors at all levels in their auditing firm, hand a written

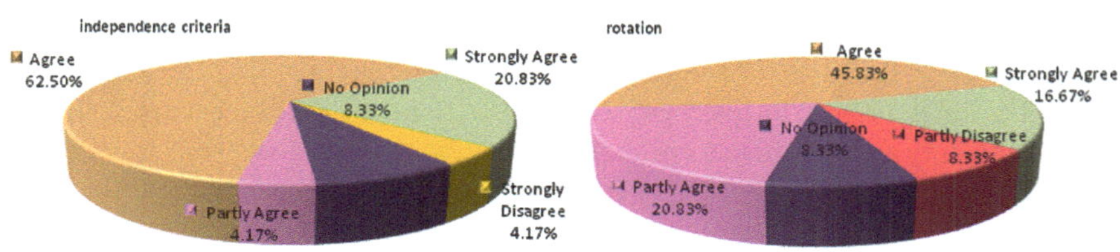

Graphic 4.9 Opinions of managers of audit firms–additional independence criteria and auditor rotation

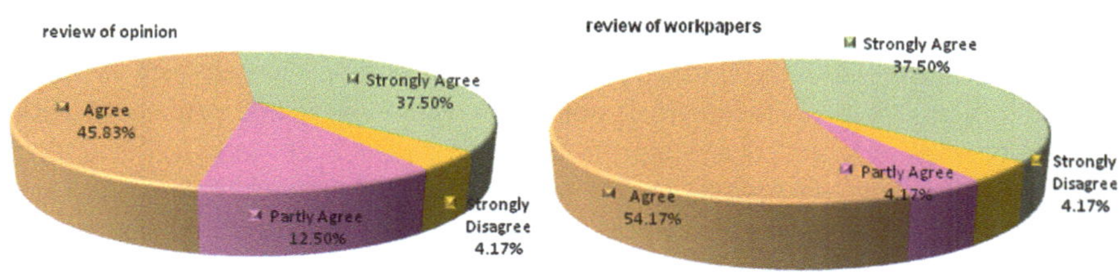

Graphic 4.10 Opinions of managers of audit firms–review of opinion and working papers

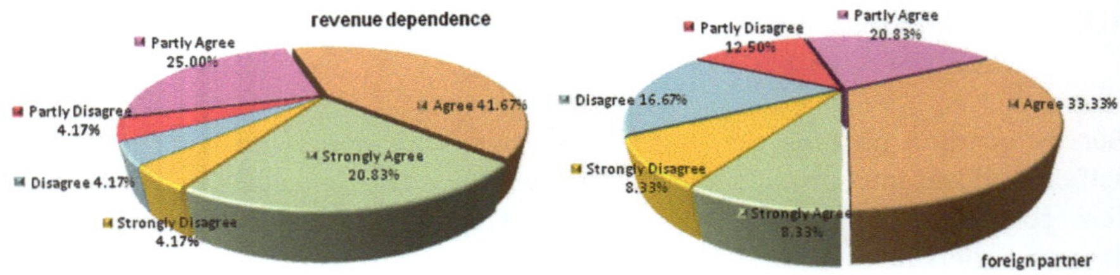

Graphic 4.11 Opinions of managers of audit firms–revenue dependence and foreign partner

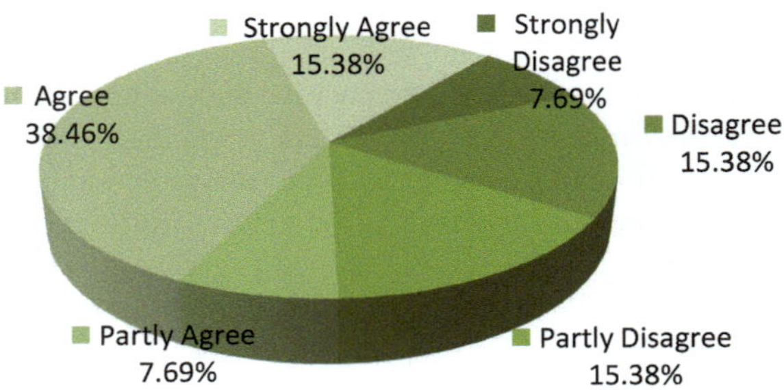

Graphic 4.12 Opinions of managers of audit firms that have a foreign partner about the impact of having a foreign partner on audit quality

declaration to the audit committee annually, make up 41.67% of the respondents; where another 16.67% have no idea, and the rest says there is no such declaration. Those, declaring absolutely, that none of any auditors at all levels of auditing firm have any relation regarding any service with the audit client other than audit, make up 66.67% of the respondents. The percentage of managers of auditing firms admitting such a relation is 12.50. The question, whether the management of the auditing firm is notified annually and in written form about this kind of relation, gets "yes" answer from two-thirds of respondents. For quality control purposes, it is advised that auditors at all levels ought to notify the audit committee annually in written form about situations threatening their independence. This statement is supported by 83.33% of the responding auditing firms' managers, who say their auditors at all levels make this notification. About the annual written notification to the audit committee about the precautions the auditor takes against these kinds of threats that would impair their independence, 62.51% affirms there is such a notification, and 25% doesn't. Similar to this statement, 20.83% of the managers of auditing firms reject the statement by saying that auditors at all levels of their firm do not make any annual written notification about all kinds of relationships may be suppressing their independence, and 66.66% of them admit such a notification. Any kind of advantage afforded by the audit client or parties related to the audit client is apt to immediate written notification to the management of the auditing firm. Saying that there is such a notification gets support from 79.17% of the respondents. The percentage does not change for the statement pointing to a promise of such favor. Managers support the statement about the immediate written notification to the audit firm management in case there is any partnership relationship of an auditor with the audit client or any related party, by 83.33%. Graphic 4.13 displays the responses to this question, and also summarizes the responses to some other questions. One of the disappointing questions of the survey is that 25% of the managers of auditing firms confess they do not have an ethics handbook; 25% say that their workforce did not read it, and 25% declare that they do not browse the ethics handbook from time to time. Around 50% of the auditing firms' managers say that at least 90% of previous year enrolled auditors continue working with the auditing firm in the current year. Those saying that at least 75% of the newcomers continue working, make up 70.83% of the respondents. For continuation level of 50% of the newcomers, yes answers are 75% of the responding auditing firms' managers. While assessing turnover questions of the survey, the facts that the responding managers of auditing firms represent the most prominent auditing firms in Turkey, the audit industry is homogeneous in Turkish audit market, and unemployment rate of Turkey is not relieving in the short run are to be kept in mind.

Another audit team related question is about the sufficiency of capacity of the auditing firm, and except for 14.29% of respondents, the rest of managers of auditing firms asserts sufficient capacity. A similar portion comes for training policies; 14.29% say they have no such training policy. The answers to the question about the average yearly training hours per audit professionals except for fresh comers is as follows; 50% declares minimum 90 training hours per professional, minimum 60 training hours per professional is declared by 25%, minimum 30 training hours per professional is verified by 70.84 and minimum 12 h is welcomed by 74.99%.

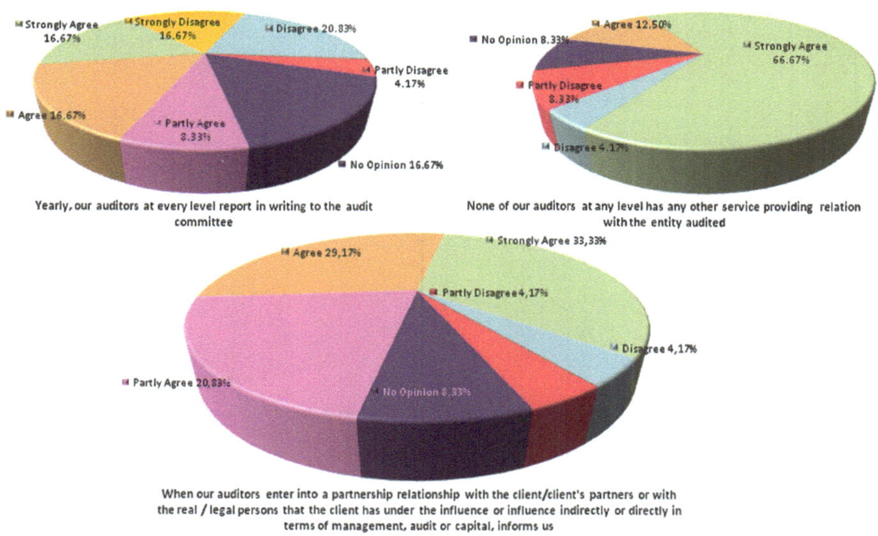

Graphic 4.13 Opinions of managers of audit firms about written notifications and other service relations with the audit client

The nine prohibited activities for a registered accounting firm performing an independent audit of a public company according to Sarbanes–Oxley Act (SOX) (SOX, Title II, Section 201; SmartPros.com 2002) are as follows:

(1) Bookkeeping or other services relating to the accounting records or financial statements of the audit client;
(2) Financial information systems design and implementation;
(3) Appraisal or evaluation services, fairness opinions or contribution-in-kind reports;
(4) Actuarial services;
(5) Internal audit outsourcing services;
(6) Management functions or human resources;
(7) Broker or dealer, investment advisor, or investment banking services;
(8) Legal services and expert services unrelated to the audit; and
(9) Any other service that the accounting board determines, by regulation, is impermissible.

Though the prevailing regulations in Turkey do not prohibit attestation service to the existing audit client, giving them under the same package impairs independence, which in turn negatively impacts the audit quality (Yılancı and Yıldız 2001;

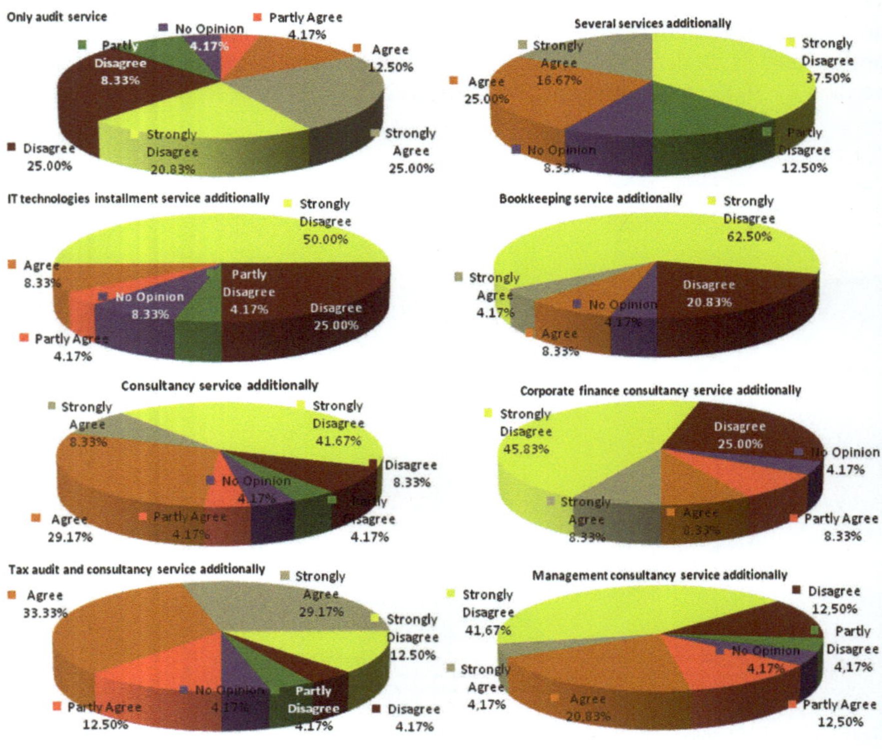

Graphic 4.14 Services audit firms give to their audit clients

Uzay 2004). As the author, I give emphasis on independence at utmost level. Therefore, the question(s) of surveys about this topic mean a lot for researchers to depict the stance of related parties of an audit.

Only 37.5% of the managers of auditing firms say that they only render audit service to the audit client, and 58.33% admit they provide other kinds of services. Auditing firms' managers saying that they do not provide Information Technologies System installation, make up 75% of the respondents, one fourth provides such a service. According to the auditing firms' managers responding the survey, 12.50% undertakes bookkeeping; 41.67% advises the audit client, 24.99% accepts corporate consulting service, 74.99 gives tax audit and consultation service, and management consultation to audit client is rendered by 37.50% of the respondents (Graphic 4.14).

4.2.3.4 Survey of Audit Clients' Managers

The audit client entities' managers' survey with 58 questions is answered by 148 stock exchange quoted companies, which are audited by 24 different auditing firms and, are from 28 different sectors. The sectors with at least ten respondents are Real Estate Activities, Banks and Special Finance Corporations, Financial Institutions, Chemicals, Petroleum Rubber and Plastic Products, Food, Beverage, and Tobacco. These companies represent 40.41% of total assets and 46.81% of total net worth of 516 Borsa Istanbul stock exchange quoted companies. This helped us to depict the stance of managers of audit client companies.

4.2.3.5 About Audit Client Companies

Managers of audit client companies taking part in the survey are 42 years old, have 18 years nine months of experience, and average tenure is nine years and four months, with a maximum tenure of 35 years eight months. Managers of audit client companies are mainly positioned at accounting department—27.70%; management—27.03%; finance and financial affairs departments in total—22.97%; where 10.81% of the respondents are general manager, 16.89% are CFO, and 35.81% are the director of their department.

Some of demographics about audit client entities' managers are displayed in Table 4.2, and Graphic 4.15.

Table 4.2 Demographics of audit client entities' managers

	Average	Minimum	Maximum
Age	42.13	26.62	65.52
Professional Tenure	18.78	1.93	38.93
Tenure with the Current Company	9.36	0.13	35.67

Note All data in years

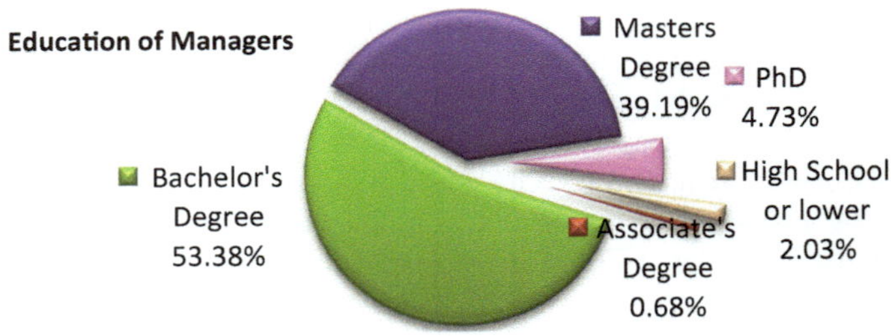

Graphic 4.15 Education of audit client entities' managers

Graphic 4.16 displays the experience of the members of the board of directors.

Out of 148 audit client companies, 15.76% don't have an audit committee, and responding companies' committee members are composed of auditors—69%; financiers—81%; economists—78%; and accountants—79%. The professions of audit committee members matters, as it is considered as an audit quality impacting factor (Graphic 4.17).

Though 29.05% do not believe, 70.95% of managers of audit client companies agree on merits of auditing firm choice to be done by the audit committee. At differing levels respondents agree on audit committee composed by experienced members positively impact audit quality—91.22%; and appointment of financiers and/or accounting based members positively impacts—91.22%. The professional backgrounds of audit committee members are shown in Graphic 4.17. In reality, 61% of the audit clients benefit from an audit committee for auditor choice; 34% do not. As audit firm choice decision considered; less than 6% of the respondents say that this decision is solely taken by the general manager, 16% say it is up to the CEO, another 16% think that CFO or the like choose the auditor, and 66% state that the Board of Directors makes this decision. This diversity of answers implies that a combination of the alternatives is valid for audit firm choice decision. Graphic 4.18 displays the body of the audit client choosing the audit firms.

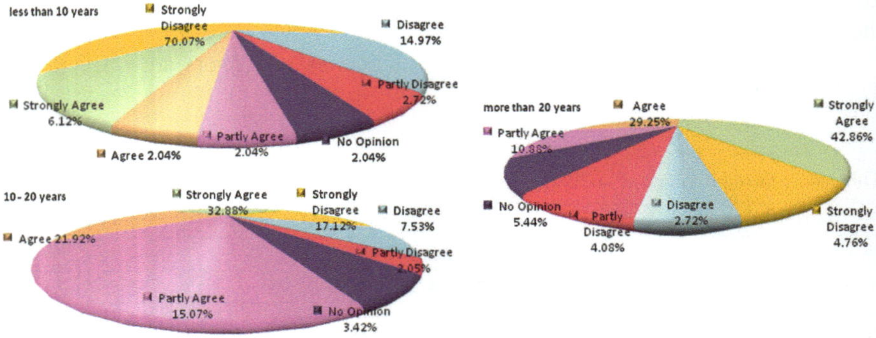

Graphic 4.16 Experience of board of directors of audit client entities in years

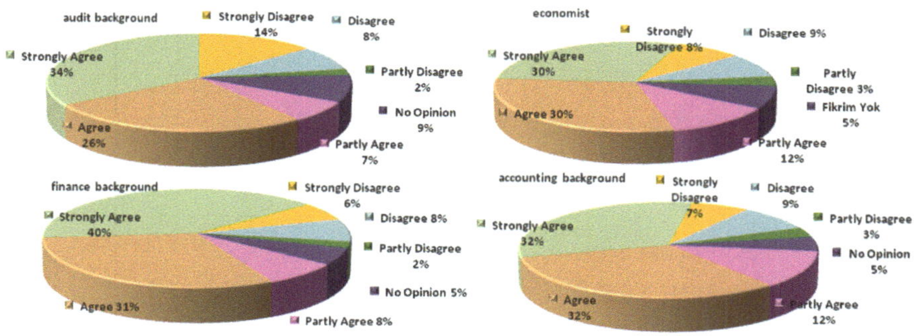

Graphic 4.17 Professional background of audit committee members of audit clients

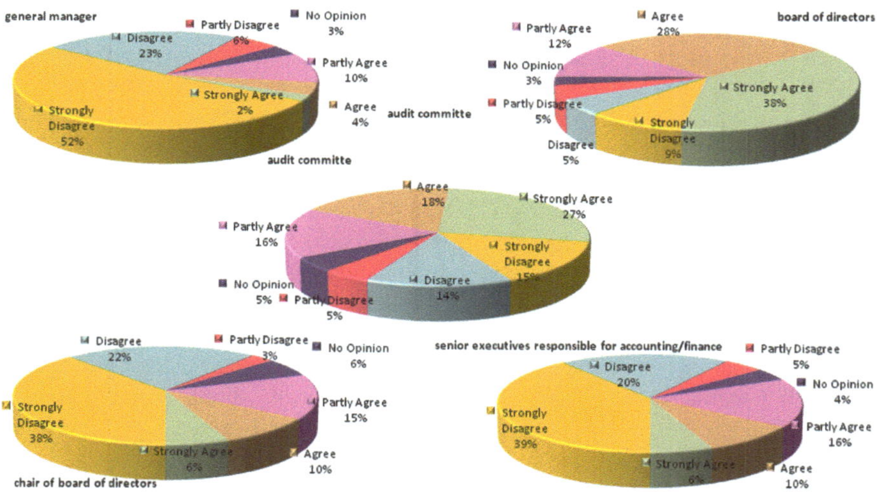

Graphic 4.18 The Body making audit firm choice

Audit quality literature supports an efficient internal control system of the audit client as a positively impacting factor. There are questions of the survey aiming to find these out. Out of 148 audit client companies, 83.11% has an internal control system, and 70.75% claim their system is efficient. Companies, with an internal control team composed by at least three persons are 45.58%; teams composed by three at most make up 28.58%, and teams with a single member are 13.6% of the respondents. Not only the size but also the qualifications of internal control team make sense. The existence of members with experience more than ten years is supported by 73.46%; at least five-year experience is valid for 64.38%, and teams with members with less than five years experience make up 25.94% of the responding audit client companies. The question, whether certain professionals have a seat in internal control team is answered as; auditors—76.18%, accountants—75.68%, financiers—75.51%, bankers—45.58%, and engineers—28.56% (Graphic 4.19).

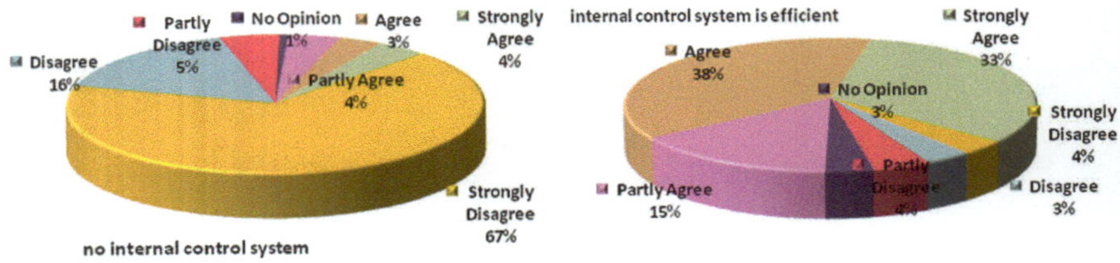

Graphic 4.19 Existence and efficiency of the internal control system

Abidance to corporate governance principles is another would be audit quality impacting factor. Among managers of audit client companies, 59.86% believes that his/her company absolutely follows corporate governance principles, and 29.25% says "yes." There are two managers out of 148, stating that their company does not follow principles. Incentive pay for performance is a noxious factor to audit quality. Sometimes the roots of creative accounting stem from incentive pay for performance. However, 72.11% of the respondents declare such pay to managers, and 21.77% say they do not have it.

The disappointing point here is that, as seen from Graphic 4.20, only 11.56% of the respondents are against such payment, and 87.76 are pro it.

Turkish Standards on Auditing (TSA) 220, "Quality Control for an Audit of Financial Statements" (www.kgk.gov.tr, TSA 220 2014: 15) points to audit client's integrity. As Pacini states in lecturing notes "*material errors and irregularities, fraud are more likely when management is dishonest.*" According to him, those client firms, which face potential significant legal claims and/or financial distress, raise the probability of an auditor lawsuit. Therefore, he suggests that the auditor should talk to management and creditors, review credit reports, and filings with regulatory agencies (Pacini 2003). This is why emphasis is given to the questions directed to the honesty of the audit client management. The possibility of board members of having ever stood a trial due practice is assessed by managers of audit client companies as follows; 12.00% does not have an idea, 9.00% says there has been such a trial, and the rest absolutely disclaim such a trail. As further asked, whether there came out a punishment following such a trial, only 3.00% says "yes," 8.00% has no idea, and the rest defend the idea that there is no such punishment. Due to tendency of concealment and sweeping these kind disgraces under the carpet, the frank answers did not come out of these questions. The data are shown in Graphic 4.21.

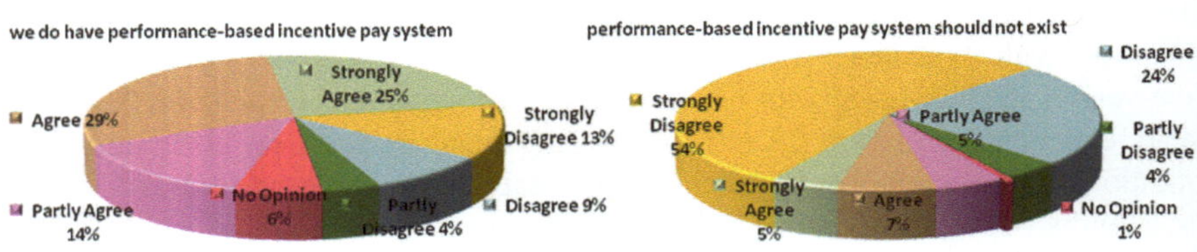

Graphic 4.20 Performance-based incentive pay system

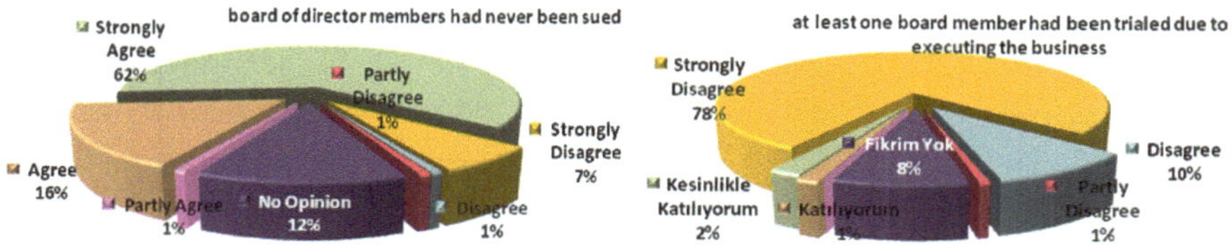

Graphic 4.21 Whether board of director members had ever been trialed due to their executive roles

4.2.3.6 Audit Client Managers' Opinions About Auditor's Merits and Demographics

About *auditor's age*, 56.76% of the respondents agree that auditor's age impacts audit quality significantly, and the rest do not believe that age is a significant factor. *Auditor's gender* is not an impacting factor according to 85.72% of the responding managers of audit client companies. *Educational background of the auditor* seems to be a significant factor for 95.27% of the auditing firms' managers, whereas 3.38% of think it is not that important.

Managers of audit clients, who think that the *experience of the auditor* absolutely impacts audit quality make up 50.00%, those who partially agree and agree with it make up 48.65% of the respondents. Managers of audit client companies agreeing that professional competence positively counts, make up 98.65% of the respondents; same support comes for independence. Except for partially disagreeing group—0.68%, and those opting out this statement—1.35%, the rest of the respondents finds auditor's trustworthiness as a positively and significantly impacting factor on audit quality. Professionalism—98.65%; professional care and due diligence and ethical understanding of the auditor— 99.32% each are positively impacting factors, as well. Except for those, who say they do not have an opinion—4.73%, and disagreeing managers—2.03%, the rest believe the audit quality perceived by the auditor significantly impacts the quality of the audit. The statements saying that conducting an audit in a sector where auditor is already specialized, and for a client well known by the auditor would impact audit quality, finds support from 92.57 and 97.00% of respondents respectively. Statement about auditor's regular declaration of property/wealth is supported only by than 57.43% of the respondents.

4.2.3.7 Opinions of Managers of Audit Clients About the Audit Itself and the Auditing Process

Among the managers of audit client companies, 32.43% believe that there is no harm to the audit quality in getting a package of services, like consultancy, accounting, external auditing, and tax consultation from a single CPA firm. Those thinking that there would not be harm to the audit quality, in case their company gets consultancy, installation of an accounting system and the like, from their audit firm make up 23.65% of the respondents—Graphic 4.22. The survey question pointing the positive and significant impact on audit quality of self-created and interiorized additional independence criteria created by the auditing firm, got 89.19% of the respondents' approval. For rotation of the audit team members at certain intervals collected 92.62% of the respondents' agreement.

Managers of audit clients responding the survey agree that; a review of the auditor's opinion by a non-audit team member auditor at the completion phase of the audit will enhance the audit quality—89.18% and review of the working papers at the same phase on the same basis is supported by 90.53% of the respondents. The statement that generation of an auditing firm's revenue from a diversity of clients instead of an individual client has positive and significant impact on audit quality got rejection from 21.63% of the respondents, and 6.08% pretend they have no opinion. This is the core point of audit quality studies, since revenue dependency impairs independence. Opinions of managers of audit clients about the audit itself and the auditing process related issues are shown in the Graphic 4.23.

The opinion that, 'auditing firm having a foreign partner or affiliated to an international network, may have a positive impact on audit quality', finds support from managers of audit clients by 67.57 %; where 64.29% of managers of audit client companies audited by an auditing firm with a foreign affiliate, are among these—Graphic 4.22. Though being audited by an auditing firm affiliated to an international network, 21.42% of the managers of audit clients do not agree with this opinion.

4.2.3.8 Auditors' Survey

The auditors' survey, which directs 28 questions, is answered by 26 auditing partners and 67 auditors, totally by 93 auditors, where 85 of them are engaged with 35 different auditing firms and eight are anonymous. Some of the demographic factors about auditors are displayed in Table 4.3, and in Graphic 4.24.

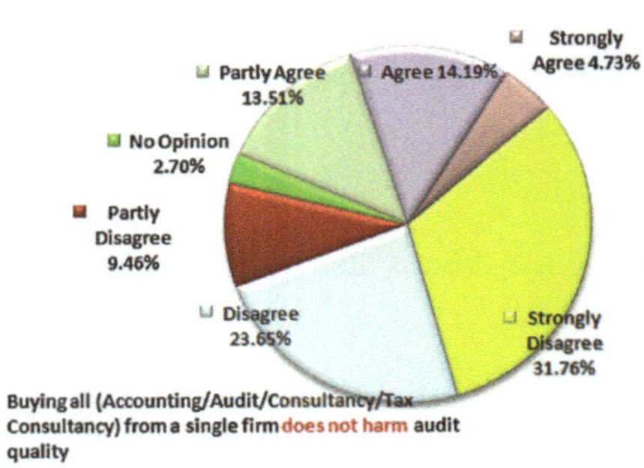

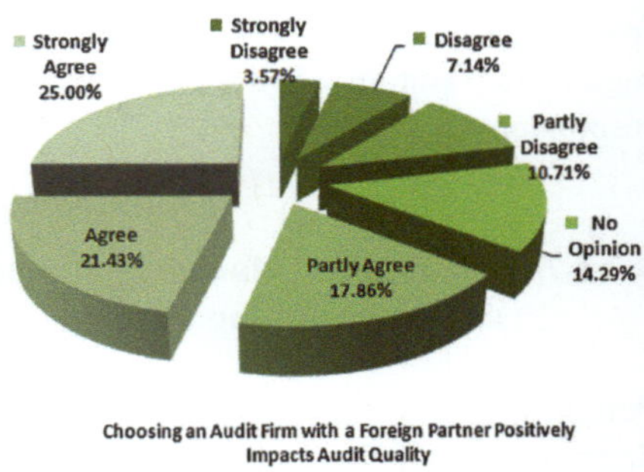

Graphic 4.22 Opinions of managers of audit clients about the audit itself and the auditing process-I

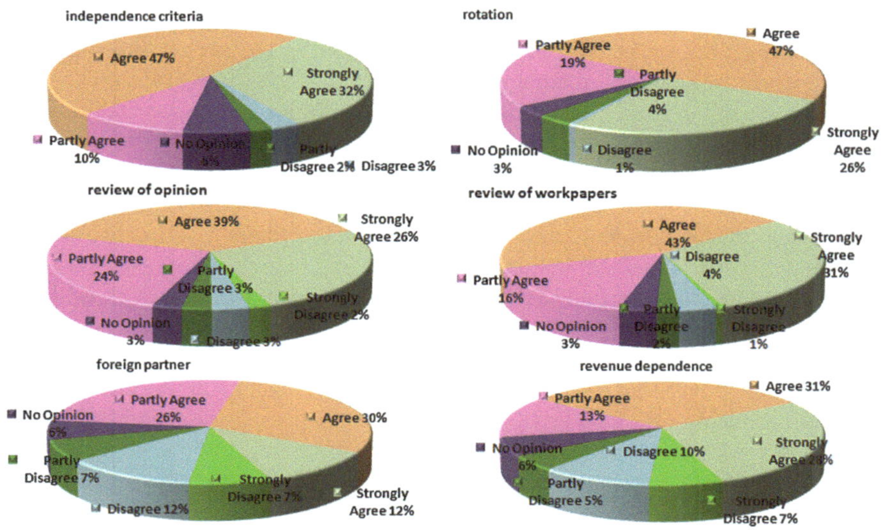

Graphic 4.23 Opinions of managers of audit clients about the audit itself and the auditing process-II

Table 4.3 Demographics of auditors-I

	Average	Minimum	Maximum
Age	36.45	23.24	63.13
Experience auditor	10.09	0.31	32.31
Tenure at the last audit firm	7.62	0.29	30.90
Tenure as audit firm partner	5.46	0.31	19.65

Note All data in years

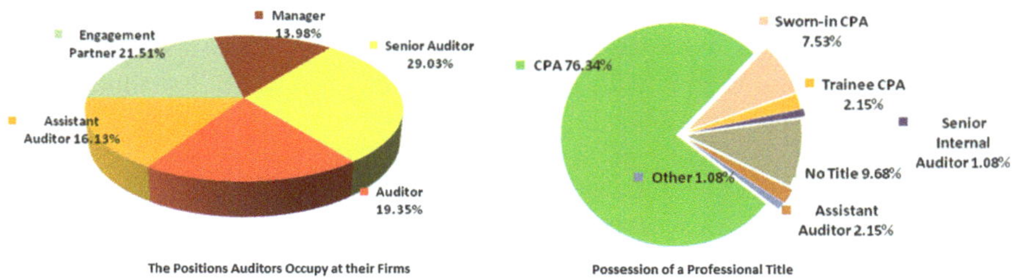

Graphic 4.24 Demographics of auditors-II

Auditors saying that, there are no *quality control policies and procedures* within their auditing firm, make up 7.53% of those answering the survey. According to 12.90% of the respondents, there are quality control policies and procedures within their firm, though they are informed only about their duties and responsibilities. Just orally informed auditors make up 6.45%; auditors informed only by a written notice make up 15.05%, and auditors informed both orally and written make up 53.76% of the respondents.

Another critical question tries to find out, whether there is a *quality control department* or not within the auditing firm. According to the auditors 24.73% of the auditing firms have not established a quality control department yet. Out of those, which already have one, 11.83% of the auditors evaluate the quality control department as ineffective; 25.81% of the auditors believe that the department would work more effectively, and 37.63% of the auditors are content with the effectiveness of the department.

Auditor' merits and demographic information are thought to be impacting the audit quality. *Auditor's age* is one of these; and 15.06% of the auditors responding believe that age is absolutely not significant, while 22.58% think it is, and 45.16% partially find age as significant. *Auditor's gender* is not an impacting factor according to 71.24% of the responding auditors, and those who think it is, make up 18.28%. *Educational background of the auditor* seems to be one of the factors, where there is almost a consensus among auditors—96.77% of the respondents evaluate it as a heavily impacting factor.

Auditors who think that the *experience of the auditor* absolutely impacts audit quality make up 61.29%, those who partially agree and agree with it make up 37.64% of the respondents. Auditors agreeing that professional competence positively counts make up 96.76% of the respondents, and except 2.16% of the respondents agree that professionalism of the auditor positively impacts the quality of the audit conducted. The ratio of the auditors believing that the independence of the auditor has importance on audit quality and the ratio of auditors having the opinion that trustworthiness of auditor has considerable impact on audit quality are unique—95.83%; whereas, 97.84% of them accredit ethical understanding of the auditor positively impacting audit quality.

Though differing at degree of agreeing; 97.85% of the respondents find professional care and due diligence as an important factor on audit quality, and except for those who say they don't have an opinion—4.30%, and those who disagree—3.24%; the rest believe the audit quality perceived by the auditor significantly impacts the quality of the audit.

Hypothetically, conducting an audit in a sector where auditor has already specialized would impact audit quality. Same is thought to be valid for an audit conducted for a client well known by the auditor. The results of the survey support both statements by 94.62%. A would be factor impacting audit quality is auditor's regular declaration of property/wealth; however, only 32.25% of the respondents support this idea.

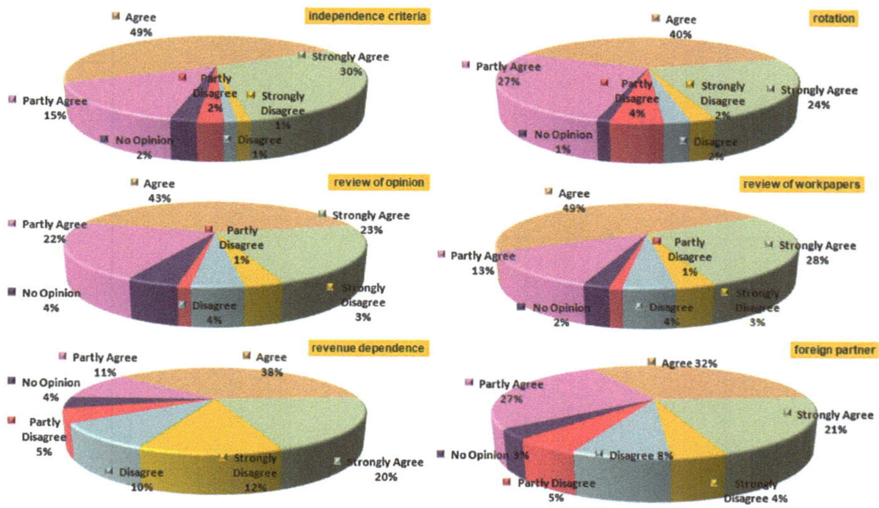

Graphic 4.25 Opinions of auditors about the audit itself and the auditing process

Another aim of the survey is finding out the opinions of auditors about the audit itself and the auditing process. In literature, there are opinions pro self-created and naturalized additional independence criteria of the auditing firm itself. The question of the survey pointing the positive and significant impact of such criteria on audit quality got 93.55% of the respondents' approval. Rotation of the audit team members at certain intervals is another would be determinant of audit quality. The question, intending to unveil the opinions of auditors about rotation, collected more than 90% of the respondents' agreement.

Auditors responding the survey agree that; review of the auditor's opinion by a non-audit team member auditor at the completion phase of the audit, will enhance the audit quality—87.1%. Similarly; the review of the working papers at the same phase on the same basis collects approval of the 89.25% of the responding auditors. Generation of an auditing firm's revenue from a diversity of clients instead of an individual client has positive and significant impact on audit quality. This sentence received approval only from 68.81% of the responding auditors. Some of the above-mentioned opinions of auditors are summarized in the Graphic 4.25.

In order to assist the comparison of opinions of three groups responding the questionnaires, three additional tables. In Table 4.4 the auditor qualifications are presented in percentages, and Table 4.5 displays the mean and standard deviations of the same data. The third table compares the opinions of the three groups regarding the audit process (Table 4.6).

Table 4.4 Comparative table of degrees of agreeing with the statements about the auditor qualifications in percentages

Statements	Managers of audit firms %							Managers of Audit Clients %							Auditors %						
	1	2	3	4	5	6	7	1	2	3	4	5	6	7	1	2	3	4	5	6	7
Auditor's age	12.50	4.17	29.17	0	20.83	16.66	16.66	9.46	18.92	10.17	4.73	35.14	17.57	4.05	7.53	10.75	10.75	3.23	45.16	16.13	6.45
Auditor's gender	50.00	29.17	4.17	8.33	8.33	0	0	59.46	22.30	4.05	6.76	4.73	2.70	0	41.94	29.03	6.45	4.30	8.60	5.38	4.30
Auditor's education	4.17	4.17	8.33	4.17	16.67	41.67	20.83	0	1.35	2.03	1.35	14.86	43.24	37.16	2.15	0	1.08	0	22.58	47.31	26.88
Auditor's experience	4.17	0	0	0	8.33	41.67	45.83	0	0	0.68	0.68	4.73	43.92	50.00	1.08	0	0	0	3.23	34.41	61.29
Auditor's professional competence at a specific level	4.17	0	0	0	0	32.50	62.50	0	0	0	1.35	4.73	38.51	55.41	1.08	0	1.08	1.08	5.38	27.96	63.44
Auditor's independence	4.17	0	0	0	4.17	33.33	58.33	0	0	0.68	0.68	3.38	28.38	66.89	1.08	0	1.08	1.08	7.53	31.18	58.06
Auditor's integrity	4.17	0	0	0	8.33	33.33	54.17	0	0	0.68	1.35	5.41	33.11	59.46	1.08	0	0	2.15	10.75	36.56	49.46
Auditor's professionalism	4.17	0	0	0	0	50.00	45.83	0	0	0	1.35	4.73	40.54	53.38	1.08	0	1.08	0	8.60	36.56	52.69
Auditor's ethical understanding	4.17	0	0	0	4.17	41.67	50.00	0	0	0	0.68	6.08	39.19	54.05	1.08	0	1.08	0	8.60	40.86	48.39
Auditor auditing in a sector where he/she experienced	4.17	0	4.17	0	16.67	37.50	37.50	0	2.03	4.05	1.35	9.46	37.16	45.95	1.08	0	3.23	1.08	18.28	45.16	31.18
Auditor's professional care and due diligence	4.17	0	0	0	8.33	29.17	58.33	0	0	0	0.68	2.70	35.81	60.81	1.08	0	1.08	0	2.15	34.41	61.29
Auditor's perceived audit quality	0	0	0	4.17	16.67	37.50	41.67	0.68	1.35	0.68	4.73	13.51	44.59	34.46	1.08	1.08	1.08	4.30	12.90	53.76	25.81
Auditor's knowledge about audit client company	4.17	0	0	0	4.17	50.00	41.67	0	1.35	0.68	0.68	10.81	41.89	44.59	1.08	0	2.15	2.15	6.45	37.63	50.54
Auditor's declaration of property to professional chambers regularly	16.67	41.67	4.17	8.33	8.33	12.50	8.33	6.08	10.14	8.11	18.24	26.35	21.62	9.46	21.51	0	11.83	15.05	17.20	15.05	0

Table 4.5 Table of comparison of agreeing with the statements about the auditor qualifications

Statements	Managers of audit firms $n = 24$		Audit client entities' managers $n = 148$		Auditors $n = 93$	
	Mean M	Standard Deviation *St*	Mean M	Standard Deviation *St*	Mean M	Standard Deviation *St*
Auditor's age	3.75	1.57	3.30	1.53	3.61	1.42
Auditor's gender	1.54	1.02	1.49	1.04	2.06	1.48
Auditor's education	4.38	1.58	5.07	1.03	4.94	0.94
Auditor's experience	5.21	1.10	5.41	0.76	5.54	0.73
Auditor's professional competence at a specific level	5.46	1.06	5.44	0.87	5.46	0.98
Auditor's independence	5.38	1.10	5.59	0.75	5.39	1.00
Auditor's integrity	5.29	1.12	5.46	0.90	5.24	1.13
Auditor's professionalism	5.29	1.04	5.42	0.87	5.38	0.83
Auditor's ethical understanding	5.29	1.08	5.45	0.76	5.33	0.83
Auditor auditing in a sector where he/she experienced	4.96	1.20	5.16	1.10	4.97	1.04
Auditor's professional care and due diligence	5.33	1.13	5.55	0.71	5.53	0.76
Auditor's perceived audit quality	5.04	1.30	4.89	1.39	4.82	1.33
Auditor's knowledge about audit client company	5.21	1.06	5.25	0.90	5.25	1.15
Auditor's declaration of property to professional chambers regularly	2.58	1.77	3.21	1.99	2.42	1.68

Table 4.6 Comparison of opinions regarding audit process

Survey Questions Regarding The Audit Process	Managers of audit firms $n = 24$		Audit client entities' managers $n = 148$		Auditors $n = 93$	
	Mean M	Standard Deviation *St*	Mean M	Standard Deviation *St*	Mean M	Standard Deviation *St*
Apart from legal and professional regulations, the fact that the audit firm has its own independence criteria has an important and positive effect on the quality of the audit	4.58	1.72	4.79	1.49	4.92	1.16
Each of the auditors constituting the audit team shall be subject to rotation in specific time frames, and assigned to the engagements with different clients has an important and positive influence on the quality of the audit	4.38	1.58	4.82	1.21	4.68	1.18
In the completion phase of the audit, the review of the auditor's opinion by an engagement partner who is not on the audit team has an important and positive influence on the quality of the audit	5.08	1.10	4.65	1.34	4.52	1.50
The fact that the work papers are reviewed by an engagement partner who is not on the audit team during the completion of the audit has an important and positive influence on the quality of the audit	5.17	1.05	4.81	1.34	4.76	1.36
The fact that a significant portion of the audit firm's total revenue is not earned from a single client or a single group of companies has an important and positive effect on the quality of the audit	4.58	1.25	4.18	1.86	4.01	1.85
The audit firm having a partnership with a foreign audit firm or making an agreement affects the audit quality positively	3.79	1.50	3.75	1.71	4.27	1.53

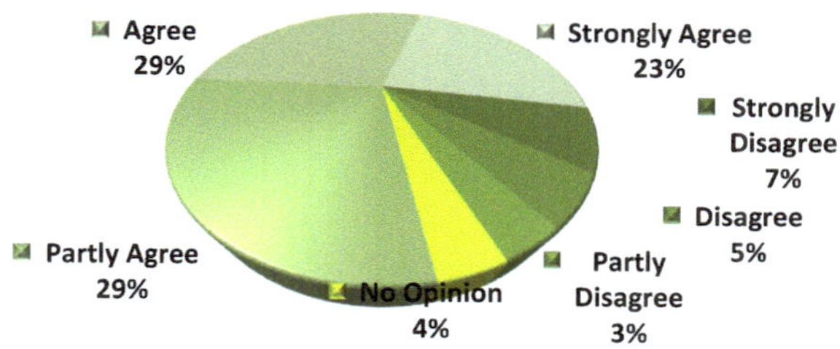

Graphic 4.26 Opinions of auditors of audit firms that have a foreign partner: "having a foreign partner positively impacts the audit quality"

The auditing firm having a foreign partner or affiliation to an international network may have a positive impact on audit quality. The opinion finds support from auditors by 79.57%; where 73.77% of the agreeing auditors are recruited by an auditing firm with a foreign affiliation. Auditors who do not agree with this opinion are distributed as follows; 16.67% of them work at an auditing firm with no foreign partner and 83.33% work at an auditing firm, which has foreign affiliation (Graphic 4.26).

Summary and Discussion

While conducting the survey, questions about the existence of quality control policies and procedures, and the way of sharing them within the auditing firm, have been asked both to managers of auditing firms and to the auditors. Auditing firms' managers affirmed the existence of quality control policies and procedures, and their transfer to auditors both in written and oral form by 62.50 and 53.76% of auditors did so. Starting from this determination, it can be concluded that auditing firms in Turkey have not yet established quality control policies and procedures outright, put them in black and white, and share of information to the auditors is not adequate and satisfactory.

Similar to this, both groups answered the questions about the existence and the functionality of the quality control department. Auditors admit their existence and functionality by 37.63% and managers of auditing firms did so by 33.33%. From this, it is commented that auditing firms in Turkey should generally pay more attention to this issue.

Annual declaration of independence is an ethical issue. One-third of the managers of auditing firms say that auditors at all levels within the auditing firm hand a written declaration to the audit committee annually. Annual written notification by all auditors at all levels within the auditing firm, about the existence of any other employment of any service besides audit by the audit client, is confirmed by half of the managers of auditing firms. The percentage of the auditing firms' managers believing that all auditors at all levels within the auditing firm inform the audit committee annually in written form, about any circumstance threatening their independence, is 50%. This group of questions related to auditors' notifications to the related authorities concerned got positive answers from the managers of auditing firms by 60% on the average. Half of the threats on independence, 42% of the relationships suppressing independence, and 37.5% of possible favors from the audit client are missing as notifications by auditors. Having the remaining 40% on the average, on the non-confirming side, apparently reflects the peril of low audit quality.

I. Kesimli, *External Auditing and Quality*, Accounting, Finance, Sustainability, Governance & Fraud: Theory and Application,
https://doi.org/10.1007/978-981-13-0526-9

An audit industry lacking the emphasis on independence will be far from being efficient. Therefore, further high-quality, satisfactory, and more frequent training about professional ethics and independence is advised. In addition to this, transparency reports prepared by auditing firms should be properly and effectively overseen by public authorities.

Factors Related to the Auditing Firm

(1) Organizational structure—network, local office/partner, Web design;
(2) Secondary partnerships and indirect partners;
(3) Business model;
(4) Variety of services supplied by the auditing firm, and their effects on independence;
(5) Independence—the level and sustainability of it;
(6) Law abidance, abidance to standards, ethics policies, and policy implementations;
(7) Human resources policies and procedures, and training policies;
(8) Ratio of professional staff to audit partners;
(9) Professional chargeable hours managed per audit partner;
(10) Chargeable hours per audit professional;
(11) Annual professional staff retention;
(12) Yearly training hours per audit professional;
(13) Quality control system;
(14) Number of audit clients;
(15) Time spent on a unique audit by the audit team; and
(16) Who pays the audit fee, and satisfactoriness of it.

Factors Related to the Auditor

(1) Independence of the auditor

- Law abidance, abidance to standards, ethics policies, and policy implementations;

(2) Years of experience; number of audits realized

- Knowledge about audit client and it's industry; experience in that specific industry;

(3) Rotation;
(4) Modified opinions/statements;
(5) Professional skepticism; and
(6) Overconfidence in auditor abilities.

Factors Related to the Audit Client

(1) Characteristics of the board of directors;

(2) Characteristics of the audit committee;
(3) Effectiveness of the internal control;
(4) Restatement of financial tables;
(5) Organizational structure;
(6) Corporate governance;
(7) Social responsibility;
(8) Existence of performance-based payment; and
(9) Law abidance, abidance to standards, ethics policies, and policy implementations.

Factors Related to the Public Authority

(1) Effectiveness of the public oversight;
(2) Peer review;
(3) Autonomy—independence from political power;
(4) Organizational structure;
(5) Efficient controls; and
(6) Penalties for those who do not abide laws, standards, and ethics.

Suggestions

Under suggestions, the Audit Firms Quality Index (AFQI) and the Payment Pool are handled. The purpose of the Index is mediating the process of the choice of the specific audit firm by facilitating the audit client to make a rational choice, where the choice will be based on objective criteria. The purpose of the Payment Pool is to increase auditor's independence, hence improving audit quality. While Audit Firms Quality (AFQI) is discussed in detail, the Payment Pool is a suggestion open for further discussions. PCAOB has a project to enhance audit quality by determining audit quality indicators. The Board's project on audit quality indicators seeks to develop a portfolio of quantitative measures that provide new insight into audit quality and explore how those measures might be deployed in a manner that best promotes quality. These indicators would be designed to help audit committees, investors, and others seeking the services of auditors to evaluate a firm's potential performance (Harris 20.03.2014). The PCAOB's project has similarities to the index proposed here, but Audit Firms Quality Index (AFQI) is original. The legislative requirements are not included in the index to function as parameters. Several institutions exercise their specific quality control inspections. What are questioned in the index are the audit quality-impacting indicators not covered by these inspections. The index is a unique and incremental tool that will help enhancing audit quality.

Audit Firms Quality Index (AFQI)

The audit market has an oligopolistic market structure, and this has many indicators. Auditing firms must comply with the various regulations introduced by regulators; most of the regulations further protect the oligopoly and make it more solid. Regulations punish audit firms' international growth in favor of the Big Four, thus causing concentration. For example, only two of the companies listed on the S&P 500 work with an audit firm other than the Big Four, and the Big Four get two-thirds of the revenue of the accounting industry. Companies believe that small audit firms do not have the required skill packages. Despite numerous legal violations during the course of their own engagements and the bankruptcy of Lehman

I. Kesimli, *External Auditing and Quality*, Accounting, Finance, Sustainability, Governance & Fraud: Theory and Application,
https://doi.org/10.1007/978-981-13-0526-9

Brothers-like customers, accounting circles pointed out that they were able to parry them without much damage. Aiming to help breaking down the oligopolistic structure and to rationalize the preferences of the audit client firms, this study recommends the **Audit Firms Quality Index (AFQI)**. The purpose of the index is mediating audit client's rational choice of the specific audit firm by facilitating objective criteria. Having high scores from this index, thus ranking high will be criteria for audit clients in choosing their audit engagement firms. Besides, the index will serve as a feedback instrument for audit firms, from which they can benefit as an input in their audit process.

In the future, the index is recommended to be combined with the ratings of the audit client companies, especially public companies listed in stock exchanges. Such a combined rating that influences the rational choice of investors based on objective criteria will function much more effectively and will be bounding. The index is to be updated and published periodically. Making the audit firm choice by considering the prominent criteria listed as Main Indicators of Audit Quality on Table 3.10 will impact audit quality positively. For the audit to be high quality, the audit firm's organizational structure is to be well designed; the audit firm should not have affiliates, side and/or indirect partners aiming to take advantage of casus omissus[1]; should not have side and/or indirect partners to provide the services that are no allowed by legislation; and have an ethical business model are prerequisites.

An audit firm, which confirms to the law and audit standards, establishes ethic policies and procedures, has a quality control system, and is to be preferred at the first hand. In case the audit firm has any foreign partner, within the frame of this partnership, experts of the foreign partner are required to assess the quality of the work performed, and the audit approach of the affiliate/local firm and its policies. Otherwise, there will not be any advantage of having a foreign partner or being a member of an international network regarding the audit quality. Here comes another reservation to be taken into consideration—the extent of the foreign partner's records being respectable—and how it is assessed against audit quality indicators are significant determiners.

One of the questions is asked in all three surveys. It is the statement "*The audit firm having a partnership with a foreign audit firm or making an agreement affects the audit quality positively.*" The audit client entities' managers agree with this statement by 67.57%, while 26.43% did not agree that a foreign partner's existence makes a positive contribution. As these responses are re-evaluated regarding the foreign partners of respondents if any, it is seen that managers of audit client entities that currently have a foreign partner agree at 64.29–21.42% disagree. Responses of those from three groups, who took the questionnaire, are tabulated in Table 1.

As it is not that easy to reveal the impacts of having a foreign partner or being a part of an international network, an analysis of audit firms responsible in the accounting scandals lived during 1980–2014 may give a hint about this issue.

[1]**casus omissus**: a case not provided for by the statute

Table 1 Opinions of respondents about the statement related to foreign partner

The audit firm having a partnership with a foreign audit firm or making an agreement affects the audit quality positively				Mean M	Agree Disagree
Managers of audit firms	1	Strongly disagree	8.33%	3.79	37.50
	2	Disagree	16.67%		
	3	Partly disagree	12.50%		
	4	No opinion	0.00%		0.00
	5	Partly agree	20.83%		62.50
	6	Agree	33.33%		
	7	Strongly agree	8.33%		
Audit client entities' managers	1	Strongly disagree	7.43%	3.75	26.35
	2	Disagree	12.16%		
	3	Partly disagree	6.76%		
	4	No opinion	6.08%		6.08
	5	Partly agree	26.35%		67.57
	6	Agree	29.73%		
	7	Strongly agree	11.49%		
Auditors	1	Strongly disagree	4.30%	4.27	17.20
	2	Disagree	7.53%		
	3	Partly disagree	5.38%		
	4	No opinion	3.23%		3.23
	5	Partly agree	26.88%		79.57
	6	Agree	32.26%		
	7	Strongly agree	20.43%		

Table 2 is a shorter one of Table 1.5 focusing on the role they undertook in accounting scandals before and after Enron Scandal.

Analyzing the table may help to overcome prejudicial approaches in audit firm choice. This is not an issue specific to Turkey, but a worldwide one to deal with. First, the investors and then the audit clients should be aware of functioning merits of an audit firm; it is not a matter of being popular, but performing high-quality audits by abiding the rules and legislation.

Table 2 Top five audit firms involved in 1980–2014 accounting scandals

Auditing firm	Scandals	Share (%)
Ernst & Young	**12**	**20.69**
Deloitte & Touche	**11**	**18.97**
PricewaterhouseCoopers	**10**	**17.24**
KPMG	**7**	**12.07**
Big Four	**40**	**68.97**
Arthur Andersen	**11**	**18.97**
Others	7	12.06
Total	58	100.00

The variety of the services the audit firm provides and the impacts of these services on independence are to be evaluated. The party paying audit fee, the satisfactoriness of this fee and the bondage to an audit client for generation of the revenue, and independence within this context are altogether important issues to be taken into consideration, while making the audit firm choice. The human resource policies and procedures, training policies, average yearly training hours of audit personnel are very important. Following and assimilating the current legislation and practices and providing their implementation will be possible with continuous education/training. The human resource policies and procedures directly affect the audit professional retention rate. Each audit conducted reaching the desired/ acceptable level of quality and sustaining the quality obtained regarding all audits are the keys. The ratio of audit professionals to partners that is defined as leverage; chargeable hours per audit professional; professional chargeable hours managed per audit partner; time spent on an audit are the indicators of audit quality. Having local office or partner and the number of companies audit firm audits are the other indicators.

There are 51 quality-impacting indicators listed as Main Indicators of Audit Quality in Table 3.10. First group of indicators are audit firm related; some are under the control of the firm, shaped under the organizational structure and human resources it has. Even though it cannot be isolated from the audit firm itself, some of the quality-impacting indicators are auditor related. The environment the auditor is brought up, the personality, and his/her education are altogether audit quality-impacting factors. The audit firms have some kind of control of auditor-related indicators by recruiting the most appropriate auditors, and adding value to them, which in turn will positively enhance the qualifications of audit firm's human resources. The third group of indicators is audit client related. The organizational structure of their entities, their management styles, characters of their managers, the nearby and distant environments they are in, and the like. Some of these seem to be neither reportable nor controllable, thus not auditable. Therefore, these indicators are not considered to be evaluated for index creation purposes. However, in case this is desired, then with the help of the degrees of their compliance to laws and legislation and their corporate governance indices will be a factor in calculating Audit Firms Quality Index (AFQI). As seen from Table 3.10, the last group of indicators is those related to the regulating institutions; thus similar to the audit client related indicators, these are not controllable factors, thus excluded from calculations.

The logic behind inventing such an index lies in the fact that any component to be used in index calculation has to be observable, measurable, reportable, and comparable. Another point to be emphasized is that the regulating institutions' power is needed in assuring data flow from audit firms to indexing body. As discussed so far, the index does not have a claim to benefit from all indicators listed in the Main Indicators of Audit Quality. The explanation of index formulas follows. Creation of this index emphasizes the transparency of audit firms and reminds that the cost of sustainable quality is to be taken into consideration.

There are two alternative equations proposed for Audit Firms Quality Index (AFQI). Each equation benefits from the same factors as ***coefficients***, and the difference is that the first equation sums the factors, where the second one multiplies them. Both have merits and demerits. The methods are explained below.

$$\mathbf{AFQI} = (\mathbf{i}) \times (\mathbf{ii}) \times (\mathbf{iii}) \times (\mathbf{iv}) \times (\mathbf{v}) \times (\mathbf{vi}) \times (\mathbf{vii}) \quad (1)$$

The first equation given above multiplies the coefficients calculated. The second equation below summates the multiplication of each coefficient by the weight assigned. The weights are not yet assigned and are expected to be determined following discussions and research in the future.

$$\mathbf{AFQI} = \mathbf{w}_1(\mathbf{i}) + \mathbf{w}_2(\mathbf{ii}) + \mathbf{w}_3(\mathbf{iii}) + \mathbf{w}_4(\mathbf{iv}) + \mathbf{w}_5(\mathbf{v}) + \mathbf{w}_6(\mathbf{vi}) + \mathbf{w}_7(\mathbf{vii}) \quad (2)$$

w = weight

When Eq. 1 is applied, the ideal audit firm would have a score of 100, where another audit firm, each of the seven coefficients of which are 99%, will score 93.207. Another audit firm that provides mediocre audit quality and has coefficients around 50% each will score 0.781, less than one. If the constant weight assigned to each seven coefficients is to be criticized, then it will be considered assigning weights to coefficients following research in this area. Another suggestion regarding Eq. 1 is adding up the coefficients of each audit firms, accepting the highest scoring audit firm as the ideal one, and dividing any audit firm's score to the ideal audit firm's score. The scores of audit firms will be proportionate to the ideal audit firm's score.

Coefficients

Coefficients are (i) **Auditor Experience Year Multiplier,** (ii) **Leverage**, (iii) **Chargeable Hours per Audit Staff**, (iv) **Workload Coefficient**, (v) **Annual Professional Staff Retention Rate**, (vi) **Training Hours Coefficient**, and (vii) **Audit Firm Independence Coefficient Factor**. The minuscules (lowercase Roman numerals) are representing the coefficients in equations.

(i) **Auditor Experience Year Multiplier**: The weighted average years of experience of audit firm's audit professionals at all levels after becoming licensed as a CPA.

A hypothetical audit firm is designed to calculate the auditor experience year multiplier. The audit firm is assumed to have a balanced audit staff, composed of three staff assistants, eleven auditors, ten senior auditors, eight managers, and eight engagement partners. By assuming it this way, each level of auditors has a balanced share in audit staff, and the shares are calculated. Thus, 20% of audit staff of any audit firm ideally is to be engagement partners, 20% managers, 25% senior auditors, 27.5% auditors, and 7.5% staff assistants. Another hypothetical factor in calculating **Auditor Experience Year Multiplier** is the years of experiences of each personnel. An experience of minimum 27 years is advised for an engagement partner, 26 years for managers, 18 years for senior auditors, nine years for auditors, and one year for assistant staff. The third component of **Auditor Experience Year Multiplier** is the weight assigned to each level. Hypothetical weights assigned are 40, 35, 21, 3, and 1, respectively. These weights are used in the formula below.

	Engagement partner	Manager	In-charge auditor	Auditor	Staff assistant	Title
100.00	40.00	35.00	21.00	3.00	1.00	Weight
40	8	8	10	11	3	Audit staff
100.00	20.00	20.00	25.00	27.50	7.50	Weight in audit staff (%)
	27	26	18	9	1	Years of experience
5.000	2.160	1.820	0.945	0.074	0.001	Score

$$\textbf{Score} = \sum_{u}^{n}\left[\frac{\text{weight}}{100} \times \text{Weight in Audit Staff} \times \text{Years of Experience}\right]$$

u = title

According to the above-given formula, a hypothetical ideal audit firm will score 5.000. Audit firms' calculated scores will be divided by 5.000, and the multiplier will be determined. Naturally, the hypothetical ideal audit firm's multiplier will be 100%.

$$\textbf{Score} = \left[\frac{40}{100} \times 20\% \times 27\right] + \left[\frac{35}{100} \times 20\% \times 26\right] + \left[\frac{21}{100} \times 25\% \times 18\right] + \left[\frac{3}{100} \times 27.5\% \times 9\right] + \left[\frac{1}{100} \times 7.5\% \times 1\right]$$

$$Score = 5.000$$

$$\textbf{Years of Experience Factor} = \frac{\textbf{Audit Firm's Years of Experience Factor}}{5.000}$$

(ii) **Leverage**: Ratio of professional staff to audit partners.

In calculating the leverage, the formula given below will be used. In order to get healthy results, audit firms are expected to timely and transparently report to public oversight institutions. The leverage calculated for any audit firm will be compared to the leverage of the hypothetical ideal firm's leverage; thus, the leverage multiplier will be calculated.

$$\textbf{Leverage} = \frac{\text{number of audit professionals}}{\text{number of engagement partners}}$$

$$\textbf{Leverage Coefficient} = \frac{\text{Leverage}_{\text{Ideal Audit Firm}}}{\text{Leverage}_{\text{Audit Firm}}}$$

The comparison of audit staff of the auditing firms having license agreements with Deloitte & Touche, Ernst & Young, KPMG and PricewaterhouseCoopers, and others is given in Table 2.7. The ratio of audit professionals to partners is defined as ***leverage***. Generally, the leverage is calculated with the help of the formula given below:

$$\text{Leverage} = \frac{\text{Number of Non} - \text{Partner Audit Staff}}{\text{Number of Partners}}$$

The leverage is discussed under the title 2.2.1. The Profile of Auditing Firms in Turkey. As seen from the calculations, the leverage of Big Four is 12.93 in 2012–2013 era and is almost four times of the leverage of the remaining auditing firms. The gap enlarged in 2015 and Big Four leverage reached 20.12, which is almost 5.34 times of the leverage of the remaining 91 auditing firms. The leverages for the two time periods are comparatively tabulated in Table 2.8. As seen from Table 2.8, among Big Four, Akis CPA has the highest leverage—23.85. The lowest leverage among all auditing firms is 0.25 and belongs to BD CPA, the audit staff of which consists eight partners and two staff assistants. As stated earlier, auditors and/or auditing firms with a higher proportion of non-audit services (NAS) in their product mix are expected to have higher leverage (Deltas and Doogar 2005: 13). The average of the leverages of all audit firms is 5.27 in 2012–2013 era and 6.75 in 2015. It is and will be emphasized throughout the text that the composition of the audit team has an effect on audit quality. Nonetheless, quantitative criteria solely do not become an indicator; they act as determinants in assessing the audit quality. According to Robert Conway, a depressed leverage is one of the factors positively impacting audit quality (Conway 25.11.2009: 11).

(iii) **Chargeable Hours per Audit Staff**: The average of the chargeable hours per audit staff at each level.

In order to calculate chargeable hours per audit staff, at the first step for each of the audit staff the hours required to conduct proper audits within an ideal workload under a yearly plan will be determined. The next step will be determining the average hours each staff at every level to complete audits yearlong. The division of these two will generate the average for an audit firm. This will be compared to the average of the hypothetical ideal audit firm's average, and the deviation will be found.

$$\textbf{Professional Chargeable Hours} = \sum_{u}^{n} \text{an auditor's total hours spent on audits in a year}$$

$$\textbf{Average Hours Worked} = \frac{\sum_{u}^{n} \text{auditor's total hours spent on audits in a year}}{\text{number of auditors}}$$

Chargeable Hours per Audit Staff Coefficient

$$= \frac{\text{Average Hours Worked}_{\text{Ideal Audit Firm}}}{\text{Average Hours Worked}_{\text{Audit Firm}}}$$

(iv) **Workload Coefficient**: Professional chargeable hours managed per audit partner.

Professional Chargeable Hours calculated in the previous coefficient will be divided to the numbers of partners to find the **workload**. This will be compared to the workload of the hypothetical ideal audit firm; thus the coefficient will be calculated.

$$\textbf{Workload} = \frac{\text{Professional chargeable hours}}{\text{Number of Partners}}$$

$$\textbf{Workload Coefficient} = \frac{\text{Workload}_{\textbf{Ideal Audit Firm}}}{\text{Workload}_{\textbf{Audit Firm}}}$$

This calculation will have an effect of diminishing the multipliers of audit firms that have higher workloads.

(v) **Annual Professional Staff Retention Rate**: The percentage of professionals employed a year ago, who are still employed to date.

$$\textbf{Rate} = \frac{\text{the number of professionals employed a year ago, who are still employed to date}}{\text{the number of professionals employed a year ago}}$$

The rate probably will be less than 100%; for audit firms with higher rates it will bring positive comments and impact the index positively.

(vi) **Training Hours Coefficient**: The weighted training hours are calculated, based on training programs planned and realized and the numbers of audit personnel at all levels attending these.

First, training hours of each auditor at each level will be calculated, and the sum will be taken for the audit staff, and then total training hours will be divided in the total number of audit profession of the audit firm. The audit firm's average will be compared to the hypothetical ideal audit firm's average, and the coefficient will be determined.

$$\textbf{Total Training Hours} = \textbf{Score} = \sum_{u}^{n} [\text{Training hours of each auditor}]$$

u = title

$$\textbf{Average Training Hours} = \frac{\sum_{u}^{n} [\text{Training hours of each auditor}]}{\text{Total number of audit professionals}}$$

$$\textbf{Training Hours Coefficient} = \frac{\text{Average Training Hours}_{\text{Audit Firm}}}{\text{Average Training Hours}_{\text{Ideal Audit Firm}}}$$

Probably the rate will be less than 100%; for audit firms with higher rates it will bring positive comments and impact the index positively.

(vii) **Audit Firm Independence Coefficient Factor**: The weighted average of the independence factor of each auditor at each level assigned to audits, and the overall independence factor of the audit firm.

Audit Firm Independence Coefficient Factor will compose of two components. The first one is the one related to the audit firm itself **Audit Firm Engagement Independence Coefficient**. This coefficient will be calculated by taking into consideration the services the audit firm provides to its audit clients, under different names, or by a CPA and/or CPA firm to the audit client's affiliates, or third parties in relation with the audit client. Providing any service forbidden by laws will score null, and an engagement that does not include any service against regulations will score one. Since a zero will cause serious problems in Eq. 1, an audit firm in this category will encounter problems. However, in Eq. 2, the audit firm will end up with a lower index score.

As stated in Independent Audit By-Law [22](5), audit firms and auditors cannot render any service to the audited entity other than ratification, tax consultancy, and tax audit and carry out them through related audit firms and other firms included in the audit network. Services rendered by the natural entity partners of the audit firm, its auditors, and key management personnel also fall within this scope. Table 3 displays these services and scores assigned. In light of data in this table, **Audit Firm Engagement Independence Coefficient** is to be calculated as follows.

$$\textbf{Audit Firm Engagement Independence Coefficient} = \frac{\sum_{i=1}^{n} [\text{Score of Service Provided}]}{\text{Number of services rendered}}$$

The second component is **Audit Team Independence Score**. Principally, it is suggested that quarterly auditors should hand a written *notification of independence*. This notification will be done through the Web site of POA personally by the auditors; the employer of the auditor will keep a track as well. The audit firms having additional independence criteria on their own are much more desirable. This

Table 3 Services audit firms are allowed to provide to their audit clients and the scores assigned

Service	Laws and regulations	Score
Independent audit	Allowed	1
Tax consultancy	Allowed	1
Assertion and certified councillorship (CPA)	Allowed	1
Tax audit	Allowed	1
Finance consultancy	Forbidden	0
Legal consultancy	Forbidden	0
Training	Forbidden	0
Management consultancy	Forbidden*	0
Accounting services	Forbidden	0
Internal audit	Forbidden	0
Outsourcing	Forbidden	0
Change management	Forbidden	0
Investment consultancy	Forbidden	0
Human resource	Forbidden	0
Tourism consultancy	Forbidden	0
Information Technology consultancy	Forbidden	0
Customs advisor	Forbidden	0

is to guarantee that auditors are independent in substance and appearance. This system would also enable the **Audit Team Independence Score** to be calculated almost automatically. This score is to be calculated by disregarding the titles the auditors carry. Then, the score of each auditor will be summed and divided in the total numbers of auditors in the audit team. In case the auditors in audit team are from related CPA firms, or are CPAs not employed by the audit firms, this will be a matter to be taken care of. If there is any relation not allowed by the law, then the score will be null. A fully law-abiding audit firm will score one. These relations are like having shares of the other firm, or board membership.

$$\textbf{Audit Team Independence Score} = \sum_{i=1}^{n} [\text{Auditors}' \text{ Independence Score}]$$

i = team members

$$\begin{array}{l}\textbf{Audit Engagement Team}\\ \textbf{Independence Coefficient}\end{array} = \frac{\sum_{i=1}^{n} [\text{Auditors Independence Score}]}{\text{Numbers of Auditors in the Engagement Team}}$$

Multiplication of both coefficients will generate **Audit Firm Independence Coefficient**. When the average of all audits the audit firm carries throughout a calendar year is taken, **Audit Firm Independence Coefficient Factor** will be calculated.

$$\textbf{Audit Firm Independence Coefficient} = \text{Audit Firm Engagement Independence Coefficient} \times \text{Audit Engagement Independence Coefficient}$$

$$\textbf{Audit Firm Independence Coefficient Factor} = \frac{\sum_{i=1}^{n} [\text{Audit Firm Independence Coefficient}]}{\text{Number of Engagements}}$$

Assigning the revenue earned from each audit as weight will make it more meaningful. In this way, the importance level of independence is generated. By evaluating the survey responses of managers of audit firms regarding the staff retention data, the table given below is created:

Staff retention rate (%)	25	50	75	90
Opinions: strongly agree and agree (%)	62.50	75.00	70.83	50.53
Opinions: disagree and strongly disagree (%)	20.83	8.33	8.34	8.33
Other opinions: no opinion and partly agree/disagree (%)	16.67	16.67	20.83	41.14

Relying on the data that is to be provided by audit firms about their staff, the rate will be easily calculated. The quality of each component of the index is as important as its quantity. For example, while calculating **Training Hours Coefficient**, along with the data about how many hours the training was, the content of the training is also very significant. Developments and changes in standards and legislation, current good practices, ethics training, issues related to unfair competition, and the like are to be covered in these trainings as well. The restriction of the licenses of auditors who are not able to document the training and/or those who do not attend required trainings would be another precaution.

Payment Pool

Arrangements regarding the payment of audit fee are among the precautions to enhance audit quality. The opinion that the audit fee being paid by the company that is audited hits independence at the very beginning of the work (Turner 2008; Blay and Geiger 2013; Duflo et al. 2013; Tanç and Uzay 2013) finds advocators from a broad spectrum—from members of regulating institutions, academics, and the like. As one of the studies about audit fee and audit quality, the findings of Tanç and Uzay, supports the opinion that audit fee being paid by the audit client harms audit quality (2013: 22). A solution would be making audit fee payments from a pool of funds. This solution can be supported by a system, where audit firms will be assigned to audit clients randomly. These will enhance audit quality.

Therefore, **Payment Pool** is suggested here. The Payment Pool will be designed by answering the question "who benefits from audited financial statements?" There are a number of stakeholders who make use of financial statements audited by audit firms; therefore, these parties are to make the payment. Payment of the audit fee by public authorities is not suggested, and this would be an extra burden on taxpayers.

Any contribution of financial statements users to the Payment Pool should be proportionate to the benefit they get from audited financial statements. A sample Payment Pool contributors are suggested below:

(1) Domestic and foreign investors, both real persons and corporate bodies, who invest in and trade financial instruments, like stock exchanges, bonds and the like;
(2) Management of investment funds, which invest in all kinds of financial instruments;
(3) Individual pension funds that invest in all kinds of financial instruments;
(4) Foreign and domestic creditors lending to audited entities;
(5) Regulatory institutions like BRSA, EMRA, Borsa Istanbul, POA and similar regulating bodies; and
(6) Audited entities.

Within the frame of the suggestion, the formula for calculating the contributions would be as stated below:

$$\textbf{Funds to be Collected in the Pool}(\textbf{FCP}) = \left| \begin{array}{c} \text{Audit fee to be determined} \\ \times \\ \text{Coefficient of the audit client entity to be audited} \end{array} \right|$$

The coefficient of the audit client entity to be audited would be a combination of difficulty level and the scope of the audit to be performed and the size of the entity to be audited.

Funds to be collected in the Pool (FCP) =	Domestic and foreign investors—real persons and corporate bodies	6%
	Management of investment funds	7%
	Individual pension funds	7%
	Foreign and domestic creditors	7%
	Revenue Administration	7%
	(1) BRSA (2) EMRA (3) Borsa Istanbul, (4) POA and the like *in this group, the payment will be done by the institutions whichever has interest in the audit	16%
	Audit clients	50%

The weights in the table are suggestions only and are open for discussion. The way how contributions are to be collected is the next thing to be determined. Especially, collections from the real person investor may be complicated. A fee may be collected based on their daily trade. Same is to be applied for funds investing in securities exchanges. The size of their portfolio, or their trade volume, and may be the frequency of their transactions would serve as good direction for fee collection.

The second and very crucial part of Payment Pool suggestion is random auditor and/or audit firm assignment. The merits of audit firms and auditors, the sector expertise, their experiences, etc., will all determine to which audit client they will be assigned. Random assignment and rotation will both enhance audit quality. The dependence of audit firms on their clients and the stress of performing as the audit client desires will be terminated. Consequently, the auditors will feel independence and act independently. The Audit Firms Quality Index (AFQI) will also be used in the Payment Pool, where public oversight bodies will take the scores listed in the index into consideration when randomly assigning audit firms to the audit clients.

It is very well understood that audit has a plain and clear effect on business world. The historical experiences lead the way to quality audits. Contrary to the abundance of the foreign accounting scandal data, there is no data about Turkish accounting scandals. Cultural merits of Turkish society are the cause of this lack. Low financial literacy, callousness to unethical behavior, the weakness of ethical perception, and several other factors do not let accounting and business scandals to come on earth. Therefore, I tried to draw attention to some of the universal accounting scandals that are lived in a specific era—from 1980 to 2014—and tried to link these to some weaknesses in financial reporting and audit function. Most of these scandals are from cultures where whistle-blowing mechanisms are effective, and sanctions against financial crime exist. Starting from this point, I tried to draw the profile of audit industry in Turkey. What I witnessed is that the audit circles are like a closed book. Therefore, all analyses are to be done over reports and the data available on Web sites of related institutions and audit firms. The obstacles are to overcome. Increased transparency of audit firms will help to detect problematic issues and to find solutions. The triangle of the audit client, public oversight and regulators, the audit firms, from now on, has to transform into a rectangular, where the fourth corner becomes all remaining stakeholders. This is the society in general. Being an investor or not should not matter. The society as a whole has to demand high-quality audits.

In this book, I tried to define the quality, which is an abstract attribute of a work done, over several factors. The outcome is the Index I invented, and the Payment Pool I suggest. The impact of the Index will be stronger if it is applied together with the Payment Pool. I hope Audit Firms Quality Index (AFQI) will be useful in the future and enlighten the path of stakeholders.

Appendix A
Auditing Firms Performing in Turkey (2014)

Registered name	Capital	Number of partners	Share of the biggest partner	Share of the second biggest partner	Structure of the board of directors[a]	Total number of auditors	Partner	Partner not participating audits	Manager	Senior auditor	Auditor	Staff assis-tant	Licensing foreign institution	PCAOB Category unless registered 2015 (A-B-C-D-E)[b]
Total: 87 auditing firms	(000)	780	%	%		2725	410	37	211	212	351	1541		16
A-1 YEMİNLİ MALİ MÜŞAVİRLİK VE BAĞIMSIZ DENETİM A.Ş.	50	17	59.50	3.75	1 + 0 + 4 + 2	16	6	0	3	7	0	0	–	
AAC BAĞIMSIZ DENETİM DANIŞMANLIK VE YEMİNLİ MALİ MÜŞAVİRLİK A.Ş.	50	8	35.00	8.50	1 + 1 + 1 + 2	8	3	0	4	1	0	0	–	
AC İSTANBUL ULUSLARARASI BAĞIMSIZ DENETİM VE SMMM A.Ş.	50	5	49.90	49.90	1 + 1 + 1 + 0	14	3	1	0	3	0	8	Enterprise Network Worldwide	
ADALYA ULUSLARARASI BAĞIMSIZ DENETİM SERBEST MUHASEBECİ MALİ MÜŞAVİR A.Ş.	100	11	58.00	12.00	1 + 1 + 1 + 0	13	8	0	0	1	0	4	–	
ADAY BAĞIMSIZ DENETİM VE SERBEST MUHASEBECİ MALİ MÜŞAVİRLİK A.Ş.	50	5	44.00	44.00	1 + 1 + 1 + 0	10	2	0	0	2	3	3	–	

(continued)

I. Kesimli, *External Auditing and Quality*, Accounting, Finance, Sustainability, Governance & Fraud: Theory and Application,
https://doi.org/10.1007/978-981-13-0526-9

(continued)

Registered name	Capital	Number of partners	Share of the biggest partner	Share of the second biggest partner	Structure of the board of directors[a]	Total number of auditors	Partner	Partner not participating audits	Manager	Senior auditor	Auditor	Staff assis-tant	Licensing foreign institution	PCAOB Category unless registered 2015 (A-B-C-D-E)[b]
Total: 87 auditing firms	(000)	780	%	%		2725	410	37	211	212	351	1541		16
ADM Bağımsız Denetim A.Ş.	0													
AKADEMİK BAĞIMSIZ DENETİM DANIŞMANLIK VE YEMİNLİ MALİ MÜŞAVİRLİK A.Ş.	50	13	43.75	25.75	1 + 1 + 1 + 1	18	8	0	0	0	4	6	–	
AKİS BAĞIMSIZ DENETİM VE SERBEST MUHASEBECİ MALİ MÜŞAVİRLİK A.Ş.	50	14	25.00	15.00	1 + 1 + 1 + 1	380	13	1	4	9	7	347	KPMG	B
AKT BAĞIMSIZ DENETİM A.Ş.	50	10	48.02	12.25	1 + 0 + 2 + 1	11	3	0	3	0	4	1	–	
AKTAN BAĞIMSIZ DENETİM VE YEMİNLİ MALİ MÜŞAVİRLİK A.Ş.	160	8	33.00	31.00	1 + 1 + 2 + 1	10	6	0	1	1	1	1	–	
Alternatif Bağımsız Denetim A.Ş.**	160	5	100.00	0.00	1 + 1 + 0 + 0	5	4	0	1	0	0	0	–	
ANIL YEMİNLİ MALİ MÜŞAVİRLİK VE BAĞIMSIZ DENETİM A.Ş.	270	15	90.00	5.00	1 + 1 + 1 + 0	29	3	0	12	0	10	4	–	
ARILAR BAĞIMSIZ DENETİM VE YEMİNLİ MALİ MÜŞAVİRLİK A.Ş.	400	5	75.00	15.00	1 + 1 + 3 + 0	12	3	0	3	2	2	2	NEXIA INTERNA-TIONAL	

(continued)

(continued)

Registered name	Capital	Number of partners	Share of the biggest partner	Share of the second biggest partner	Structure of the board of directors[a]	Total number of auditors	Partner	Partner not participating audits	Manager	Senior auditor	Auditor	Staff assis-tant	Licensing foreign institution	PCAOB Category unless registered 2015 (A-B-C-D-E)[b]
Total: 87 auditing firms	(000)	780	%	%		2725	410	37	211	212	351	1541		16
ARKAN ERGİN ULUSLARARASI BAĞIMSIZ DENETİM VE SMMM A.Ş.	175	6	46.29	6.57	1 + 1 + 2 + 0	29	3	0	0	3	3	20	JPA INTERNA-TIONAL	
ARTI DEĞER ULUSLARARASI BAĞIMSIZ DENETİM VE YEMİNLİ MALİ MÜŞAVİRLİK AŞ	100	7	73.00	20.00	1 + 1 + 1 + 0	12	4	0	5	2	0	1	JHI JEFFREYS HENRY INTERNA-TIONAL	
AS BAĞIMSIZ DENETİM VE YMM A. Ş.	50	7	59.80	39.70	1 + 1 + 1 + 0	49	2	0	3	4	6	34	NEXİA INTERNA-TIONAL LTD	
ATA ULUSLARARASI BAĞIMSIZ DENETİM VE SMMM A.Ş.	310	5	69.50	10.00	1 + 1 + 2 + 0	41	5	0	0	2	3	31	KRESTON INTERNA-TIONAL	
AVRASYA BAĞIMSIZ DENETİM VE YEMİNLİ MALİ MÜŞAVİRLİK A.Ş.	50	5	26.00	25.00	1 + 1 + 2 + 1	13	5	0	1	1	2	4	–	
AYK BAĞIMSIZ DIŞ DENETİM VE DANIŞMANLIK A.Ş.	50	11	32.00	32.00	1 + 0 + 2 + 0	9	2	0	3	2	2	0	–	
BAKIŞ YEMİNLİ MALİ MÜŞAVİRLİK VE BAĞIMSIZ DENETİM A.Ş.	50	11	28.00	23.00	1 + 1 + 1 + 0	15	2	0	1	8	2	2	IPG INTERNA-TIONAL	

(continued)

(continued)

Registered name	Capital	Number of partners	Share of the biggest partner	Share of the second biggest partner	Structure of the board of directors[a]	Total number of auditors	Partner	Partner not participating audits	Manager	Senior auditor	Auditor	Staff assis-tant	Licensing foreign institution	PCAOB Category unless registered 2015 (A-B-C-D-E)[b]
Total: 87 auditing firms	(000)	780	%	%		2725	410	37	211	212	351	1541		16
													PRATICE GROUP	
BAN-DEN BAĞIMSIZ DENETİM HİZMETLERİ A.Ş.	250	13	17.20	17.00	1 + 1 + 1 + 0	11	3	4	0	0	8	0	–	
BAŞARAN NAS BAĞIMSIZ DENETİM VE SERBEST MUHASEBECİ MALİ MÜŞAVİRLİK A.Ş	50	29	7.14	7.14	1 + 1 + 13 + 0	410	26	2	8	16	45	315	PRICE WATER HOUSE COOPERS	D
BATI YEMİNLİ MALİ MÜŞAVİRLİK VE BAĞIMSIZ DENETİM A.Ş.	138	5	51.00	47.51	1 + 1 + 1 + 0	8	2	0	1	2	3	0	–	
BD BAĞIMSIZ DENETİM VE YEMİNLİ MALİ MÜŞAVİRLİK A.Ş.	100	10	15.95	15.95	1 + 0 + 2 + 0	15	9	0	3	0	2	1	–	
BDD BAĞIMSIZ DENETİM VE DANIŞMANLIK A.Ş.	50	19	51.48	5.00	1 + 1 + 1 + 0	17	8	0	3	3	3	0	–	
BDO DENET BAĞIMSIZ DENETİM YEMİNLİ MALİ MÜŞAVİRLİK A.Ş.	50	14	20.96	20.96	1 + 1 + 1 + 0	21	4	1	1	1	2	13	BDO INTERNA-TIONAL	
BİLGİ BAĞIMSIZ DENETİM VE YEMİNLİ MALİ MÜŞAVİRLİK A.Ş.	50	8	91.50	5.50	1 + 1 + 1 + 0	7	2	0	4	1	0	0	–	

(continued)

(continued)

Registered name	Capital	Number of partners	Share of the biggest partner	Share of the second biggest partner	Structure of the board of directors[a]	Total number of auditors	Partner	Partner not participating audits	Manager	Senior auditor	Auditor	Staff assis-tant	Licensing foreign institution	PCAOB Category unless registered 2015 (A-B-C-D-E)[b]
Total: 87 auditing firms	(000)	780	%	%		2725	410	37	211	212	351	1541		16
BİLGİLİ BAĞIMSIZ DENETİM VE YMM A. Ş.	50	7	60.00	10.00	1 + 1 + 1 + 10	21	3	0	6	4	3	5	AGN INTERNA-TIONAL LTD	D
BİRLEŞİK UZMANLAR YEMİNLİ MALİ MÜŞAVİRLİK VE BAĞIMSIZ DENETİM A.Ş.	250	6	55.25	18.75	1 + 1 + 4 + 0	36	3	2	1	0	3	29	Prime Global	
BİRLEŞİM BAĞIMSIZ DENETİM VE YMM A. Ş.	200	5	64.98	32.50	1 + 1 + 1 + 0	8	3	0	0	1	2	2	HAZLEMS FENTON	
CONSULTA BAĞIMSIZ DENETİM VE YEMİNLİ MALİ MÜŞAVİRLİK A.Ş.	50	4	99.60	0.20	1 + 1 + 1 + 0	20	4	0	3	5	7	1	INAA GROUP	
CPA BAĞIMSIZ DENETİM VE YMM A. Ş.	50	6	26.00	25.00	1 + 1 + 3 + 0	8	3	0	3	0	1	1	–	
Crowe Horwath Olgu Bağımsız Denetim ve Yeminli Mali Müşavirlik A.Ş.	660	20	32.87	29.31	1 + 1 + 1 + 0	25	4	0	6	7	7	1	CROWE HORWATH	
ÇAĞDAŞ BAĞIMSIZ DENETİM SMMM A.Ş.	50	5	51.00	41.40	1 + 1 + 1 + 0	8	2	0	0	3	1	2	IAPA INTERNA-TIONAL	

(continued)

(continued)

Registered name	Capital	Number of partners	Share of the biggest partner	Share of the second biggest partner	Structure of the board of directors[a]	Total number of auditors	Partner	Partner not participating audits	Manager	Senior auditor	Auditor	Staff assis-tant	Licensing foreign institution	PCAOB Category unless registered 2015 (A-B-C-D-E)[b]
Total: 87 auditing firms	(000)	780	%	%		2725	410	37	211	212	351	1541		16
DEĞER BAĞIMSIZ DENETİM VE YEMİNLİ MALİ MÜŞAVİRLİK A.Ş.	112	11	29.25	28.25	1 + 0 + 5 + 0	23	8	0	9	0	1	5	ECOVIS EUROPE	
DENGE BAĞIMSIZ DENETİM SERBEST MUHASEBECİ MALİ MÜŞAVİRLİK A.Ş.	100	13	74.00	12.50	1 + 1 + 9 + 0	48	6	1	3	3	2	34	MAZARS SOCIÉTÉ COOPÉRA-TIVE À RESPON-SABILITÉ LIMITÉE	D
DETAY BAĞIMSIZ DENETİM VE DANIŞMANLIK A.Ş.	50	8	55.67	21.67	1 + 1 + 1 + 0	11	6	1	0	5	0	0	INTERNA-TIONAL EXPERTS AND CONSUL-TANTS IECnet	
DMR Bağımsız Denetim ve Danışmanlık A.Ş.	250	8	50.00	45.60	1 + 0 + 0 + 0	8	4	1	0	0	4	0	Kudos International Network	
DMF SİSTEM ULUSLARARASI BAĞIMSIZ DENETİM DANIŞMANLIK VE YMM A.Ş.	250	8	95.70	1.00	1 + 1 + 5 + 1	8	2	0	2	2	2	0	RUSSELL BEDFORD INTERNA-TIONAL	
DRT BAĞIMSIZ DENETİM VE SERBEST	50	30	48.77	8.40	1 + 0 + 6 + 0	98	25	0	9	29	35	0	DELOITTE TOUCHE TOHMATSU	A

(continued)

(continued)

Registered name	Capital	Number of partners	Share of the biggest partner	Share of the second biggest partner	Structure of the board of directors[a]	Total number of auditors	Partner	Partner not participating audits	Manager	Senior auditor	Auditor	Staff assis-tant	Licensing foreign institution	PCAOB Category unless registered 2015 (A-B-C-D-E)[b]
Total: 87 auditing firms	(000)	780	%	%		2725	410	37	211	212	351	1541		16
MUHASEBECİ MALİ MÜŞAVİRLİK A.Ş.													INTERNA-TIONAL	
EGE YEMİNLİ MALİ MÜŞAVİRLİK VE BAĞIMSIZ DENETİM A.Ş.	100	15	99.25	0.10	1 + 1 + 0 + 2	14	3	1	1	1	5	4	CH INTERNA-TIONAL	
ELİT BAĞIMSIZ DENETİM VE YEMİNLİ MALİ MÜŞAVİRLİK A.Ş.	50	4	33.33	33.33	1 + 0 + 2 + 0	22	3	0	0	0	4	15	CPA ASSOCIATES INTERNA-TIONAL INC.-USA	
ENGİN BAĞIMSIZ DENETİM VE SERBEST MUHASEBECİLİK MALİ MÜŞAVİRLİK A.Ş.	100	6	30.40	29.20	1 + 1 + 1 + 0	46	3	0	1	4	3	35	GRANT THORNTON	
ERCİYES YEMİNLİ MALİ MÜŞAVİRLİK VE BAĞIMSIZ DENETİM A.Ş.	100	6	50.00	35.00	1 + 1 + 1 + 0	14	2	1	3	4	3	2	–	D
EREN BAĞIMSIZ DENETİM ve YEMİNLİ MALİ MÜŞAVİRLİK A.Ş.	50	7	29.51	29.51	1 + 1 + 2 + 0	63	3	0	3	2	9	46	GRANT THORNTON	
GÜÇBİR BAĞIMSIZ DENETİM A.Ş.	50	8	56.63	18.69	1 + 1 + 1 + 0	12	8	0	0	2	1	1	IAPA INTERNA-TIONAL	

(continued)

(continued)

Registered name	Capital	Number of partners	Share of the biggest partner	Share of the second biggest partner	Structure of the board of directors[a]	Total number of auditors	Partner	Partner not participating audits	Manager	Senior auditor	Auditor	Staff assis-tant	Licensing foreign institution	PCAOB Category unless registered 2015 (A-B-C-D-E)[b]
Total: 87 auditing firms	(000)	780	%	%		2725	410	37	211	212	351	1541		16
Güncel Bağımsız Denetim Danışmanlık ve YMM A.Ş.	50	5	60.00	20.00	1 + 1 + 1 + 0	13	3	0	0	0	10	0	Groupe Laviale Sohaco	
GÜNEY BAĞIMSIZ DENETİM VE SERBEST MUHASEBECİ MALİ MÜŞAVİRLİK A.Ş.	90	17	7.14	7.14	1 + 1 + 4 + 0	416	17	0	4	17	4	374	ERNST& YOUNG GLOBAL LIMITED	D
GÜRELİ YEMİNLİ MALİ MÜŞAVİRLİK VE BAĞIMSIZ DENETİM HİZMETLERİ A.Ş.	200	19	62.49	10.50	1 + 1 + 3 + 0	109	9	0	14	14	10	62	BAKER TILLY INTERNA-TIONAL	
HLB SAYGIN YEMİNLİ MALİ MÜŞAVİRLİK VE BAĞIMSIZ DENETİM A.Ş.	90	7	99.60	0.32	1 + 1 + 1 + 0	15	5	1	3	1	2	4	HLB INTERNA-TIONAL	
IHY BAĞIMSIZ DENETİM VE YEMİNLİ MALİ MÜŞAVİRLİK A.Ş.	1,000	7	76.15	5.00	1 + 0 + 2 + 0	17	5	0	4	1	2	5	Kingston Sorel International	D
IŞIK YEMİNLİ MALİ MÜŞAVİRLİK ve BAĞIMSIZ DENETİM A.Ş.	260	8	25.00	24.81	1 + 0 + 2 + 0	16	7	0	3	1	5	0	BKR INTERNA-TIONAL	D
İRFAN BAĞIMSIZ DENETİM VE YEMİNLİ MALİ MÜŞAVİRLİK A.Ş.	820	6	31.95	31.95	1 + 1 + 1 + 1	18	3	0	3	2	5	5	-	D

(continued)

(continued)

Registered name	Capital	Number of partners	Share of the biggest partner	Share of the second biggest partner	Structure of the board of directors[a]	Total number of auditors	Partner	Partner not participating audits	Manager	Senior auditor	Auditor	Staff assis-tant	Licensing foreign institution	PCAOB Category unless registered 2015 (A-B-C-D-E)[b]
Total: 87 auditing firms	(000)	780	%	%		2725	410	37	211	212	351	1541		16
İTİMAT BAĞIMSIZ DENETİM A.Ş.	100	8	51.00	40.00	1 + 0 + 2 + 0	6	3	0	1	0	2	0	FIDUNION INTERNA-TIONAL	D
KAPİTAL KARDEN BAĞIMSIZ DENETİM VE YEMİNLİ MALİ MÜŞAVİRLİK A.Ş.	120	11	46.58	46.58	1 + 1 + 1 + 0	18	3	3	0	0	6	9	RSM INTERNA-TIONAL	
KARMA BAĞIMSIZ DENETİM A.Ş.	50	8	37.00	37.00	1 + 1 + 1 + 0	8	2	0	1	2	3	0	PARKER RANDALL INTERNA-TIONAL	
KAVRAM BAĞIMSIZ DENETİM VE YEMİNLİ MALİ MÜŞAVİRLİK A.Ş.	155	6	45.19	45.19	1 + 0 + 3 + 0	16	4	0	3	2	5	2	CROWE HORWATH INTERNA-TIONAL	
KÖKER YEMİNLİ MALİ MÜŞAVİRLİK VE BAĞIMSIZ DENETİM A.Ş.	75	6	58.50	20.00	1 + 1 + 1 + 0	16	3	2	1	2	2	8	AGN INTERNA-TIONAL	
LEGAL YÖNET BAĞIMSIZ DENETİM YEMİNLİ MALİ MÜŞAVİRLİK A.Ş.	50	5	91.00	8.00	1 + 0 + 2 + 0	8	2	2	3	2	0	1	LEA Global	
MBK Bağımsız Denetim ve Serbest Muhasebeci Mali Müşavirlik A.Ş.	100	5	52.00	45.00	1 + 1 + 1 + 0	29	3	0	2	2	3	19	Moore Stephens International LTD	

(continued)

(continued)

Registered name	Capital	Number of partners	Share of the biggest partner	Share of the second biggest partner	Structure of the board of directors[a]	Total number of auditors	Partner	Partner not participating audits	Manager	Senior auditor	Auditor	Staff assis-tant	Licensing foreign institution	PCAOB Category unless registered 2015 (A-B-C-D-E)[b]
Total: 87 auditing firms	(000)	780	%	%		2725	410	37	211	212	351	1541		16
MED YEMİNLİ MALİ MÜŞAVİRLİK VE BAĞIMSIZ DENETİM A.Ş.	100	5	93.00	3.00	1 + 0 + 2 + 1	9	4	0	1		0	4	RG TREUHAND MÜTH AND PARTNER GMBH	D
Mega Global Uluslar Arası Bağımsız Denetim Anonim Şirketi	50	11	47.50	47.50	1 + 1 + 1 + 0	11	2	0	5	2	1	1	Jeffreys Henry International	
MERCEK BAĞIMSIZ DENETİM VE YEMİNLİ MALİ MÜŞAVİRLİK A.Ş.	400	18	15.50	15.50	1 + 1 + 2 + 0	21	7	0	3	0	6	5	–	D
Meridyen Kurumsal Çözüm ve Bağımsız Denetim Anonim Şirketi	0													
MGI BAĞIMSIZ DENETİM VE YEMİNLİ MALİ MÜŞAVİRLİK A.Ş.	50	10	61.80	31.00	1 + 1 + 8 + 0	19	6	0	8	1	2	2	MGI Business Solutions Worldwide	
MOD BAĞIMSIZ DENETİM SERBEST MUHASEBECİ MALİ MÜŞAVİRLİK A.Ş.	250	8	90.00	4.00	1 + 1 + 1 + 1	12	3	0	1	0	4	4	–	
OLUŞUM BAĞIMSIZ DIŞ DENETİM VE DANIŞMANLIK A.Ş.	50	8	41.62	24.90	1 + 0 + 3 + 0	10	4	0	1	1	4	0	NEXIA INTERNA-TIONAL	

(continued)

(continued)

Registered name	Capital	Number of partners	Share of the biggest partner	Share of the second biggest partner	Structure of the board of directors[a]	Total number of auditors	Partner	Partner not participating audits	Manager	Senior auditor	Auditor	Staff assis-tant	Licensing foreign institution	PCAOB Category unless registered 2015 (A-B-C-D-E)[b]
Total: 87 auditing firms	(000)	780	%	%		2725	410	37	211	212	351	1541		16
ÖNDER BAĞIMSIZ DENETİM VE DANIŞMANLIK A.Ş.	50	5	51.00	42.00	1 + 0 + 2 + 0	15	3	0	0	0	8	4	–	
PÜR BAĞIMSIZ DENETİM YEMİNLİ MALİ MÜŞAVİRLİK A.Ş.	50	5	59.80	30.00	1 + 1 + 1 + 0	10	2	0	2	0	3	3	–	
RANDIMAN DENETİM YEMİNLİ MALİ MÜŞAVİRLİK VE BAĞIMSIZ DENETİM A.Ş.	70	5	99.86	0.40	1 + 0 + 1 + 0	13	3	0	3	1	1	5	–	
RASYONEL BAĞIMSIZ DENETİM VE YEMİNLİ MALİ MÜŞAVİRLİK A.Ş.	50	6	47.00	46.50	1 + 1 + 2 + 0	15	2	0	7	1	1	4	EURAUDIT INT	
Referans Bağımsız Denetim ve Danışmanlık A.Ş.	50	6	41.00	12.25	1 + 0 + 3 + 0	13	7	0	0	2	2	2	–	
REHBER BAĞIMSIZ DENETİM VE YEMİNLİ MALİ MÜŞAVİRLİK A.Ş.	100	8	49.60	48.02	1 + 1 + 1 + 0	11	3	3	2	1	2	3	ANTEA Alliance of Independent Firms	

(continued)

(continued)

Registered name	Capital	Number of partners	Share of the biggest partner	Share of the second biggest partner	Structure of the board of directors[a]	Total number of auditors	Partner	Partner not participating audits	Manager	Senior auditor	Auditor	Staff assis-tant	Licensing foreign institution	PCAOB Category unless registered 2015 (A-B-C-D-E)[b]
Total: 87 auditing firms	(000)	780	%	%		2725	410	37	211	212	351	1541		16
REPORT BAĞIMSIZ DENETİM VE SERBEST MUHASEBECİ MALİ MÜŞAVİRLİK A.Ş.	50	14	35.00	18.00	1 + 1 + 2 + 0	13	3	0	4	0	0	6	–	
SAMDEN SAMSUN BAĞIMSIZ DIŞ DENETİM VE SMMM A.Ş.	120	10	84.17	2.50	1 + 0 + 0 + 1	14	3	0	5	0	6	0	–	D
SER-BERKER BAĞIMSIZ DENETİM VE YEMİNLİ MALİ MÜŞAVİRLİK A.Ş.	500	9	44.00	43.88	1 + 1 + 1 + 0	22	5	4	0	3	9	5	DFK INTERNA-TIONAL	
SUN BAĞIMSIZ DIŞ DENETİM YEMİNLİ MALİ MÜŞAVİRLİK A.Ş.	62	8	48.43	48.43	1 + 1 + 2 + 0	28	8	0	5	1	8	6	PKF WORLD WIDE	
TAM BAĞIMSIZ DENETİM VE DANIŞMANLIK A.Ş.	50	11	30.00	21.00	1 + 1 + 1 + 0	7	3	0	2	0	2	0	-	
TÜRKERLER BAĞIMSIZ DENETİM YEMİNLİ MALİ MÜŞAVİRLİK A.Ş.	50	5	57.25	30.15	1 + 1 + 1 + 0	11	5	0	1	1	2	2	Premier International Associates	

(continued)

(continued)

Registered name	Capital	Number of partners	Share of the biggest partner	Share of the second biggest partner	Structure of the board of directors[a]	Total number of auditors	Partner	Partner not participating audits	Manager	Senior auditor	Auditor	Staff assis-tant	Licensing foreign institution	PCAOB Category unless registered 2015 (A-B-C-D-E)[b]
Total: 87 auditing firms	(000)	780	%	%		2725	410	37	211	212	351	1541		16
TÜRKMEN BAĞIMSIZ DENETİM VE YEMİNLİ MALİ MÜŞAVİRLİK A.Ş.	50	7	94.75	5.00	1 + 0 + 2 + 0	13	2	0	0	4	4	3	International Practice Group	A
ULUSAL BAĞIMSIZ DENETİM VE YEMİNLİ MALİ MÜŞAVİRLİK A.Ş.	100	14	15.40	11.72	1 + 0 + 2 + 7	15	7	6	0	3	0	5	The International Accounting Group	D
UZMAN YEMİNLİ MALİ MÜŞAVİRLİK VE BAĞIMSIZ DENETİM A.Ş.	50	6	79.91	19.97	1 + 1 + 1 + 0	11	2	0	3	1	2	3	UHY URBACH HACKER YOUNG INTERNA-TIONAL LTD.	
YEDİTEPE BAĞIMSIZ DENETİM A.Ş.	60	14	18.00	15.00	1 + 1 + 3 + 0	15	8	0	0	0	7	0	Praxity-Global Alliance Ltd.	
YILDIZLAR BAĞIMSIZ DENETİM VE YEMİNLİ MALİ MÜŞAVİRLİK A.Ş.	60	6	30.00	28.33	1 + 1 + 1 + 1	7	4	0	0	0	3	0	–	D
YKY BAĞIMSIZ DENETİM VE YEMİNLİ MALİ MÜŞAVİRLİK A.Ş.	50	6	74.69	24.90	1 + 1 + 0 + 0	8	3	0	1	1	3	0	–	
YORUM YEMİNLİ MALİ MÜŞAVİRLİK VE BAĞIMSIZ DENETİM A.Ş.	65	6	57.99	42.00	1 + 1 + 1 + 0	7	2	0	1	0	4	0	–	

(continued)

(continued)

Registered name	Capital	Number of partners	Share of the biggest partner	Share of the second biggest partner	Structure of the board of directors[a]	Total number of auditors	Partner	Partner not participating audits	Manager	Senior auditor	Auditor	Staff assis-tant	Licensing foreign institution	PCAOB Category unless registered 2015 (A-B-C-D-E)[b]
Total: 87 auditing firms	(000)	780	%	%		2725	410	37	211	212	351	1541		16
YÖNTEM YEMİNLİ MALİ MÜŞAVİRLİK ve BAĞIMSIZ DENETİM A.Ş.	60	8	99.48	0.10	1 + 0 + 0 + 0	14	6	0	0	0	3	5	NEXIA INTERNA-TIONAL	

[a]Board Chairman + Vice Board Chairman + Number of Board Members + Number of auditors assigned according to Turkish Code of Commerce

[b]Category: *A* Audit report for at least one issuer, *B* No audit reports for issuers but played a substantial role in the audit of at least one issuer, *C* Audit reports for at least one broker-dealer, *D* No audit reports for broker-dealers, but substantial role in audit of at least one broker-dealer, *E* None of the above, *F* No Form 2 filed

Source

(1) Public Company Accounting Oversight Board (PCOAB). Registration & Reporting. Registered Firms. http://pcaobus.org/Registration/Firms/Pages/RegisteredFirms.aspx. Accessed 06 May 2012

(2) BRSA. Bankacılık Düzenleme ve Denetleme Kurumu (BDDK). Kuruluşlar, Bağımsız Denetim kuruluşları. http://www.bddk.org.tr/WebSitesi/turkce/Kuruluslar/Bagimsiz_Denetim_Kuruluslari/Finansal_Denetim/Finansal_Denetim.aspx. Accessed 03 May 2012

(3) EMRA. EPDK, T.C.. Bağımsız Denetim. Bağımsız Denetim Kuruluşları. http://www2.epdk.org.tr/denetim/bagimsiz/kurulus/adresbilgisi.asp. Accessed 13 May 2012

(4) CMB. Sermaye Piyasası Kurulu. Kurumlar. Bağımsız Denetim Kuruluşları. Bağımsız Denetimle Yetkili Kuruluşlarhttp://www.spk.gov.tr/apps/msd/iletisim.aspx?submenuheader=9. Accessed 24 Apr 2012

(5) Treasury. Hazine Müsteşarlığı, T.C. Başbakanlık. Sigortacılık ve Özel Emeklilik. Kurumlar. Bağımsız Denetim Kuruluşları. http://www.hazine.gov.tr/irj/portal/anonymous?NavigationTarget=navurl://4d00dc5ed3455e78d888a06d22227f9a. Accessed 13 May 2012

(6) Public Oversight—Accounting and Auditing Standards Authority. Kamu Gözetimi Kurumu. http://www.kgk.gov.tr/dk/index.aspx. Accessed 03 May 2014

Appendix B
Sarbanes–Oxley Act Frame Plan

CHAPTER 98	PUBLIC COMPANY ACCOUNTING REFORM AND CORPORATE RESPONSIBILITY
SHORT TITLE	SARBANES–OXLEY ACT OF 2002
	SUBCHAPTER I—PUBLIC COMPANY ACCOUNTING OVERSIGHT BOARD
	SUBCHAPTER II—AUDITOR INDEPENDENCE
	SUBCHAPTER III—CORPORATE RESPONSIBILITY
	SUBCHAPTER IV—ENHANCED FINANCIAL DISCLOSURES
SEC. 7201.	DEFINITIONS
(1)	APPROPRIATE STATE REGULATORY AUTHORITY
(2)	AUDIT
(3)	AUDIT COMMITTEE
(4)	AUDIT REPORT
(5)	BOARD
(6)	COMMISSION
(7)	ISSUER
(8)	NON-AUDIT SERVICES
(9)	PERSON ASSOCIATED WITH A PUBLIC ACCOUNTING FIRM
(10)	PROFESSIONAL STANDARDS
(11)	PUBLIC ACCOUNTING FIRM
(12)	REGISTERED PUBLIC ACCOUNTING FIRM
(13)	RULES OF THE BOARD
(14)	SECURITY
(15)	SECURITIES LAWS
(16)	STATE

(continued)

I. Kesimli, *External Auditing and Quality*, Accounting, Finance, Sustainability, Governance & Fraud: Theory and Application,
https://doi.org/10.1007/978-981-13-0526-9

(continued)

CHAPTER 98	PUBLIC COMPANY ACCOUNTING REFORM AND CORPORATE RESPONSIBILITY
(17)	FOREIGN AUDITOR OVERSIGHT AUTHORITY
SEC. 7202.	COMMISSION RULES AND ENFORCEMENT
SUBCHAPTER I	PUBLIC COMPANY ACCOUNTING OVERSIGHT BOARD
SEC. 101	ESTABLISHMENT; ADMINISTRATIVE PROVISIONS
(A)	ESTABLISHMENT OF BOARD
(B)	STATUS
(C)	DUTIES OF THE BOARD
(D)	COMMISSION DETERMINATION
(E)	BOARD MEMBERSHIP
(F)	POWERS OF THE BOARD
(G)	RULES OF THE BOARD
(H)	ANNUAL REPORT TO THE COMMISSION
SEC. 102	REGISTRATION WITH THE BOARD
(A)	MANDATORY REGISTRATION
(B)	APPLICATIONS FOR REGISTRATION
(C)	ACTION ON APPLICATIONS
(D)	PERIODIC REPORTS
(E)	PUBLIC AVAILABILITY
(F)	REGISTRATION AND ANNUAL FEES
SEC. 103	AUDITING, QUALITY CONTROL, AND INDEPENDENCE STANDARDS AND RULES
(A)	AUDITING, QUALITY CONTROL, AND ETHICS STANDARDS
(B)	INDEPENDENCE STANDARDS AND RULES
(C)	COOPERATION WITH DESIGNATED PROFESSIONAL GROUPS OF ACCOUNTANTS AND ADVISORY GROUPS
(D)	EVALUATION OF STANDARD SETTING PROCESS
SEC. 104	INSPECTIONS OF REGISTERED PUBLIC ACCOUNTING FIRMS
(A)	IN GENERAL
(B)	INSPECTION FREQUENCY
(C)	PROCEDURES
(D)	CONDUCT OF INSPECTIONS
(E)	RECORD RETENTION
(F)	PROCEDURES FOR REVIEW
(G)	REPORT
(H)	INTERIM COMMISSION REVIEW
SEC. 105	INVESTIGATIONS AND DISCIPLINARY PROCEEDINGS
(A)	IN GENERAL
(B)	INVESTIGATIONS
(C)	DISCIPLINARY PROCEDURES

(continued)

(continued)

CHAPTER 98	PUBLIC COMPANY ACCOUNTING REFORM AND CORPORATE RESPONSIBILITY
(D)	REPORTING OF SANCTIONS
(E)	STAY OF SANCTIONS
SEC. 106	FOREIGN PUBLIC ACCOUNTING FIRMS
(A)	APPLICABILITY TO CERTAIN FOREIGN FIRMS
(B)	PRODUCTION OF DOCUMENTS
(C)	EXEMPTION AUTHORITY
(D)	SERVICE OF REQUESTS OR PROCESS
(E)	SANCTIONS
(F)	OTHER MEANS OF SATISFYING PRODUCTION OBLIGATIONS
(G)	DEFINITION
SEC. 107	COMMISSION OVERSIGHT OF THE BOARD
(A)	GENERAL OVERSIGHT RESPONSIBILITY
(B)	RULES OF THE BOARD
(C)	COMMISSION REVIEW OF DISCIPLINARY ACTION TAKEN BY THE BOARD
(D)	CENSURE OF THE BOARD; OTHER SANCTIONS
SEC. 108	ACCOUNTING STANDARDS
(A)	OMITTED
(B)	COMMISSION AUTHORITY
(C)	NO EFFECT ON COMMISSION POWERS
(D)	STUDY AND REPORT ON ADOPTING PRINCIPLES-BASED ACCOUNTING
SEC. 109	FUNDING
(A)	IN GENERAL
(B)	ANNUAL BUDGETS
(C)	SOURCES AND USES OF FUNDS
(D)	ANNUAL ACCOUNTING SUPPORT FEE FOR THE BOARD
(E)	ANNUAL ACCOUNTING SUPPORT FEE FOR STANDARD SETTING BODY
(F)	LIMITATION ON FEE
(G)	ALLOCATION OF ACCOUNTING SUPPORT FEES AMONG ISSUERS
(H)	ALLOCATION OF ACCOUNTING SUPPORT FEES AMONG BROKERS AND DEALERS
(I)	OMITTED
(J)	RULE OF CONSTRUCTION
(K)	START-UP EXPENSES OF THE BOARD
SEC. 7220.	DEFINITIONS
(1)	AUDIT
(2)	AUDIT REPORT

(continued)

(continued)

CHAPTER 98	PUBLIC COMPANY ACCOUNTING REFORM AND CORPORATE RESPONSIBILITY
(3)	BROKER
(4)	DEALER
(5)	PROFESSIONAL STANDARDS
(6)	SELF-REGULATORY ORGANIZATION
SUBCHAPTER II	AUDITOR INDEPENDENCE
SEC. 201	SERVICES OUTSIDE THE SCOPE OF PRACTICE OF AUDITORS
(A)	PROHIBITED ACTIVITIES
(B)	EXEMPTION AUTHORITY
SEC. 202	PREAPPROVAL REQUIREMENTS
(A)	IN GENERAL
(B)	DISCLOSURE TO INVESTORS
(C)	DELEGATION AUTHORITY
(D)	APPROVAL OF AUDIT SERVICES FOR OTHER PURPOSES
SEC. 203	AUDIT PARTNER ROTATION
SEC. 204	AUDITOR REPORTS TO AUDIT COMMITTEES
SEC. 205	CONFORMING AMENDMENTS
(A)	DEFINITIONS
(B)	AUDITOR REQUIREMENTS
(C)	OTHER REFERENCES
(D)	CONFORMING AMENDMENT
SEC. 206	CONFLICTS OF INTEREST
SEC. 207	STUDY OF MANDATORY ROTATION OF REGISTERED PUBLIC ACCOUNTING FIRMS
(A)	STUDY AND REVIEW REQUIRED
(B)	REPORT REQUIRED
(C)	DEFINITION
SEC. 208	COMMISSION AUTHORITY
(A)	COMMISSION REGULATIONS
(B)	AUDITOR INDEPENDENCE
SEC. 209	CONSIDERATIONS BY APPROPRIATE STATE REGULATORY AUTHORITIES
SUBCHAPTER III	CORPORATE RESPONSIBILITY
SEC. 301	PUBLIC COMPANY AUDIT COMMITTEES
(A)	COMMISSION RULES
(B)	RESPONSIBILITIES RELATING TO REGISTERED PUBLIC ACCOUNTING FIRMS
(C)	INDEPENDENCE
(D)	COMPLAINTS
(E)	AUTHORITY TO ENGAGE ADVISERS
(F)	FUNDING

(continued)

(continued)

CHAPTER 98	PUBLIC COMPANY ACCOUNTING REFORM AND CORPORATE RESPONSIBILITY
SEC. 302	CORPORATE RESPONSIBILITY FOR FINANCIAL REPORTS
(A)	REGULATIONS REQUIRED
(B)	FOREIGN REINCORPORATIONS HAVE NO EFFECT
(C)	DEADLINE
SEC. 303	IMPROPER INFLUENCE ON CONDUCT OF AUDITS
(A)	RULES TO PROHIBIT
(B)	ENFORCEMENT
(C)	NO PREEMPTION OF OTHER LAW
(D)	DEADLINE FOR RULEMAKING
SEC. 304	FORFEITURE OF CERTAIN BONUSES AND PROFITS
(A)	ADDITIONAL COMPENSATION PRIOR TO NONCOMPLIANCE WITH COMMISSION FINANCIAL REPORTING REQUIREMENTS
(B)	COMMISSION EXEMPTION AUTHORITY
SEC. 305	OFFICER AND DIRECTOR BARS AND PENALTIES
(A)	UNFITNESS STANDARD
(B)	EQUITABLE RELIEF
SEC. 306	INSIDER TRADES DURING PENSION FUND BLACKOUT PERIODS
(A)	PROHIBITION OF INSIDER TRADING DURING PENSION FUND BLACKOUT PERIODS
(B)	NOTICE REQUIREMENTS TO PARTICIPANTS AND BENEFICIARIES UNDER ERISA EMPLOYEE RETIREMENT INCOME SECURITY ACT
(C)	EFFECTIVE DATE
SEC. 307	RULES OF PROFESSIONAL RESPONSIBILITY FOR ATTORNEYS
SEC. 308	FAIR FUNDS FOR INVESTORS
(A)	CIVIL PENALTIES ADDED TO DISGORGEMENT FUNDS FOR THE RELIEF OF VICTIMS
(B)	ACCEPTANCE OF ADDITIONAL DONATIONS
(C)	STUDY REQUIRED
SUBCHAPTER IV	ENHANCED FINANCIAL DISCLOSURES
SEC. 401	DISCLOSURES IN PERIODIC REPORTS
(A)	DISCLOSURES REQUIRED
(B)	COMMISSION RULES ON PRO FORMA FIGURES
(C)	STUDY AND REPORT ON SPECIAL PURPOSE ENTITIES
SEC. 402	ENHANCED CONFLICT OF INTEREST PROVISIONS
(A)	PROHIBITION ON PERSONAL LOANS TO EXECUTIVES
SEC. 403	DISCLOSURES OF TRANSACTIONS INVOLVING MANAGEMENT AND PRINCIPAL STOCKHOLDERS

(continued)

(continued)

CHAPTER 98	PUBLIC COMPANY ACCOUNTING REFORM AND CORPORATE RESPONSIBILITY
SEC. 404	MANAGEMENT ASSESSMENT OF INTERNAL CONTROLS
(A)	RULES REQUIRED
(B)	INTERNAL CONTROL EVALUATION AND REPORTING
SEC. 405	EXEMPTION
SEC. 406	CODE OF ETHICS FOR SENIOR FINANCIAL OFFICERS
(A)	CODE OF ETHICS DISCLOSURE
(B)	CHANGES IN CODES OF ETHICS
(C)	DEFINITION
(D)	DEADLINE FOR RULEMAKING
SEC. 407	DISCLOSURE OF AUDIT COMMITTEE FINANCIAL EXPERT
(A)	RULES DEFINING "FINANCIAL EXPERT"
(B)	CONSIDERATIONS
(C)	DEADLINE FOR RULEMAKING.
SEC. 408	ENHANCED REVIEW OF PERIODIC DISCLOSURES BY ISSUERS
(A)	REGULAR AND SYSTEMATIC REVIEW
(B)	REVIEW CRITERIA
(C)	MINIMUM REVIEW PERIOD
SEC. 409	REAL TIME ISSUER DISCLOSURES
SUBCHAPTER V	ANALYST CONFLICTS OF INTEREST
SEC. 501	TREATMENT OF SECURITIES ANALYSTS BY REGISTERED SECURITIES ASSOCIATIONS AND NATIONAL SECURITIES EXCHANGES
(A)	RULES REGARDING SECURITIES ANALYSTS.
(B)	DISCLOSURE
(C)	COMMISSION AUTHORITY
SUBCHAPTER VI	COMMISSION RESOURCES AND AUTHORITY
SEC. 601	AUTHORIZATION OF APPROPRIATIONS
SEC. 602	APPEARANCE AND PRACTICE BEFORE THE COMMISSION
(A)	AUTHORITY TO CENSURE
(B)	DEFINITION
SEC. 603	FEDERAL COURT AUTHORITY TO IMPOSE PENNY STOCK BARS
(A)	SECURITIES EXCHANGE ACT OF 1934 - AUTHORITY OF A COURT TO PROHIBIT PERSONS FROM PARTICIPATING IN AN OFFERING OF PENNY STOCK
(B)	SECURITIES ACT OF 1933 - AUTHORITY OF A COURT TO PROHIBIT PERSONS FROM PARTICIPATING IN AN OFFERING OF PENNY STOCK

(continued)

(continued)

CHAPTER 98	PUBLIC COMPANY ACCOUNTING REFORM AND CORPORATE RESPONSIBILITY
SEC. 604	QUALIFICATIONS OF ASSOCIATED PERSONS OF BROKERS AND DEALERS
(A)	BROKERS AND DEALERS
(B)	INVESTMENT ADVISERS
(C)	CONFORMING AMENDMENTS
TITLE VII	STUDIES AND REPORTS
SEC. 701	GAO STUDY AND REPORT REGARDING CONSOLIDATION OF PUBLIC ACCOUNTING FIRMS
(A)	STUDY REQUIRED
(B)	CONSULTATION
(C)	REPORT REQUIRED
SEC. 702	COMMISSION STUDY AND REPORT REGARDING CREDIT RATING AGENCIES
(A)	STUDY REQUIRED
(B)	REPORT REQUIRED
SEC. 703	STUDY AND REPORT ON VIOLATORS AND VIOLATIONS
(A)	STUDY REQUIRED
(B)	REPORT REQUIRED
SEC. 704	STUDY OF ENFORCEMENT ACTIONS
(A)	STUDY REQUIRED
(B)	REPORT REQUIRED
SEC. 705	STUDY OF INVESTMENT BANKS
(A)	GAO STUDY
(B)	REPORT
TITLE VIII	CORPORATE AND CRIMINAL FRAUD ACCOUNTABILITY
SEC. 801	SHORT TITLE
SEC. 802	CRIMINAL PENALTIES FOR ALTERING DOCUMENTS
(A)	DESTRUCTION, ALTERATION, OR FALSIFICATION OF RECORDS IN FEDERAL INVESTIGATIONS AND BANKRUPTCY
(B)	DESTRUCTION OF CORPORATE AUDIT RECORDS
SEC. 803	DEBTS NONDISCHARGEABLE IF INCURRED IN VIOLATION OF SECURITIES FRAUD LAWS
SEC. 804	STATUTE OF LIMITATIONS FOR SECURITIES FRAUD
SEC. 805	REVIEW OF FEDERAL SENTENCING GUIDELINES FOR OBSTRUCTION OF JUSTICE AND EXTENSIVE CRIMINAL FRAUD
SEC. 806	PROTECTION FOR EMPLOYEES OF PUBLICLY TRADED COMPANIES WHO PROVIDE EVIDENCE OF FRAUD
SEC. 807	CRIMINAL PENALTIES FOR DEFRAUDING SHAREHOLDERS OF PUBLICLY TRADED COMPANIES

(continued)

(continued)

CHAPTER 98	PUBLIC COMPANY ACCOUNTING REFORM AND CORPORATE RESPONSIBILITY
TITLE IX	WHITE-COLLAR CRIME PENALTY ENHANCEMENTS
SEC. 901	SHORT TITLE
SEC. 902	ATTEMPTS AND CONSPIRACIES TO COMMIT CRIMINAL FRAUD OFFENSES
SEC. 903	CRIMINAL PENALTIES FOR MAIL AND WIRE FRAUD
SEC. 904	CRIMINAL PENALTIES FOR VIOLATIONS OF THE EMPLOYEE RETIREMENT INCOME SECURITY ACT OF 1974
SEC. 905	AMENDMENT TO SENTENCING GUIDELINES RELATING TO CERTAIN WHITE-COLLAR OFFENSES
SEC. 906	CORPORATE RESPONSIBILITY FOR FINANCIAL REPORTS
(A)	FAILURE OF CORPORATE OFFICERS TO CERTIFY FINANCIAL REPORTS
TITLE X	CORPORATE TAX RETURNS
TITLE XI	CORPORATE FRAUD ACCOUNTABILITY

Appendix C
Independent Audit By-Law

Wednesday, December 26th, 2012 Official Gazette Number: 28509

English version of the Independent Audit By-Law is meant purely as a documentation tool. In the case of any disputes regarding the implementation and interpretation, the original Turkish version will prevail and the POA does not assume any liability for their contents.

REGULATIONS
From Public Oversight, Accounting, and Auditing Standards Authority:
INDEPENDENT AUDIT BY-LAW
PART ONE
Purpose, Scope, Grounds, and Definitions
Purpose

ARTICLE 1—(1) The purpose of this By-law is to regulate the procedures and principles in relation to statutory auditors, audit firms, and statutory audit that will be conducted within the framework of Turkish Commercial Code dated 13/1/2011 and numbered 6102 and Statutory Decree dated 26/9/2011 and numbered 660 on the Organization and Duties of Public Oversight, Accounting, and Auditing Standards Authority.

Scope

ARTICLE 2—(1) This By-law covers the statutory audit that will be conducted within the framework of the Law 6102 and of the Statutory Decree 660, the authorization of audit firms and statutory auditors, keeping of their register entries, their obligations and responsibilities, examination and inspection of the latter by the Authority, and administrative sanctions applicable to them.

I. Kesimli, *External Auditing and Quality*, Accounting, Finance, Sustainability, Governance & Fraud: Theory and Application,
https://doi.org/10.1007/978-981-13-0526-9

Grounds

ARTICLE 3—(1) This By-law has been issued on the basis of Articles 9, 25, and 27 to the Statutory Decree dated 26/9/2011 and numbered 660 on the Organization and Duties of Public Oversight, Accounting, and Auditing Standards Authority.

Definitions

ARTICLE 4—(1) In this By-law,

(a) "Statutory auditor" means the natural persons authorized by the Authority to perform statutory audit among members of the profession, who acquired certified public accountant or sworn-in certified public accountant license in accordance with the Law dated 1/6/1989 and Numbered 3568 on Certified Public Accountancy and Sworn-in Certified Public Accountancy;
(b) "Statutory audit" means the auditing of financial statements and other financial details on books, records, and documents by applying required statutory audit techniques specified in the auditing standards with the aim of obtaining sufficient and appropriate statutory audit evidences, which would ensure a reasonable assurance with regard to their compliance with financial reporting standards and accuracy, then evaluating and reporting them;
(c) "Audit team" means a team consisting of a key audit partner and statutory auditors that conduct their duties under the responsibility of the key audit partner to perform a certain statutory audit duty on behalf of an audit firm;
(d) "Audit firm" means an equity capital company that is authorized by the Authority to carry out statutory audits and the partners of which are the members of the profession, who acquired certified public accountant or sworn-in certified public accountant license;
(e) "Statutory audit public register (Register)" means the public register that is kept electronically by the Authority and where the records of audit firms and statutory auditors are monitored;
(f) "Audit network" means a structure for cooperation that aims at profit or cost sharing or shares common ownership, control or management, common quality control policies and procedures, a common business strategy, the use of a common brand or trade name or a significant part of professional resources regardless of the fact that if there is a legal connection between audit firms or statutory auditors;
(g) "Audited entity" means an entity that has entered into a contract with an audit firm or a statutory auditor for the purpose of having a statutory audit conducted;
(h) "Financial statements" mean the financial statements that is required to be issued according to Turkish Accounting Standards;
(i) "Related audit firm and other entities" mean other audit firms and other entities that directly or indirectly control the audit firm or that are directly or indirectly controlled by the same;
(j) "Quality assurance system" means the system organized by the Authority to ensure that the statutory audits of the statutory auditors and audit firms would

be performed in compliance with specified standards and principles with the aim of ensuring quality in the statutory audit and confidence of public opinion toward the statutory audits being performed;

(k) "Quality control system" means the system organized by audit firms within their organizations in accordance with the Authority's arrangements to achieve the required quality in audits;

(l) "Public institutions" mean the institutions included in the lists annexed to the Law 5018 dated 10/12/2003 on Public Financial Management and Control Law;

(m) "Public interest entities (PIE)" mean publicly-held companies, banks, insurance, reassurance and pension companies, factoring companies, financing companies, financial lease companies, asset management companies, pension funds, issuers as defined by the Capital Markets Law dated 28/7/1981 and numbered 2499 and the entities, which are evaluated in this scope by the Authority since they significantly concern the public interest regarding their fields of activity, trading volumes, number of personnel they employ;

(n) "Key management personnel" mean the persons, including the members of managing body, that directly or indirectly have the authority and responsibility for planning, managing, and controlling the firm's activities;

(o) "The Board" means the Public Oversight, Accounting and Auditing Standards Board;

(p) "The Authority" means the Public Oversight, Accounting and Auditing Standards Authority;

(q) "Member of the profession" means Certified Public Accountants and Sworn-in Certified Public Accountants that have obtained their licenses in scope of the Law 3568;

(r) "Partner" means the shareholders of joint-stock companies and the partners of limited companies and commandite companies;

(s) "Equity capital company" means the companies classified as equity capital companies under Turkish Commercial Code dated 13/1/2011 and numbered 6102;

(t) "Exam" means statutory auditor exam;

(u) "Responsible auditor" means the statutory auditor that an audit firm holds responsible for carrying out a certain statutory audit activity and authorizes to sign on behalf of the audit firm the report relevant to that audit;

(v) "Turkish Auditing Standards" mean including the statutory audit of information systems, education, ethics, quality control, and auditing standards within the field of statutory audit together with other arrangements in connection with this field, which comply with international standards, approved by the Board and issued with the name of the Turkish Auditing Standard in compliance with the Statutory Decree numbered 660;

(w) "Turkish Accounting Standards" mean accounting standards approved by the Board in compliance with the Statutory Decree numbered 660 and issued with the name of the Turkish Accounting Standards and Turkish Financial Reporting Standards together with other arrangements in connection with this field;

(x) "Certificate of authorization" means the Audit Firm Certificate or Statutory Auditor Certificate that is granted by the Authority to audit firms and statutory auditors in relation to their approval where the conditions prescribed in this By-law are met;
(y) "Annual report" means the report prepared by the management bodies of equity companies or by the parent company's managing body in case of a group of companies in compliance with Article 516 and 518 to the Law 6102 and the relevant legislation; and
(z) "Managing body" means the board of directors in case of joint-stock companies, the manager or managers in case of partnership companies, the capital of which is divided into shares, and the director or directors in case of limited companies.

(2) Definitions used in this By-law have such meanings attributed to them in Turkish Accounting Standards and Turkish Auditing Standards, and in this By-law, audit means statutory audit, auditor means statutory auditor, and audit firm means independent audit firms.

PART TWO

Principles of Audit

Purpose and scope of statutory audit

ARTICLE 5—(1) An audit is carried out for the purpose of forming an opinion that will provide users assurance within the framework of Turkish Auditing Standards whether the issues, including financial statements and other financial information, subject to the audit comply with the predefined criteria or not.

(2) Audit provides the users with reasonable or limited assurance relating to the compliance of the audit subject with the audit criterion. Where it is not explicitly expressed in the relevant legislation or audit engagement that it will provide limited assurance, the audit will be carried out to give a reasonable assurance. The audit scope required by a reasonable and limited assurance level will be defined within the framework of Turkish Auditing Standards.

(3) An audit covers obtaining sufficient and appropriate audit evidence about the statutory audit subject within the framework of Turkish Auditing Standards through abiding by the principles of professional ethics with a professional skepticism and forming and reporting an opinion on the basis of this evidence.

(4) Elements of an audit are made up of the audit subject, parties, criterion, evidence, and audit report.

Audit subject

ARTICLE 6—(1) An audit should be carried out about the matters that are subject to statutory audit according to the provisions of the Law numbered 6102, Statutory Decree numbered 660, and other legislation.

(2) An audit should cover the financial statements, annual activity reports, and systems for the early detection and management of risks that are subject to statutory audit under the provisions of the Law numbered 6102 and other matters that need to be directly or indirectly audited, reviewed, or assessed by audit firms and statutory auditors in accordance with the other legislation.

Parties of an audit

ARTICLE (7)—(1) The audited entity, auditor, and the intended users as defined by the relevant legislation are the parties of an audit.

Audit criterion

ARTICLE 8—(1) An audit should be based on predefined criteria whereby the audit subject's compliance is assessed. Turkish Accounting Standards should constitute the audit criterion in terms of financial statements, while provisions of the Law 6102 and the relevant legislation on audit criterion in terms of early risk detection and management, and arrangements about audit criterion or the rules referred to by the same in terms of the audit subjects that fall within the scope of the other legislation.

(2) In the cases where the other legislation envisages the fulfillment of a direct or indirect audit by audit firms and auditors, but does not express the criteria that the audit subjects should comply with, the Authority will define the audit criterion. In the audits carried out on a voluntary basis, those requesting the audit will define it.

Audit evidence

ARTICLE 9—(1) Audit evidence consists of the information, documents, and representations that are sufficient and appropriate for the predefined assurance level and obtained by the auditor for the purpose of expressing an opinion in order to give assurance about whether there are material non-compliances about the audit within the framework of audit criterion. This evidence is obtained and documented by planning and carrying out the audit within the framework of Turkish Auditing Standards and with professional skepticism.

(2) An audit should be planned and carried out with professional skepticism considering that the conditions resulting in material audit non-compliances may exist. When materiality is assessed within the framework of the existing conditions, it depends on the size or nature of the non-compliance or both between the audit subject and audit criterion.

Audit report

ARTICLE (10)—(1) Audit report is a document, which is prepared in line with the Authority's arrangements for the purpose of forming the audit opinion and other noteworthy matters, if any, that are formed according to the predefined assurance level as a result of assessing the audit evidence within the framework of Turkish Auditing Standards available to users and the responsibility of which is assumed by the undersigned audit firm or the statutory auditor.

PART THREE

Authorization

Those authorized to carry out an audit

ARTICLE 11—(1) Audit should only be carried out by audit firms or auditors that are authorized by the Authority within the framework of their respective authorities.

(2) Audit firms and statutory auditors start exercising their authorities following the announcement of authorization by the Authority.

(3) The audit of PIEs and the entities, which are included in this scope by the Authority in terms of their fields of activity, trading volumes, number of personnel they employ, and similar criteria, should only be carried out by audit firms, while the audit of others is carried out by audit firms or auditors.

Certificates of Authorization

ARTICLE 12—(1) Audit Firm Certificate is granted to equity capital companies, and Statutory Auditor Certificate is granted to the members of profession, the applications of which are accepted by the Authority within the frame of this By-law.

Authorization of audit firms

ARTICLE 13—(1) Save for the conditions set out in the Law 3568 and the relevant legislation, a firm that files an application for audit activities must:

(a) be an equity capital company;
(b) have registered shares certificates;
(c) have a field of activity exclusively for statutory audit or the professional field falling within the scope of the Law 3568;
(d) have the phrase of statutory audit in its trade name;
(e) have the articles of association that do not contain such matters that are contrary to the provisions of audit legislation;
(f) have a capital and voting rights owned by auditors by more than half and all the partners of which must be the members of profession;
(g) have such auditors that bear Statutory Auditor Certificates within the framework of Article 14;
(h) employ auditors on a full-time basis and for one reporting period as a minimum;
(i) have at least two responsible auditors that meet the conditions set out in Article 28;
(j) have audit staff of such quality and width that can, as a minimum, constitute the audit teams as defined in Article 27;
(k) have the members of managing body entirely composed of the members of profession and majority of them must be the auditors permanently employed by it, provided that it does not exceed seventy-five percent;
(l) not employ the auditors, partners, and key management personnel that act as the partners, key management personnel, or auditors at another audit firm or another real or natural entity carrying out statutory audit activities or that carry out statutory audit activities on their behalf;
(m) have written policies and procedures of quality control system, the principles of which are set out by the Authority, including audit guides;
(n) have such organization, office, technical equipment, document, and recording facilities at a level to be accepted by the Authority in order to carry out the audit activities efficiently;
(o) not have the approval that was withdrawn by the Authority previously; and
(p) not have the legal entity and partners that have disrepute and the partners must not be in a position that compromises the reputation required by audit profession.

(2) Firms that want to carry out audit activities file applications with the Authority together with the information and documents evidencing that they meet the conditions prescribed by paragraph one. The firms that are approved by the Authority with regard to the required conditions following onsite examinations, where necessary, will be recorded in the register and announced provided that they pay the required charges and fees and file a registration application with the Authority within ninety days at the latest. Audit Firm Certificates will be granted to these firms following the registration procedure.

(3) Without prejudice to the other legislation provisions, the transfer, demerger, merger, and type modification procedures of audit firms are subject to the Authority's permission.

(4) By obtaining the opinions of such authorities, boards, or organizations that are responsible for the regulation and audit of certain areas, the Authority may define additional requirements for the audit firms that will carry out audit in these areas and it will separately announce the audit firms that meet these requirements in lists. Apart from these, new audit firm lists can be made under such requirements determined by the Authority for auditing the entities that will be identified on the basis of trading volume, fields of activity, the nature of respective regulations, and similar matters governing the entity to be audited.

(5) The Authority can grant approval to the firms that have such trade names without the phrase of statutory audit, provided that they modify their trade names within three months, and such modification is announced in the Turkish Trade Registry Gazette. The approval of those that fail to modify their trade name within this period is canceled.

(6) Audit firms exercise the auditing authority through and under the responsibility of responsible auditors that have the qualifications set out in Article 28 and that are authorized to sign the audit report on behalf of the firm. This responsibility does not relieve the audit firm and its key management personnel from responsibility.

Authorization of statutory auditors

ARTICLE 14—(1) Those who want to carry out statutory audit activities must:

(a) have a bachelor's degree as a minimum obtained from faculties and graduate schools or from foreign higher education institutions, the equivalency of which are accepted by Council of Higher Education, that give education in the branches of law, economics, public finance, business administration, accounting, banking, public administration, and political sciences, or where they graduated from other education branches, have a master's degree as a minimum obtained from the disciplines set out in this paragraph;
(b) be the member of profession;
(c) be domiciled in Turkey;
(d) be competent to exercise their civil rights;
(e) have completed the applied practical training set out in Article 15;
(f) have passed the statutory auditor exam set out in Article 16;

(g) not have been convicted for the crimes against the national security, the crimes against the constitutional order and the functioning of this order, the crimes against the national defense, the crimes against the state secrets and espionage, crimes of embezzlement, corruption, bribery, theft, fraud, forgery, abuse of confidence, fraudulent bankruptcy, bid rigging, conspiracy to avoid contractual obligations, laundering of illegally obtained assets, or smuggling even if the periods set out in Article 53 to the Turkish Penal Code dated 26/9/2004 and numbered 5237 are expired and sentenced to imprisonment for one year and more as a result of a malicious crime or benefited from amnesty or the announcement of judgment is deferred;

(h) not have the approval that was withdrawn by the Authority previously; and

(i) not have disrepute and be in a position that compromises the reputation required by statutory audit profession.

(2) The members of profession that want to become auditors file applications to the Authority together with the information and documents evidencing that they meet the conditions prescribed by paragraph one. Applications are filed personally or through the audit firms where they are employed. The applicants that are approved by the Authority with regard to the required conditions will be recorded in the register and announced provided that they pay the required charges and fees and file a registration application with the Authority. Statutory Auditor Certificates, auditor identification card, and auditor seal will be granted to these persons following the registration procedure.

(3) By obtaining the opinions of such authorities, boards, or organizations that are responsible for the regulation and audit of certain areas, the Authority can define additional requirements for the auditors that will carry out statutory audit in these areas.

Practical Training

ARTICLE 15—(1) Persons who want to become auditors must have received practical training on professional subjects including auditing of financial statements, for a minimum period of 3 years at an audit firm or from a statutory auditor. Periods spent in ratification and tax audit services within the framework of the Law 3568 and periods spent by those having the audit authorization at the public institutions and agencies falling within the scope of paragraph two of Article 6 to the same Law at such public institutions and agencies will be included in the practical training period.

(2) Those having a minimum professional experience of fifteen years are not subject to the requirement of practical training.

(3) In implementing this By-law, professional experience means the period actually spent in statutory audit. However, the periods spent in professional activities falling within the scope of the Law 3568 or in apprenticeship and services accepted as apprenticeship are also taken into account in calculating this period. The periods of undergraduate and graduate studies in the disciplines set out in subparagraph (a) of paragraph one Article 14 are included in this period with the limitation of 4 years. The calculation of this period is based on the activity

commencement date and, with the exception of periods spent in public institutions and agencies, the periods of discontinuation in these activities for more than one year are excluded.

(4) Those receiving applied practical training have the title of assistant auditors during the practical training period, and they participate in audit activities in company with auditors. In this period, those employing assistant auditors with them take all kinds of measures to ensure that assistant deputies gain the required professional competence for the purpose of putting theoretical knowledge into implementation. Auditors are authorized and obliged in the issues such as giving assignment in audits to assistant auditors, making them to attend the interviews held with the audited entities, overseeing their activities, and reviewing the working papers prepared by them.

(5) Practical training starts with the delivery of information and documents evidencing the satisfaction of required conditions to the Authority by the relevant audit firm, statutory auditor, or assistant auditor within the period of notification to the Social Security Institution.

(6) The Authority regulates the issues relating to the practical training, auditors that can give practical training and trainees, and their follow-up.

Statutory auditor exam

ARTICLE 16—(1) The Authority conducts the statutory auditor exam for the purpose measuring the theoretical and practical knowledge of examinees in the areas relevant to statutory audit.

(2) The graduation condition set out in subparagraph (a) of paragraph one of Article 14 is sought for taking the exam.

(3) Statutory auditor exam covers the following main subjects:

(a) Accounting (General accounting, cost and management accounting);
(b) Accounting Standards (Turkish Accounting Standards, and regulations and standards included in the legislation for preparing the annual and consolidated financial statements);
(c) Corporate Governance Principles and Financial Management;
(d) Audit (Turkish Auditing Standards, and other legislation regarding professional ethics, independence, risk management, and internal control and audit);
(e) General Legal Legislation (Commercial Law, Law of Obligations, Execution and Bankruptcy Law, Civil Law, Tax Law, Social Security Legislation, Administrative Law); and
(f) Legislation on capital market, banking, insurance, and individual retirement,

(4) Certified Public Accountants are subject to an exam for the subjects set out in subparagraphs (b), (c), (d), and (f) and Sworn-in Certified Public Accountants in (b), (d), and (f).

(5) Those that will not carry out statutory audit activities in the fields of capital market, banking, insurance, and individual retirement are not subject to an exam for the subjects set out in subparagraph (f) of paragraph three of this Article.

(6) Exam results are valid for two years. The Authority decides on the unification and separation of the exam by subjects, content of subjects, announcement,

application method, place, time, form, duration, announcement of results, fee, conditions for passing the exam, exam committee, and other issues relating to the exam.

PART FOUR

Statutory Audit Public Register

Registration and announcement

ARTICLE 17—(1) Authorization, warning, and approval's suspension, withdrawal, and cessation procedures in relation to auditors and audit firms are recorded in a register kept by the Authority electronically and these are announced publicly in an up-to-date manner. Authorization enters into force upon registration and announcement.

(2) The Authority grants a number to each audit firm and auditor.

(3) Those unregistered cannot carry out audit activities.

Register Information

ARTICLE 18—(1) In the register kept by the Authority, the following information on the audit firms is recorded followed up:

(a) Trade name and trade register number;
(b) Register number granted by the Authority;
(c) Address of head office and addresses of branch offices (the audit network, if any, that they are included and this network's legal and structural nature, their related audit firms and other entities and these firms' legal and structural nature);
(d) Web site address;
(e) Partners' names and surnames, Turkish identification numbers, and shares in the corporate capital together with share percentages and amounts;
(f) Addresses and other contact details of partners;
(g) Turkish identification numbers of those charged in the managing body and their duties, if any, in other companies;
(h) List and register numbers of statutory auditors;
(i) Information on their registrations, if any, by the competent authorities of other countries; and
(j) Other information considered necessary by the Authority.

(2) In the register kept by the Authority, the following information on the statutory auditors is recorded followed up:

(a) Name, surname, and Turkish identification number;
(b) Trade name and trade register number, if any;
(c) Register number granted by the Authority;
(d) Contact details;
(e) Web site address, if any;
(f) Information on the Statutory Auditor Certificate;
(g) The trade name, trade register number, Web site address, if any, and contact details of the audit firm of which she or he is a partner or employee;

(h) Information on their registrations, if any, by the competent authorities of other countries; and
(i) Other information considered necessary by the Authority.

(3) Certain information on auditors or audit firms recorded in the register may not be announced publicly as decided by the Authority.

PART FIVE

Obligations of Audit Firms and Statutory Auditors

Ensuring the quality and reliability in statutory audits

ARTICLE 19—(1) Audit firms and auditors conduct their activities in such a manner that enables them to carry out reliable and high-quality audits.

(2) Audit activities of audit firms and auditors cover the other actions and processes that aim at ensuring the continuity, quality, and reliability of audits in addition to the audit process.

(3) An audit process commences with the entity's audit offer for each accounting period; it is planned, scheduled, and implemented in accordance with Turkish Auditing Standards and ends with the reporting of the audit result. Provisions on the obligations after the delivery of report are reserved. Audit process is documented within the framework of Turkish Auditing Standards.

(4) For the purpose of ensuring the continuity, quality, and reliability of audits, the provisions of this part are observed, mainly those relating to the professional ethics and quality control system, both during statutory audit processes and outside the audit processes.

Establishing a quality control system

ARTICLE 20—(1) Audit firms must carry out their activities within the framework of a quality control system, the minimum conditions of which are defined by the Authority. In implementing this system, the written policies and procedures that are established according to the Authority's arrangements and notified to the Authority are observed. The policies and processes are updated and implemented in line with the Authority's arrangements.

(2) Where there is a difference between the written policies and procedures of the audit firm's quality control system and the Authority's arrangements, on which these are based, or in case an application outside the audit firm's written policies and procedures is more advisable due to the specific reasons of the current conditions, it is possible to deviate from the written policies and processes in question. This situation and reason thereof must be submitted by the statutory auditor to the audit firm in writing for archiving.

Compliance with professional ethics

ARTICLE 21—(1) Audit firms and statutory auditors must comply with the professional ethics, the following details of which will be identified by the Authority:

(a) Integrity: to be fair, frank, honest, and reliable in all of their professional and business relations;
(b) Objectivity: to prevent prejudices, biases, conflicts of interest, and others that fraud on their powers from affecting their professional of business judgments or decisions;

(c) Professional competence and due care: to maintain the professional knowledge and skills at such a level that ensures the audited entities to receive sufficient statutory audit services and to act in due care and in accordance with Turkish Auditing Standards in the light of the current developments in legislation and statutory audit techniques;
(d) Confidentiality: to observe the confidentiality of information obtained when carrying out a statutory audit; to refrain from disclosing this information to third parties and from using the same for the benefits of themselves or third parties, without prejudice to any legal or professional right or duty to disclose the information in question; and
(e) Professional behavior: to comply with the relevant legislation and to avoid from such actions and behaviors that damage the statutory audit profession's reputation.

(2) Audit firms will, prior to each audit and once a year as a minimum in any case, obtain a written promise from auditors and those participating in audits to the extent that they act and will act in compliance with firm's policies and processes in relation to independence, objectivity, and confidentiality. Auditors and those participating in audits should inform in writing the audit firm about the matters that may arise following the commencement of an audit and that can negatively impact the matters listed in subparagraph one.

Independence and maintenance of independence

ARTICLE 22—(1) Audit firms and auditors carry out audits in independent of mind and independent in appearance.

(a) Independence of mind is the expressing of an opinion by the statutory auditor free from the influences that can impact her/his professional judgment in order to ensure acting within the framework of integrity, objectivity, and professional skepticism.
(b) Independence in appearance is the avoidance of situations and behaviors that can make an impression for the third persons, who assess the entire circumstances and conditions of the subject, that the audit firm, auditor, or the member of an audit team makes concessions of integrity, objectivity, and professional skepticism.

(2) Audit firms and auditors must be objective and independent from the audited entity when carrying out an audit, and they can by no means take part in the decision-making mechanisms of the audited entities. Additionally, audit firms and auditors must not be subject to such special conditions that can eliminate their independence.

(3) Independence is deemed to have been eliminated where audit firms or auditors are of the opinion that the independence has been impaired. Some of the conditions that impair or eliminate the independence are as follows:

(a) Direct or indirect borrowing and lending relationship other than ordinary economic relations between statutory auditors and the audit firm's partners, key management personnel, statutory auditors and their spouses, even if divorced, and relatives by blood and marriage up to (and including) third degree or the entity audited by the audit firm of those being in relation with the audited entity;

(b) Failure by the audited entity to pay an audit fee for the previous periods without a valid reason;

(c) Making the audit fee conditional on audit results and resulting of this condition in uncertainties about the audit quality and setting of this fee on the basis of other services provided to the audited entity outside the scope of the audit; and

(d) Emergence of other conditions that impair independence.

(4) Where factors compromising the independence arise, measures should be taken to protect the independence. Where it is understood that the measures taken are insufficient to eliminate the threats, the independence will be deemed to have been impaired. Audit firms and auditors must record the threats emerging against the independence and measures taken in response to them when carrying out an audit in writing and maintain these records. Conditions where the independence is impaired or eliminated are notified to the Authority, and the relevant audit engagement is terminated by obtaining the Authority's approval.

(5) Audit firms and auditors cannot render any service to the audited entity other than ratification, tax consultancy, and tax audit and carry out them through related audit firms and other firms included in the audit network. Services rendered by the natural entity partners of the audit firm, its auditors, and key management personnel also fall within this scope.

Advertisement ban

ARTICLE 23—(1) Audit firms and auditors cannot advertise directly or indirectly and involve in such activities that fall within the scope of advertisement. They cannot use any title other than their professional and academic titles in their trade names, signboards, or printed papers.

(2) However, audit firms and auditors can prepare and distribute brochures that contain corporate introductory information, place advertisements for seeking personnel for them or for audited entities, prints scientific works on the professional subjects, and organize meetings such as seminars and conferences and give education in relation to the professional subjects.

(3) When conducting the activities referred in subparagraph two, it is required

(a) To refrain from making a promise and commitment in relation to the result of the work;

(b) To observe the seriousness and prudence required by the work;

(c) To refrain from including exaggerative emotional expressions, images, and information that are wrong, mislead and delude the public opinion, and misuse the lack of experience such as concealing the information that must be announced for taking healthy decisions, and leaving such an impression;

(d) To refrain from creating expectations that do not have a concrete background for the works and services that can be done; and

(e) To refrain from comparing the audit firm or the auditor with another audit firm or the auditor.

Unfair competition ban

ARTICLE 24—(1) The audit firms and the auditors cannot act in such a manner that it may in any way negatively impact the quality of audit activity or harm their colleagues, without prejudice to the unfair competition conditions included in other arrangements.

(2) Audit firms and auditors cannot accept the audit service request of an audited entity for the same period when its audit service relation with another audit firm or auditor continues, except for the conditions permitted by the Authority.

Continuing education

ARTICLE 25—(1) Auditors are educated on a continuous basis for the purpose of keeping their theoretical knowledge and professional skills at a sufficient level, complying with professional ethics, following up changes in the professional field, and ensuring their professional development.

(2) Continuing education obligation starts as from the registration of auditors and implemented as defined by the Authority.

(3) Following their registration, auditors must meet the continuing education requirements once in five years.

(4) Audit firms should take the measures required for enabling the auditors to complete their continuing education programs.

(5) The Authority regulates the matters relating to continuing education by obtaining the relevant organizations' opinions, where necessary.

(6) For the purpose of ensuring the audit objectivity and independence and improving the reliance in and the quality of audit, the Authority takes required measures for educating auditors and the members of profession or improving their level of education within the framework of this By-law in addition to continuing education.

Limitations on the audit activity

ARTICLE 26—(1) Audit firms and auditors cannot undertake the following audits:

(a) The audits that they cannot undertake under the Law 6102;
(b) The audits that will impair independence;
(c) The audits where the number, quality, or experience of audit staff is insufficient in relation to the audited entity's characteristics;
(d) Audits for the entities that were carried out for seven years within the last decade for audit firms and five years within the last seven years for auditors, including the ones employed at an audit firm, unless a three-year period passes;
(e) The audits that are contrary to the arrangements made by the Authority in relation to the contract acceptance process; and
(f) The audits that cannot be carried out healthily as a result of the workload of audit firms or auditors.

(2) In calculating the period in subparagraph (d) of paragraph one, the periods spent for audits carried out by the firms and related audit firms included in the same audit network are considered altogether. The periods spent by a statutory auditor in the same audited entity will be considered together, regardless of the audit firm where the auditor was employed.

(3) Auditors cannot take charge of the key management personnel position at such entities and their subsidiaries for which they carried out audits during the last two years, unless a two-year period passes.

(4) Auditors can carry out audits only at one audit firm. Unless their relations with the audit firm that employs them terminate, they cannot carry out audit activities at another audit firm or on their own.

Audit teams

ARTICLE 27—(1) The audits that must only be carried out by audit firms within the framework of the legislation are carried out by such audit teams that consist of the auditors in the number and qualification required by the audit. Audit teams are comprised of the auditors in sufficient number and with such authority, knowledge, experience, and skills to carry out the audit in compliance with the Authority's arrangements considering the audited entity's trading volume, activities, and the regulations relevant to that entity. However, audit teams consist of three statutory auditors as a minimum. At least one substitute auditor will be assigned for each of the responsible auditor position and certain positions in audit teams. The substitute statutory auditors must have such qualifications that enable them to undertake the responsibilities of those they replace. The Authority may define different minimum numbers of auditors and substitute auditors depending on the characteristics of audited entities.

(2) By obtaining the opinions of such authorities, boards, or organizations that are responsible for the regulation and audit of certain areas, the Authority can define additional conditions for those that will carry out audit in these areas. All of the auditors included in the audit team should meet the additional conditions prescribed by the Authority according to the characteristics of audited entities.

(3) Auditors that are not authorized in relation to the audit in question and assistant statutory auditors, experts that will provide technical information including the audit of information systems, and other persons that assist the audit can also take part in audit teams, provided that they are not assigned as statutory auditors. Auditors or experts that meet the conditions prescribed by the Authority on the subject of information systems' audit should be made available in sufficient numbers for the audit of banks as defined in Banking Law dated 19/10/2005 and numbered 5411 and other entities set out by the Authority. These persons should work under the responsibility, supervision, and control of auditors, but they cannot take a decision-making position at any stage of the audit. These persons are not taken into account in calculating the minimum number of auditors and held responsible for the audit without prejudice to general provisions and their obligations of independence, objectivity, and secrecy.

(4) Audit teams should carry out statutory audits under the supervision and administration of the responsible auditor.

(5) Audit firms can give the titles of auditor, senior statutory auditor, and to statutory auditors. Senior statutory title should not be given to those that have not served in auditing for six year and chief auditor title to those that have not served in auditing for ten years.

Conditions for becoming a responsible auditor

ARTICLE 28—(1) Responsible auditors are authorized to sign audit reports on behalf of audit firms, and they are assigned by the managing body of audit firms among the auditors that meet the following conditions:

(a) For audits to be carried out at PIEs, having fifteen-year professional experience and having carried out audits actually for two years as a minimum during this period in the areas envisaged by legislation with title of auditor, senior statutory auditor, or chief statutory auditor;
(b) For other audits, having minimum ten-year professional experience and having carried out audits actually for one year as a minimum during this period with title of auditor, senior statutory auditor, or chief statutory auditor; and
(c) Having been authorized to sign audit reports on behalf of the audit firm.

(2) Information and documents evidencing that the auditors meet the conditions prescribed in paragraph one should be delivered to the Authority for approval by the audit firm with the decision of the managing body.

Audit engagement

ARTICLE 29—(1) The audit engagement that is drawn in writing up between the audit firm or statutory auditor and the audited entity must contain the following matters as a minimum:

(a) The date and number of the general assembly decision or court order that forms a basis for the engagement;
(b) Purpose, scope, period, and special reasons, if any, of the audit;
(c) Subject and criterion of the statutory audit;
(d) Responsibilities of the parties;
(e) A provision to the extent that the audit will be carried out and completed according to Turkish Auditing Standards and relevant legislation;
(f) A provision to the extent that an unlimited access will be provided for all of the records, documents, and other information requested in connection with the audit;
(g) Names and titles and envisaged working periods of auditors, including their substitutes, assigned in the audit team together with the detailed breakdown of fees for each of them and total audit fee;
(h) A provision to the extent that the responsible auditor and his/her substitute are authorized to sign the audit report on behalf of the audit firm;
(i) Commencement and ending dates of the audit and report delivery date;
(j) A provision to the extent that professional liability insurance policy will be bought;
(k) Audited entity's obligation to inform the auditor about the events that occur after the report date, but prior to the announcement of financial statements or annual report and that will affect them; and
(l) A provision to the extent that the engagement can only be canceled in accordance with the legislation.

(2) No service can be envisaged in the engagement other than the audit service, and the payment of audit fee can only be made conditional on the audit service.

(3) The audit engagement will be concluded for the accounting period for which the audit firm or the auditor is selected under the Law 6102;

(4) The auditor can only be removed from the audit function where another statutory auditor is appointed and as prescribed in subparagraph four of Article 39 to the Law 6102. The auditor can only cancel the audit engagement where there is a valid reason or where a removal action is filed against him/her. Audit firms and auditors can terminate the engagements where there are reasons justifiable by the Authority.

Obligation to issue an audit reportand express an opinion

ARTICLE 30—(1) As a result of the statutory audit activity, an audit report is issued according to the form and principles defined by the Authority.

(2) This report should contain the following under the title of opinion:

(a) An unqualified opinion where there is not any non-compliances or misstatements on the statutory audit subject that can be considered material according to audit criterion separately and collectively;
(b) A qualified opinion where there are separately or collectively material non-compliances or misstatements on the audit subject or where sufficient appropriate audit evidence cannot be obtained, but this does not affect the audit subject in general;
(c) An adverse opinion where, after obtaining the sufficient appropriate audit evidence, the non-compliances or misstatements detected are separately or collectively material and affect the audit subject in general; and
(d) A disclaimer of opinion where sufficient appropriate audit evidence cannot be obtained that will constitute the basis of the audit opinion for the material matters that affect the audit subject in general or where uncertainties, which impede forming an opinion although sufficient evidence is obtained, arise subsequently.

Subsequent events

ARTICLE 31—(1) The audit firm and statutory auditor have the obligation of including in their report the events that occur after the balance sheet date, but prior to the audit report date and that require restatement or explanation in the financial statements or annual activity report within the framework of Turkish Auditing Standards and relevant legislation.

(2) Where the audit firm and auditor become aware of the events that occur after the audit report date, but prior to the announcement date of financial statements or annual activity report and that will affect these, they will assess the requirement of restatement or explanation in financial statements or annual activity report and carry out the required procedures in line with Turkish Auditing Standards and relevant legislation.

(3) Where the audit firm and auditor become aware of the events that occur after the period of announcement of the financial statements and annual report and that will affect these, they will assess the requirement of restatement or explanation in

financial statements or annual report and carry out the required procedures in line with Turkish Auditing Standards and relevant legislation.

Fee Tariff

ARTICLE 32—(1) Audit fee is determined in such a manner that it ensures the audit independence, objectivity, and quality. Where the services permitted in line with the legislation are rendered in connection with the audited entity, this does not affect the audit fee.

(2) The Authority can determine the fee tariffs for audit service in relation with the relevant period.

(3) In the years where the fee tariff is not determined, the amounts that are calculated through increasing fee amounts applied in the previous period by the revaluation percentages set and announced for that year by the Ministry of Finance will apply.

Professional liability insurance

ARTICLE 33—(1) Audit firms and auditors must buy professional liability insurance policies that will cover all of the audits starting from the first audit work that they undertake.

(2) Matters relating to the professional liability insurance are regulated by the Authority after obtaining the opinion of the Undersecretariat of Treasury.

Notifications

ARTICLE 34—(1) Audit firms and auditors will notify the following to the Authority:

(a) Modifications to any information that has been previously notified to the Authority, including register information, within following 10 days at the latest;
(b) Information to be requested by the Authority in connection with the audit engagements and contracts for other services within 10 days at the latest following the signing date;
(c) Procedures relating to engagement cancelation and withdrawal under Article 39 to the Law 6102 within 10 days at the latest following the procedure date;
(d) Professional liability insurance drawing date and modifications to the policy and insurance company within 10 days at the latest following the date of modifications;
(e) Their revenues for the last calendar year until the end of the fifteenth day of May in line with the form set out by the Authority; and
(f) Other notifications and other information to be requested by the Authority within the period set out by the legislation or the Authority.

Obligation of retention and submission

ARTICLE 35—(1) Audit firms have the obligation of retention of their commercial books, audit reports, and all types of documents regarding the audit activities and quality control system, including the ones kept electronically, mechanically, and in other environments, for a period of ten years together with their appendices. This provision also applies to the persons carrying out audit on their own.

(2) Audit firms and auditors have the obligation of presenting all information and documents together with the ones that must be kept under subparagraph one that are requested by the persons assigned by the Authority and of delivering a copy thereof to the assigned persons and making available an environment for their review.

(3) All of the documents and appendices thereof, including the ones that are kept electronically, mechanically, and in other environments in connection with each audit activity, must be filed. Audit files should be created during the audit.

Preparation and publication of transparency reports

ARTICLE 36—(1) The audit firm that carried out the audit of PIEs in a calendar year should notify the Authority the transparency report and publish the same on their Web sites within three months of the end of each calendar year.

(2) The chairman of the audit firm's managing body will sign this report, and it will contain the following information as a minimum on the audit firm:

(a) A description of its legal structure and partners;
(b) A description of its key management personnel and responsible auditors;
(c) A description of the legal and structural attributes of the audit network that it belongs to;
(d) A description of the related audit firms and other entities and of the nature of these relations;
(e) A description of its organizational structure;
(f) An indication of when the last quality assurance review took place;
(g) The list of PIEs for which the audit firm has carried out statutory audits during the preceding year;
(h) A statement on the policy followed by the audit firm concerning the continuing education of statutory auditors;
(i) In relation to the independence practices, a statement confirming that the compliance with the principles of independence has been reviewed;
(j) Financial information indicating the weight of audit activities such as the distribution of total revenues by the audit of financial statements, other audits, and non-audit services;
(k) Information concerning the basis of the responsible auditors' remuneration;
(l) An introduction of the quality control system and the declaration of the audit firm to the extent that this system functions efficiently; and
(m) Other information requested by the Authority.

(3) Where there is an imminent significant threat to the personal safety and there is such a request, information on the audited entity may not be included in the explanation given in connection with subparagraph (g) of paragraph two by obtaining the Authority's approval.

(4) The audit firms that have not carried out a PIE audit within a calendar year although they were included in the lists for PIE audits will explain this in their Web site's section for transparency reports.

(5) Where the report is updated through a transparency report, the original and updated versions of the report will separately be made available to public opinion for five years.

Obligations arising out of Turkish Commercial Code

ARTICLE 37—(1) Audit firms and auditors should also fulfil the following obligations during statutory audits that they carry out under the Law 6102:

(a) To report and present the statutory audit results in compliance with the Law 6102 and this By-law and to make statements to the general assembly about statutory audit activities and results thereof;
(b) To propose the establishment of a committee for the early detection and management of risks where necessary under Article 378 to the Law 6102 and, in case such a system exists, to draw up a separate report explaining its structure and practices and present the same to the board of directors together with the audit report;
(c) To abide by the provisions regarding the assignment and removal of statutory auditors, and cancellation of engagements referred in Article 399 to the Law 6102;
(d) Where the audit engagement is canceled, to draw up a report about the results obtained until the cancellation date according Article 402 to the Law 6102 and to present the same to the general assembly; and
(e) In connection with the statutory audit, to perform the other obligations envisaged in the Law 6102 and relevant legislation other than the arrangements of the Statutory Decree numbered 660 and secondary legislation.

PART SIX

Examination, Inspection, and Administrative Sanctions to be Imposed by the Authority

Examinations and inspections

ARTICLE 38—(1) The Authority examines and inspects the audit firms and statutory auditors within the framework of selected statutory audit files sufficient number and other information, notifications, documents under the quality assurance system to be established by it. Examination and inspection activities are carried out within the scope of an annual examination and inspection plan that is prepared annually by the Authority by obtaining the opinions of relevant institutes. Examination results are declared to public every year with a report.

(2) Examinations and inspections conducted at audit firms cover the assessments in relation to the inspection of statutory audit activities, which were carried out by audit firms, under the legislation, and audit of these firms' activities in relation to their compliance with the legislation, and qualifications and quantities of resources spent, audit fees received, and the audit firm's internal control system.

(3) Minimum triennial examination and inspection will be conducted for the audit firms that audit PIEs, while the examination and inspection of others will be conducted per six years and statutory auditors will be subject to such inspection and audit when deemed necessary by the Authority.

(4) In addition to the planned examination and inspections, the Authority conducts examinations and inspections in case of denouncements, complaints, and notifications and in other cases deemed necessary.

(5) The Authority may carry out the examinations and inspections through either its own personnel or the relevant inspection units of the institutions and boards specified in Article 25 to the Statutory Decree numbered 660.

(6) Examinations and inspections are carried out in compliance with the procedures and methods set out by the Authority.

(7) Administrative sanctions will apply against those that violate the legislation as a result of the examinations and inspections conducted. Audit firms and statutory auditors must take the required measures in relation to the matters detected as a result of examinations and inspections.

(8) Where the Authority requests a competent justice of peace with a letter containing the grounds in case of a failure to present or deliver the reports, books, documents, working papers, and all of the records, including the ones kept electronically, magnetically, and in similar environments, and the means that contain similar information to be requested by those appointed for examination under paragraph seven of Article 25 to the Statutory Decree 660 or in other necessary cases, a search can be made before the concerned entities if the justice of peace adjudges in favor of making a search at requested sites.

Administrative sanctions

ARTICLE 39—(1) Depending on the violations detected, the following sanctions will be applicable against those that act in violation of the statutory audit provisions and Authority's arrangements in their statutory audit activities following the examinations and inspections, denouncements and complaints, and notifications of other institutes and agencies:

(a) Warning;
(b) Suspension of approval; and
(c) Withdrawal of approval.

Warning

ARTICLE 40—(1) The warning sanction will be imposed against audit firms or statutory audits in case of

(a) Carrying out statutory audit activities in violation of Turkish Auditing Standards in such a manner that it does not involve a heavier sanction depending on the committed act's aggravation;
(b) Failing to take required measures in relation to the matters that compromise independence and to record the assessments thereon;
(c) Failing to establish the quality control system set out in Article 20;
(d) Failing to make the commitment referred in subparagraph two of Article 21;
(e) Failing to comply with the advertisement ban set out in Article 23;
(f) Violating the provisions of Article 24;
(g) Failing to ensure participation in the continuing education programs set out in Article 25 or to complete the education programs by the end of the envisaged period;
(h) Assigning responsible auditors other than those approved within the framework of Article 28;

(i) Acting in violation of the provisions of Article 29;
(j) Failing to buy the professional liability insurance policy referred in Article 33;
(k) Failing to make the required notifications to the Authority timely, completely, and correctly;
(l) Acting in violation of the provisions of Article 35;
(m) Failing in preparing, notifying to the Authority in due time, or publishing the transparency report as set out in Article 36;
(n) Failing to comply with the fee tariff set by the Authority;
(o) Failing to complete the statutory audit reports in due time or duly sending the prepared reports to the relevant recipients under the legislation;
(p) Acting in violation of the provisions of Article 37; and
(q) Detection of other similar matters that involve warning sanction according to the other relevant legislation, although not included in this By-law.

Suspension of approval

ARTICLE 41—(1) Where the following violations are detected, the approvals of audit firms and statutory auditors will be suspended for a period to be determined by the Board, provided that this period does not exceed two years on the basis of the committed act's aggravation:

(a) Continuance of an act that involves the warning sanction in spite of a warning or recurrence thereof within two years following the finalization of sanction or commitment, within this period, of different acts that involve the warning sanction for the third time;
(b) Misstatements without required professional competence and due care within the framework of Turkish Auditing Standards;
(c) During the statutory audit activities carried out, failure to comply with integrity, objectivity, independence, professional competence and due care, confidentiality, professional behavior, and other ethical principles and to carry out reliable and high quality statutory audits;
(d) Rendering services for the audited entity in violation of paragraph five of Article 22;
(e) Failure to comply with the limitations set out in Article 26;
(f) Acting in violation of the conditions sought for audit teams under Article 27 in case of the statutory audits that must only be carried out by the audit firms according to the legislation; and
(g) Detection of other matters that involve the suspension of their approvals according to the legislation.

Withdrawal of approval

ARTICLE 42—(1) Where the following violations are detected, the approvals of audit firms or statutory auditors will be suspended in perpetuity:

(a) Recurrence of an act that involves the suspension of approval within two years following the finalization of sanction or commitment, within this period, of different acts that involve the suspension of approval for the third time;

(b) Obtaining the certificate of authorization by making incorrect or misleading statements deliberately or by other illegal ways;
(c) Subsequently understating that they do not meet the authorization conditions or subsequent loss of these conditions by them;
(d) In the letters of opinion to be released under Article 30, to deliberately release an adverse opinion, where it was required to release an unmodified opinion, an unmodified opinion where it was required to release an adverse opinion, and an unmodified opinion where it was required to release a disclaimer of opinion;
(e) Loss of independence and objectivity in such a manner that it impairs the reliance in the statutory audit or invalidates the statutory audit; and
(f) Detection of other matters that involve the withdrawal of their approvals according to the legislation.

(2) Audit firms and statutory auditors cannot file an application of re-approval for withdrawn approvals.

(3) Audit firms and statutory auditors, the approvals of whom are withdrawn, will return their seals, certificates of authorization, and identification card within the period set out by the Authority. Any act in violation of this provision will be denounced to the Public Prosecutor's Office.

Other provisions on the administrative sanctions

ARTICLE 43—(1) As a result of the examinations and inspections carried out by the Authority and where it is possible to remedy, the Authority may grant a separate period for remedying the violations and deficiencies detected prior to taking a decision for sanction. Where it is detected that the violations and deficiencies are not remedied by the end of the period so granted, the corresponding administrative sanctions will apply.

(2) A minimum period of ten days will be granted to the persons concerned for a defense. Those failing to defend within the granted period will be deemed to have renounced their right of defense.

(3) The Authority is entitled to impose a sanction heavier by one degree with the reasons thereof considering the act's aggravation.

(4) The decisions taken by the Board after the required assessments are notified to the concerned persons. The Board decisions are final and unobjectionable with a right to resort to the jurisdiction. The Board decisions are recorded in the register of the concerned persons.

(5) Imposing sanctions on the statutory auditors employed by reason of the violations detected at audit firms does not relieve the audit firms from legal and criminal liabilities.

(6) Where the violation is not attributable to audit firms and auditors, the Authority will conduct the required procedures.

(7) The sanction and injunction decisions taken against audit firms and auditors under this Article will also be notified to the other institutes as deemed necessary by the Authority.

(8) Those against whom a suspension of approval decision has been taken cannot enter into new engagements during this period, while those against whom a

withdrawal of approval decision has been taken cannot enter into any new engagement following the decision of withdrawal. However, the Board may take a decision favoring the continuance of their activities limited with the completion of their ongoing audit works.

(9) The Board can cease the statutory audit activities of an audit firm or statutory auditor in the following cases:

(a) Loss of the auditor's juridical capacity as a result of disappearance, mental loss, disability, and similar reasons or termination of the audit firm's activities actually or in registration or subsequent impossibility to carry out the audit activities as a result of an injunction adjudged by the court against it; and
(b) Where there is a possibility that the continuance of the audit firm or auditor its activities will result in irreparable losses by reason of a situation that involves suspension or withdrawal of the approval following the first assessments made within the framework of the annual inspection plan or in connection with the denouncements and complaints or notification from other institutes.

PART SEVEN
Miscellaneous Provisions
Responsibility in statutory audits

ARTICLE 44—(1) Audit firms and statutory auditors are severally liable for losses that may arise in connection with the non-compliance of audit reports with Turkish Auditing Standards and incorrect, deficient, and misleading information and opinions contained in these reports.

(2) Administrative sanctions are applicable against the audit firms and statutory auditors for whom the violations of legislation have been detected. In the cases deemed necessary by the Authority, sanctions will also be applicable against such auditors that are assigned in audit teams and that bring about the violation of legislation as a result of their acts and operations.

(3) The responsibility for the violations of legislation brought about by such persons included in audit teams for assistance purposes other than the ones assigned in the capacity of auditors will reside with the audit firms and auditors, under the surveillance of whom they work, in terms of administrative sanctions. The responsibility of those participating in audits for assistance purposes arising out of their obligations of independence, objectivity, and secrecy is reserved.

Force majeure

ARTICLE 45—(1) The periods referred hereunder do not count between the occurrence and termination dates of a force majeure case.

(2) The cases that can be accepted as force majeure to preclude the fulfillment of an obligation are as follows:

(a) Disasters such as fire, earthquake, and flood;
(b) Strikes;
(c) Severe accidents, severe illnesses, and imprisonment;
(d) Disappearance within the meaning of Article 4721 and involuntary loss of books and documents; and

(e) Other similar cases that can be accepted by the Authority.

(3) A force majeure case is notified to the Authority within twenty days following the date of occurrence. Where it is impossible to make the notification, this period will start counting as from the actual termination date of the impossibility.

(4) The force majeure case must not stem from a fault attributable to the audit firm or auditor, it must be impossible for the audit firm or auditor to eliminate this impediment, and the force majeure case must be notified to the Authority with the documents evidencing its occurrence. For the force majeure cases that are widely known, no notification and evidencing document will be sought.

Notifications

ARTICLE 46—(1) Notifications to be hereunder are subject to the provisions of the Notification Law dated 11/2/1959 and numbered 7201.

Form of notifications to be served with the Authority

ARTICLE 47—(1) Notifications to be served with the Authority hereunder are made electronically in the form requested by the Authority according to the Law on Electronic Signature dated 15/1/2004 and numbered 5070, unless otherwise provided.

Remuneration for the Authority's services

ARTICLE 48—(1) The Authority is entitled to determine a fee for the services of training, exam, authorization, registering, and other services to be rendered hereunder.

Authorization

ARTICLE 49—(1) The Authority is authorized to regulate the matters in relation to the implementation of this By-law.

PART EIGHT

Provisional and Final Provisions

Transitional provisions relating to the statutory auditors

TEMPORARY ARTICLE 1—(1) Without prejudice to the other conditions prescribed for becoming a statutory auditor, the exam condition as set out in Article 16 will not be sought for

(a) Those that have been entitled to obtain the statutory audit license from public institutions under the relevant legislation prior to the publication of this By-law as a result of an exam or benefit from an exemption granted by the legislation in relation to the exam; and
(b) Those that have been entitled to obtain the license as a result of the statutory auditor exams announced by public institutions prior to the date of 2/11/2011, when the Statutory Decree numbered 660 was published and the complementary exams to be organized in connection therewith until 31/12/2012 should they file an application until 31/12/2014 and except for the exam subjects on insurance and individual retirement legislation.

(2) In order to have the possibility to carry out audits in the fields of insurance and individual pensions, those falling within the scope of paragraph one must meet the conditions sought for carrying out audits in this field under the Insurance Law

dated 3/6/2007 and numbered 5684 and relevant legislation or must pass the exam to be conducted in this field by the Authority, or must have completed the training to be organized by the Authority. The training to be organized within the scope of this paragraph may also be carried out in cooperation with public entities or universities.

(3) The scores obtained by those taking the statutory audit exams organized by the public institutions prior to 1/1/2013 for the subjects that they passed in these exams will be considered in the exam to be organized for them here under or in the exam to be conducted for those falling within the scope of paragraph four within the validity period set out in the relevant legislation and upon their requests.

(4) If they file applications together with their licenses until 31/12/2014, those entitled to become Sworn-in Certified Public Accountants and those having a 15-year professional experience and entitled to become Certified Public Accountants as of the publication date hereof will

(a) Be deemed to have met the exam condition set out in Article 14 regarding the subjects that they passed, provided that they meet the conditions sought under Article 14 to become statutory auditors, except for the condition of exam, and they successfully complete the training programs envisaged by the Authority in respect of exam subjects set out in Article 16.
(b) Those rendered the services qualified as apprenticeship under the Law 3568 and having a 15-year professional experience as of the publication date hereof will fall within the scope of this paragraph, should they become the members of profession until 31/12/2014.
(c) The members of profession that fall within the scope of this paragraph can also take the exams organized by the Authority instead of participating in the training program set out in subparagraph (a). They will not be subject to a separate training for the exam subject that they have passed.
(d) The members of profession that fall within the scope of this paragraph are not subject to the conditions set out in subparagraph (b) of paragraph one or Article 28 until 31/12/2015 and in Article 15.
(e) Training to be organized under subparagraph (a) will be organized in connection with the exam subjects specified for the members of profession in paragraph four of Article 16. This training can also be carried out in cooperation with public entities or universities.

(5) In the authorizations to be made until 31/12/2015, those having 10-year professional experience as of the publication date hereof should spend at least 1 year of applied practical training with an auditor or at an audit firm, while others should spend at least 2 years.

(6) In connection with the accounting period ending before 1/1/2014, the members of profession that fall within the scope of paragraph four can carry out audits within the framework of the provisions hereof with the Authority's approval, provided that these audits are limited to their taxpayers that entered into an engagement with them under the Law 3568 for the accounting period of 2012 and without prejudice to the limitations set out in Article 26 hereof and in the Law 6102.

Statutory Auditor Certificate, identification card, and seal will not be granted to them. This provision does not constitute an acquired right after the accounting period in question.

(7) Training activities envisaged by the Authority under this Article will be completed until 31/12/2015.

Transitional provisions relating to the existing audit firms

TEMPORARY ARTICLE 2—(1) The audit firms that obtained authorization from public institutions for the purpose of carrying out audit activities have the authority to carry out audit activities for accounting periods starting prior to 1/1/2014, provided that they file an application with the Authority together with the certificates evidencing their authorization within one month following the publication date hereof. These firms must adapt the provisions hereof until 1/1/2014, and they will be authorized and registered by the Authority as of their adaptation date; otherwise, no approval will be granted to them. The members of profession that act as auditors at these firms without the statutory audit certificate as of the publication date hereof cannot be assigned in the capacity of auditors at audits for accounting periods starting on and after 1/1/2014 without the statutory audit certificate.

Transitional provisions relating to the existing audit firms authorized for the first time

TEMPORARY ARTICLE 3—(1) The condition for establishing the quality control system referred in subparagraph (m) of paragraph one of Article 13 in the audit firm that file an application for authorization between the publication date of the Statutory Law 660 and 31/12/2013 is not sought provided that audit guides have been created as a component of the quality control system. These firms will establish the quality control system within 6 months following the authorization date. In case of a failure to establish the quality control system within this period, the required administrative sanctions will apply. The audit guides whereby the audit processes to be followed and methods to be implemented are set out in detail are established within the framework of the accounting and auditing legislation in force and international practices. Those falling within the scope of this Article are not entitled to carry out PIE audits.

Implementing the existing regulations

TEMPORARY ARTICLE 4—(1) The implementation of existing regulations will continue until the standards and regulations to be published by the Authority in line with the Statutory Law 660 enter into force for audits.

(2) The condition of seventy-five percent set out in subparagraph (k) of paragraph one of Article 13 will not be applied until the end of the year when full membership to the EU is achieved.

Renewal of the existing audit engagements

TEMPORARY ARTICLE 5—(1) The engagements that were signed prior to the publication date hereof and that cover the periods starting after 31/12/2012 will be restructured within the framework of this By-law in line with the provisions of the Law 6102 on the assignment of auditors. (2) In calculating the periods referred in subparagraph (d) of paragraph one of Article 26, the periods spent in audits carried out under the relevant legislation before 1/1/2013.

Entry into force

ARTICLE 50—(1) This By-law enters into force on its publication date.

Implementation

ARTICLE 51—(1) The provisions of this By-law will be implemented by the Chairman of the Authority.

Appendix D
International Standard on Quality Control 1

INTERNATIONAL STANDARD ON QUALITY CONTROL 1
QUALITY CONTROL FOR FIRMS THAT PERFORM AUDITS AND REVIEWS OF FINANCIAL STATEMENTS, AND OTHER ASSURANCE AND RELATED SERVICES ENGAGEMENTS
(Effective as of December 15, 2009)

CONTENTS

(continued)

I. Kesimli, *External Auditing and Quality*, Accounting, Finance, Sustainability, Governance & Fraud: Theory and Application,
https://doi.org/10.1007/978-981-13-0526-9

(continued)

CONTENTS	
Elements of a System of Quality Control	A2–A3
Leadership Responsibilities for Quality within the Firm	A4–A6
Relevant Ethical Requirements	A7–A17
Acceptance and Continuance of Client Relationships and Specific Engagements	A18–A23
Human Resources	A24–A31
Engagement Performance	A32–A63
Monitoring	A64–A72
Documentation of the System of Quality Control	A73–A75

International Standard on Quality Control (ISQC) 1, *Quality Control for Firms that Perform Audits and Reviews of Financial Statements, and Other Assurance and Related Services Engagements,* should be read in conjunction with ISA 200, *Overall Objectives of the Independent Auditor and the Conduct of an Audit in Accordance with International Standards on Auditing.*

Introduction

Scope of this ISQC

1. This International Standard on Quality Control (ISQC) deals with a firm's responsibilities for its system of quality control for audits and reviews of financial statements, and other assurance and related services engagements. This ISQC is to be read in conjunction with relevant ethical requirements.
2. Other pronouncements of the International Auditing and Assurance Standards Board (IAASB) set out additional standards and guidance on the responsibilities of firm personnel regarding quality control procedures for specific types of engagements. ISA 220, for example, deals with quality control procedures for audits of financial statements.
3. A system of quality control consists of policies designed to achieve the objective set out in paragraph 11 and the procedures necessary to implement and monitor compliance with those policies.

Authority of this ISQC

4. This ISQC applies to all firms of professional accountants in respect of audits and reviews of financial statements, and other assurance and related services engagements. The nature and extent of the policies and procedures developed by an individual firm to comply with this ISQC will depend on various factors such as the size and operating characteristics of the firm, and whether it is part of a network.
5. This ISQC contains the objective of the firm in following the ISQC, and requirements designed to enable the firm to meet that stated objective. In addition, it contains related guidance in the form of application and other explanatory material, as discussed further in paragraph 8, and introductory material that provides context relevant to a proper understanding of the ISQC, and definitions.
6. The objective provides the context in which the requirements of this ISQC are set, and is intended to assist the firm in:

   - Understanding what needs to be accomplished; and
   - Deciding whether more needs to be done to achieve the objective.

7. The requirements of this ISQC are expressed using "shall."
8. Where necessary, the application and other explanatory material provides further explanation of the requirements and guidance for carrying them out. In particular, it may:

   - Explain more precisely what a requirement means or is intended to cover; and
   - Include examples of policies and procedures that may be appropriate in the circumstances.

   While such guidance does not in itself impose a requirement, it is relevant to the proper application of the requirements. The application and other explanatory material may also provide background information on matters addressed in this ISQC. Where appropriate, additional considerations specific to public sector audit organizations or smaller firms are included within the application and other explanatory material. These additional considerations assist in the application of the requirements in this ISQC. They do not, however, limit or reduce the responsibility of the firm to apply and comply with the requirements in this ISQC.
9. This ISQC includes, under the heading "Definitions," a description of the meanings attributed to certain terms for purposes of this ISQC. These are provided to assist in the consistent application and interpretation of this ISQC, and are not intended to override definitions that may be established for other purposes, whether in law, regulation, or otherwise. The Glossary of Terms relating to International Standards issued by the IAASB in the *Handbook of International Quality Control, Auditing, Review, Other Assurance, and Related Services Pronouncements* published by IFAC includes the terms defined in this ISQC. It also includes descriptions of other terms found in this ISQC to assist in common and consistent interpretation and translation.

Effective Date

10. Systems of quality control in compliance with this ISQC are required to be established by December 15, 2009.

Objective

11. The objective of the firm is to establish and maintain a system of quality control to provide it with reasonable assurance that:

    (a) The firm and its personnel comply with professional standards and applicable legal and regulatory requirements; and
    (b) Reports issued by the firm or engagement partners are appropriate in the circumstances.

Definitions

12. In this ISQC, the following terms have the meanings attributed below:

    (a) Date of report—The date selected by the practitioner to date the report.
    (b) Engagement documentation—The record of work performed, results obtained, and conclusions the practitioner reached (terms such as "working papers" or "workpapers" are sometimes used).
    (c) Engagement partner—The partner or other person in the firm who is responsible for the engagement and its performance, and for the report that is issued on behalf of the firm, and who, where required, has the appropriate authority from a professional, legal, or regulatory body.
    (d) Engagement quality control review—A process designed to provide an objective evaluation, on or before the date of the report, of the significant judgments the engagement team made and the conclusions it reached in formulating the report. The engagement quality control review process is for audits of financial statements of listed entities, and those other engagements, if any, for which the firm has determined an engagement quality control review is required.
    (e) Engagement quality control reviewer—A partner, other person in the firm, suitably qualified external person, or a team made up of such individuals, none of whom is part of the engagement team, with sufficient and appropriate experience and authority to objectively evaluate the significant judgments the engagement team made and the conclusions it reached in formulating the report.
    (f) Engagement team—All partners and staff performing the engagement, and any individuals engaged by the firm or a network firm who perform procedures on the engagement. This excludes external experts engaged by the firm or a network firm.
    (g) Firm—A sole practitioner, partnership or corporation or other entity of professional accountants.

(h) Inspection—In relation to completed engagements, procedures designed to provide evidence of compliance by engagement teams with the firm's quality control policies and procedures.
(i) Listed entity—An entity whose shares, stock, or debt are quoted or listed on a recognized stock exchange, or are marketed under the regulations of a recognized stock exchange or other equivalent body.
(j) Monitoring—A process comprising an ongoing consideration and evaluation of the firm's system of quality control, including a periodic inspection of a selection of completed engagements, designed to provide the firm with reasonable assurance that its system of quality control is operating effectively.
(k) Network firm—A firm or entity that belongs to a network.
(l) Network—A larger structure:

    (i) That is aimed at cooperation, and
    (ii) That is clearly aimed at profit or cost-sharing or shares common ownership, control or management, common quality control policies and procedures, common business strategy, the use of a common brand name, or a significant part of professional resources.

(m) Partner—Any individual with authority to bind the firm with respect to the performance of a professional services engagement.
(n) Personnel—Partners and staff.
(o) Professional standards—IAASB Engagement Standards, as defined in the IAASB's *Preface to the International Standards on Quality Control, Auditing, Review, Other Assurance and Related Services*, and relevant ethical requirements.
(p) Reasonable assurance—In the context of this ISQC, a high, but not absolute, level of assurance.
(q) Relevant ethical requirements—Ethical requirements to which the engagement team and engagement quality control reviewer are subject, which ordinarily comprise Parts A and B of the International Ethics Standards Board for Accountants' *Code of Ethics for Professional Accountants* (IESBA Code) together with national requirements that are more restrictive.
(r) Staff—Professionals, other than partners, including any experts the firm employs.
(s) Suitably qualified external person—An individual outside the firm with the competence and capabilities to act as an engagement partner, for example, a partner of another firm, or an employee (with appropriate experience) of either a professional accountancy body whose members may perform audits and reviews of historical financial information, or other assurance or related services engagements, or of an organization that provides relevant quality control services.

Requirements

Applying, and Complying with, Relevant Requirements

13. Personnel within the firm responsible for establishing and maintaining the firm's system of quality control shall have an understanding of the entire text of this ISQC, including its application and other explanatory material, to understand its objective and to apply its requirements properly.
14. The firm shall comply with each requirement of this ISQC unless, in the circumstances of the firm, the requirement is not relevant to the services provided in respect of audits and reviews of financial statements, and other assurance and related services engagements. (Ref: Para. A1)
15. The requirements are designed to enable the firm to achieve the objective stated in this ISQC. The proper application of the requirements is therefore expected to provide a sufficient basis for the achievement of the objective. However, because circumstances vary widely and all such circumstances cannot be anticipated, the firm shall consider whether there are particular matters or circumstances that require the firm to establish policies and procedures in addition to those required by this ISQC to meet the stated objective.

Elements of a System of Quality Control

16. The firm shall establish and maintain a system of quality control that includes policies and procedures that address each of the following elements:
    (a) Leadership responsibilities for quality within the firm.
    (b) Relevant ethical requirements.
    (c) Acceptance and continuance of client relationships and specific engagements.
    (d) Human resources.
    (e) Engagement performance.
    (f) Monitoring.
17. The firm shall document its policies and procedures and communicate them to the firm's personnel. (Ref: Para. A2–A3)

Leadership Responsibilities for Quality within the Firm

18. The firm shall establish policies and procedures designed to promote an internal culture recognizing that quality is essential in performing engagements. Such policies and procedures shall require the firm's chief executive officer (or equivalent) or, if appropriate, the firm's managing board of partners (or equivalent) to assume ultimate responsibility for the firm's system of quality control. (Ref: Para. A4–A5)
19. The firm shall establish policies and procedures such that any person or persons assigned operational responsibility for the firm's system of quality control by the firm's chief executive officer or managing board of partners has sufficient and appropriate experience and ability, and the necessary authority, to assume that responsibility. (Ref: Para. A6)

Relevant Ethical Requirements

20. The firm shall establish policies and procedures designed to provide it with reasonable assurance that the firm and its personnel comply with relevant ethical requirements. (Ref: Para. A7–A10)

Independence

21. The firm shall establish policies and procedures designed to provide it with reasonable assurance that the firm, its personnel and, where applicable, others subject to independence requirements (including network firm personnel) maintain independence where required by relevant ethical requirements. Such policies and procedures shall enable the firm to: (Ref: Para. A10)

    (a) Communicate its independence requirements to its personnel and, where applicable, others subject to them; and
    (b) Identify and evaluate circumstances and relationships that create threats to independence, and to take appropriate action to eliminate those threats or reduce them to an acceptable level by applying safeguards, or, if considered appropriate, to withdraw from the engagement, where withdrawal is possible under applicable law or regulation.

22. Such policies and procedures shall require: (Ref: Para. A10)

    (a) Engagement partners to provide the firm with relevant information about client engagements, including the scope of services, to enable the firm to evaluate the overall impact, if any, on independence requirements;
    (b) Personnel to promptly notify the firm of circumstances and relationships that create a threat to independence so that appropriate action can be taken; and
    (c) The accumulation and communication of relevant information to appropriate personnel so that:

        (i) The firm and its personnel can readily determine whether they satisfy independence requirements;
        (ii) The firm can maintain and update its records relating to independence; and
        (iii) The firm can take appropriate action regarding identified threats to independence that are not at an acceptable level.

23. The firm shall establish policies and procedures designed to provide it with reasonable assurance that it is notified of breaches of independence requirements and to enable it to take appropriate actions to resolve such situations. The policies and procedures shall include requirements for: (Ref: Para. A10)

    (a) Personnel to promptly notify the firm of independence breaches of which they become aware;

(b) The firm to promptly communicate identified breaches of these policies and procedures to:

   (i) The engagement partner who, with the firm, needs to address the breach; and
   (ii) Other relevant personnel in the firm and, where appropriate, the network, and those subject to the independence requirements who need to take appropriate action; and

(c) Prompt communication to the firm, if necessary, by the engagement partner and the other individuals referred to in subparagraph 23(b)(ii) of the actions taken to resolve the matter, so that the firm can determine whether it should take further action.

24. At least annually, the firm shall obtain written confirmation of compliance with its policies and procedures on independence from all firm personnel required to be independent by relevant ethical requirements. (Ref: Para. A10–A11)
25. The firm shall establish policies and procedures: (Ref: Para. A10)

(a) Setting out criteria for determining the need for safeguards to reduce the familiarity threat to an acceptable level when using the same senior personnel on an assurance engagement over a long period of time; and
(b) Requiring, for audits of financial statements of listed entities, the rotation of the engagement partner and the individuals responsible for engagement quality control review, and, where applicable, others subject to rotation requirements, after a specified period in compliance with relevant ethical requirements. (Ref: Para. A12–A17)

Acceptance and Continuance of Client Relationships and Specific Engagements

26. The firm shall establish policies and procedures for the acceptance and continuance of client relationships and specific engagements, designed to provide the firm with reasonable assurance that it will only undertake or continue relationships and engagements where the firm:

(a) Is competent to perform the engagement and has the capabilities, including time and resources, to do so; (Ref: Para. A18, A23)
(b) Can comply with relevant ethical requirements; and
(c) Has considered the integrity of the client, and does not have information that would lead it to conclude that the client lacks integrity. (Ref: Para. A19–A20, A23)

27. Such policies and procedures shall require:

(a) The firm to obtain such information as it considers necessary in the circumstances before accepting an engagement with a new client, when deciding whether to continue an existing engagement, and when considering acceptance of a new engagement with an existing client. (Ref: Para. A21, A23)

(b) If a potential conflict of interest is identified in accepting an engagement from a new or an existing client, the firm to determine whether it is appropriate to accept the engagement; and
(c) If issues have been identified, and the firm decides to accept or continue the client relationship or a specific engagement, the firm to document how the issues were resolved.

28. The firm shall establish policies and procedures on continuing an engagement and the client relationship, addressing the circumstances where the firm obtains information that would have caused it to decline the engagement had that information been available earlier. Such policies and procedures shall include consideration of:

(a) The professional and legal responsibilities that apply to the circumstances, including whether there is a requirement for the firm to report to the person or persons who made the appointment or, in some cases, to regulatory authorities; and
(b) The possibility of withdrawing from the engagement or from both the engagement and the client relationship. (Ref: Para. A22–A23)

Human Resources

29. The firm shall establish policies and procedures designed to provide it with reasonable assurance that it has sufficient personnel with the competence, capabilities, and commitment to ethical principles necessary to:

(a) Perform engagements in accordance with professional standards and applicable legal and regulatory requirements; and
(b) Enable the firm or engagement partners to issue reports that are appropriate in the circumstances. (Ref: Para. A24–A29)

Assignment of Engagement Teams

30. The firm shall assign responsibility for each engagement to an engagement partner and shall establish policies and procedures requiring that:

(a) The identity and role of the engagement partner are communicated to key members of client management and those charged with governance.
(b) The engagement partner has the appropriate competence, capabilities, and authority to perform the role; and
(c) The responsibilities of the engagement partner are clearly defined and communicated to that partner. (Ref: Para. A30)

31. The firm shall also establish policies and procedures to assign appropriate personnel with the necessary competence, and capabilities to:

(a) Perform engagements in accordance with professional standards and applicable legal and regulatory requirements; and
(b) Enable the firm or engagement partners to issue reports that are appropriate in the circumstances. (Ref: Para. A31)

Engagement Performance

32. The firm shall establish policies and procedures designed to provide it with reasonable assurance that engagements are performed in accordance with professional standards and applicable legal and regulatory requirements, and that the firm or the engagement partner issue reports that are appropriate in the circumstances. Such policies and procedures shall include:

    (a) Matters relevant to promoting consistency in the quality of engagement performance; (Ref: Para. A32–A33)
    (b) Supervision responsibilities; and (Ref: Para. A34)
    (c) Review responsibilities. (Ref: Para. A35)

33. The firm's review responsibility policies and procedures shall be determined on the basis that work of less-experienced team members is reviewed by more experienced engagement team members.

Consultation

34. The firm shall establish policies and procedures designed to provide it with reasonable assurance that:

    (a) Appropriate consultation takes place on difficult or contentious matters.
    (b) Sufficient resources are available to enable appropriate consultation to take place.
    (c) The nature and scope of, and conclusions resulting from, such consultations are documented and are agreed by both the individual seeking consultation and the individual consulted; and
    (d) Conclusions resulting from consultations are implemented. (Ref: Para. A36–A40)

Engagement Quality Control Review

35. The firm shall establish policies and procedures requiring, for appropriate engagements, an engagement quality control review that provides an objective evaluation of the significant judgments made by the engagement team and the conclusions reached in formulating the report. Such policies and procedures shall:

    (a) Require an engagement quality control review for all audits of financial statements of listed entities;
    (b) Set out criteria against which all other audits and reviews of historical financial information and other assurance and related services engagements shall be evaluated to determine whether an engagement quality control review should be performed; and (Ref: Para. A41)
    (c) Require an engagement quality control review for all engagements, if any, meeting the criteria established in compliance with subparagraph 35(b).

36. The firm shall establish policies and procedures setting out the nature, timing, and extent of an engagement quality control review. Such policies and

procedures shall require that the engagement report not be dated until the completion of the engagement quality control review. (Ref: Para. A42–A43)

37. The firm shall establish policies and procedures to require the engagement quality control review to include:

    (a) Discussion of significant matters with the engagement partner;
    (b) Review of the financial statements or other subject matter information and the proposed report;
    (c) Review of selected engagement documentation relating to significant judgments the engagement team made and the conclusions it reached; and
    (d) Evaluation of the conclusions reached in formulating the report and consideration of whether the proposed report is appropriate. (Ref: Para. A44)

38. For audits of financial statements of listed entities, the firm shall establish policies and procedures to require the engagement quality control review to also include consideration of the following:

    (a) The engagement team's evaluation of the firm's independence in relation to the specific engagement;
    (b) Whether appropriate consultation has taken place on matters involving differences of opinion or other difficult or contentious matters, and the conclusions arising from those consultations; and
    (c) Whether documentation selected for review reflects the work performed in relation to the significant judgments and supports the conclusions reached. (Ref: Para. A45–A46)

Criteria for the Eligibility of Engagement Quality Control Reviewers

39. The firm shall establish policies and procedures to address the appointment of engagement quality control reviewers and establish their eligibility through:

    (a) The technical qualifications required to perform the role, including the necessary experience and authority; and (Ref: Para. A47)
    (b) The degree to which an engagement quality control reviewer can be consulted on the engagement without compromising the reviewer's objectivity. (Ref: Para. A48)

40. The firm shall establish policies and procedures designed to maintain the objectivity of the engagement quality control reviewer. (Ref: Para. A49–A51)
41. The firm's policies and procedures shall provide for the replacement of the engagement quality control reviewer where the reviewer's ability to perform an objective review may be impaired.

Documentation of the Engagement Quality Control Review

42. The firm shall establish policies and procedures on documentation of the engagement quality control review which require documentation that:

    (a) The procedures required by the firm's policies on engagement quality control review have been performed;
    (b) The engagement quality control review has been completed on or before the date of the report; and

(c) The reviewer is not aware of any unresolved matters that would cause the reviewer to believe that the significant judgments the engagement team made and the conclusions it reached were not appropriate.

Differences of Opinion

43. The firm shall establish policies and procedures for dealing with and resolving differences of opinion within the engagement team, with those consulted and, where applicable, between the engagement partner and the engagement quality control reviewer. (Ref: Para. A52–A53)
44. Such policies and procedures shall require that:

(a) Conclusions reached be documented and implemented; and
(b) The report not be dated until the matter is resolved.

Engagement Documentation

Completion of the assembly of final engagement files

45. The firm shall establish policies and procedures for engagement teams to complete the assembly of final engagement files on a timely basis after the engagement reports have been finalized. (Ref: Para. A54–A55)

Confidentiality, safe custody, integrity, accessibility, and retrievability of engagement documentation

46. The firm shall establish policies and procedures designed to maintain the confidentiality, safe custody, integrity, accessibility and retrievability of engagement documentation. (Ref: Para. A56–A59)

Retention of engagement documentation

47. The firm shall establish policies and procedures for the retention of engagement documentation for a period sufficient to meet the needs of the firm or as required by law or regulation. (Ref: Para. A60–A63)

Monitoring

Monitoring the firm's quality control policies and procedures

48. The firm shall establish a monitoring process designed to provide it with reasonable assurance that the policies and procedures relating to the system of quality control are relevant, adequate, and operating effectively. This process shall:

(a) Include an ongoing consideration and evaluation of the firm's system of quality control including, on a cyclical basis, inspection of at least one completed engagement for each engagement partner;
(b) Require responsibility for the monitoring process to be assigned to a partner or partners or other persons with sufficient and appropriate experience and authority in the firm to assume that responsibility; and
(c) Require that those performing the engagement or the engagement quality control review are not involved in inspecting the engagement. (Ref: Para. A64–A68)

Evaluating, Communicating and Remedying Identified Deficiencies

49. The firm shall evaluate the effect of deficiencies noted as a result of the monitoring process and determine whether they are either:

(a) Instances that do not necessarily indicate that the firm's system of quality control is insufficient to provide it with reasonable assurance that it complies with professional standards and applicable legal and regulatory requirements, and that the reports issued by the firm or engagement partners are appropriate in the circumstances; or
(b) Systemic, repetitive, or other significant deficiencies that require prompt corrective action.

50. The firm shall communicate to relevant engagement partners and other appropriate personnel deficiencies noted as a result of the monitoring process and recommendations for appropriate remedial action. (Ref: Para. A69)
51. Recommendations for appropriate remedial actions for deficiencies noted shall include one or more of the following:

(a) Taking appropriate remedial action in relation to an individual engagement or member of personnel;
(b) The communication of the findings to those responsible for training and professional development;
(c) Changes to the quality control policies and procedures; and
(d) Disciplinary action against those who fail to comply with the policies and procedures of the firm, especially those who do so repeatedly.

52. The firm shall establish policies and procedures to address cases where the results of the monitoring procedures indicate that a report may be inappropriate or that procedures were omitted during the performance of the engagement. Such policies and procedures shall require the firm to determine what further action is appropriate to comply with relevant professional standards and applicable legal and regulatory requirements and to consider whether to obtain legal advice.
53. The firm shall communicate at least annually the results of the monitoring of its system of quality control to engagement partners and other appropriate individuals within the firm, including the firm's chief executive officer or, if appropriate, its managing board of partners. This communication shall be sufficient to enable the firm and these individuals to take prompt and appropriate action where necessary in accordance with their defined roles and responsibilities. Information communicated shall include the following:

(a) A description of the monitoring procedures performed.
(b) The conclusions drawn from the monitoring procedures.
(c) Where relevant, a description of systemic, repetitive, or other significant deficiencies and of the actions taken to resolve or amend those deficiencies.

54. Some firms operate as part of a network and, for consistency, may implement some of their monitoring procedures on a network basis. Where firms within a network operate under common monitoring policies and procedures designed to comply with this ISQC, and these firms place reliance on such a monitoring system, the firm's policies and procedures shall require that:

    (a) At least annually, the network communicate the overall scope, extent, and results of the monitoring process to appropriate individuals within the network firms; and
    (b) The network communicate promptly any identified deficiencies in the system of quality control to appropriate individuals within the relevant network firm or firms so that the necessary action can be taken, in order that engagement partners in the network firms can rely on the results of the monitoring process implemented within the network, unless the firms or the network advise otherwise.

Complaints and Allegations

55. The firm shall establish policies and procedures designed to provide it with reasonable assurance that it deals appropriately with:

    (a) Complaints and allegations that the work performed by the firm fails to comply with professional standards and applicable legal and regulatory requirements; and
    (b) Allegations of non-compliance with the firm's system of quality control. As part of this process, the firm shall establish clearly defined channels for firm personnel to raise any concerns in a manner that enables them to come forward without fear of reprisals. (Ref: Para. A70)

56. If during the investigations into complaints and allegations, deficiencies in the design or operation of the firm's quality control policies and procedures or non-compliance with the firm's system of quality control by an individual or individuals are identified, the firm shall take appropriate actions as set out in paragraph 51. (Ref: Para. A71–A72)

Documentation of the System of Quality Control

57. The firm shall establish policies and procedures requiring appropriate documentation to provide evidence of the operation of each element of its system of quality control. (Ref: Para. A73–A75)
58. The firm shall establish policies and procedures that require retention of documentation for a period of time sufficient to permit those performing monitoring procedures to evaluate the firm's compliance with its system of quality control, or for a longer period if required by law or regulation.

59. The firm shall establish policies and procedures requiring documentation of complaints and allegations and the responses to them.

Application and Other Explanatory Material

Applying, and Complying with, Relevant Requirements

Considerations Specific to Smaller Firms (Ref: Para. 14)

A1. This ISQC does not call for compliance with requirements that are not relevant, for example, in the circumstances of a sole practitioner with no staff. Requirements in this ISQC such as those for policies and procedures for the assignment of appropriate personnel to the engagement team (see paragraph 31), for review responsibilities (see paragraph 33), and for the annual communication of the results of monitoring to engagement partners within the firm (see paragraph 53), are not relevant in the absence of staff.

Elements of a System of Quality Control (Ref: Para. 17)

A2. In general, communication of quality control policies and procedures to firm personnel includes a description of the quality control policies and procedures and the objectives they are designed to achieve, and the message that each individual has a personal responsibility for quality and is expected to comply with these policies and procedures. Encouraging firm personnel to communicate their views or concerns on quality control matters recognizes the importance of obtaining feedback on the firm's system of quality control.

Considerations Specific to Smaller Firms

A3. Documentation and communication of policies and procedures for smaller firms may be less formal and extensive than for larger firms.

Leadership Responsibilities for Quality within the Firm

Promoting an Internal Culture of Quality (Ref: Para. 18)

A4. The firm's leadership and the examples it sets significantly influence the internal culture of the firm. The promotion of a quality-oriented internal culture depends on clear, consistent, and frequent actions and messages from all levels of the firm's management that emphasize the firm's quality control policies and procedures, and the requirement to:

(a) perform work that complies with professional standards and applicable legal and regulatory requirements; and
(b) issue reports that are appropriate in the circumstances. Such actions and messages encourage a culture that recognizes and rewards high quality work. These actions and messages may be communicated by, but are not limited to, training seminars, meetings, formal or informal dialogue, mission statements, newsletters, or briefing memoranda. They may be incorporated in the firm's internal documentation and training materials, and in partner and staff appraisal procedures such that they will support and reinforce the firm's view on the importance of quality and how, practically, it is to be achieved.

A5. Of particular importance in promoting an internal culture based on quality is the need for the firm's leadership to recognize that the firm's business strategy is subject to the overriding requirement for the firm to achieve quality in all the engagements that the firm performs. Promoting such an internal culture includes:

(a) Establishment of policies and procedures that address performance evaluation, compensation, and promotion (including incentive systems) with regard to its personnel, in order to demonstrate the firm's overriding commitment to quality;
(b) Assignment of management responsibilities so that commercial considerations do not override the quality of work performed; and
(c) Provision of sufficient resources for the development, documentation, and support of its quality control policies and procedures.

Assigning Operational Responsibility for the Firm's System of Quality Control (Ref: Para. 19)

A6. Sufficient and appropriate experience and ability enables the person or persons responsible for the firm's system of quality control to identify and understand quality control issues and to develop appropriate policies and procedures. Necessary authority enables the person or persons to implement those policies and procedures.

Relevant Ethical Requirements

Compliance with Relevant Ethical Requirements (Ref: Para. 20)

A7. The IESBA Code establishes the fundamental principles of professional ethics, which include:

(a) Integrity;
(b) Objectivity;
(c) Professional competence and due care;
(d) Confidentiality; and
(e) Professional behavior.

A8. Part B of the IESBA Code illustrates how the conceptual framework is to be applied in specific situations. It provides examples of safeguards that may be appropriate to address threats to compliance with the fundamental principles and also provides examples of situations where safeguards are not available to address the threats.

A9. The fundamental principles are reinforced in particular by:

- The leadership of the firm;
- Education and training;
- Monitoring; and
- A process for dealing with non-compliance.

Definition of "Firm," "Network," and "Network Firm" (Ref: Para. 20–25)

A10. The definitions of "firm," network," or "network firm" in relevant ethical requirements may differ from those set out in this ISQC. For example, the IESBA Code defines the "firm" as:

(a) A sole practitioner, partnership or corporation of professional accountants;
(b) An entity that controls such parties through ownership, management, or other means; and
(c) An entity controlled by such parties through ownership, management, or other means.

The IESBA Code also provides guidance in relation to the terms "network" and "network firm."

In complying with the requirements in paragraphs 20–25, the definitions used in the relevant ethical requirements apply in so far as is necessary to interpret those ethical requirements.

Written Confirmation (Ref: Para. 24)

A11. Written confirmation may be in paper or electronic form. By obtaining confirmation and taking appropriate action on information indicating noncompliance, the firm demonstrates the importance that it attaches to independence and makes the issue current for, and visible to, its personnel.

Familiarity Threat (Ref: Para. 25)

A12. The IESBA Code discusses the familiarity threat that may be created by using the same senior personnel on an assurance engagement over a long period of time and the safeguards that might be appropriate to address such threats.

A13. Determining appropriate criteria to address familiarity threat may include matters such as:

- The nature of the engagement, including the extent to which it involves a matter of public interest; and
- The length of service of the senior personnel on the engagement.

Examples of safeguards include rotating the senior personnel or requiring an engagement quality control review.

A14. The IESBA Code recognizes that the familiarity threat is particularly relevant in the context of financial statement audits of listed entities. For these audits, the IESBA Code requires the rotation of the key audit partner after a predefined period, normally no more than seven years, and provides related standards and guidance. National requirements may establish shorter rotation periods.

Considerations specific to public sector audit organizations

A15. Statutory measures may provide safeguards for the independence of public sector auditors. However, threats to independence may still exist regardless of any statutory measures designed to protect it. Therefore, in establishing the policies and procedures required by paragraphs 20–25, the public sector auditor may have regard to the public sector mandate and address any threats to independence in that context.

A16. Listed entities as referred to in paragraphs 25 and A14 are not common in the public sector. However, there may be other public sector entities that are significant due to size, complexity, or public interest aspects, and which consequently have a wide range of stakeholders. Therefore, there may be instances when a firm determines, based on its quality control policies and procedures, that a public sector entity is significant for the purposes of expanded quality control procedures.

A17. In the public sector, legislation may establish the appointments and terms of office of the auditor with engagement partner responsibility. As a result, it may not be possible to comply strictly with the engagement partner rotation requirements envisaged for listed entities. Nonetheless, for public sector entities considered significant, as noted in paragraph A16, it may be in the public interest for public sector audit organizations to establish policies and procedures to promote compliance with the spirit of rotation of engagement partner responsibility.

Acceptance and Continuance of Client Relationships and Specific Engagements

Competence, Capabilities, and Resources (Ref: Para. 26(a))

A18. Consideration of whether the firm has the competence, capabilities, and resources to undertake a new engagement from a new or an existing client involves reviewing the specific requirements of the engagement and the existing partner and staff profiles at all relevant levels, and including whether:

- Firm personnel have knowledge of relevant industries or subject matters.
- Firm personnel have experience with relevant regulatory or reporting requirements, or the ability to gain the necessary skills and knowledge effectively;
- The firm has sufficient personnel with the necessary competence and capabilities;
- Experts are available, if needed;
- Individuals meeting the criteria and eligibility requirements to perform engagement quality control review are available, where applicable; and
- The firm is able to complete the engagement within the reporting deadline.

Integrity of Client (Ref: Para. 26(c))

A19. With regard to the integrity of a client, matters to consider include, for example:

- The identity and business reputation of the client's principal owners, key management, and those charged with its governance.
- The nature of the client's operations, including its business practices.
- Information concerning the attitude of the client's principal owners, key management and those charged with its governance toward such matters as aggressive interpretation of accounting standards and the internal control environment.
- Whether the client is aggressively concerned with maintaining the firm's fees as low as possible.
- Indications of an inappropriate limitation in the scope of work.
- Indications that the client might be involved in money laundering or other criminal activities.
- The reasons for the proposed appointment of the firm and non-reappointment of the previous firm.
- The identity and business reputation of related parties.

The extent of knowledge a firm will have regarding the integrity of a client will generally grow within the context of an ongoing relationship with that client.

A20. Sources of information on such matters obtained by the firm may include the following:

- Communications with existing or previous providers of professional accountancy services to the client in accordance with relevant ethical requirements, and discussions with other third parties.
- Inquiry of other firm personnel or third parties such as bankers, legal counsel and industry peers.
- Background searches of relevant databases.

Continuance of Client Relationship (Ref: Para. 27(a))

A21. Deciding whether to continue a client relationship includes consideration of significant matters that have arisen during the current or previous engagements, and their implications for continuing the relationship. For example, a client may have started to expand its business operations into an area where the firm does not possess the necessary expertise.

Withdrawal (Ref: Para. 28)

A22. Policies and procedures on withdrawal from an engagement or from both the engagement and the client relationship address issues that include the following:

- Discussing with the appropriate level of the client's management and those charged with its governance the appropriate action that the firm might take based on the relevant facts and circumstances.
- If the firm determines that it is appropriate to withdraw, discussing with the appropriate level of the client's management and those charged with its governance withdrawal from the engagement or from both the engagement and the client relationship, and the reasons for the withdrawal.
- Considering whether there is a professional, legal, or regulatory requirement for the firm to remain in place, or for the firm to report the withdrawal from the engagement, or from both the engagement and the client relationship, together with the reasons for the withdrawal, to regulatory authorities.
- Documenting significant matters, consultations, conclusions, and the basis for the conclusions.

Considerations Specific to Public Sector Audit Organizations (Ref: Para. 26–28)

A23. In the public sector, auditors may be appointed in accordance with statutory procedures. Accordingly, certain of the requirements and considerations regarding the acceptance and continuance of client relationships and specific engagements as set out paragraphs 26–28 and A18–A22 may not be relevant. Nonetheless, establishing policies and procedures as described may provide valuable information to public sector auditors in performing risk assessments and in carrying out reporting responsibilities.

Human Resources (Ref: Para. 29)

A24. Personnel issues relevant to the firm's policies and procedures related to human resources include, for example:

- Recruitment.
- Performance evaluation.
- Capabilities, including time to perform assignments.
- Competence.
- Career development.
- Promotion.
- Compensation.
- The estimation of personnel needs.

Effective recruitment processes and procedures help the firm select individuals of integrity who have the capacity to develop the competence and capabilities necessary to perform the firm's work and possess the appropriate characteristics to enable them to perform competently.

A25. Competence can be developed through a variety of methods, including the following:

- Professional education.
- Continuing professional development, including training.
- Work experience.
- Coaching by more experienced staff, for example, other members of the engagement team.
- Independence education for personnel who are required to be independent.

A26. The continuing competence of the firm's personnel depends to a significant extent on an appropriate level of continuing professional development so that personnel maintain their knowledge and capabilities. Effective policies and procedures emphasize the need for continuing training for all levels of firm personnel, and provide the necessary training resources and assistance to enable personnel to develop and maintain the required competence and capabilities.

A27. The firm may use a suitably qualified external person, for example, when internal technical and training resources are unavailable.

A28. Performance evaluation, compensation, and promotion procedures give due recognition and reward to the development and maintenance of competence and commitment to ethical principles. Steps a firm may take in developing and maintaining competence and commitment to ethical principles include:

- Making personnel aware of the firm's expectations regarding performance and ethical principles;
- Providing personnel with evaluation of, and counseling on, performance, progress and career development; and

- Helping personnel understand that advancement to positions of greater responsibility depends, among other things, upon performance quality and adherence to ethical principles and that failure to comply with the firm's policies and procedures may result in disciplinary action.

Considerations Specific to Smaller Firms

A29. The size and circumstances of the firm will influence the structure of the firm's performance evaluation process. Smaller firms, in particular, may employ less formal methods of evaluating the performance of their personnel.

Assignment of Engagement Teams

Engagement Partners (Ref: Para. 30)

A30. Policies and procedures may include systems to monitor the workload and availability of engagement partners so as to enable these individuals to have sufficient time to adequately discharge their responsibilities.

Engagement Teams (Ref: Para. 31)

A31. The firm's assignment of engagement teams and the determination of the level of supervision required include, for example, consideration of the engagement team's:

- Understanding of, and practical experience with, engagements of a similar nature and complexity through appropriate training and participation;
- Understanding of professional standards and applicable legal and regulatory requirements;
- Technical knowledge and expertise, including knowledge of relevant information technology;
- Knowledge of relevant industries in which the clients operate;
- Ability to apply professional judgment; and
- Understanding of the firm's quality control policies and procedures.

Engagement Performance

Consistency in the Quality of Engagement Performance (Ref: Para. 32(a))

A32. The firm promotes consistency in the quality of engagement performance through its policies and procedures. This is often accomplished through written or electronic manuals, software tools or other forms of standardized documentation, and industry or subject matter-specific guidance materials.

Matters addressed may include:

- How engagement teams are briefed on the engagement to obtain an understanding of the objectives of their work.
- Processes for complying with applicable engagement standards.
- Processes of engagement supervision, staff training and coaching.
- Methods of reviewing the work performed, the significant judgments made, and the form of report being issued.

- Appropriate documentation of the work performed and of the timing and extent of the review.
- Processes to keep all policies and procedures current.

A33. Appropriate teamwork and training assist less-experienced members of the engagement team to clearly understand the objectives of the assigned work.

Supervision (Ref: Para. 32(b))

A34. Engagement supervision includes the following:

- Tracking the progress of the engagement;
- Considering the competence and capabilities of individual members of the engagement team, whether they have sufficient time to carry out their work, whether they understand their instructions, and whether the work is being carried out in accordance with the planned approach to the engagement;
- Addressing significant matters arising during the engagement, considering their significance and modifying the planned approach appropriately; and
- Identifying matters for consultation or consideration by more experienced engagement team members during the engagement.

Review (Ref: Para. 32(c))

A35. A review consists of consideration of whether:

- The work has been performed in accordance with professional standards and applicable legal and regulatory requirements;
- Significant matters have been raised for further consideration;
- Appropriate consultations have taken place, and the resulting conclusions have been documented and implemented;
- There is a need to revise the nature, timing, and extent of work performed;
- The work performed supports the conclusions reached and is appropriately documented;
- The evidence obtained is sufficient and appropriate to support the report; and
- The objectives of the engagement procedures have been achieved.

Consultation (Ref: Para. 34)

A36. Consultation includes discussion at the appropriate professional level, with individuals within or outside the firm who have specialized expertise.

A37. Consultation uses appropriate research resources as well as the collective experience and technical expertise of the firm. Consultation helps to promote quality and improves the application of professional judgment.

Appropriate recognition of consultation in the firm's policies and procedures helps to promote a culture in which consultation is recognized as a strength and encourages personnel to consult on difficult or contentious matters.

A38. Effective consultation on significant technical, ethical, and other matters within the firm or, where applicable, outside the firm can be achieved when those consulted:

- Are given all the relevant facts that will enable them to provide informed advice; and
- Have appropriate knowledge, seniority, and experience, and when conclusions resulting from consultations are appropriately documented and implemented.

A39. Documentation of consultations with other professionals that involve difficult or contentious matters that is sufficiently complete and detailed contributes to an understanding of:

- The issue on which consultation was sought; and
- The results of the consultation, including any decisions taken, the basis for those decisions and how they were implemented.

Considerations Specific to Smaller Firms

A40. A firm needing to consult externally, for example, a firm without appropriate internal resources, may take advantage of advisory services provided by:

- Other firms;
- Professional and regulatory bodies; or
- Commercial organizations that provide relevant quality control services.

Before contracting for such services, consideration of the competence and capabilities of the external provider helps the firm to determine whether the external provider is suitably qualified for that purpose.

Engagement Quality Control Review

Criteria for an Engagement Quality Control Review (Ref: Para. 35(b))

A41. Criteria for determining which engagements, other than audits of financial statements of listed entities, are to be subject to an engagement quality control review may include, for example:

- The nature of the engagement, including the extent to which it involves a matter of public interest.
- The identification of unusual circumstances or risks in an engagement or class of engagements.
- Whether laws or regulations require an engagement quality control review.

Nature, Timing, and Extent of the Engagement Quality Control Review (Ref: Para. 36–37)

A42. The engagement report is not dated until the completion of the engagement quality control review. However, documentation of the engagement quality control review may be completed after the date of the report.

A43. Conducting the engagement quality control review in a timely manner at appropriate stages during the engagement allows significant matters to be promptly resolved to the engagement quality control reviewer's satisfaction on or before the date of the report.

A44. The extent of the engagement quality control review may depend, among other things, on the complexity of the engagement, whether the entity is a listed entity, and the risk that the report might not be appropriate in the circumstances. The performance of an engagement quality control review does not reduce the responsibilities of the engagement partner.

Engagement Quality Control Review of a Listed Entity (Ref: Para. 38)

A45. Other matters relevant to evaluating the significant judgments made by the engagement team that may be considered in an engagement quality control review of an audit of financial statements of a listed entity include:

- Significant risks identified during the engagement and the responses to those risks.
- Judgments made, particularly with respect to materiality and significant risks.
- The significance and disposition of corrected and uncorrected misstatements identified during the engagement.
- The matters to be communicated to management and those charged with governance and, where applicable, other parties such as regulatory bodies.

These other matters, depending on the circumstances, may also be applicable for engagement quality control reviews for audits of the financial statements of other entities as well as reviews of financial statements and other assurance and related services engagements.

Considerations specific to public sector audit organizations

A46. Although not referred to as listed entities, as described in paragraph A16, certain public sector entities may be of sufficient significance to warrant performance of an engagement quality control review.

Criteria for the Eligibility of Engagement Quality Control Reviewers

Sufficient and Appropriate Technical Expertise, Experience and Authority (Ref: Para. 39(a))

A47. What constitutes sufficient and appropriate technical expertise, experience and authority depend on the circumstances of the engagement. For example, the engagement quality control reviewer for an audit of the financial statements of a listed entity is likely to be an individual with sufficient and appropriate experience and authority to act as an audit engagement partner on audits of financial statements of listed entities.

Consultation with the Engagement Quality Control Reviewer (Ref: Para. 39(b))

A48. The engagement partner may consult the engagement quality control reviewer during the engagement, for example, to establish that a judgment made by the engagement partner will be acceptable to the engagement quality control reviewer. Such consultation avoids identification of differences of opinion at a late stage of the engagement and need not compromise the engagement quality control reviewer's eligibility to perform the role. Where the nature and extent of the consultations become significant, the reviewer's objectivity may be compromised unless care is taken by both the engagement team and the reviewer to maintain the reviewer's objectivity. Where this is not possible, another individual within the firm or a suitably qualified external person may be appointed to take on the role of either the engagement quality control reviewer or the person to be consulted on the engagement.

Objectivity of the Engagement Quality Control Reviewer (Ref: Para. 40)

A49. The firm is required to establish policies and procedures designed to maintain objectivity of the engagement quality control reviewer. Accordingly, such policies and procedures provide that the engagement quality control reviewer:

- Where practicable, is not selected by the engagement partner;
- Does not otherwise participate in the engagement during the period of review;
- Does not make decisions for the engagement team; and
- Is not subject to other considerations that would threaten the reviewer's objectivity.

Considerations specific to smaller firms

A50. It may not be practicable, in the case of firms with few partners, for the engagement partner not to be involved in selecting the engagement quality control reviewer. Suitably qualified external persons may be contracted where sole practitioners or small firms identify engagements requiring engagement quality control reviews. Alternatively, some sole practitioners or small firms may wish to use other firms to facilitate engagement quality control reviews.

Where the firm contracts suitably qualified external persons, the requirements in paragraphs 39–41 and guidance in paragraphs A47–A48 apply.

Considerations specific to public sector audit organizations

A51. In the public sector, a statutorily appointed auditor (for example, an Auditor General, or other suitably qualified person appointed on behalf of the Auditor General) may act in a role equivalent to that of engagement partner with overall responsibility for public sector audits. In such circumstances, where applicable, the selection of the engagement quality control reviewer includes consideration of the need for independence from the audited entity and the ability of the engagement quality control reviewer to provide an objective evaluation.

Differences of Opinion (Ref: Para. 43)

A52. Effective procedures encourage identification of differences of opinion at an early stage, provide clear guidelines as to the successive steps to be taken thereafter, and require documentation regarding the resolution of the differences and the implementation of the conclusions reached.

A53. Procedures to resolve such differences may include consulting with another practitioner or firm, or a professional or regulatory body.

Engagement Documentation

Completion of the Assembly of Final Engagement Files (Ref: Para. 45)

A54. Law or regulation may prescribe the time limits by which the assembly of final engagement files for specific types of engagement is to be completed. Where no such time limits are prescribed in law or regulation, paragraph 45 requires the firm to establish time limits that reflect the need to complete the assembly of final engagement files on a timely basis. In the case of an audit, for example, such a time limit would ordinarily not be more than 60 days after the date of the auditor's report.

A55. Where two or more different reports are issued in respect of the same subject matter information of an entity, the firm's policies and procedures relating to time limits for the assembly of final engagement files address each report as if it were for a separate engagement. This may, for example, be the case when the firm issues an auditor's report on a component's financial information for group consolidation purposes and, at a subsequent date, an auditor's report on the same financial information for statutory purposes.

Confidentiality, Safe Custody, Integrity, Accessibility and Retrievability of Engagement Documentation (Ref: Para. 46)

A56. Relevant ethical requirements establish an obligation for the firm's personnel to observe at all times the confidentiality of information contained in engagement documentation, unless specific client authority has been given to disclose information, or there is a legal or professional duty to do so. Specific laws or regulations may impose additional obligations on the firm's personnel to maintain client confidentiality, particularly where data of a personal nature are concerned.

A57. Whether engagement documentation is in paper, electronic, or other media, the integrity, accessibility, or retrievability of the underlying data may be compromised if the documentation could be altered, added to or deleted without the firm's knowledge, or if it could be permanently lost or damaged. Accordingly, controls that the firm designs and implements to avoid unauthorized alteration or loss of engagement documentation may include those that:

- Enable the determination of when and by whom engagement documentation was created, changed, or reviewed;
- Protect the integrity of the information at all stages of the engagement, especially when the information is shared within the engagement team or transmitted to other parties via the Internet;
- Prevent unauthorized changes to the engagement documentation; and
- Allow access to the engagement documentation by the engagement team and other authorized parties as necessary to properly discharge their responsibilities.

A58. Controls that the firm designs and implements to maintain the confidentiality, safe custody, integrity, accessibility, and retrievability of engagement documentation may include the following:

- The use of a password among engagement team members to restrict access to electronic engagement documentation to authorized users.
- Appropriate backup routines for electronic engagement documentation at appropriate stages during the engagement.
- Procedures for properly distributing engagement documentation to the team members at the start of the engagement, processing it during engagement, and collating it at the end of engagement.
- Procedures for restricting access to, and enabling proper distribution and confidential storage of, hardcopy engagement documentation.

A59. For practical reasons, original paper documentation may be electronically scanned for inclusion in engagement files. In such cases, the firm's procedures designed to maintain the integrity, accessibility, and retrievability of the documentation may include requiring the engagement teams to:

- Generate scanned copies that reflect the entire content of the original paper documentation, including manual signatures, cross-references, and annotations;
- Integrate the scanned copies into the engagement files, including indexing and signing off on the scanned copies as necessary; and
- Enable the scanned copies to be retrieved and printed as necessary. There may be legal, regulatory, or other reasons for a firm to retain original paper documentation that has been scanned.

Retention of Engagement Documentation (Ref: Para. 47)

A60. The needs of the firm for retention of engagement documentation, and the period of such retention, will vary with the nature of the engagement and the firm's circumstances, for example, whether the engagement documentation is needed to provide a record of matters of continuing significance to future engagements. The retention period may also depend on other factors, such as whether local law or regulation prescribes specific retention periods for certain types of engagements, or whether there are generally accepted retention periods in the jurisdiction in the absence of specific legal or regulatory requirements.

A61. In the specific case of audit engagements, the retention period would ordinarily be no shorter than five years from the date of the auditor's report, or, if later, the date of the group auditor's report.

A62. Procedures that the firm adopts for retention of engagement documentation include those that enable the requirements of paragraph 47 to be met during the retention period, for example, to:

- Enable the retrieval of, and access to, the engagement documentation during the retention period, particularly in the case of electronic documentation since the underlying technology may be upgraded or changed over time;
- Provide, where necessary, a record of changes made to engagement documentation after the engagement files have been completed; and

- Enable authorized external parties to access and review specific engagement documentation for quality control or other purposes.

Ownership of engagement documentation

A63. Unless otherwise specified by law or regulation, engagement documentation is the property of the firm. The firm may, at its discretion, make portions of, or extracts from, engagement documentation available to clients, provided such disclosure does not undermine the validity of the work performed, or, in the case of assurance engagements, the independence of the firm or its personnel.

Monitoring

Monitoring the Firm's Quality Control Policies and Procedures (Ref: Para. 48)

A64. The purpose of monitoring compliance with quality control policies and procedures is to provide an evaluation of:

- Adherence to professional standards and applicable legal and regulatory requirements;
- Whether the system of quality control has been appropriately designed and effectively implemented; and
- Whether the firm's quality control policies and procedures have been appropriately applied, so that reports that are issued by the firm or engagement partners are appropriate in the circumstances.

A65. Ongoing consideration and evaluation of the system of quality control include matters such as the following:

- Analysis of:
  - New developments in professional standards and applicable legal and regulatory requirements, and how they are reflected in the firm's policies and procedures where appropriate;
  - Written confirmation of compliance with policies and procedures on independence;
  - Continuing professional development, including training; and
  - Decisions related to acceptance and continuance of client relationships and specific engagements.
- Determination of corrective actions to be taken and improvements to be made in the system, including the provision of feedback into the firm's policies and procedures relating to education and training.
- Communication to appropriate firm personnel of weaknesses identified in the system, in the level of understanding of the system, or compliance with it.
- Follow-up by appropriate firm personnel so that necessary modifications are promptly made to the quality control policies and procedures.

A66. Inspection cycle policies and procedures may, for example, specify a cycle that spans three years. The manner in which the inspection cycle is organized, including the timing of selection of individual engagements, depends on many factors, such as the following:

- The size of the firm.
- The number and geographic location of offices.
- The results of previous monitoring procedures.
- The degree of authority both personnel and offices have (for example, whether individual offices are authorized to conduct their own inspections or whether only the head office may conduct them).
- The nature and complexity of the firm's practice and organization.
- The risks associated with the firm's clients and specific engagements.

A67. The inspection process includes the selection of individual engagements, some of which may be selected without prior notification to the engagement team. In determining the scope of the inspections, the firm may take into account the scope or conclusions of an independent external inspection program. However, an independent external inspection program does not act as a substitute for the firm's own internal monitoring program.

Considerations Specific to Smaller Firms

A68. In the case of small firms, monitoring procedures may need to be performed by individuals who are responsible for design and implementation of the firm's quality control policies and procedures, or who may be involved in performing the engagement quality control review. A firm with a limited number of persons may choose to use a suitably qualified external person or another firm to carry out engagement inspections and other monitoring procedures. Alternatively, the firm may establish arrangements to share resources with other appropriate organizations to facilitate monitoring activities.

Communicating Deficiencies (Ref: Para. 50)

A69. The reporting of identified deficiencies to individuals other than the relevant engagement partners need not include an identification of the specific engagements concerned, although there may be cases where such identification may be necessary for the proper discharge of the responsibilities of the individuals other than the engagement partners.

Complaints and Allegations

Source of Complaints and Allegations (Ref: Para. 55)

A70. Complaints and allegations (which do not include those that are clearly frivolous) may originate from within or outside the firm. They may be made by firm personnel, clients, or other third parties. They may be received by engagement team members or other firm personnel.

Investigation Policies and Procedures (Ref: Para. 56)

A71. Policies and procedures established for the investigation of complaints and allegations may include, for example, that the partner supervising the investigation:

- Has sufficient and appropriate experience;
- Has authority within the firm; and
- Is otherwise not involved in the engagement.

The partner supervising the investigation may involve legal counsel as necessary.

Considerations specific to smaller firms

A72. It may not be practicable, in the case of firms with few partners, for the partner supervising the investigation not to be involved in the engagement.

These small firms and sole practitioners may use the services of a suitably qualified external person or another firm to carry out the investigation into complaints and allegations.

Documentation of the System of Quality Control (Ref: Para. 57)

A73. The form and content of documentation evidencing the operation of each of the elements of the system of quality control is a matter of judgment and depends on a number of factors, including the following:

- The size of the firm and the number of offices.
- The nature and complexity of the firm's practice and organization.

For example, large firms may use electronic databases to document matters such as independence confirmations, performance evaluations, and the results of monitoring inspections.

A74. Appropriate documentation relating to monitoring includes, for example:

- Monitoring procedures, including the procedure for selecting completed engagements to be inspected.
- A record of the evaluation of:
  - Adherence to professional standards and applicable legal and regulatory requirements;
  - Whether the system of quality control has been appropriately designed and effectively implemented; and
  - Whether the firm's quality control policies and procedures have been appropriately applied, so that reports that are issued by the firm or engagement partners are appropriate in the circumstances.
- Identification of the deficiencies noted, an evaluation of their effect, and the basis for determining whether and what further action is necessary.

Considerations Specific to Smaller Firms

A75. Smaller firms may use more informal methods in the documentation of their systems of quality control such as manual notes, checklists, and forms.

http://www.ifac.org/sites/default/files/downloads/a007-2010-iaasb-handbook-isqc-1.pdf, 25.02.2012.

Curriculum Vitae

She was born in Üsküdar Istanbul, attended elementary school at Babaeski Cumhuriyet Primary School, secondary school and high school at Istanbul Erkek Lisesi. Following the English Preparation School of Boğaziçi University, with honors degree she first graduated from Vocational School of Management and got her B.A. from Business Administration.

Within the "10 Young Executive Candidates" program of Türkiye Tütüncüler Bankası (Turkish Tobacco Producers' Bank) and Irving Trust Bank, which were partners at the time, she got training at all departments of the Bank in Izmir and assigned as assistant manager and became the assistant to the CEO Dr. Antonio Puja. Following the break of the partnership of two banks, she worked as assistant personnel manager until leaving the bank, which moved the headquarters to Istanbul, and started working at Raks Holding as Assistant Manager of Budgeting and Planning Department. Following the radical management changes at the company, she decided to work as freelancer and assisted budgeting processes of BMC OMPAŞ A.Ş., Rapak Ambalaj, etc., until becoming the partner and manager of Bilda Bilgisayar Sistemleri Ltd. Şti., a software company. Ownership of a trading company and trade life followed.

After two decades of private sector experience, she started lecturing at vocational schools. In the meantime, she got her MBA from Business Administration at Trakya University and enrolled with PhD program at the same university, which is completed successfully in 2015. She is affiliated to Kırklareli University, Lüleburgaz Vocational School as Head of Accounting and Taxation Program and lectures at Lüleburgaz Vocational School. She speaks German and English as foreign languages.

I. Kesimli, *External Auditing and Quality*, Accounting, Finance, Sustainability, Governance & Fraud: Theory and Application,
https://doi.org/10.1007/978-981-13-0526-9

References

Abma R (10.12.2009). Eumedion Corporate Governance Forum. IOSCO Consultation Report Comment Letter, p. 1, 3, 5. http://www.iosco.org/library/pubdocs/pdf/IOSCOPD339.pdf. Accessed 05 May 2012

ACFE. Association of Certified Fraud Examiners. Fraud Resources (2016) Report to the Nations on Occupational Fraud and Abuse. https://s3-us-west-2.amazonaws.com/acfepublic/2016-report-to-the-nations.pdf. Accessed 03 Apr 2016

ACFE. Association of Certified Fraud Examiners. Fraud Resources (1996) Report to the Nations on Occupational Fraud and Abuse

ACFE. Association of Certified Fraud Examiners. Fraud Resources (2002) Report to the Nations on Occupational Fraud and Abuse

ACFE. Association of Certified Fraud Examiners. Fraud Resources (2004) Report to the Nations on Occupational Fraud and Abuse

ACFE. Association of Certified Fraud Examiners. Fraud Resources (2006) Report to the Nations on Occupational Fraud and Abuse

ACFE. Association of Certified Fraud Examiners. Fraud Resources (2008) Report to the Nations on Occupational Fraud and Abuse

ACFE. Association of Certified Fraud Examiners. Fraud Resources (2010) Report to the Nations on Occupational Fraud and Abuse. http://www.acfe.com/rttn-archive.aspx. Accessed 12 Nov 2012

ACFE. Association of Certified Fraud Examiners. Fraud Resources (2012) Report to the Nations on Occupational Fraud and Abuse. http://www.acfe.com/uploadedFiles/ACFE_Website/Content/rttn/2012-report-to-nations.pdf. Accessed 12 Nov 2012

ACFE. Association of Certified Fraud Examiners. Fraud Resources (2014) Report to the Nations on Occupational Fraud and Abuse. http://www.acfe.com/rttn-download-2014.aspx. Accessed 25 May 2014

Adamson G (2011) Making money in CPA firms in these turbulent economic times. Adamson Advisory Practice Management Consultants. http://www.adamsonadvisory.com/397/making-money-in-cpa-firms-in-these-turbulent-economic-times/. Accessed 31 Jan 2015

Altıntaş T (2007) A study on the perception of audit quality in Turkey (Doctoral Thesis, Istanbul University). Istanbul

American Institute of Certified Public Accountants. AICPA. Home. Research. Standards. Audit & Attest Standards. Statements on Quality Control Standards. SQCS No. 8. A firm's system of quality control (Redrafted). http://www.aicpa.org/Research/Standards/AuditAttest/Pages/SQCS.aspx. Accessed 13 Jun 2015

I. Kesimli, *External Auditing and Quality*, Accounting, Finance, Sustainability, Governance & Fraud: Theory and Application,
https://doi.org/10.1007/978-981-13-0526-9

American Institute of Certified Public Accountants. AICPA. Research. Standards. Audit & Attest Standards. AU Section 329, Analytical Procedures. http://www.aicpa.org/research/standards/auditattest/pages/sas.aspx#SAS43. Accessed 10 May 2012

American Institute of Certified Public Accountants. AICPA. http://www.aicpa.org/About/MissionandHistory/Pages/History%20of%20the%20AICPA.aspx. Accessed 04 Nov 2012

American Institute of Certified Public Accountants. AICPA. About. http://www.aicpa.org/About/Pages/About.aspx. Accessed 08 Feb 2013. http://www.aicpa.org/about/governance/aicpacouncil/pages/aicpa%20council.aspx. Accessed 08 Feb 2013, 09 Nov 2017

American Institute of Certified Public Accountants. AICPA. Become a CPA. http://www.aicpa.org/BecomeACPA/Licensure/Pages/default.aspx. Accessed 16 Jan 2015

American Institute of Certified Public Accountants. AICPA. State & Territory Requirements. https://www.thiswaytocpa.com/exam-licensure/state-requirements/NY/. Accessed 16 Jan 2015

Arens AA, Elder RJ, Beasley MS (2012) Auditing and assurance services, 14th edn. Prentice Hall, Boston, MA

Bailey RL, Dickins D, Reisch JT (2010) A discussion of public identification of US audit engagement partners: who benefits? who pays? International Journal of Disclosure & Governance 7(4):334–343. https://doi.org/10.1057/jdg.2010.13,12.12.2011

Baillot V (2007) International Organization of Securities Commissions. IOSCO Roundtable. Paris (01 Jul 2007). Quality of Public Company Audits from a Regulatory Perspective. http://www.iasplus.com/en/binary/iosco/0706roundtable.pdf. Accessed 19 Sept 2012

Ball R, Robin A, Wu JS (2003) Incentives versus standards: properties of accounting income in four East Asian countries. J Acc Econ 36:235–270

Banker RD, Chang H, Cunningham R (2003) The public accounting industry production function. J Acc Econ 35(2):255-281, ISSN 0165-4101, https://doi.org/10.1016/s0165-4101(03)00021-1

Banking Regulation and Supervision Agency (BRSA). Bankacılık Düzenleme ve Denetleme Kurumu (BDDK). Kuruluşlar, Bağımsız Denetim kuruluşları. http://www.bddk.org.tr/WebSitesi/turkce/Kuruluslar/Bagimsiz_Denetim_Kuruluslari/Finansal_Denetim/Finansal_Denetim.aspx. Accessed 03 May 2012. http://www.bddk.org.tr/WebSitesi/turkce/Kurum_Bilgileri/BDDK_Hakkinda/5802bddk_kitapcik_14_07_2014_tur.pdf. Accessed 09 Nov 2014. http://www.bddk.org.tr/WebSitesi/turkce/Kuruluslar/DenetciDenetlenen/125242013_yili_bagimsiz_denetim_sozlesmeleri.pdf. Accessed 23 Feb 2015

Barth ME, Landsman WR, Lang M, Williams C (March 2006) Accounting quality: international accounting standards and US GAAP. Working paper series. http://public.kenan-flagler.unc.edu/faculty/langm/bllw_0302.pdf . Accessed 15 Feb 2014

Başoğlu U, Ceylan A, Parasız I (2009) Finans, Teori - Kurum - Uygulama, 2nd edn. Ekin Basım Yayın Dağıtım, Bursa

Beck PJ, Wu MGH (2006) Learning by doing and audit quality. Contemp Acc Res 23(1):1–30

Birkett BS (1986) The Recent history of corporate audit committees. Acc Historians J 13(2). http://www.accountingin.com/accounting-historians-journal/volume-13-number-2/. Accessed 25 Mar 2017

Blay AD, Geiger MA (2013) Auditor fees and auditor independence: evidence from going concern reporting. Contemporary Accounting Research 30(2):579–606. https://doi.org/10.1111/j.1911-3846.2012.01166.x

Block CC (2011) Report on Sino-Forest Corporation. Muddy Waters Initiating Coverage on TRE.TO, OTC:SNOFF—Strong Sell. Muddy Waters Research. http://www.muddywatersresearch.com/research/tre/initiating-coverage-treto. Accessed 05 Apr 2013

Bouton D (2007) International Organization of Securities Commissions. IOSCO Roundtable. Paris (01.07.2007). Quality of Public Company Audits from a Regulatory Perspective. http://www.iasplus.com/en/binary/iosco/0706roundtable.pdf. Accessed 19 Sep 2012

Bozkurt N (2006) *Muhasebe Denetimi*, 4th edn. Alfa Basım Yayın Dağıtım, Istanbul

Brazel JF, Agoglia CP (2004) The effects of computer assurance specialist competence and auditor AIS expertise on auditor planning judgments. Working Paper, North Carolina State University. http://ssrn.com/abstract=497287, 04.04.2015 or https://doi.org/10.2139/ssrn.497287

Brazel JF, Bierstaker JL, Choi J-H, Glover SM, Myers LA (2011) Comments by the Auditing Standards Committee of the Auditing Section of the American Accounting Association on the European Commission Green Paper on Audit Policy: lessons from the crisis. Curr Issues Audit 5(1):C1–C7. https://doi.org/10.2308/ciia.2011.5.1.C1

Brown A (15.01.2010) European Group of International Accounting Networks and Associations—EGIAN's IOSCO Consultation Report Comment Letter, p 5. http://www.iosco.org/library/pubdocs/pdf/IOSCOPD339.pdf. Accessed 05 May 2012

Brown GR (1962) Changing audit objectives and techniques. Acc Rev 37(4):696

BusinessDictionary. Definition. Full time equivalent FTE. http://www.businessdictionary.com/definition/full-time-equivalent-FTE.html. Accessed 03 Feb 2013

BusinessDictionary. Definition. compliance audit. http://www.businessdictionary.com/definition/compliance-audit.html. Accessed 26 Mar 2013

California Corporations Code. Corporation Code. Section 100–195. Item: 171.5. https://leginfo.legislature.ca.gov/faces/codes_displayText.xhtml?lawCode=CORP&division=1.&title=1.&part=&chapter=1.&article=. Accessed 05 Jun 2017; http://www.leginfo.legislature.ca.gov/cgi-bin/displaycode?section=corp&group=00001-01000&file=100-195. Accessed 17 Jan 2015

Çalıyurt KT, Kesimli IG (2015) Avrupa'da Bağımsız Denetimde Mevzuat Açısından Gelişmeler ve Türkiye Yansımaları. 'Developments on the Legislation of External Audit in Europe and Its Reflections in Turkey.' Finans Politik & Ekonomik Yorumlar 52(602):13–24

Cambridge University Press. http://www.cambridge.org/. Professional English Online. clawback option. http://peo.cambridge.org/index.php?view=article&id=140%3Aclawback&option=com_content&Itemid=4. Accessed 06 Jan 2015. http://dictionary.cambridge.org/dictionary/english/clawback?fallbackFrom=turkish#translations. Accessed 05 Mar 2017

Cameran M, Campa D, Pettinicchio A (2014) IFRS adoption among private companies: impact on earnings quality. J Acc Audit Finance 29(3):278–305. Accessed 06 Jan 2015

Cameran M, Prencipe A, Trombetta M (2013) Mandatory audit firm rotation and audit quality: evidence from the Italian setting. European Accounting Review Forthcoming. Retrieved from http://ssrn.com/abstract=2420370, http://www.uam.es/otros/catedraccc/docs/prencipe.pdf. Accessed 31 Jan 2015

Capital Markets Board of Turkey (CMB). Legal Framework. Sermaye Piyasasında Bağımsız Denetim Standartları Hakkında Tebliğ. The Communiqué Regarding Independent Auditing in Capital Markets (Communiqué) (Serial: X, No. 22). Retrieved from http://www.spk.gov.tr/apps/teblig/displayteblig.aspx?id=295&ct=f&action=dis. Accessed 18 Feb 2012

Capital Markets Board of Turkey (CMB). About Us. Organization. http://www.cmb.gov.tr/Sayfa/AltSayfa/49#. Accessed 17 Nov 2017

Capital Markets Board of Turkey (CMB). http://www.cmb.gov.tr/Sayfa/Index/0/0#. Accessed 17 Nov 2017

Capital Markets Board of Turkey (CMB). CMB Introductory Booklet, p 7. http://www.cmb.gov.tr/Sayfa/Index/0/5. Accessed 17 Nov 2017

Capital Markets Board of Turkey (CMB). http://www.cmb.gov.tr/Sayfa/Index/1/1. Accessed 17 Nov 2017. http://www.spk.gov.tr/duyurugoster.aspx?aid=20140411&subid=0&ct=c&submenuheader=null. Accessed 08 Feb 2015. http://www.spk.gov.tr/indexcont.aspx?action=showpage&showmenu=yes&menuid=0&pid=0&subid=2&submenuheader=0. Accessed 09 Nov 2014

Cazes C (27.01.2010) Compagnie Nationale des Commissaires aux Comptes CNCC. IOSCO Consultation Report Comment Letter. p 3. http://www.iosco.org/library/pubdocs/pdf/IOSCOPD339.pdf. Accessed 05 May 2012

Chartered Institute of Management Accountants (CIMA). Thought Leadership, Reports and Research by Topic, Sustainability and Ethics. http://www.cimaglobal.com/Documents/Thought_leadership_docs/Sustainability%20and%20Climate%20Change/sustainability_report_v7_web.pdf. Accessed 25 Feb 2012

Choy AK, Fields T, King RR (2008) Social responsibility of the auditor as independent gatekeeper: an experimental investigation (August 8, 2008). http://ssrn.com/abstract=1248342. Accessed 04 Aug 2014 or https://doi.org/10.2139/ssrn.1248342

Christensen HB, Lee E, Walker M (6 March 2008) Incentives or standards: what determines accounting quality changes around IFRS adoption? AAA 2008 Financial Accounting and Reporting Section (FARS).http://ssrn.com/abstract=1013054, or https://doi.org/10.2139/ssrn.1013054. Accessed 08 Nov 2012

Clikeman PM (May 2003) The Greatest Frauds of the (Last) Century. Monograph. http://www.newaccountantusa.com/newsFeat/wealthManagement/Clikeman_Greatest_Frauds.pdf. Accessed 15 Mar 2008

Coffee J (13.05.2004). Gatekeeper failure and reform: the challenge of fashioning relevant reforms. Law and Economics Workshop UC Berkeley. http://www.escholarship.org/uc/item/8xr2120q. Accessed 09 Jan 2015

Cohen JR, Krishnamoorthy G, Wright A (2009) Waste is our business, Inc.: the importance of non-financial information in the audit planning process. http://ssrn.com/abstract=1088444, 05.06.2015 or https://doi.org/10.2139/ssrn.1088444

Colby EE (23.03.2004) Financial statement fraud, Part 1. Chartered Professional Accountants. PD Net. http://www.cga-pdnet.org/Non_VerifiableProducts/ArticlePublication/FinStatFraud/FinStatFraud_p1.pdf. Accessed 07 Jan 2015

Committee on Basic Auditing Concepts, 1969–71 (1972) Accounting Review 47(4):14–74

Company Corporation. Professional Corporations & Professional Limited Liability Companies. https://www.incorporate.com/professional_corporation.html. Accessed 16 Jan 2015

Conway R (25.11.2009) IOSCO Consultation report comment letter, p 11. http://www.iosco.org/library/pubdocs/pdf/IOSCOPD339.pdf. Accessed 05 May 2012

Cook M (2007) International Organization of Securities Commissions. IOSCO Roundtable. Paris (01 Jun 2007). Quality of Public Company Audits from a Regulatory Perspective. 1st Panel: audit quality: evaluating external audits in today's environment. http://www.iasplus.com/en/binary/iosco/0706roundtable.pdf. Accessed 19 Sep 2012

Cook TM, Russell RA (1981) Introduction to management science, 2nd edn. Prentice Hall Inc, New Jersey

Cox J (2007) International Organization of Securities Commissions. IOSCO Roundtable. Paris (01 Jun 2007). Quality of Public Company Audits from a Regulatory Perspective. 3rd Panel: audit firm concentration: potential effects on audit quality. http://www.iasplus.com/en/binary/iosco/0706roundtable.pdf. Accessed 19 Sep 2012

Croft J (23.01.2012) Law courts correspondent. Nadir stole millions from Polly Peck, court told. Financial Times. http://www.ft.com/intl/cms/s/0/ab1e8684-45cb-11e1-acc9-00144feabdc0.html#axzz1opmd6wkr. Accessed 11 Mar 2012

van Damme H (13 Jan 2010) Fédération des Experts comptables Européens (FEE). IOSCO Consultation Report Comment Letter. p 14. Retrieved from http://www.iosco.org/library/pubdocs/pdf/IOSCOPD339.pdf. Accessed 05 May 2012

Dang L (2004) Assessing actual audit quality (Doctoral Thesis, Drexel University). Philadelphia

De La Martiniere G (2007) International Organization of Securities Commissions. IOSCO Roundtable. Paris (01.07.2007). Impacts of auditor liability on behaviour and quality. http://www.iasplus.com/en/binary/iosco/0706roundtable.pdf. Accessed 19 Sep 2012

DeAngelo LE (1981a) Auditor independence, 'low balling,' and disclosure regulation. J Acc Econ 3(2):113–127

DeAngelo LE (1981b) Auditor size and audit quality. J Acc Econ 3(3):183–199 (North-Holland Publishing Company)

DeFond ML, Hung M, Carr E, Zhang J (2011) Was the Sarbanes-Oxley act good news for corporate bondholders? Acc Horizons (0888–7993) 25(3):465–485. (http://search.ebscohost.com/login.aspx?authtype=ip,uid&profile=ehost&defaultdb=bth). http://search.ebscohost.com/login.aspx?direct=true&db=bth&site=ehost-live&AN=65823368. Accessed 01 Jan 2011

Dehaan E, Hodge F, Shevlin T (2013) Does voluntary adoption of a clawback provision improve financial reporting quality? Contemp Acc Res 30(3):1027–1062. https://doi.org/10.1111/j.1911-3846.2012.01183.x

Delespaul J-C (13 Dec 2005) Audit regulation—public oversight. Transparency and audit regulation. 5th FCM Conference in Istanbul. Text of speech on behalf of DIPAC. http://www.fcmweb.org/activities.asp?mode=2&IDDocumento=84. Accessed 10 Mar 2013

Deloitte Touche Tohmatsu (15.01.2010). In their comment letter to IOSCO Consulting Report. p 2. http://www.iosco.org/library/pubdocs/pdf/IOSCOPD339.pdf. Accessed 05 May 2012

Deltas G, Doogar R (09 Jan 2005) Product and cost differentiation by large audit firms. In: 2005 ASSA Conference—expanding the frontiers of economics—Oligopoly markets and antitrust, Philadelphia

Department of Treasury. Government of Western Australia. Economic Audit. http://www.treasury.wa.gov.au/Treasury/Economic_Audit/Economic_Audit/. Accessed 29 Jan 2017. http://www.treasury.wa.gov.au/cms/content.aspx?id=2163. Accessed 26 Feb 2012

Dicksee LR (1907) Auditing: a practical manual for auditors, 7th edn. (First printed in August 1892). Gee&Co. Printers and Publishers, London

Dictionary.com. auditor. http://dictionary.reference.com/browse/auditor. 29.06.2015.

Doogar R, Easley RF (1998) Concentration without differentiation: a new look at the determinants of audit market concentration. J Acc Econ 25:235–253

Duflo E, Greenstone M, Pande P, Ryan N (2013) Truth-telling by third-party auditors and the response of polluting firms: experimental evidence from India. Q J Econ 128(4):1499–1545

Durukan BM, Ikiz AK (2007) (Models related to audit quality, quality and service quality: Conceptual Framework) "Denetim Kalitesi, Kalite ve Hizmet Kalitesine İlişkin Modeller: Kavramsal Çerçeve". Malî Çözüm Dergisi/Financial Analysis (82):35–62

e-conomic.com. auditor. https://www.e-conomic.com/accountingsoftware/accounting-words/auditor, 29.06.2015

ET Bureau. The Economic Times. India Times (30.08.2011) Auditors should be paid from a pool of funds. http://articles.economictimes.indiatimes.com/2011-08-30/news/29945171_1_auditors-corporate-governance-companies-bill. Accessed 03 Nov 2013

EUR-Lex. Access to European Union Law. Directive2014/56/EU of the European Parliament and of the Council amending Directive 2006/43/EC on statutory audits of annual accounts and consolidated accounts 16 April 2014. http://eur-lex.europa.eu/legal-content/EN/TXT/PDF/?uri=CELEX:32014L0056&from=EN. Accessed 07 Feb 2015

EUR-Lex. Access to European Union Law. Directive2006/43/EC of the European Parliament and of the Council on statutory audits of annual accounts and consolidated accounts, amending Council Directives 78/660/EEC and 83/349/EEC and repealing Council Directive 84/253/EEC 17 May 2006. http://eur-lex.europa.eu/legal-content/EN/TXT/HTML/?uri=CELEX:32006L0043. Accessed 19 Sep 2012

EUR-Lex. Access to European Union Law. Eighth Council Directive 84/253/EEC of 10 April 1984 based on Article 54(3)(g) of the Treaty on the approval of persons responsible for carrying out statutory audits of accounting documents. http://eurlex.europa.eu/legalcontent/EN/TXT/PDF/?uri=CELEX:31984L0253&qid=1423170797029&from=EN. Accessed 05 Feb 2015

Energy Market Regulatory Board (EMRA). Enerji Piyasası Düzenleme Kurumu (EPDK), T.C. Bağımsız Denetim. Bağımsız Denetim Kuruluşları. http://www2.epdk.org.tr/denetim/bagimsiz/kurulus/adresbilgisi.asp. 13.05.2012. http://www.epdk.org.tr/index.php/epdk-denetim/bagimsiz-denetim?id=51. Accessed 09 Nov 2014

Erickson M, Mayhew BW, Felix Jr WL (2000) Why do audits fail? Evidence from Lincoln savings and loan. J Acc Res 38(1):165–194

European Commission (Oct 2007) The EU single market, internal market, auditing, docs. Oxera Report. "Ownership Rules of Audit Firms and their Consequences for Audit Market Concentration". http://ec.europa.eu/internal_market/auditing/docs/market/oxera_report_en.pdf. Accessed 12 Mar 2012

European Commission (October 2010) Green Paper. Audit policy: lessons from the crisis. Brussels. Retrieved from http://ec.europa.eu/internal_market/consultations/docs/2010/audit/green_paper_audit_en.pdf. Accessed 04 Feb 2015

European Commission (October 2010) Green Paper. Audit policy: lessons from the crisis. Brussels. Retrieved from http://europa.eu/rapid/press-release_STATEMENT-14-104_en.htm. Accessed 04 Feb 2015. http://www.europarl.europa.eu/news/en/news-room/content/20140331IPR41179/html/Reforming-EU-audit-services-to-restore-investors%27-confidence. Accessed 11 May 2015

Eurostat. Statistics Explained. Glossary. http://ec.europa.eu/eurostat/statistics-explained/index.php/Glossary:Full-time_equivalent_(FTE). Accessed 12 Jun 2015

Financenmoney. https://financenmoney.wordpress.com/2011/02/17/impact-of-inflation-on-corporate-finance. Accessed 06 Jan 2015

Financial Accounting Standards Board. Facts about FASB. http://www.fasb.org/facts/index.shtml#structure. Accessed 06 Jul 2013, and 25 Oct 2017

Financial Reporting Council (2006) Audit Inspection Unit 2005/6 Audit Quality Inspections Public Report July 2006. Retrieved from http://www.frc.org.uk/pob/publications/index.cfm?mode=list&year=2006. Accessed 25 Feb 2012. Retrieved from http://www.frc.org.uk/images/uploaded/documents/AIU%20Annual%20Report%202010-11.pdf. Accessed 25 Feb 2012

Financial Reporting Council (2008) Promoting audit quality. Audit Quality Framework 2008. https://www.frc.org.uk/Our-Work/Publications/FRC-Board/The-Audit-Quality-Framework-(1)-File.pdf. Accessed 05 May 2012

Financial Reporting Council (May 2008) Our Work. Publications. Choice in the UK and Audit Market: Progress Report and Further Consultation. https://frc.org.uk/Our-Work/Publications/FRC-Board/First-Progress-Report-on-the-implementation-of-the-File.pdf. Accessed 31 Jan 2015

Financial Reporting Council. Our Work. Conduct. Audit Quality Review. http://www.frc.org.uk/Our-Work/Conduct/Audit-Quality-Review.aspx. Accessed 05 May 2013

Francis JR (2006) Researching audit quality. American Accounting Association. 2006 Auditing Doctoral Consortium in conjunction with the Auditing Section 2006 Midyear Conference. 12 Jan 2006. Los Angeles, California.

Francis JR, Michas PN, Seavey SE (2013) Does audit market concentration harm the quality of audited earnings? Evidence from audit markets in 42 Countries. Contemp Account Res 30 (1):325–355. https://doi.org/10.1111/j.1911-3846.2012.01156.x

Francis JR (2011) A framework for understanding and researching audit quality. Auditing 30 (2):125–152. https://doi.org/10.2308/ajpt-50006

Fraser J, Lindsay H (2004) 20 questions directors should ask about internal audit. Toronto. Canadian Institute of Chartered Accountants. National Library of Canada Cataloguing in Publication, p 7. ISBN 1-55385-092-0

Fraser NP (2010) A single set of worldwide auditing standards: the road is long…. Int J Discl Gov 7(4):298–309. https://doi.org/10.1057/jdg.2010.20

Free Online Dictionary. Audit. http://www.thefreedictionary.com/audit. Accessed 23 Feb 2012

Free Online Dictionary. aufsichtsrat. http://de.thefreedictionary.com/aufsichtsrat. Accessed Aug 2012

Free Online Dictionary. Blackout periods. http://financial-dictionary.thefreedictionary.com/Blackout+Periods. Accessed 10 Mar 2012

Free Online Dictionary. Historically Black Colleges. http://encyclopedia.thefreedictionary.com/Historically+Black+Colleges. Accessed 13 Jan 2011

Free Online Dictionary. Industry. http://www.thefreedictionary.com/industry. Accessed 29 Oct 2013

Free Online Dictionary. Strategy. http://www.thefreedictionary.com/strategy. Accessed 21 Nov 2014

Free Online Dictionary. vorstand. http://de.thefreedictionary.com/vorstand. Accessed 10 Aug 2012

Gaetano C (18.10.2013) Study: audit quality rests on who pays. Compliance Week. http://www.nysscpa.org/blog/2013/10/18/study-audit-quality-rests-who-pays. Accessed 03 Nov 2013

Garside J (24.08.2014) Autonomy deals raise questions as HP row escalates. The Guardian. http://www.theguardian.com/business/2014/aug/24/hewlett-packard-questions-autonomy-deals-middlemen. Accessed 09 Jan 2015

Gentner S (02.04.2014) Public Company Accounting Oversight Board's April 2, 2014 Public Meeting on the Auditor's Reporting Model. http://pcaobus.org/News/Webcasts/Pages/04022014_PublicMeeting.aspx, 11.05.2015

Georgiades G (15 Mar 2011) AICPA Statement on Auditing Standards, quality control for an engagement conducted in accordance with Generally Accepted Auditing Standards. GAAS Update Service 11(5), s1

Green PB, Calderon TG (1994) Using real-world cases to illustrate the power of analytical procedures. J Acc Educ 12(3):245–268. http://deepblue.lib.umich.edu/bitstream/2027.42/31473/1/0000395.pdf. Accessed 11 Mar 2012

Gönen S, Uzay Ş (2009) Türkiye'de Bağımsız Denetim Kuruluşlarının Görünümü (Outlook of the Auditing Firms in Turkey). Trakya Üniversitesi İktisâdi ve İdarî Bilimler Fakültesi. *1. Ulusal Kurumsal Yönetim, Yolsuzluk, Etik ve Sosyal Sorumluluk Konferansı*, 11–14 Jun 2009. Edirne. Bildiri Kitabı. Editör: Doç. Dr. Kıymet Tunca Çalıyurt. 143–162

Göğer T (2006) The factors that determine the quality of an independent audit within independent audit practices and a survey on the audit firms in Turkey (Master Thesis, Marmara University). Istanbul

Gülen F (1998) Finansal Denetim. First Edition. Ankara, T.C. Sayıştay Başkanlığı. p 1, 3. http://www.sayistay.gov.tr/yayin/yayin2.asp?id=39. Accessed 26 Feb 2012

Haddrill S (22.12.2009) Financial Reporting Council. IOSCO Consultation Report Comment Letter. p 1. Retrieved from http://www.iosco.org/library/pubdocs/pdf/IOSCOPD339.pdf. Accessed 05 May 2012

Hanson JD (24.10.2014) The PCAOB and Audit Committees—Common Goals. University of California—Irvine Audit Committee Summit. Irvine, CA. Public Company Accounting Oversight Board (PCOAB). News Releases. Event65s & Public Company Accounting Oversight Board Meetings. Speeches & Statements. http://pcaobus.org/News/Speech/Pages/10242014_Audit_Committee_Summit.aspx. Accessed 29 Oct 2014

Harris SB (20.03.2014) The importance of auditing and audit regulation to the capital markets. American University Kogod School of Business. Washington, DC. Public Company Accounting Oversight Board (PCOAB). News Releases. Events & Public Company Accounting Oversight Board Meetings. Speeches & Statements. http://pcaobus.org/News/Speech/Pages/03202014_American.aspx. Accessed 28 Mar 2014

Hayes R, Dassen R, Schilder A, Wallage P (2005) Principles of auditing—an introduction to international standards on auditing, 2nd edn. Pearson Education Limited, Essex

Hollis Ashbaugh, (2001) Non-US Firms' Accounting Standard Choices. Journal of Accounting and Public Policy 20 (2):129-153

Hornby AS (1977) Oxford advanced learners' dictionary of current english, New edn. Oxford University Press, Oxford, p 51

Humphrey C, Kausar A, Loft A, Woods M (2011) Regulating audit beyond the crisis: a critical discussion of the EU Green Paper. Eur Acc Rev 20(3):431–457. https://doi.org/10.1080/09638180.2011.597201

Hunton JE, Wright AM, Wright S (2004) Are financial auditors overconfident in their ability to assess risks associated with enterprise resource planning systems? J Inf Syst 18(2):7–28

Institute of Internal Auditors (IIA). About Us. About the Profession. About Internal Auditing. https://na.theiia.org/about-us/about-ia/Pages/About-the-Profession.aspx. Accessed 15 Jan 2015

International Federation of Accountants (IFAC). Retrieved from http://www.ifac.org/sites/default/files/downloads/a007-2010-iaasb-handbook-isqc-1.pdf. Accessed 25 Feb 2012

International Federation of Accountants (IFAC). About IFAC. http://www.ifac.org/about-ifac/organization-overview/history. Accessed 06 Feb 2013, 08 Feb 2015 and 04 Nov 2017

International Federation of Accountants (IFAC). http://www.ifac.org/auditing-assurance/about-iaasb, http://www.ifac.org/auditing-assurance/about-iaasb/iaasb-members. Accessed 06 Feb 2013. http://www.iaasb.org/about-iaasb/members. Accessed 08 Nov 2017

International Federation of Accountants (IFAC). Complete exposure draft, reporting on audited financial statements. http://www.ifac.org/sites/default/files/publications/files/Complete%20ED,%20Reporting%20on%20Audited%20Financial%20Statements.pdf. Accessed 08 Sep 2013

International Federation of Accountants (IFAC). Handbook of the code of ethics for professional accountants. http://www.ifac.org/system/files/publications/files/2012-IESBA-Handbook.pdf. Accessed 26 Jan 2018

International Federation of Accountants (IFAC) (Dec 2007) Transnational Auditors Committee. Forum of Firms. Tone at the top and audit quality. https://www.ifac.org/about-ifac/forum-firms-and-transnational-auditors-committee. Accessed 01 Dec 2011

International Federation of Accountants (IFAC). http://www.ifac.org/sites/default/files/downloads/a007-2010-iaasb-handbook-isqc-1.pdf. Accessed 25 Feb 2012. http://www.ifac.org/sites/default/files/downloads/a010-2010-iaasb-handbook-isa-220.pdf. Accessed 25 Feb 2012. http://www.ifac.org/bio/jean-claude-delespaul. Accessed 14 Mar 2013

International Organization of Securities Commissions. IOSCO (September 2009) Technical Committee. Transparency of firms that audit public companies: consultation report. Retrieved from http://www.iosco.org/library/pubdocs/pdf/IOSCOPD302.pdf. Accessed 05 May 2012. Retrieved from http://www.iasplus.com/iosco/0909transparency.pdf. Accessed 12 Mar 2012

International Organization of Supreme Audit Institutions (INTOSAI). Mexico Declaration on Independence. http://www.intosai.org/issai-executive-summaries/view/article/issai-10-the-mexico-declaration-on-sai-independence.html. Accessed 28 Jan 2017

International Organization of Supreme Audit Institutions (INTOSAI). Performance audit. ISSAI 3100. http://www.issai.org/en_us/site-issai/issai-framework/4-auditing-guidelines.htm. Accessed 29 Jan 2017

Investopedia. Dictionary. 401(k) plan. http://www.investopedia.com/terms/1/401kplan.asp. Accessed 28 Mar 2014

Investopedia. Dictionary. Aggressive accounting. http://www.investopedia.com/terms/a/aggressiveaccounting.asp. Accessed 31 Jan 2014

Investopedia. Dictionary. Auditor. http://www.investopedia.com/terms/a/auditor.asp. Accessed 29 Jun 2015

Investopedia. Dictionary. Cook the books. http://www.investopedia.com/terms/c/cookthebooks.asp. Accessed 31 Jan 2014

Investopedia. Dictionary. Cookie jar accounting. http://www.investopedia.com/terms/c/cookiejaraccounting.asp#axzz2DAdPXYt0. Accessed 10 Mar 2012

Investopedia. Dictionary. Creative-accounting. http://www.investopedia.com/terms/c/creative-accounting.asp. Accessed 31 Jan 2014

Investopedia. Dictionary. Financial-shenanigans. http://www.investopedia.com/terms/f/financial-shenanigans.asp. Accessed 31 Jan 2014

Investopedia. Dictionary. ponzischeme. http://www.investopedia.com/terms/p/ponzischeme.asp#ixzz1okMQB6a4. Accessed 10 Mar 2012

Investopedia. Dictionary. Pump and dump. http://www.investopedia.com/terms/p/pumpanddump.asp#axzz2DAdPXYt0. Accessed 10 Mar 2012

Investopedia. Dictionary. Thrift savings plan. http://www.investopedia.com/articles/personal-finance/062513/what-federal-employees-retirement-system-fers-and-how-does-it-work.asp. Accessed 28 Mar 2014

Itimat Bağımsız Denetim ve Yeminli Mali Müşavirlik A.Ş. (Itimat CPA) Kurumsal (Corporate). Organizasyon Yapısı (Organizational Structure. http://www.itimat-ymm.com/uploads/201283011141441%C4%B0T%C4%B0MAT%20A.%C5%9E.%20ORGAN%C4%B0ZASYON%20YAPISI.pdf. Accessed 16 Oct 2013. Şeffaflık Raporu (Transparency Report). http://www.itimat-ymm.com/uploads/2014411168892013-Seffaflik-Raporu.pdf. Accessed 14 Apr 2014

Jennings J (2007) International Organization of Securities Commissions. IOSCO Roundtable. Paris (01.07.2007) Quality of public company audits from a regulatory perspective. 2. Panel: "Impacts of Auditor Liability on Behaviour and Quality". http://www.iasplus.com/en/binary/iosco/0706roundtable.pdf. Accessed 19 Sep 2012

Johnson GL, Gentry JA (1980) Finney and Miller's principles of accounting, 10th edn. Prentice Hall, Inc., New Jersey

Jones A, Binham C (29.11.2012) KPMG disputes role in autonomy writedown. Financial Times. http://www.ft.com/cms/s/0/5f610688-3a1f-11e2-baac-00144feabdc0.html#axzz3OKYW2Ert. Accessed 09 Jan 2015

Karaian J (2013) Beyond the Big Four—Why regulators and clients can't break the audit oligopoly. Quarz. http://qz.com/136346/beyond-the-big-four-why-regulators-and-clients-cant-break-the-audit-oligopoly/. Accessed 17 Oct 2013

Kaval H (2008) Muhasebe Denetimi, 3rd edn. Gazi Kitabevi, Ankara

Kaymaz Ö, Karaibrahimoglu YZ (2011) Early observations on the quality of IFRS reports: evidence from Turkey. Glob J Bus Res 5(3):27–40. http://ssrn.com/abstract=1874257. Accessed 13 Oct 2011

Kesimli I (2015) Assessment of Turkish auditing firms from the perspective of international quality control standard. (unpublished Doctoral Thesis, Trakya University). Trakya University, Turkey

Kinney Jr WR (1986/03) Audit technology and preferences for auditing standards. J Acc Econ 8 (1):73–89. http://deepblue.lib.umich.edu/handle/2027.42/26243. Accessed 29 Jan 2015

Kinney Jr WR (1999) Auditor independence: a burdensome constraint or core value? Acc Horizons 13(1):69–75

Kishali Y, Güner MF, Pehlivanlı D (2013) "Modül I, Denetim Standartları". *KGK. Geçiş Dönemi Eğitim Dokümanları. Beykent Üniversitesi.*http://www.kgk.gov.tr/content_detail-326-782–.html. Accessed 21 May 2015

Knechel WR, Krishnan GV, Pevzner M, Shefchik LB, Velury UK (2013) Audit quality: insights from the academic literature. Auditing J Pract Theor (32):385–421. https://doi.org/10.2308/ajpt-50350

Koçel T (2001) İşletme Yöneticiliği (Business Management), 8th edn. Beta Basım Yayım Dağıtım A.Ş, Istanbul

Land N (02.04.2014) Speech. Public Company Accounting Oversight Board's April 2, 2014 Public Meeting on the Auditor's Reporting Model. http://pcaobus.org/News/Webcasts/Pages/04022014_PublicMeeting.aspx. Accessed 11 May 2015

Lee T-H, Azham MA (2008) The evolution of auditing: an analysis of the historical development. J Mod Acc Auditing 4(12):1–8

LexisNexis. InfoPro. Zimmerman's research guide. https://law.lexisnexis.com/infopro/zimmermans/disp.aspx?z=1895. Accessed 31 Jan 2013

Löhlein L (Oct 2014) How independent are public audit oversight systems? An interdisciplinary approach to comparing accounting regulation. In: 11th international accounting conference. Istanbul, p1

Löhlein L (2015) Same but different—comparing European Union Audit Oversight Regulation. Audit Financiar 13(126):74–80

MacKenzie A (15.01.2010) Grant Thornton International Ltd. IOSCO Consultation Report Comment Letter, p 6. http://www.iosco.org/library/pubdocs/pdf/IOSCOPD339.pdf. Accessed 05 May 2012

Macías M, Muiño F (2011) Examining dual accounting systems in Europe. Int J Acc 46:51–78

Maersk. http://www.maersk.com/pages/default.aspx. Accessed 04 Oct 2013

McKenna F (20.11.2012) HewlettPackard's autonomy allegations: a material writedown puts all four audit firms on the spot. Forbes. http://www.forbes.com/sites/francinemckenna/2012/11/20/hewlett-packards-autonomy-allegations-a-material-writedown-puts-all-four-audit-firms-on-the-spot/. Accessed 09 Jan 2015

Mod Bağımsız Denetim Serbest Muhasebeci Mali Müşavirlik A.Ş. (Mod CPA) Hakkımızda (About Us). Şeffaflık Raporu (Transparency Report). http://www.moddenetim.com.tr/2010-yili-seffaflik-raporu.pdf. Accessed 16 Oct 2013. http://www.moddenetim.com.tr/wp-content/uploads/2014/03/internet-sitesine-konulcak-%C5%9Feffafl%C4%B1k-raporu.pdf. Accessed 14 May 2014

Montgomery RH (1919) Auditing, theory and practice, 2nd edn (First printed in August 1912). The Ronald Press Company, New York

National Audit Office of Finland (2007) Performance Audit Manual. International Publications of the National Audit Office of Finland. Edita Prima Ltd., Helsinki. ISBN 978-952-499-027-1. http://www.vtv.fi/files/20/Perforormance_Audit_Manual_netti.pdf . Accessed 26 Feb 2012

National Audit Office of England. Finance Manual May 2009.https://www.nao.org.uk/freedom-of-information/wp-content/uploads/sites/13/2013/03/NAO_Finance_Manual.pdf. Accessed 22 Jan 2017

National Audit Office of England. http://www.nao.org.uk/idoc.ashx?docId=6415DDEC-E721-4F73-BBE9-762DEC5DDF5E&version=-1. Accessed 26 Feb 2012

National Audit Office of England. NAO General Report of the Comptroller and Auditor General 2002–03. https://www.nao.org.uk/wp-content/uploads/2004/03/0304365es.pdf. Accessed 05 Jan 2015

Nolo. Law for all. Legal topics. Limited partnerships and limited liability partnerships. http://www.nolo.com/legal-encyclopedia/limited-partnerships-limited-liability-partnerships-29748.html. Accessed 16 Jan 2015

Norris F (29.11.2012) A clash of auditors in H.P. Deal and Loss. New York Times. http://www.nytimes.com/2012/11/30/business/auditors-clash-in-hp-deal-for-autonomy.html?emc=tnt&tntemail1=y. Accessed 30 Nov 2012

Okur M (Nov 2007) The audit of external audit. "Bağımsız Denetimin Denetimi". SPK Muhasebe Standartları Dairesi. Yeterlik Etüdü. Ankara. http://www.spk.gov.tr/yayin.aspx?type=yay02&submenuheader=-1. Accessed 18 Oct 2013

Oxford Advanced Learners' Dictionary. http://oald8.oxfordlearnersdictionaries.com/dictionary/audit. Accessed 23 Feb 2012

Özyurt A (2010) A research on features of the independent auditors affecting the independent audit quality. Master's Thesis, Hacettepe University, Ankara

PCAOB Release No. 2009-005. July 28, 2009. PCAOB Rulemaking Docket Matter No. 029. http://pcaobus.org/Search/pages/results.aspx?k=audit%20partner%20signs%20audit%20report. Accessed 11 May 2015

Pacini CJ (17.10.2003) Independent Audit I Course Notes. Florida Gulf Coast University. Retrieved from ruby.fgcu.edu/courses/cpacini/courses/acg4632/ch7audnotes.pdf. Accessed 11 Apr 2016

Parlakkaya R, Akmeşe H, Akmeşe KA (2014) Status Quo of International Financial Reporting Standards and International Standards on Auditing: a research on the accounting professionals in Konya. Emerging Markets Queries in Finance and Business (EMQ 2013) Procedia Economics and Finance 15:1663–1670. http://www.sciencedirect.com/science/article/pii/S2212567114006388#bbib0010. Accessed 12 Feb 2017

Pirgaip B (May 2004) Sermaye Piyasasında Bağımsız Denetim Standartlarının Uluslararası Denetim Standartları ile Harmonizasyonu. SPK Muhasebe Standartları Dairesi. Yeterlik Etüdü. Ankara. http://www.spk.gov.tr/yayin.aspx?type=yay02&submenuheader=-1. Accessed 18 Oct 2013

Platt E, Kawa L (20.11.2012) 16 Financial Shenanigans that got companies into tons of trouble. www.businessinsider.com/financial-accounting-shenanigans-2012-11?op=1. Accessed 31 Jan 2014

Psaros J, Trotman KT (2004) The impact of the type of accounting standards on preparers' judgments. Abacus 40(1):76–93. https://doi.org/10.1111/j.1467-6281.2004.00144.x

Public Company Accounting Oversight Board (PCOAB). News. Events. Documents. http://pcaobus.org/news/events/documents/05152013_sagmeeting/audit_quality_indicators.pdf. Accessed 29 Jan 2015

Public Company Accounting Oversight Board (PCOAB). About the PCAOB. http://pcaobus.org/About/Board/Pages/default.aspx. Accessed 08 Feb 2013, and 11 Jan 2015. http://pcaobus.org/About/History/Pages/default.aspx. Accessed 09 Nov 2014

Public Company Accounting Oversight Board (PCOAB). Registration & Reporting. Registered Firms. http://pcaobus.org/Registration/Firms/Pages/RegisteredFirms.aspx. Accessed 04 Jun 2017, 12 Jan 2015 and 06 May 2012

Public Company Accounting Oversight Board (PCOAB). Registration. Application fees and annual fees. http://pcaobus.org/Registration/rasr/Pages/AnnualFees.aspx. Accessed 01 Jun 2017 and 16 Jan 2015

Public Company Accounting Oversight Board (PCOAB). Registration. http://pcaobus.org/Registration/Pages/default.aspx. Accessed 01 Jun 2017 and 16 Jan 2015

Public Company Accounting Oversight Board (PCOAB). Inspections. http://pcaobus.org/Inspections/Pages/default.aspx. Accessed 17 Jan 2015. http://pcaobus.org/International/Inspections/Pages/IssuerClientsWithoutAccess.aspx. Accessed 17 Jan 2015

Public Company Accounting Oversight Board (PCOAB). Standards. Auditing. AS 2401: consideration of fraud in a financial statement audit. https://pcaobus.org/Standards/Auditing/Pages/AS2401.aspx. Accessed 22.01.2018

Public Company Accounting Oversight Board (PCOAB). Standards. Auditing. https://pcaobus.org/Standards/Auditing/Documents/ReorganizedandPreReorganizedNumbering.pdf. Accessed 21 Jan 2018. http://pcaobus.org/Standards/Auditing/Pages/Auditing_Standard_16.aspx, http://pcaobus.org/Standards/Auditing/Pages/Auditing_Standard_16_Appendix_C.aspx. Accessed 19 Jan 2013. http://pcaobus.org/Standards/Auditing/Pages/Auditing_Standard_1.aspx. Accessed 16 Jan 2015

Public Company Accounting Oversight Board (PCOAB). Rules. SAG. http://pcaobus.org/Rules/Rulemaking/Docket%20004/2003-06-30_Release_2003-009.pdf, 06.02.2013. http://pcaobus.org/Rules/PCAOBRules/Documents/Bylaws.pdf. Accessed 06 Feb 2013. http://pcaobus.org/Enforcement/Documents/Release2003-015.pdf. Accessed 16 Jan 2015

Public Oversight—Accounting and Auditing Standards Authority (POA). Institutional. Institution Organization Chart. http://www.kgk.gov.tr/content_list-256-baskan-yardimcilari.html. Accessed 03 Mar 2013

Public Oversight—Accounting and Auditing Standards Authority (POA). Institutional. http://www.kgk.gov.tr/content_detail-178-733-kgk-teskilat.html. Accessed 30 May 2014

Public Oversight—Accounting and Auditing Standards Authority (POA). Institutional. Legislation. Bylaw. http://www.kgk.gov.tr/content_detail-219-516-teskilat-ve-gorevleri-hakkinda-yonetmelik.html. Accessed 03 Mar 2012

Public Oversight—Accounting and Auditing Standards Authority (POA). Institutional. http://www.kgk.gov.tr/content_detail-219-1020-bagimsiz-denetim-yonetmeligi.html. Accessed 01 Jan 2015. http://www.kgk.gov.tr/Portalv2Uploads/files/Duyurular/v1/Mevzuat/660_KHK.pdf. Accessed 15 Oct 2017

Public Oversight—Accounting and Auditing Standards Authority (POA). Announcements. http://www.kgk.gov.tr/contents/files/seffaflik.pdf. Accessed 25 Apr 2014

Public Oversight—Accounting and Auditing Standards Authority (POA). Announcements. http://www.kgk.gov.tr/content_detail-191-1006-rotasyon-surelerinin-hesaplanmasina-iliskin-duyuru-(09102014).html. Accessed 09 Oct 2014

Public Oversight—Accounting and Auditing Standards Authority (POA). List of audit firms. http://www.kgk.gov.tr/dk/index.aspx, 03–16 May 2014

Public Oversight—Accounting and Auditing Standards Authority (POA). Institutional. Institution Organization Chart. Service Units/Departments. http://www.kgk.gov.tr/content_detail-301-633-%E2%98%BC-gozetim-ve-denetim-daire-baskanligi-.html. Accessed 25 Sep 2015

Public Oversight—Accounting and Auditing Standards Authority (POA). Board Members. http://www.kgk.gov.tr/UnitMembers/3/1/KURUL-U%CC%88YELERI%CC%87. Accessed 15 Oct 2017
Public Oversight—Accounting and Auditing Standards Authority (POA). Standards. Accounting Standards. TAS 1. Turkish Accounting Standard 1. Presentation of Financial Tables. http://www.kgk.gov.tr/content_detail-345-1055-tms-tfrs-2014-seti.html. Accessed 02 Jan 2015. http://kgk.gov.tr/Portalv2Uploads/files/DynamicContentFiles/T%C3%BCrkiye%20Muhasebe%20Standartlar%C4%B1/TMSTFRS2016Seti/TMS1.pdf. Accessed 19 Feb 2017
Public Oversight—Accounting and Auditing Standards Authority (POA). Standard on Quality Control 1 (QCS 1). Retrieved from http://www.kgk.gov.tr/content_detail-315-792.html. Accessed 19 Oct 2013
Public Oversight—Accounting and Auditing Standards Authority (POA). http://www.kgk.gov.tr/contents/files/KOBI_TFRS.pdf. Accessed 06 Jan 2015
Public Oversight—Accounting and Auditing Standards Authority (POA). Standards. Turkish Standards on Auditing. Retrieved from http://www.kgk.gov.tr/content_detail-315-792.html. Accessed 12 July 2014
Public Oversight—Accounting and Auditing Standards Authority (POA). TSA 210. Agreeing the terms of audit engagements
Public Oversight—Accounting and Auditing Standards Authority (POA). TSA 220. Quality control for an audit of financial statements
Public Oversight—Accounting and Auditing Standards Authority (POA). Ethical codes of conduct for independent auditors. http://www.kgk.gov.tr/contents/files/Pdf/BagimsizDenetcilerIcinEtikKurallar04062014.pdf. Accessed 12 Jul 2014
Public Oversight—Accounting and Auditing Standards Authority (POA). TSA 240. The auditor's responsibilities relating to fraud in an audit of financial statements
Public Oversight—Accounting and Auditing Standards Authority (POA). TSA 250. Consideration of laws and regulations in an audit of financial statements
Public Oversight—Accounting and Auditing Standards Authority (POA). TSA 260. Communication with those charged with governance
Public Oversight—Accounting and Auditing Standards Authority (POA). TSA 265. Communicating deficiencies in internal control to those charged with governance and management
Public Oversight—Accounting and Auditing Standards Authority (POA). TSA 300. Planning an audit of financial statements
Public Oversight—Accounting and Auditing Standards Authority (POA). TSA 315. Identifying and assessing the risks of material misstatement through understanding the entity and its environment
Public Oversight—Accounting and Auditing Standards Authority (POA). TSA 330. The auditor's responses to assessed risks
Public Oversight—Accounting and Auditing Standards Authority (POA). TSA 450. Evaluation of misstatements identified during the audit
Public Oversight—Accounting and Auditing Standards Authority (POA). TSA 500. Audit evidence
Public Oversight—Accounting and Auditing Standards Authority (POA). TSA 501. Audit evidence—specific considerations for selected items
Public Oversight—Accounting and Auditing Standards Authority (POA). TSA 505. External confirmations
Public Oversight—Accounting and Auditing Standards Authority (POA). TSA 510. Initial audit engagements—opening balances
Public Oversight—Accounting and Auditing Standards Authority (POA). TSA 540. Auditing accounting estimates, including fair value accounting
Public Oversight—Accounting and Auditing Standards Authority (POA). TSA 550. Related parties

Public Oversight—Accounting and Auditing Standards Authority (POA). TSA 560. Subsequent events

Public Oversight—Accounting and Auditing Standards Authority (POA). TSA 570. Going concern

Public Oversight—Accounting and Auditing Standards Authority (POA). TSA 600. Special considerations—audits of group financial statements (Including the work of component auditors)

Public Oversight—Accounting and Auditing Standards Authority (POA). TSA 610. Using the work of internal auditors

Public Oversight—Accounting and Auditing Standards Authority (POA). Code of Ethics for Professional Accountants (Ethical codes of conduct for independent auditors). http://www.kgk.gov.tr/contents/files/Pdf/20150521-10-1-BagimsizDenetcilerIcinEtikKurallar.pdf. Accessed 21 May 2015

Public Oversight—Accounting and Auditing Standards Authority (POA). TSA 705. Issuing an opinion other than unqualified opinion in the independent auditor's report

Public Oversight—Accounting and Auditing Standards Authority (POA). TSA 706. Emphasis of matter paragraphs and other matter paragraphs in the independent auditor's report

Public Oversight—Accounting and Auditing Standards Authority (POA). TSA 710. Comparative information—corresponding figures to prior periods and comparative financial statements

Public Oversight—Accounting and Auditing Standards Authority (POA). TSA 720. The auditor's responsibilities relating to other information in documents containing audited financial statements

Public Oversight—Accounting and Auditing Standards Authority (POA). Independent Audit Firms. Transparency reports. http://www.kgk.gov.tr/DynamicContentDetail/5304/Bag%CC%86%C4%B1ms%C4%B1z-Denetim-Kurulus%CC%A7lar%C4%B1n%C4%B1n-S%CC%A7effafl%C4%B1k-Raporlar%C4%B1-ile-S%CC%A7effafl%C4%B1k-Raporlar%C4%B1na-I%CC%87lis%CC%A7kin-Ac%CC%A7%C4%B1klamalar%C4%B1. Accessed 29 Jan 2018

Redmayne NB (05 Aug 2013) Audit quality—an academic's perspective. New Zealand Institute of Chartered Accountants. Home. News. News archive. 2013. August. https://www.nzica.com/News/Archive/2013/August/Audit-quality-an-academics-perspective.aspx. Accessed 07 Mar 2014

Reece D (12 Jan 2004) Deloitte UK boss 'lacked competence'. The Independent. http://www.independent.co.uk/news/business/news/deloitte-uk-boss-lacked-competence-572728.html. Accessed 11 Mar 2012

Rezaee Z, Riley R (2009) Financial statement fraud: prevention and detection, 2nd edn. ISBN: 978-0-470-54323-8. Wiley, Hoboken. http://media.johnwiley.com.au/product_data/excerpt/05/04704557/0470455705.pdf. Accessed 11 Mar 2012

Rittenberg LE, Johnstone KM, Gramling AA (2012) Auditing: a business risk approach, 8th edn. South-Western, Cengage Learning, Ohio. ISBN-13: 978-0-538-47624-9

Sarbanes-Oxley Act (SOX) (2002) Retrieved from https://www.google.com.tr/#hl=en&q=To+protect+investors+by+improing+the+accuracy+and+reliability+of+corporate+disclosures+made+pursuant+to+the+securities+laws,+and+for+other+purposes.&gws_rd=cr,ssl. Accessed 10 Apr 2016

Serpa LB (2013) Keynote Speaker. In: 3rd Organisational Governance Conference. Copenhagen, Denmark 8–9 August 2013. Copenhagen Business School and the Centre for Research into Organisational Governance, De Montfort University

Skinner DJ, Srinivasan S (July 01, 2011) Audit quality and auditor reputation: evidence from Japan. Chicago Booth Research Paper, No 10–15; Harvard Business School Accounting & Management Unit Working Paper No. 10–088. Retrieved from http://ssrn.com/abstract=1557231. Accessed 13 Oct 2011

SmartPro (November 2002) Defining "Non Audit" services: the audit committee's role. Retrieved from http://accounting.smartpros.com/x35824.xml. Accessed 10 Apr 2016

Soo Young K, Youngdeok L, Simnett R (2014) The effect of mandatory audit firm rotation on audit quality and audit fees: empirical evidence from the Korean audit market. Auditing J Pract Theor 33(4):167–195. https://doi.org/10.2308/ajpt-50814

Suseno NS (2013) An empirical analysis of auditor independence and audit fees on audit quality. Int J Manage Bus Stud 3(3):81–87

Tanç ŞG, Uzay Ş (Oct 2013) The impact of audit company size and audit fee on audit quality: a survey on audit companies operating in Turkey (Denetim Şirketinin Büyüklüğünün ve Denetim Ücretinin Denetimin Kalitesi Üzerine Etkisi: Türkiye'de Faaliyet Gösteren Denetim Şirketleri Üzerine Bir Araştırma), p 21. In: 10th International Accounting Conference. Istanbul.

Taşkın K (01.04.2011) Computer assisted audit tools and techniques. Presentation, Edirne Chamber of Accountants

The Economist (08.12.2012) The Big Four auditors accountable. Two controversies ensnare the Big Four. The Economist. http://www.economist.com/news/finance-and-economics/21567953-two-controversies-ensnare-big-four-accountable. Accessed 09 Jan 2015

The Sarbanes-Oxley Forum. http://www.soxlaw.com/index.htm. Accessed 09 Mar 2012

Tomasic R (1992) Auditors and the reporting of illegality and financial fraud. Complex commercial fraud: Proceedings of a Conference held 20–23 August 1991/edited by Peter N. Grabosky. Australian Institute of Criminology, Canberra (AIC Conference Proceedings; No 10); 43–63. http://citeseerx.ist.psu.edu/viewdoc/download?doi=10.1.1.197.6443&rep=rep1&type=pdf. Accessed 11 Mar 2012

Turkish Code of Commerce (TCC). Law No. 6102 Date 13/01/2011, 14 February 2011 Monday Official Gazette No. 27846. Retrieved from http://www.resmigazete.gov.tr/main.aspx?home=http://www.resmigazete.gov.tr/eskiler/2011/02/20110214.htm&main=http://www.resmigazete.gov.tr/eskiler/2011/02/20110214.htm. Accessed 03 Aug 2011 and 12 Feb 2013

Turkish Court of Accounts. Mexico Declaration on Independence. http://www.sayistay.gov.tr/tr/Upload/95906369/files/bilgi_notlari/MexicoDeklarasyonu.pdf. Accessed 28 Jan 2017. T.C. Sayıştay Başkanlığı. e-Kütüphane. Sayıştayların (Yüksek Denetim Kurumlarının) Bağımsızlığı Hakkında Mexico Deklârasyonu. http://www.sayistay.gov.tr/yayin/elek/elekicerik/57_MexicoDeklarasyonu.pdf. Accessed 26 Feb 2012

Turkish Language Association (TLA). Türk Dil Kurumu (TDK). Audit/denetim. http://www.tdk.gov.tr/index.php?option=com_bilimsanat&arama=kelime&guid=TDK.GTS.559bfd3493a687.03410018. Accessed 28 Feb 2013

Turkish Language Association (TLA). Türk Dil Kurumu (TDK). Plân. http://www.tdk.gov.tr/index.php?option=com_bati&arama=kelime&guid=TDK.BATI.559bfce2c5a698.05684506. Accessed 21 Nov 2014

Turkish Language Association (TLA). Türk Dil Kurumu (TDK). Strateji. http://www.tdk.gov.tr/index.php?option=com_bts&arama=kelime&guid=TDK.GTS.559bfe4415c1b4.90828256. Accessed 21 Nov 2014

Turkish Language Association (TLA). Türk Dil Kurumu (TDK). Bağımsızlık. http://www.tdk.gov.tr/index.php?option=com_bts&arama=kelime&guid=TDK.GTS.559bfe4946a328.43500028. Accessed 02 Jan 2015

Turkish Language Association (TLA). Türk Dil Kurumu (TDK). Financial/mali. http://www.tdk.gov.tr/index.php?option=com_bts&arama=kelime&guid=TDK.GTS.559bfeff4d0896.01570077. Accessed 05 Jan 2015

Turner LE (2008) Dissenting statement. Advisory Committee on the Auditing Profession: Final Report, IX. http://www.treasury.gov/about/organizational-structure/offices/Documents/final-report.pdf. Accessed 03 Jan 2013

TÜSİAD. Turkish Industry and Business Association. Internal Auditing Sub—Working Group (27 May 2010, Istanbul). Ali Kamil Uzun, Özlem Aykaç, Fuat Öksüz, Şenol Toygar, Doç. Dr. Şaban Uzay, Melda Çele, Kerem Tuzlacı. Reel Sektörde İç Denetim Uygulamaları: Tespit ve Öneriler. Seminar Presentation: Şaban Uzay, cited slide no. 41–42, 44–45. http://iibf.erciyes.edu.tr/akademi/mh/suzay/a1tusiadsunum.pdf. Accessed 16 Mar 2013

U.S. Securities and Exchange Commission (SEC). About what we do. http://www.sec.gov/images/secorg.pdf. Accessed 08 Feb 2013, and 17 Nov 2017. https://www.sec.gov/Article/whatwedo.html. Accessed 12 Feb 2018

U.S. Securities and Exchange Commission (SEC). Enforcement. http://www.sec.gov/divisions/enforce/friactions.shtml. Accessed 18 Jan 2015

U.S. Securities and Exchange Commission (SEC). Accounting and Auditing Enforcement Release No. 3612/December 15, 2014–Administrative Proceeding File Nos. 3-14872, 3-15116, http://www.sec.gov/litigation/admin/2014/34-73838.pdf. Accessed 18 Jan 2015

USLegal. Legal Definitions Home. Partnerships Law & legal definition. http://definitions.uslegal.com/p/partnerships/. Accessed 16 Jan 2015

United Kingdom House of Commons Treasury Committee (2009) Banking crisis: reforming corporate governance and pay in the City, Ninth Report of Session 2008–09, HC 519. (London: The Stationery Office). http://www.parliament.the-stationery-office.co.uk/pa/cm200809/cmselect/cmtreasy/519/519.pdf. Accessed 04 Feb 2015. https://www.publications.parliament.uk/pa/cm200809/cmselect/cmtreasy/519/519.pdf. Accessed 03 Mar 2017

United States Government Accountability Office GAO (Jan 2008) Report to congressional addressees. Audits of public companies—continued concentration in audit market for large public companies does not call for immediate action. http://www.gao.gov/new.items/d08163.pdf. Accessed 31 Jan 2015

United States House of Representatives. Office of the Law Revision Counsel. Download. Title 15—Commerce and Trade. Chapter 98—Public Company Accounting Reform and Corporate Responsibility. July 30, 2002, 116 Stat. 745, known as the Sarbanes-Oxley Act of 2002. http://uscode.house.gov/download/pls/15C98.txt. Accessed 12 Dec 2011

United States Treasury (2008) ACAP. Advisory Committee on the Auditing Profession: Final Report. Retrieved from http://www.treasury.gov/about/organizational-structure/offices/Documents/final-report.pdf . Accessed 03 Jan 2013

University of Cincinnati. College of Law. Securities lawyer's deskbook. The Sarbanes-Oxley Act of 2002. http://taft.law.uc.edu/CCL/SOact/toc.html, 09.03.2012

Usta Ö (2005) *İşletme Finansı ve Finansal Yönetim*, 2nd edn. Detay Yayıncılık, Ankara

Uzay Ş (2004) Türkiye'de Denetçi Bağımsızlığı. MÖDAV. The 1st Annual International Accounting Conference, 3–5 Nov 2004. Bildiri Kitabı, Istanbul, pp 435–485

Uzay Ş (2008) An overview of operational auditing—Faaliyet Denetimine Genel Bakış. In: 2nd International Symposium on Auditing in Turkey, 25–29 April 2007. ISMMMO Yayın No. 92. Editor: Cemal Ibiş, Antalya, pp 275–307

Uzay Ş, Tanç A, Erciyes M (July 2008) Türkiye'de Muhasebe Denetimi: Geçmişten Geleceğe - 1, (a) 20–24 July 2008 Istanbul. *12. Dünya Muhasebe Tarihçileri Kongresi*. (b) *Mali Çözüm Dergisi* (95):125–140

Washington College of Law. Student Bar Association. http://www.wcl.american.edu/sba/outline_databank/outlines/BusinessAssociations_Harrison.pdf. Accessed 16 Jan 2015

Wellink N (14.01.2010) Basel Committee on Banking Supervision. IOSCO Consultation Report Comment Letter, p 1. http://www.iosco.org/library/pubdocs/pdf/IOSCOPD339.pdf. Accessed 05 May 2012

Weston FT (1966) Discussion of audit recommendations and management auditing: a case study and some remarks. J Acc Res 4(3):157–159

Wikipedia. Notable Accounting Scandals. Accounting Scandals. Notable Accounting Scandals. http://en.wikipedia.org/wiki/Accounting_scandals. Accessed 10 Mar 2012

Wikipedia. Tobashi Scheme. http://en.wikipedia.org/wiki/Tobashi_scheme. Accessed 10 Mar 2012

Wikipedia. Aufsichtsrat. http://de.wikipedia.org/wiki/Aufsichtsrat. Accessed 10 Aug 2012

Wikipedia. Ivar Kreuger. http://en.wikipedia.org/wiki/Ivar_Kreuger. Accessed 04 Nov 2012

Wikipedia. Phillip Musica. http://en.wikipedia.org/wiki/Phillip_Musica. Accessed 06 Nov 2012

Wikipedia. Savings loan crisis. http://en.wikipedia.org/wiki/Savings_%26_Loan_Crisis. Accessed 31 Jan 2013

Worldbank. http://siteresources.worldbank.org/EXTCENFINREPREF/Resources/4152117-1270824012230/stat_audit_directive_and_public_oversight.pdf. Accessed 02 Jun 2014

Yılancı M, Yıldız B (2001) Yeminli Malî Müşavir-Bağımsız Denetçi ve Tasdik-Malî Tablo Denetimi Çelişkisi: Mesleğin Gelişimine Etkileri. *Muhasebe ve Denetime Bakış*. p 5, 67–77

Index

I. Kesimli, *External Auditing and Quality*, Accounting, Finance, Sustainability, Governance & Fraud: Theory and Application,
https://doi.org/10.1007/978-981-13-0526-9

FSC
www.fsc.org
MIX
Papier | Fördert
gute Waldnutzung
FSC® C083411

Kolibri 360 GmbH
Ferdinand-Jühlke-Straße 7
99095 Erfurt, Deutschland
produktsicherheit@kolibri360.de